AF505910

European Security and Transatlantic Relations
after 9/11 and the Iraq War

Also by Ian Cuthbertson

AMERICAN FOREIGN POLICY IN THE POST-COLD WAR WORLD (*with James H. Nolt and Sherle R. Schwenniger*)

THE ANTI-TACTICAL BALLISTIC MISSILE ISSUE AND EUROPEAN SECURITY

BRITAIN'S EXPERIENCE IN COUNTER-TERRORISM: LESSONS FROM A LONG WAR

ENHANCING EUROPEAN SECURITY: *Living in a Less Nuclear World* (*with David Robertson*)

THE FAR AND DISTANT LANDS: RUSSIA, THE WEST AND THE FUTURE OF EURASIA (*edited with Jane L. Brody*)

THE GUNS FALL SILENT: *The End of the Cold War and the Future of Conventional Disarmament* (*edited with Peter M.E. Volten*)

MINORITIES: *The New Europe's Old Issue* (*edited with Jane Liebowitz*)

MINORITY RIGHTS AND RESPONSIBILITIES: *Challenges in the New Europe* (*with Jane Liebowitz*)

REDEFINING THE CSCE: *Challenges and Opportunities in the New Europe* (*ed.*)

Also by Heinz Gärtner

BETWEEN AUSTRIA AND MOSCOW: *The Dependency of Austrian Communists on the Soviet Union*

EUROCOMMUNISTS IN WESTERN EUROPE

INTERNATIONAL RELATIONS IN AUSTRIA (*with O. Höll*)

HEGEMONY AND CAUSES OF WAR

A THIRD WAY BETWEEN THE BLOCS: *the World Powers, Europe and the 'Eurocommunists'* (*edited with G. Trautmann*)

HANDBOOK FOR ARMS CONTROL

CHALLENGES OF VERIFICATION. *Smaller States and Arms Control*

THE FUTURE OF EUROPEAN SECURITY: *Between National and Collective Security*

MODELS OF EUROPEAN SECURITY AND AUSTRIA

EUROPE'S NEW SECURITY CHALLENGES (*edited with Adrian Hyde-Price and Erich Reiter*)

SMALL STATES AND ALLIANCES (*edited with Erich Reiter*)

DEFINITIONS ON INTERNATIONAL THEORY AND SECURITY

European Security and Transatlantic Relations after 9/11 and the Iraq War

Edited by

Heinz Gärtner
Senior Researcher, Austrian Institute for International Affairs, Vienna

and

Ian M. Cuthbertson
Senior Fellow, World Policy Institute, New School University, USA

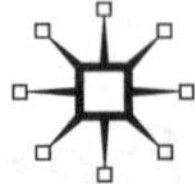

First published 2005 by
PALGRAVE MACMILLAN
Houndmills, Basingstoke, Hampshire RG21 6XS and
175 Fifth Avenue, New York, N.Y. 10010
Companies and representatives throughout the world

PALGRAVE MACMILLAN is the global academic imprint of the Palgrave
Macmillan division of St. Martin's Press, LLC and of Palgrave Macmillan Ltd.
Macmillan® is a registered trademark in the United States, United Kingdom
and other countries. Palgrave is a registered trademark in the European
Union and other countries.

ISBN-13: 978–1–4039–3685–1
ISBN-10: 1–4039–3685–4

This book is printed on paper suitable for recycling and made from fully
managed and sustained forest sources.

A catalogue record for this book is available from the British Library.

Library of Congress Cataloging-in-Publication Data
European security and transatlantic relations after 9/11 and the Iraq War /
    edited by Heinz Gärtner and Ian M. Cuthbertson.
        p.   cm.
    Includes bibliographical references and index.
    ISBN 1–4039–3685–4
    1. National security—Europe—History—21st century.   2. National
    security—United States—History—21st century.   3. Europe—Foreign
    relations—United States.   4. United States—Foreign relations—Europe.
    5. World politics—1995–2005.   I. Gärtner, Heinz.   II. Cuthbertson,
    Ian M., 1957–

    UA646.E92525 2005
    355′.031′091821—dc22

                                                          2004059168

10   9   8   7   6   5   4   3   2   1
14   13   12   11   10   09   08   07   06   05

Printed and bound in Great Britain by
Antony Rowe Ltd, Chippenham and Eastbourne

Contents

List of Tables and Figures

Tables

Figures

Notes on the Contributors

Heiko Borchert runs a political and business consultancy and is Director for Security and Defense at the Duesseldorf Institute for Foreign and Security Policy (DIAS). He is co-editor of a series of books on network centric security policy. His research interests and publications focus on the transatlantic relationship, European security policy, and security sector transformation.

Ian M. Cuthbertson is a Senior Fellow at the World Policy Institute of the New School University and Director of the WPI's Counter-Terrorism Project. He also serves as a consultant on security issues to a number of governments, international organizations and multinational companies. He is the author and editor of a number of books and articles on European military affairs, transatlantic security issues, the evolving relationship between Russia, the West and the new nations of Eurasia, counter-terrorism policy and the dangers posed by nuclear, chemical and biological weapons in the hands of terrorists.

Heinz Gärtner is Senior Researcher at the Austrian Institute for International Affairs – OIIP Vienna – since 1979. Various international Visiting Fellow- and Professorships at the Institute for East–West Security Studies, New York (1987–89); St. Hugh's College, Oxford (1992); University of British Columbia, Vancouver (1993); University of Erlangen, Germany (1994/95); University of Vienna (1999–2001); Stanford University, CA (2001–02); and Fulbright Fellowship, World Policy Institute, New York, 2001. In 1998 he received the Bruno Kreisky Award for most outstanding Political Books: 'Models of European Security'. He has published widely on European security, NATO and transatlantic relations.

Jan Willem Honig is Senior Lecturer in the Department of War Studies at King's College London. Prior to joining the Department in 1993, he taught at the University of Utrecht and at New York University. He was also a Research Associate at the Institute for East–West Security Studies in New York. In 1999–2000, Jan Honig was a Visiting Fellow at the Remarque Institute of New York University and the Centre of International Studies at Princeton University. He is the author of a number of books, including *Srebrenica: Record of a War Crime* (with Norbert Both).

P. Terrence Hopmann is Professor of Political Science and Director of the Program on Global Security of the Thomas J. Watson Jr. Institute for

International Studies at Brown University, Providence, RI, USA. His research focuses on the processes of negotiation and conflict resolution on security issues within states, regionally within Eurasia, and globally. Recent books include *The Negotiation Process and the Resolution of International Conflicts* and *Building Security in Post-Cold War Eurasia: The OSCE and US Foreign Policy*.

Adrian Hyde-Price is Professor of Politics and International Relations in the Department of Politics at the University of Leicester. He has previously lectured at the Universities of Birmingham, Southampton and Manchester, and was a Research Fellow on the International Security Programme at the Royal Institute of International Affairs (Chatham House, London). His main research interests include the European security system; coercive diplomacy; war and conflict in the international system; and EU foreign and security policy. His most recent publications include *Germany and European Order: Enlarging NATO and the EU; The International Politics of East Central Europe; European Security Beyond the Cold War: Four Scenarios for the Year 2010;* and *Security and Identity in Europe* (co-edited).

Regina Karp is Director of the Center for Regional and Global Study at Old Dominion University. She is a specialist in the topics of arms control, weapons proliferation, and international security. She has published books and articles on the issues of the Strategic Defense Initiative (SDI) and European security and defense procurement of the former Federal Republic of Germany. Recently, she has been working on the issue of security integration in the Baltic Sea region with special concentration on Sweden and Finland.

Alexander Kelle is a Lecturer in Politics and International Studies at Queen's University Belfast. Previously he held posts at the University of Bradford, Stanford University and the Peace Research Institute Frankfurt. His main areas of work are the chemical and biological weapons control regimes. He is author of several PRIF-Reports, the latest of which assesses the state of implementation of the Chemical Weapons Convention.

Daniel Maurer works in the Force Development Division of the Swiss Armed Forces Planning Staff, where he oversees long-term studies in the field of European security. He has published a monograph on European crisis management in the Balkans. He has a Master's Degree in International Relations from the University of Zurich.

Kari Möttölä is Special Adviser in security policy at the Unit for Policy Planning and Research at the Finnish Ministry for Foreign Affairs, since 1989. Former Director of the Finnish Institute of International Affairs,

Möttölä has published articles and submitted conference papers on Finnish foreign policy, the CFSP/ESDP of the European Union, regional and European security, and transatlantic relations. Graduate of University of Helsinki (MA in political science, 1969), he is a member of the International Institute for Strategic Studies and the International Studies Association.

Daniel N. Nelson (Ph.D., Johns Hopkins) became Dean of Arts and Sciences at the University of New Haven in August 2002. From January 1999 until his appointment at UNH, he served as Professor of Civil–Military Relations at the George C. Marshall Center for European Security Studies in Garmisch, Germany (2000–02) and as Scholar-in-Residence at the National Defense University (1999). Nelson is also Editor-in-Chief of the scholarly quarterly *International Politics* published by Palgrave and Senior Consultant for Global Concepts, Inc., an international consulting firm in Alexandria, Virginia. He is a member of the Council on Foreign Relations, the International Institute of Strategic Studies, and the Atlantic Council of the US and serves on the boards of several non-governmental organizations.

Susan E. Penksa is an Associate Professor of Political Science at Westmont College in Santa Barbara, CA. Her scholarly research and writing is based on extensive field experience in West and Central Europe, as well as in Bosnia, and includes work on security and foreign policy, CFSP/ESDP, the Balkans, and transatlantic security relations. Her most recent publication is 'EU Security Cooperation and the Transatlantic Relationship' (co-author, Warren Mason); *Cooperation and Conflict*; September 2003.

Friedrich Steinhäusler is currently Chairman of the US/German Trans-atlantic ERP Expert Group 'Global Fight Against terrorism', and the NATO CLG Expert Group 'Terrorism Threats against Nuclear Power Plants and Spent Fuel Transport'. Furthermore he is Co-Director of the NATO ARW 'Catastrophic Terrorism and First responders: Threats and Countermeasures'. Prof. Steinhäusler was Programme Coordinator for 'Security' and Project Manager for 'Protection of Nuclear material against Theft and Sabotage' at Stanford University, California, from 1999 to 2003. He organized the EU High-Level Scientific Conference on 'Physical Protection of Nuclear Material (NUMAT)' in Salzburg (Austria) in September 2002.

Christian Tuschhoff has been a Visiting Associate Professor at Emory University since 2002. He served as the Ralph I. Straus Visiting Professor at Harvard University in 2000 and as a Robert Bosch Foundation Fellow at the American Institute for Contemporary German Studies in 2001. He received his Ph.D (1988) and *Habilitation* (1998) degrees from the Free University in Berlin and an MA (1984) from the University of Munich. His main research interests are transatlantic relations and NATO cohesion.

Georg Witschel joined the German Foreign Office in 1983 and has been Federal Government Commissioner for Combating International Terrorism since 2002. He has a Ph.D in international law and has published in the fields of international law and of terrorism and on economic questions relating to Slovenia.

Preface and Acknowledgements

This book represents a major milestone in the on-going work of a group of European and American security and international relations specialists who have come together periodically since the end of the Cold War to address the challenges that face the West in the new global security environment. The majority of the authors of this book are well known to each other, having met numerous times over the years to discuss and analyze the myriad of issues involved in determining the current state and future prospects for the Transatlantic relationship and European security.

We first met as a group during the 1990s to assess the myriad implications of the end of the East-West conflict, a process that resulted in a number of books and articles being published. After the tragic events of 11 September 2001, the group focused its attentions on the likely consequences for European security of the new war on terrorism. Our examination of the issues included a full review of the new challenges that faced Europeans in this new global conflict; an analysis of threat perceptions as viewed from both sides of the Atlantic; the risks posed by the proliferation of WMD, and finally; what the implications of the new security environment after 9/11 and the wars in Afghanistan and Iraq were for the future of NATO and the evolution of the new European Security System?

The first in this latest series of meetings took place at Stanford University in the spring of 2002, at a time when Heinz Gärtner was teaching and carrying out research as a visiting professor at Stanford. During the presentations and discussion of the conference participants' papers, it became clear that there were sharp differences of opinion within our group, especially on the scale and consequences of the new threats and their implications on the future of NATO as a collective defense organization. A great deal of work went into making this first meeting a success and it would not have been possible without the organizational and financial support the European Forum. In particular, we wish to thank Timothy Josling, who was director of the Forum at that time, and Tamara Danoyan, who provided all of the administrative support that made the meeting run smoothly.

As a result of the lively exchange of views that the meeting engendered, participants were asked to review and refine their arguments in preparation for the group's next meeting. Some of the papers from this initial conference were subsequently published in a Special Feature of the Journal *International Politics* (March 2003). As further follow-up to our initial meeting, in 2003 some of our conference participants these authors presented their ideas on these critical issues on a panel at the Annual Convention of the International Studies Association in Portland, Oregon.

Building upon this solid foundation of review and analysis, the next meeting of the group took place at the Austrian Institute for International Affairs (OIIP) in Vienna in April 2004. At this conference, participants presented their revised and updated manuscripts, which reflected the dramatic changes in the transatlantic relationship that resulted from the build up to and the launching of the war in Iraq. While there was broad agreement on many issues, a number of the long-standing controversies remain and we continue to explore these issues as part of the on-going work of the group. A good example of the continuing debate is that while there was broad agreement on the type of measures necessary to combat terrorism, there remains a wide range of different opinions on modern terrorism's origins and how to address the problems that are seen as its precursor conditions.

The Vienna meeting was a great success, with an informed and thoughtful debate between the participants and lively questions from the equally well-qualified audience who attended our various sessions. We wish to thank the OIIP and its director, Otmar Höll, for generously providing the facilities for the meeting and Lilli Gneisz for the outstanding administrative work she provided, a commitment that allowed the conference to run smoothly. Lilli also ensured that all of this book's authors stayed on schedule with their revisions to their manuscripts, and, as a result, the chapters of this book were all delivered on time, a few short weeks after the meeting. Thomas Pankratz and Philip Primer helped to set out the chapters consistently with each other. We remain profoundly grateful for the gracious financial support for the conference that was provided by the U.S. Embassy in Vienna, the Bureau of Security Policy of the Austrian Defense Ministry, the Dr. Karl Renner-Institute of the Social Democratic Party and the Austrian Federal Chancellery. The final versions of the chapters were presented at the 2005 convention of the International Studies Association in Honolulu, Hawaii, in March 2005.

We would be remiss if we did not thank all of our colleagues for their wholehearted participation in what has been a very intense process of writing, presenting and revising their chapters. It is their hard work and dedication that has allowed us to produce such a timely volume. Finally, we wish to thank Alison Howson at Palgrave/Macmillan for her unstinting support of our work and for her patience as we moved this book towards publication.

Heinz Gärtner/Ian Cuthbertson

Introduction

Heinz Gärtner and Ian M. Cuthbertson

This book is an exploration of the post-9/11 global security situation at a moment in history when profound changes are dramatically altering the traditional dynamics of international affairs. American unilateralism in international security matters, most clearly demonstrated by the build-up to and conduct of the war in Iraq, co-exists uneasily with a continued US desire to involve as many active and reliable partners as possible in the war on terrorism. At a time when Europeans are more committed than ever to seeking peaceful and multilateral solutions to global challenges, the specific focus of our investigation is to examine the impact of the policy realignments that are now taking place in both the United States and Europe, with a detailed examination of the scope and nature of the future security challenges that face Europe, the transatlantic relationship and the wider international system after 9/11 and the Iraq war. In particular, the book examines the ongoing evolution in the long-standing security relationship between the United States and Europe. The authors in this book explore a wide range of issues, attitudes, policies and general approaches in an attempt to identify which of the various options currently available can contribute most to strengthening international security and stability.

The events of 9/11 marked a sea change in how the world regarded terrorism. With the murders of 2976 innocent civilians, a critical threshold of horror was crossed. Until 11 September, it was commonly assumed that most terrorist acts were carried out with the least practicable level of violence directed against members of the general public, and that death tolls would be kept relatively low by the terrorists. This was believed to be the case because the primary objective of such attacks, while wishing to instill a degree of fear in the targeted population, was mainly to generate publicity and bring attention, from public, media and the political establishment, to the terrorist's cause. Since 9/11, that assumption no longer applies. 9/11 branded a new type of terrorist, one with the ambition of inflicting the maximum possible amount of casualties and damage, onto the public consciousness.

Some have claimed that the attacks merely acted as a catalyst to accelerate a transformation processes in American and international security that was already underway. From this viewpoint, 9/11 may in the end only represent a kind of tragic aberration in the evolution of American national security. A second stream of analysis, however, views the events of 9/11 and their aftermath, beginning with the war in Afghanistan and all subsequent American actions, as a fundamental turning point not only in America's national security thinking, but as the basis for undertaking a complete and fundamental reassessment of the overall scope and nature of the global security environment. From this point of view, what is necessary is the creation of an entirely new set of rules and international political and legal regimes that are tailored to fit a world in which the danger of terrorism, particularly if it involves the use of weapons of mass destruction, is now the greatest security threat to face all nations and peoples.

The tensions between the two viewpoints found their most concrete expression to date in the conflicts that erupted in early 2003 between the United States and other members of the UN Security Council, and large sections of the wider international community, over the legitimacy of launching a full-scale military campaign against Iraq. For a US administration that saw apparent links between Iraq and Islamic terrorism, it was clear that if incontrovertible proof could not be produced by Saddam Hussein's regime to UN weapons inspectors that Iraq had, as required, destroyed all of its weapons of mass destruction, then the security of the United States required that Saddam Hussein be deposed and his WMD destroyed. To many others in the international community, the lack of any unambiguous connection between the secular Baathist regime in Iraq and the radical Islamic fundamentalist of al Qaeda, who had long regarded Saddam Hussein secularism as anathema, meant the case was much less clear cut. The failure of the UN inspectors to find WMD, and their seeming inability to fully document the destruction of such weapons was seen as sufficient reason for more time to be given for greater clarity to emerge on what the true situation was in Iraq. But for America and some of its allies, post 9/11, struggling with the possibility of another massive terrorist attack, perhaps this time involving nuclear, biological, chemical, or radiological weapons, time and patience were two commodities that were in very short supply. For Americans, the stately pace of UN diplomacy no longer had a place in a world where terrorists could kill thousands without any warning. For those less seized with a vision of terrorism not only as a clear and present danger, but also as an overwhelming threat, 9/11, although serious, was not viewed as a sufficient rationale to abandon the more than 50 years of multilateral diplomacy that had created the current international system. It is this divergence of opinion on the future nature of the global security system this book sets out to explore.

Traditional security thinking dominated the Cold War, with reliance on significant and credible military capabilities being seen as the primary strategy necessary to achieve greater security. The dramatic shift in threat perceptions brought about by the fall of communism have been further confirmed by a wide variety of post-9/11 developments: wars between competing political ideologies and inter-state conflicts are no longer seen as the prime dangers to international security, at least in much of the developed world. In the post-1989, and in particular post-9/11 world, a broader and more complex concept of security has emerged. Such a construct is required because, while the threat of inter-state conflict has receded, Western societies face a multiplicity of lesser dangers that cumulatively could be just as dangerous and destructive as the wars of the past century.

This book focuses on the empirical and analytical concerns surrounding the nature of, and policy responses to, the future development of European and transatlantic security within the new security environment. Two historic developments are reshaping the structural dynamics of the global system, both of which have profound implications for European security and the transatlantic relations security: the aftermath of 11 September 2001 and the consequences of the war in Iraq of 2003. The changes to the West's security agenda that occurred as a result of these events have raised serious questions about traditional ways of conceptualizing security. A great deal of academic analysis has tended to be channeled within well-established disciplinary boundaries: but in the rapidly evolving security environment in which we now find ourselves, one with a multiple and and multi-dimensional new security challenges, this is no longer an appropriate or acceptable approach to examining new policy options.

Traditional security concepts are based on the realist notion of 'balance of power.' For realists, the causes of war and peace are mainly a function of the balance of power and the distribution of power within the system. The connection between alliances and a potential threat is inseparable. For Hans Morgenthau,[1] alliances are the 'most important manifestation of the balance of power.' Stephen Walt[2] modifies this concept. For him, alliances are the result of a 'balance of threat.' And for Kenneth Waltz, the members of any alliance have only negative common interests: the fear of other states.

NATO provides an excellent example of realist thinking. NATO certainly played a critical role in preventing World War III and helping the West win the Cold War. Nevertheless, NATO, like the Warsaw Pact, was fundamentally the concrete manifestation of the bipolar distribution of power in Europe during the Cold War. It was that balance of power, not the two alliances *per se*, that provided the key to maintaining stability on the continent. NATO was at root an American tool for managing power in the face of the Soviet threat. According to the realist school, alliances cannot remain cohesive without a sufficient threat. How can an alliance endure in the absence of a worthy opponent, was their question? Thus, with the collapse of the Soviet Union, realists argued that NATO could not remain as it had been during the Cold War and should either disappear or reconstitute its structure and mission to reflect the new distribution of power in Europe.[3] As a consequence of this analysis, Kenneth Waltz was moved to conclude that: 'NATO's days are not numbered but its years are'.[4]

Fifteen years after the end of the Cold War, however, NATO still shows no signs of imminent demise. In this respect, the prediction that all alliances dissolve without a tangible threat to give them cohesion appears to be wrong.[5] NATO looks like it may be an exception to these rules and cornerstones of alliance theory. Nevertheless the theorists do have a point: the core of the NATO's Cold War nuclear deterrence policy and collective defense, enshrined in Art. V of NATO's founding treaty, is rapidly diminishing in importance. What realists overlooked in their analysis, however, was that like the overall security environment, NATO also changed.

Liberal institutionalism, which argues that international institutions make a significant difference in conjunction with the realities of power politics, offers no straightforward solution to the new challenges Europe faces, because one can fairly safely assume that any future European security framework will not revert to the collective defense of the realist Cold War model. To promote cooperation, facilitate communication, provide information, develop common principles, norms, rules and constrain aggressive behavior to keep the peace[6] among the members of the Atlantic Community creates no major problems for European security and transatlantic relations. By and large, we have achieved these requirements. They are necessary and useful but they focus on the challenges of the past.

Likewise the concept of a 'security community' developed by Karl Deutsch has recently been applied to the transatlantic relations by a number of scholars.[7] According to Deutsch: 'common social problems must and can be resolved by processes of peaceful change [that is, the] assurance that members will not fight each other physically, but will settle their disputes in some other way.'[8] No country within the transatlantic region really expects to go to war with another and, apart from Greece and Turkey, none devotes any financial or organizational resources, or has developed military contingency plans to address the possibility of war with one of its neighbors and allies.

September 11 brought the concepts of the Cold War, which had been withering quietly since the fall of the Berlin Wall on the night of 9 November 1989, to a definitive end. Since 9/11 and the launching of the global war on terrorism, the overall nature of international security has been undergoing dramatic changes: it is becoming much more complex, and this in turn necessitates a more conceptually sophisticated set of analytical tools. The main effort of this book is to address the key issues that confront the evolving environment of both European and transatlantic security that has been emerging since 11 September and the war in Iraq. Traditional approaches to security are increasingly seen as inadequate to deal with the new security agenda. Thus, it is necessary to develop a broader and more complex approach to security. Future security challenges will not primarily focus on the traditional needs of territorial defence. While states will continue to pay residual attention to their territorial defense needs, it has become abundantly clear that other security challenges are inevitably going to demand the lion's share of attention in the future.

The new risk factors include the proliferation of both weapons of mass destruction (WMD) and conventional weapons, large-scale, homicidal terrorism, the instability and chaos that are the consequences of failed and failing states, the increasing barbarisation of war-torn societies and the return of warlordism, uncontrolled and illegal mass migration, genocidal ethnic conflicts, the explosive growth of sophisticated and murderously ruthless international organized crime syndicates, political and financial instability in many regions of the world, caused at least in part by large-scale public and private corruption, the impact of climate changes, the spread of infectious diseases, and continuing poverty and high birth-rates in many countries. These new threats blur both the traditional distinction between internal and external security, and also those between the various individual sectors,[9] military, political, social, economic and environmental that together go towards making up the security picture as a whole.

Nothing better illustrates the need for exploring new security approaches than the need to include non-state actors as major factors in any analysis. The campaign against terrorism involves not only military cooperation but also diplomatic, financial, economic, intelligence, customs and police cooperation. This wider approach to security is reflected in the fact that peace-, state-, and nation-building have all moved to the center of the contingency planning process for all of the major security institutions, in particular the UN, NATO, EU and OSCE.

Many contemporary security problems affect both American and European interests. The essence of security during the Cold War was against a universally perceived and agreed upon external threat. September 11 did not reverse this trend. But while Americans and Europeans often have similar threat perceptions they sometimes have very different views on the best methods of how to respond to them. A comprehensive survey of American and European public opinion that was published in September 2004[10] shows sharp divisions over when to use force and under what auspices. Although willing to use force in certain scenarios, Europeans are much less willing to use force to maintain peace or obtain justice, and they are broadly unwilling to use force without multilateral approval. These differences are reflected in the often sharp differences of priorities and opinon that often characterize NATO, EU and the OSCE's decision-making processes.

As part of the response to these new dangers, European states have conducted a thorough review of their situation and the range of responses available to them to meet the challenges their various societies face in this dramatically altered international security environment. As a result of this in-depth review, the new European Security Strategy outlines the main threats to the EU and calls for a 'more active, more coherent and more capable' response. The strategy also asserts the clear need and role for the European Union in global security and in any actions, including the use of military force, deemed necessary to achieve that security. The frontiers between internal and external security, between the police and the military, between crisis prevention and crisis management, combating organized crime and financial crime, detecting terrorism and managing 'failed states', have all become blurred and artificial. Since the risks are global and the world is interdependent, the response also has to be global. It is for this reason that the adaptation of the cooperative security system to new tasks calls for the elaboration of new principles and norms that are adequate to the requirements of the contemporary world, one in which terrorism and the proliferation of WMD together pose a qualitatively new threat to our societies. The various chapters of this book address all of these important issues.

To test of the hypothesis that the key security challenges that face the West remain multidimensional, the book examines the nature of the aims of security and the question of how and why they have changed after 9/11. Terrorism is only the most obvious of the new security threats that seriously challenge the traditional security system, but it is the challenge that most obviously highlights the reality that the current construct, one that Western nations have continued to cling to in the years since 1989, can no longer be considered adequate to confront a world that is in ever greater flux. Facing this reality means being willing to look at security issues from a global perspective, one that includes non-state actors as perhaps the central factor in the analysis, one that is able to assess the relationship between economic inequality and political radicalization, as well as fully understand the relationship between domestic and international security.

It needs to be clearly grasped, however, that even where there exists a commonality of perspective, there remain major differences between a number of the most important European countries and the US on how to deal with these new challenges. Speaking of the primacy of the United States in international affairs, Charles Krauthammer, who coined the phrase of the 'unipolar moment'[11] at the beginning of the 1990s, now speaks of 'the new unilateralism'[12] as if it might be a permanent or at least a long-lasting moment. It is a unilateralism that is based heavily on the militarily unipolarity of the world. The US administration of George W. Bush seems willing to embrace a narrow definition of security, a strategy which has seen a reemphasis on purely military measures as a response to threats, in stark contrast to the pre-9/11 situation which had seen military power effectively relegated to become just one option amongst a range of possible responses (political, economic, diplomatic, and so on) to the problems the US and its allies faced in the world.

The world after 11 September is not more unipolar than before, but 9/11 made its unilateral contours much more visible. American unilateral measures are well known: in the military field, large increases in defense spending and the abandonment of arms control agreements (for example the Comprehensive Nuclear Test Ban, the Protocol to the Biological Weapons Convention, the Anti-Ballistic Missile Treaty); first the rejection of ratification of the Kyoto Protocol, then the utter abandonment of the treaty itself as a worthwhile environmental measure; a willingness, indeed an eagerness to act alone, regardless whether or not major allies agree and support an action, as with the decision to go to war with Iraq or the assertion of the exemption of US personnel from the jurisdiction of the International Criminal Court.

Some observers do see a multipolar system emerging from the unipolar one that followed the bipolar world of the East–West conflict. Behind this desire to see such a multipolar world coalesce is often the wish to see an effective and viable 'counterweight' to US power emerge, one that is sustainable and which can create a new 'equilibrium' in the world order. That the US would look with less favor on the emergence of such a balance of power is hardly surprising. The United States, firmly convinced of its own good intentions, sees no need for a world in which its behavior can be checked by a new great power rivalry and has actively committed itself to preventing just such a situation arising anytime in the near future. Such clarity of purpose, backed by the reality of the overwhelming military dominance the US holds over any conceivable combination of competitors, means that we may indeed be destined to live in a unipolar world for a considerable time to come.

But the fact that a unipolar may be our destiny does not necessarily mean that American policy should or will be unilateral. The value of addressing major international challenges in a cooperative manner does not disappear simply because the pre-eminent power chooses to remain aloof from the complicated and often frustrating process of building consensus. Nor do international institutions lose their value to all of their participants simply because their most powerful members view them as less central to their own needs. The UN and NATO have important roles to play in helping to build and maintain international security even if the United States has turned its attention elsewhere in pursuit of similar goals. In addition, the EU, as an institution in which unilateralism has never been an option, and where the power of the collective remains greater than its individual parts, has a critical role to play in showing the US and others who doubt the value of a cooperative approach to problem solving that such a mindset is not only of value as an abstract principle, but also pays real dividends in the gritty world of everyday politics and economics.

Even in an age of terror, when security concerns are focused on preventing catastrophic events, there is still no compelling reason why even a militarily hegemonic power should not show respect and be expected to act according to the prevailing understanding of international law, even when such law clashes with its own interests. International law is not random or capricious. If it is complicated, slow-moving and often unwieldy, it is still a system that is capable of delivering both security and justice. No state can be seen to be above the system if the system itself is to have validity and credibility. It was, after all, the United States that coined the phrase 'rogue state'. A country must be rogue from something if the label is to stick and have meaning, and those somethings are the rules laid out by international treaties and the UN Charter. If the UN as an institution and international law as currently formulated are not delivering the levels of security and responsiveness that many wish to see from them, then both the UN and the body of treaties that comprise the international legal system need to be revised and amended, not abandoned.

There are practical reasons as well why it would be of benefit to the US to pay closer heed to the views of its friends and neighbors. Europeans, both governments and ordinary citizens, would have many fewer reservations about a strategy based on preemption of threat, the approach laid out in US National Security Strategy, if there was at least some form of multilateral consultation and assessment involved. Such steps would give more legitimization than the modern world is prepared to grant to any single government, no matter how rich and powerful. Europeans do not reject military action as an option in the face of a clear threat and the European Security Strategy itself speaks of 'preventive engagement' involving both military and civilian means in the face of a clear and present danger. The caveat, however, is that the Europeans continue to stress the United Nations Charter as the 'fundamental framework for international relations' and still place 'the primary responsibility' on the United Nations Security Council for the maintenance of international peace and security. Neither side the Atlantic has a monopoly on right. Americans need to understand that for other countries, nations who lack their overwhelming military and economic power, the upending of international norms and rules is not something to be done lightly, regardless of need or provocation. Europeans should in turn recognize that the US, as the hegemonic power who alone has interests that reach into every corner of the globe, will sometimes reserve its right to act unilaterally alone if it believes its vital interests are at stake. That is the reality of power. But the difference is whether the unilateral act, when taken, is one of principle or mere expediency. It is the core difference but the most urgent and the most important. Both sides have a responsibility to recognize the difference clearly.

The distinguished authors in this volume examine a range of issues, from current threat perceptions to an investigation of religiously motivated terrorism both as a socio-political phenomenon and as a security threat, along with the relationships between state and non-state actors in the global network of terrorism. There is also an assessment of the impact of both terrorism itself and responses to it (for example new policies based on preemptive strike) on both international relations and law. The risks and special challenges posed by the proliferation of weapons of mass destruction (WMD) are examined and the viability of new arms control and disarmament regimes to tackle this danger explored. Finally, the book looks at the impact of the new security environment on the evolution of both NATO and the European Security System. Is it possible that NATO could lose, or at least have to change radically, its traditional roll of collective defense organization? Will the war on terrorism reinvigorate NATO, or will it merely become a convenient military 'toolbox' for the United States to dip into to construct 'coalitions of the willing'? What are the future prospects for creating an effective and worthwhile European Security and Defense Policy, one that would enable Europeans to play a full role internationally as partners of the US?

Structure and preview of chapters

To explore all of these issues, the book is divided up into three sections. The first of these deals with the dramatic shift in threat perceptions that occurred after the fall of communism and have been confirmed by a wide variety of post-9/11 developments. In the book's first chapter, 'Defining the Enemy: EU and US Threat Perceptions After 9/11,' Susan E. Penksa explores the impact of terrorism as one of the major new threats that the West has to face. Penksa asks what are the real risks and threats to European security. To address this question, she analyzes the continuities and changes in threat perception and security policy after the attacks on 9/11. Penksa explores whether 11 September fundamentally altered perceptions of security for both state and regional actors. Penksa's chapter provides a comparative analysis of EU and US threat perceptions and investigates whether the US and EU share a convergent set of perspectives on the new security threats. She finds that while European elites and citizens largely share the same threat and security perceptions, there is a marked divergence in outlook both between EU and US elites and between European and American citizens. While both the EU and US share concerns about terrorism, proliferation of weapons of mass destruction and failed states, after 11 September, Penska highlights that the US returned to a more traditional, militarily-focused security perspective while the EU and its member states continued to articulate an expanded understanding of security. Penska believes that unless there is an increased commitment to transatlantic dialogue and cooperation, this divergence is likely to produce increased conflict and diminished security for both pillars of the transatlantic relationship.

In his chapter, entitled: 'A Revolution in Strategy? Conducting War in an Age of Rogues,' Jan Willem Honig examines the nature of the West's political objectives in contemporary conflict – the aims of war – and the question of how and why they have changed since the end of the Cold War and after

11 September. His key conclusions are that the restricted legitimacy of contemporary wars implies limited aims of war and restraint in war. Moreover, he concludes that the West is up against actors who are relatively weak and who also pursue limited aims. Hence, the West faces the challenge of fighting limited wars and he believes that this requires strategies that are very different from the traditional Western way of making war and that their proper implementation would amount to a revolution in strategy.

In 'Strategic Terrorism: Threats and Risk Assessment,' Friedrich Steinhäusler analyzes the inherent weakness and vulnerability of both Europe and the US as open societies. He distinguishes between the traditional form of terrorism and what he describes as the new 'Strategic Terrorism' (ST) that has emerged since the early 1990s. In Steinhäusler's view, strategic terrorism differs from conventional terrorism in its objectives, as well as in the degree of sophistication, the comprehensiveness of its logistics, the attack modes and weapons it employs, the scale of harm it inflicts on targeted populations, and the socio-economic and political impacts that result from strategic terrorism attacks. Steinhäusler analyzes strategic terrorism's recruitment and training methods, the operation of its international network, its logistics and modes of attack, its targets and attack scenarios. From Steinhäusler's perspective, those who engage in strategic terrorism neither wish to negotiate with their opponents, nor do they have any constraints when it comes to inflicting mass casualties. To respond to this threat, Steinhäusler proposes a transatlantic 'Integrated System of Counter-Terrorism,' encompassing political, technological and intelligence components, as a response to the heightened threat the West now faces.

Addressing specific threats and dangers, Ian M. Cuthbertson, in his chapter 'Peering into the Abyss: Understanding and Combating NBC Terrorism,' examines the dangers posed, in an era of rapidly increasing proliferation, by the possibility of weapons of mass destruction falling into the hands of terrorists. Cuthbertson examines the rise of a new breed of terrorists who not only seek the leverage that ownership of such weapons would give them, but who are also fully committed to their use, a trend that has been fueled by the rise of terrorism inspired by religious fundamentalism, especially Islamic radicalism. Cuthbertson explores a range of measures, both active and passive, that could be employed by both governments and citizens to prevent the use of such weapons and blunt their effectiveness if the terrorists succeed in obtaining, deploying and using them. Georg Witschel, in his chapter, 'The European Response to Terrorism,' looks at the lessons to be drawn from 11 September and the various terrorist attacks since then. He argues that while Europe enjoys more security than ever in its history, it is clear that transnational terrorism has now fully emerged as the major challenge to that security, a fact dramatically re-emphasized by the March 2004 bombings in Madrid. As a result of those bombings, Witschel believes that the Declaration on Combating Terrorism of the European Council has reinvigorated the EU's resolve to fight terrorism and also led to the quick implementation of a range of decisions that had been taken in recent years. Witschel asserts that EU activities to prevent and counter terrorism encompass a firm political attitude towards the threat terrorism poses, sustained efforts to win hearts and minds, particularly amongst Muslims world-wide, significant efforts to suppress the financing of terrorism, a commitment to closing the remaining loopholes in the international legal order and a willingness to reinforce intelligence and law enforcement cooperation.

The second section of the book examines whether US–European relations are doomed after recent failures in transatlantic cooperation. Regina Karp in her chapter on 'Transatlantic Relations after 9/11 and Iraq: Continuities and Discontinuities,' argues that transatlantic relations have changed dramatically since 11 September. After the 9/11 attacks, America's grief was Europe's grief. But within the span of months, European relations with America entered a steep and rapid decline due to the shift to a policy of American unilateralism, most overtly manifest in the war in Iraq. In Karp's view, while the longer-term consequences of this shift are still unknown, it is clear that for the first time in the history of transatlantic relations the very future of the transatlantic relationship is at stake and separation has become conceivable. For Karp, to assess the future of transatlantic relations, the need is for a better understanding of the interaction between the structural implications of American primacy and of the consequences of an incomplete process of European integration. In her view, the transatlantic community, though still the source of shared Euro-American values, no longer defines common policies. Against this background of structural change, Europeans must therefore confront critical questions on the future of continental integration, especially in the areas of governance, foreign policy and defense policy. As the disagreements among European over the war in Iraq showed, Europe must also address issues of hierarchy within the EU and the role of the United States in European politics.

In his chapter, 'Three Fictions of Transatlantic Relations,' Daniel Nelson maps out the three key fictions that persist about transatlantic relations. One of these is the assertion of the existence of post-Cold War American primacy and unparalleled global dominance. The second is that NATO operates by consensus and exhibits unity of purpose and efficacy in action, and the third is the cherishing, since 1989, of an image of Europe as a single entity, 'whole and free.' These three ideas have been the cornerstones of a post-Cold War visage of Euro-Atlantic relations. Nelson forthrightly rejects these 'reassuring fictions that are either long past, or were never there.' Nelson instead addresses what he views as the reality of a NATO that has increasingly splintered as an effective operational instrument, as the US shifts its focus and military strength from Western Europe to other global regions and instead relies on NATO merely as a reservoir of more or less friendly states into which it can, as needed, dip to construct ad-hoc coalitions of the willing to meet particular needs. In his analysis of how lasting security can be achieved, Nelson promotes solutions that he believes lie in recognizing the need for a new transatlantic community based on common identities, not transient interests or institutionally-embedded norms.

According to Heinz Gärtner in his chapter, 'NATO and EU: Duplication or Division of Labor?' NATO and the EU are already well along the road toward exploring ways of developing wider and deeper cooperation. Gärtner's chapter examines the impact of developments both before and after 11 September on NATO and European security in particular, and on transatlantic relations in general. When the US acted without NATO in Afghanistan after 9/11, there was a significant risk that NATO was becoming irrelevant in a world in which terrorism has become the principal strategic threat. However, this did not happen and instead, NATO became an organization with global reach. Gärtner argues that if NATO were to incorporate the strategy of preemption into its doctrine, it would further undermine the Alliance's collective defense commitments. Gärtner argues strongly that in the case of the US, a capability to act does not only imply necessarily acting unilaterally and that the US needs to recognize the legitimate concerns on the part of its allies about both US threat assessments and the range of options that are explored as practical responses to these dangers. He also argues that there needs to be greater recognition that European military capabilities are more designed for projecting low-intensity power, peacekeeping, humanitarian action, disaster relief and post-conflict reconstruction rather than for the rapid deployment of large combat forces over long distances, and it is in this role, not war-fighting, that they have most utility and value.

Christian Tuschhoff, in 'NATO Cohesion from Afghanistan to Iraq,' firmly rejects the often-repeated arguments that NATO has become irrelevant after 11 September because of a perception that it lacks crucial capabilities to fight out of area wars and meet the challenges of the twenty-first century, such as terrorism. Rather than being caught flat-footed after 9/11, he argues that NATO was quick to offer substantive aid the United States, when it invoked the common defense clause of the Alliance's treaty. The offer of assistance was not merely symbolic, as Tuschoff argues that the Alliance had been well prepared beforehand to deal with both the political and military consequences of major terrorist attacks and, since 9/11, the Alliance has remained flexible and relevant and has continued to adjust to the new security environment created by the war on terrorism.

The final section of the book focuses on the future of European security and explores some of the institutions and mechanisms that are currently available for crisis management and conflict prevention. In his chapter, entitled 'The European "Centaur": Power and Authority in Europe's Society of States,' Adrian Hyde-Price addresses one of the fundamental questions in international relations: whether there can be an order in the international system. He goes on to ask how order arises in an anarchic international system, and how has this ordering principle changed with the end of the Cold War? Hyde-Price focuses on Europe and analyzes the nature of 'order' in European international society and argues that order is based on a mix of coercion and consent, power and authority. He follows this line of thought and argues that the five institutions of Europe's 'anarchical society' originally identified by Hedley Bull have not eradicated the struggle for power and influence in the international system, but rather have refracted, channelled and moderated it. In Hyde-Price's view, Europe remains an 'anarchical society' based on a complex mix of power and authority. His conclusion is that European democracies must learn to act cooperatively when possible, but be willing to back up their diplomacy with coercive military power when necessary.

For Kari Möttölä, in 'The European Union and Crisis Management,' it is this function that is a central feature of the European Union's identity and its profile as an international actor, as outlined in European Security Strategy. In his view, crisis management underpins the EU's position on multilateral cooperation and constitutes one of its main assets of power for shaping the international security order. Moreover, Möttölä argues that it is in American interests to have the EU take over low-intensity stabilization tasks in Europe and beyond. And he argues that for the EU to influence US policies, it will have to build upon its comprehensive non-military capability and pursue multilateralism, which highlights the significance of legitimacy. At the same time, he believes it is clear that the Union will have to adapt its doctrine and capability towards the use of force, where the US military capabilities continue to dominate.

P. Terrence Hopmann reviews 'The OSCE Response to 9/11,' in his chapter and asserts that the OSCE is distinguished as a European centric multi-lateral institution by its comprehensive concept of security, one that ranges from military through to humanitarian actions. Since the end of the Cold War, Hopmann believes that the OSCE has played an important role in conflict prevention and resolution throughout the former communist regions of Eastern Europe, the Caucasus, and Central Asia. He goes on to review and analyze the new capabilities the OSCE is attempting to build, including providing extensive technical assistance to participating states in such areas as training police in combating terrorism, improving border controls, reducing the threats from man-portable air defense systems, and regulating the flow of weapons and money illegally across borders that could assist terrorist networks.

In 'Multilateral Arms Control as a Response to NBC Proliferation – A New Transatlantic Divide?' Alexander Kelle asks if more effective arms control should be the major European response to the proliferation of weapons of mass destruction. Kelle analyzes European efforts to strengthen the nuclear, biological and chemical arms control regimes over the past few years and concludes that Europe emerges as the 'model student' of multilateral NBC arms control. Kelle assesses the US and European approaches to multilateral arms control as a response to the NBC proliferation problem and in his view, the heavy reliance Europeans place on multilateral mechanism is to a large degree the externalization of the institution building processes utilized by European countries to create security in Europe itself. The chapter concludes by placing the findings from these three areas of multilateral arms control in the wider context of US and European arms control and security thinking, in order to answer the question whether we are facing a new and deep transatlantic divide over multilateral NBC arms control as a response to proliferation.

In the final chapter of the book, 'What Future for Europe's Security and Defense Policy? Five Scenarios for the Year 2020,' Heiko Borchert and Daniel Maurer outline five widely differing scenarios (Trilateral Cooperation, Pax Americana, Europower, Resurging National Sovereignty, and Unstable Periphery) that could lie in the future of the European Union and the European Security and Defense Policy (ESDP) and discusses each of their possible consequences. The chapter examines the risks and opportunities entailed in each scenario, reflects upon the impact on conflict prevention, conflict management, and post-conflict stabilization on how situations develop and looks at the relationship between the EU and its members and those between the EU and other leading powers and international organizations. The two authors argue that as capabilities mirror political ambitions, a political process to flesh out Europe's key capabilities at the strategic level should be established as a matter of urgency.

At a time of unprecedented turmoil in the transatlantic relationship, this book addresses a number of the key issues that face decision-makers on both sides of the Atlantic, as they struggle to find solutions to the new security challenges confronting Western societies. It is our hope that this collection of essays can serve as a catalyst for an increased dialogue among policy makers and opinion formers on these and act as a conduit for building greater understanding about the complex challenges the transatlantic relationship now faces and the wide variety of options available to Western nations as they confront the issues that are going to define the political and military, not to mention social and economic, landscape of the West for the foreseeable future.

Notes

1. Hans Morgenthau, *Politics among Nations*, New York, 1985, 6th edn, 205–6.
2. Stephen M. Walt, The Origins of Alliances (Cornell University Press: Ithaca, 1987).
3. John J. Mearsheimer, 'The False Promise of International Institutions,' *International Security*, Vol. 19, no. 3 (Winter 1994/95), 13–14.
4. Kenneth N. Waltz, 'The Emerging Structure of International Politics,' *International Security*, Vol. 18, no. 2 (Fall 1993), 75–6. See also John J. Mearsheimer, 'Back to the Future,' *International Security*, Vol. 15, no. 1 (Summer 1990), 52.

5. Waltz's two explanations of NATO's survival do not contribute to the analyses of the changing security challenges: 1. NATO took on a life of its own; and 2. The US wants it to bolster its own hegemony. (Kenneth N. Watz, 'Structural Realism after the Cold War,' *International Security*, Vol. 25, no. 1 (Summer 2000), 5–42.

6. Robert O. Keohane, Joseph S. Nye and Stanley Hoffmann (eds), *After the Cold War: International Institutions and State Strategies in Europe, 1989–1991* (Cambridge: Cambridge University Press, 1993), 2.

7. Emanuel Adler and Michael Barnett (eds), *Security Communities* (Cambridge: Cambridge University Press, 1998).

8. Karl Deutsch *et al.*, *Political Community and the North Atlantic Area* (Princeton, NJ: Princeton University Press, 1957), 5.

9. B. Buzan, O. Waever and J. de Wilde, *Security: a new Framework for Analysis* (Bolder: Lynne Rienner, 1998).

10. *Transatlantic Trends 2004*, A Project of The German Marshall Fund of the United States and the Compagnia Di San Paolo with Additional Support from the Luso-American Foundation, Fundación Bbva, and the Institute for Public Affairs (Ivo), September 2004.

11. C. Krauthammer, 'The Unipolar Moment', *Foreign Affairs*, Vol. 70, No. 1 (1991) 23–33.

12. C. Krauthammer, 'Help Wanted', *Time* (1 September 2003), 72.

Part I
New Risks and Challenges

1
Defining the Enemy: EU and US Threat Perceptions After 9/11

Susan E. Penksa

Introduction

What does it mean for a state to be secure? Threats are challenges to the security of a state and to its national interests. Threat perceptions are sets of beliefs about the nature of insecurity and what constitutes an 'enemy'. To understand how states perceive security threats is to know something about how they define their security environment and what value priorities they project onto that environment. The way in which threat is defined is a major component of the security culture of a state.

In this context, it is frequently argued that the terrorist attacks of 9/11 transformed world politics by refocusing American foreign policy, redefining transatlantic relations, and increasing the scope and pace of European cooperation in the high profile fields of justice, home affairs, foreign policy and security. Since the international conflict over the war with Iraq in 2003, even more attention has been directed towards understanding the epochal influences of 11 September 2001. Many analysts have asked if 9/11 fundamentally altered perceptions of security or if it merely accelerated a dramatic shift in threat perception that had already been initiated with the end of the Cold War. For present purposes, we need to ask in what ways EU and US threat perceptions have changed since 9/11 – whether there has been a divergence in threat perception between the EU and US and/or if the recent transatlantic conflict over Iraq reveals mainly tactical differences between the two sides of the Atlantic.

Comparing EU threat perceptions with US perspectives poses at least two challenges. The first obstacle is the difference between the two decision-making systems in the field of foreign and security policy. The US makes foreign policy decisions only at the national level. The EU, on the other hand, is a system of multi-level governance in which member states retain substantial autonomy in foreign and security policy – an autonomy that must then be negotiated toward a common position in intergovernmental negotiations mediated by the EU.[1] At the same time, foreign and security policy is formed by EU officials negotiating with member state representatives. What is new in EU decision-making is the creation of EU-level institutions that add a community dimension to foreign and security cooperation. The present situation leaves in place two sometimes complementary but often different sets of security perspectives in which the interests, needs and agreed upon rhetoric of security at the EU level are not necessarily identical with those of individual member states.

A second problem of analyzing EU–US threat perceptions is methodological. How does one define security threats and measure perceptions about them? Three principal dimensions shape the perception of EU security threats. The first is the institutional context. The complex machinery of decision-making in the EU has long produced a consensus view that distills the interaction among member states and between member states and EU institutions. Second, member states retain a great deal of foreign policy autonomy and articulate an array of views as yet only partly constrained by the habits of cooperation. Finally, the specific individuals (officials, specialists, politicians) who craft and implement policy have views that often constitute a distinct and highly influential security sub-culture. Hence, EU level institutional, national and elite perceptions of security threats all contribute to a new and more complex EU security culture. In a sense, the identification of the enemy and what to do about perceived threats are and must be the subject of multi-level negotiation. A serious shortcoming of analyses of European security and transatlantic relations that are exclusively state-centric is an exclusion of non-state actors such as the EU.

To probe perceptions at the national and EU levels, it is necessary to focus primarily on a comparative analysis of the threat perceptions articulated in documents such as the *European Security Strategy (ESS)*, the *National Security Strategy (NSS)* of the US, EU and US policy statements, as well as on national and EU statements about contemporary security requirements emerging from the war on terror. Threat perceptions of operational policy elites are based upon over 60 individual interviews with foreign and defense ministry officials in Berlin, London and Paris as well as with EU, NATO and national officials in Brussels and Sarajevo.[2]

Defining the enemy: the EU perspective

Even though the development of the EU as a security actor is still incomplete, it is now possible to make a comparison between EU and US threat perceptions. Although the events of 9/11 led to swift EU action in policy agreements such as the adoption of a European arrest warrant, the freezing of terrorist assets, steps to cut off the financing of known terrorist individuals and groups and the signing of a Mutual Legal Assistance and Extradition Agreement with the United States (as well as EU and member state participation in Afghanistan), there was no attempt by EU member states to write a specific European threat analysis, similar to a national security strategy. In the aftermath of the transatlantic and European conflict over Iraq in December 2003, EU members adopted their first security strategy as well as a strategy against the proliferation of weapons of mass destruction.

As drafted by CFSP High Representative Javier Solana and his team, the *European Security Strategy (ESS)* provides more of a grand strategy than a precise statement of EU policy. EU and member state officials provide at least five reasons why the *ESS* is critical for the future of the EU as a global actor: first, the *ESS* is intended to produce the first of an ongoing effort to define a common European strategic vision to support the continued evolution of a European strategic culture; second, it is to provide a basis for dialogue among EU member states that will foster both unity of perception and unity of decision; third, it is designed to encourage both sides of the Atlantic to resume a strategic dialogue; fourth, to offer a security agenda parallel to the US *National Security Strategy (NSS)* and lastly, to serve as a framework for discussion with national parliaments, media and the European public.[3]

German Foreign Minister Fischer notes that after the attacks of 9/11, European states recognized that the strategic landscape of international politics would be irrevocably altered but that 9/11 had failed to encourage member states to produce a EU strategic analysis.[4] When the conflict over Iraq broke out, the absence of a common European threat assessment and the lack of a strategic consciousness inhibited productive dialogue with the United States. The transatlantic and European disagreements about Iraq served as the catalyst to create a European strategic statement that would articulate a European understanding about new security threats, a reality that was first experienced when war and genocide occurred in the former Yugoslavia and then again, after September 11.

The *ESS* is as much about presenting a response to the American *NSS* as it is a statement of the Union's approach to international and regional security cooperation in the post-Cold War period. After 1989, there was no longer a European fear of a traditional territorial threat from a conventional invasion from the Soviet Union; the end of the Cold War has ushered in new threats '... which are more diverse, less visible, and less predictable'.[5] The *ESS* addresses the interwoven problems of conflict, insecurity and poverty and identifies five main threats to European security: terrorism, the proliferation of weapons of mass destruction, regional conflicts (such as those in Kashmir, Africa's Great Lakes Region, the Korean peninsula and the Middle East), failed states and organized crime. As the *ESS* notes, 'taking these elements together – terrorism committed to maximum violence, the availability of weapons of mass destruction, organised crime, the weakening of the state system and the privatisation of force – we could be confronted with a very radical threat indeed'.[6] Based on the Union's past achievements in civilian security, the *ESS* acknowledges that achieving security requires more than just a military response and that a multi-faceted policy of conflict prevention may require a complex combination of diplomatic, economic, humanitarian, intelligence, judicial, policing, military and political strategies.

The *EU Strategy Against Proliferation of Weapons of Mass Destruction* identifies the spread of weapons of mass destruction and their means of delivery, especially when in the hands of terrorists, as a primary threat to international peace and security. In fact, terrorist activity was highlighted as 'a new critical dimension to this threat'.[7] In consonance with statements by EU officials such as Javier Solana and Christopher Patten, the strategy notes that the EU will approach a multilateral response to the threat, including but not limited to disarmament and non-proliferation.[8] The document affirms – as does the *ESS* – a comprehensive, multifaceted security strategy in which 'the EU will continue to address the root causes of instability including through pursuing and enhancing its efforts in the areas of political conflicts, development assistance, reduction of poverty and promotion of human rights'.[9]

Three conclusions can be drawn from both of these EU strategies. First, both statements indicate that the EU conceptualization of security is comprehensive. In a series of interviews conducted with national and EU officials since 1996, there was over 90 per cent agreement with this perspective. While the academic community still rightly desires to bring greater conceptual clarity to the area of security studies, the epistemic and operational security community in Europe seems united in their understanding of the artificial divide between internal and external security and between civilian and military forms of security strategy.[10] As expressed in a British paper on EU civil–military cooperation, 'the development of ESDP within the EU is unique in that it has the potential to deliver a fully integrated civil and military crisis management capability, internally and externally'.[11] This broad understanding of security does not imply that European actors see all international issues as potential security threats. It does suggest, however, that European security actors are operating with a paradigm for European security that is different from that of their American counterparts.

Second, there is normative convergence about the types of threats that endanger European peace and stability. The *ESS* represents a significant step in defining a European strategic vision. Stressing the indivisibility of security and the symbiotic nature of postwar security threats, national and EU officials have accelerated changes in European security policy that had already been initiated in the immediate post-Cold War environment. In fact, officials from the United Kingdom, one of the most Atlantic-oriented EU member states, admit that on most issues of international security, 'there is more European convergence than US–European convergence'.[12] Terrorism was a threat to European security before 9/11 but what changed after 11 September 2001 was an elevated perception of the urgency of the problem and the recognition of the likely combination of a 'triple-threat' of international terrorism, failed states and the proliferation of weapons of mass destruction.[13] What also is striking is normative agreement about the diffuse nature of security threats – the triple threat is not the only security concern of the EU. Ethnic conflict, organized crime and drug trafficking all may threaten the security of the extended European region.

Among the EU member states, there is a growing convergence of threat perception, a prerequisite for the establishment of a common strategic culture. Of course, each member state retains its own bilateral relationships and national foreign and defense policies in a domestic environment linked to unique geographical, historical and political particularities. But, it is also the case that member states bring to the EU national concerns that then shape the outcome of EU-level decisions, choices which then feedback into shaping the articulation of national security interests. While there is not yet a theory of EU foreign policy that allows analysts to describe adequately the complicated process of system feedback at play in European security cooperation, there is an overwhelming consensus among national and EU officials that a Union level CFSP/ESDP is increasingly framing national foreign policy decision-making. For illustration, we need only to recall that EU enlargement to Spain and Portugal brought to the Union an increased concentration on the Mediterranean region while Swedish accession sharpened the focus of ESDP to include conflict prevention and the root causes of conflict. Many of the former communist countries that joined in 2004 maintain a heightened disquiet about Russia; their insecurities have already had an impact on the further development of CFSP/ESDP.

Lastly, both agendas outline a EU security policy based upon a continuation of a post-Cold War approach to security that emphasizes multilateral cooperation, preventive engagement utilizing economic, political and military tools of leverage, and transatlantic cooperation. EU support for the Kyoto Protocol, the International Criminal Court, the whole range of WMD non-proliferation regimes, as well as EU engagement in Afghanistan, Kosovo, Moldova, Iran, North Korea and Libya, are but a few of the examples of the multilateral approach to regional and international security most often pursued by the EU. The European experience of integration and the indivisibility of post-Cold War security interests have reinforced a strong European belief that national solutions to multilateral problems are simply untenable. Interview data reveal a strong endorsement amongst both national and EU officials about the indispensability of multilateralism and the need to improve EU coherence in foreign and security policy. All EU member states seem to realize and accept that the EU is more than an organization with only a set of political and economic objectives. Inevitably, the enlargement of the security function of the Union and the expanded role of the EU beyond the immediate European region will place new requirements on the political will and institutional capacity of the Union and its member states, a phenomenon that is likely to challenge and sharpen the US security approach and clarify transatlantic differences.[14]

The *ESS* is quite clear that preventive engagement using all of the different tools of the Union is as important – if not more so – than the possible recourse to force, which is only one element of the Union's strategy. Favoring a 'stronger international society, well functioning international institutions and a rule-based international order', the *ESS* vaguely alludes to the possible use of coercive action when the rules of international organizations, regimes and treaties are violated.[15] The *EU Strategy Against Proliferation of WMD* is much clearer, however, in its statement of the relationship between preventive engagement and the application of force (Chapter II.15):

> Political and diplomatic preventative measures (multilateral treaties and export control regimes) and resort to the competent international organizations form the first line of defence against proliferation. When these measures (including political dialogue and diplomatic pressure) have failed, coercive measures under Chapter VII of the UN Charter and international law (sanctions, selective or global, interceptions of shipments and, as appropriate, the use of force) could be envisioned. The UN Security Council should play a central role.

Both EU documents affirm the centrality of multilateralism (and specifically the UN system), non-proliferation and disarmament, export control regimes, and transatlantic cooperation. While neither strategy offers concrete guidance on the use of force by the Union, both statements provide a basis from which to proceed in future discussions. Strong European opposition to waging war in Iraq does not mean that force is eliminated as a viable option to addressing the triple threat, but it does suggest that there is a need for greater clarity about the use of force as an option of last resort.

In a high-stakes situation such as the decision to wage war against Iraq, the weaknesses of CFSP prevail. There is no EU seat on the UN Security Council (UNSC), so CFSP is only possible so long as the permanent UNSC members of Britain and France reflect a EU consensus. Unlike in Afghanistan, there was no international consensus that the use of force against Iraq was warranted or justifiable. And in contrast to the war in Kosovo, there was marked disagreement about Iraq among NATO members. States such as Germany and France strongly repudiated preventive war as a strategy for addressing the Iraqi threat, a threat that, in any case, they perceived as insufficiently established in Iraq, and as a distraction from the war on terror. Perhaps most significant was the intervention of the United States in EU policy-making, an enormously influential exogenous factor. EU security cooperation is not so mature that it can resist such strong pressure from the United States. The extent to which the EU has become a security actor is also limited by the significant autonomy that EU member states retain in foreign and security policy.

Notwithstanding these observations, these are still early days for CFSP. Perhaps the European row over Iraq is better viewed as an anomaly rather than as a predictive case for the future of European security cooperation or as evidence for a divergence of European threat perception.

Defining and defeating the enemy: a comparison of EU and US perspectives

September 11 defined a new era in American foreign policy and transatlantic relations. Initially, the post-Cold War period was characterized by an expanded and more interdependent view of American national security while the post-9/11 period represents a return to a more traditional territorially and militarily focused approach to American security policy. The catastrophic attacks of 9/11 were unprecedented in scope. From that moment, the war on terrorism was perceived as the single most important foreign policy priority by the United States. Secretary of State Powell explained that 'It will remain so for as long as necessary, because terrorism – potentially linked to the proliferation of weapons of mass destruction [WMD] – now represents the greatest threat to American lives'.[16] While the *National Security Strategy (NSS)* details many other security challenges, it is unequivocal in stating that the strategic priority of the United States is to combat global terror.[17] This represents a monumental change in strategic orientation by the US.

Both the EU and US share a common focus on the triple threat. Like the *ESS*, the *NSS* acknowledges the panoply of economic, political and military sources of global insecurity which threaten to destabilize not only the American way of life, but also international peace and security. But the *NSS* outlines a comprehensive understanding of national security in which the war on terror is the most urgent. One US official put it bluntly: 'there is only one security issue on our mind now – terrorism'.[18] There is unanimous agreement amongst EU and US officials that terrorism and the proliferation of weapons of mass destruction (and their possible acquisition by terrorist networks) represent a primary threat to transatlantic and international security. European officials, however, are more apt (in well over 80 per cent of interviews) to acknowledge the interrelated security concerns of political and ethnic conflict, poverty and state failure and terrorism than are US officials (who reference multiple security concerns in only 50 per cent of interviews). In fact, European perceptions and strategies confirm a wide approach to security and a blurred distinction between civil and military forms of security, 'where none of the new threats is purely military; nor can any be tackled by purely military means'.[19] For the US, the post 9/11 period has produced a more dramatic change in worldview, in strategic perception, and in response.

Strategically, the *NSS* supports a doctrine of preemptive force to deal with emerging threats. President Bush justified this doctrine before the United Nations:

> Outlaw regimes that possess nuclear, chemical, and biological weapons –
> and the means to deliver them – would be able to use blackmail and create
> chaos in entire regions. These weapons could be used by terrorists to bring
> sudden disaster and suffering on a scale we can scarcely imagine. The
> deadly combination of outlaw regimes and terror networks and weapons
> of mass murder is a peril that cannot be ignored or wished away. If such a
> danger is allowed to fully materialize, all words, all protests, will come too
> late. Nations of the world must have the wisdom and the will to stop
> grave threats before they arrive.[20]

This is the second issue on which the *ESS* parts company with the *NSS*.
Robert Jervis explains that one of the significant components of the Bush
doctrine is 'the perception of great threats that can be defeated only by new
and vigorous policies, most notably preventive war'.[21] Jervis suggests that
unless all would-be enemies are deterred by the action of the US in Iraq,
'preventive war will have to be repeated as other threats reach a similar
threshold'.[22] Conversely, both the *ESS* and the *Strategy Against Proliferation
of WMD* emphasize multilateral actions taken in accord with strengthening
the system of international law enshrined in the UN Charter. Force is seen as
a last resort, not a primary centerpiece of strategic doctrine as in the case of
the *NSS*. In individual interviews with EU officials and national political
officers, an important qualification is usually made: while terrorism and
weapons of mass destruction are viewed as primary security threats, officials
caution that Europe is not as singularly focused on the military aspects of
fighting terrorism. In the words of the *ESS*, 'dealing with terrorism may
require a mixture of intelligence, police, judicial, military and other
means.'[23] Interviews with European officials suggest that this tactical difference of emphasis is reflected in the European perception that the United
States is unjustifiably preoccupied with military strategy and by the United
States view that the EU is too focused on civilian responses.

The debate over Iraq represents a significant rupture regarding the use of
force – a sharp difference of view about the conditions that should govern
the preemptive application of force.[24] New guidelines to govern the use of
force – to protect civilians facing a genocidal threat, to prevent a terrorist
attack or to punish states which fail to take effective measures against
terrorist actors or fail to comply with non-proliferation regimes – require
sustained discussion at both the national and international levels. The UN
Charter was written on the assumption that the main threat to international
peace and security would come from state actors, not transnational actors
such as terrorist organizations and individuals. Thus far, the Bush administration – in both policy statements and actions – has defined terrorism
largely in conventional, state-centric terms and has been reluctant
to address the long-term, diffuse causes of terrorism. Since 9/11, the two
main military operations of the United States involved an attack on two

nation-states, Afghanistan and Iraq. The EU and its member states unanimously supported military action in Afghanistan while intervention in Iraq was bitterly contested. Many European officials questioned the American administration's justification for war, a rationale that seemed inconsistent, unconvincing, and even a diversionary tactic from the more complex challenge implied by the so-called war on terror.

A third, and related, fissure between the two actors is the US preference for 'coalitions of the willing' to support US interests. In contrast, the *ESS* highlights the exigency of maintaining an international order based on international law and effective multilateralism. Europeans do not perceive effective multilateralism, embedded in international and regional institutions, as constitutive of the US approach to 'organizing coalitions – as broad as practicable – of states able and willing to promote a balance of power that favors freedom'.[25] EU and member state officials from France, Germany and the United Kingdom confirm that despite EU and US shared values about democracy, rule of law, human rights, and the threat of terrorism, there exists still unresolved conflict between the EU and US concerning the role of force, the place of international institutions, and the most efficacious means for addressing the new security threats.

What was noteworthy about the European reaction to the Madrid bombings of 11 March 2004 is that EU and member state officials emphasized the significance of improving existing *civilian* capabilities in the fight against terrorism. Moreover, Javier Solana called upon EU members to 'tackle the factors behind terrorism. No cause justifies terrorism, but nothing justifies ignoring the causes of terrorism … where these grievances are legitimate they must be addressed, not just because this is a matter of justice but also because "draining the swamp" depends on it'.[26] A European preference for and belief in conflict prevention is not simply generated out of weaknesses in military capabilities, nor should it be equated with pacifism. Even France and the United Kingdom, the two militarily dominant member states of the EU, recognize that the domestic, regional, historical and geopolitical interests of West European states may not be consonant with those of the United States. The Middle East is an excellent example where domestic and geopolitical considerations have led to EU priorities and perspectives that are quite different from those of the US. In the best of all possible worlds, these strategic and worldview differences will lead to greater complementarity and political effectiveness. In the worst of situations, it will produce European discord, transatlantic differences and decreased security.

Defining the enemy: public opinion

Is there a difference between elite threat perceptions and public opinion of security threats? Since 9/11, four significant surveys of European and American foreign and security policy attitudes have been conducted by the Chicago Council on Foreign Relations and the German Marshall Fund of the

United States (*Worldviews 2002*); the German Marshall Fund and the Compagnia Di San Paolo (*Transatlantic Trends 2003*); and two survey projects by the Pew Research Center for the People and the Press (*What the World Thinks in 2002* and *A Year After Iraq War: Mistrust of America in Europe Ever Higher, Muslim Anger Persists*).[27] Each of these studies provides rich and complex data regarding public attitudes of transatlantic relations, international institutions, American foreign policy, and international security. While public opinion surveys are sensitive to current international events and may quickly change, they nevertheless provide a critical means to gauging public sentiment about key foreign policy attitudes.

Similar to the convergence in elite threat perceptions, public opinion surveys suggest that Europeans and American share a perception of terrorism as a critical international threat. In *Transatlantic Trends 2003*, the data reveal that both Americans and Europeans (70 per cent of both populations) perceive that international terrorism is the most important international threat (a similar finding to that reported in *Worldviews 2002*).[28] The 2003 survey concludes that Americans and Europeans share similar threat perceptions (regarding terrorism, Iraq developing weapons of mass destruction, and Islamic fundamentalism), but they have different visions of how best to respond. When respondents were asked questions regarding North Korea and Iran acquiring weapons of mass destruction, as well as questions that included a hypothetical situation whereby a country was found to be harboring terrorists or was a potential nuclear threat to a neighboring state, Americans were more apt than Europeans to support the use of military force.[29] In the case of support for military action against Iran, 44 per cent of Europeans would favor it while 73 per cent of Americans responded supportively. In the case of support for military action against North Korea, only 37 per cent of Europeans would do so while 63 per cent of Americans were willing. This finding is consistent with that of the *Worldviews 2002* study which reported that a clear majority of Europeans and Americans were willing to support the deployment of military forces to assist a population struck by famine, to uphold international law, to liberate hostages, to destroy a terrorist camp and to bring peace to a region where there is a civil war. The primary difference is that more Europeans seem willing to use force for humanitarian and international conflicts, whereas a larger majority of Americans support the use of troops to combat terrorism.[30]

Regarding the perception of Iraq as a threat, *Worldviews 2002* found that 57 per cent of Europeans believed that Iraq developing weapons of mass destruction was an extremely important threat, in contrast to 86 per cent of Americans who viewed it as critical.[31] Important to note is that while both European and American citizens expressed concern about Iraq as a potential military threat, more Americans were worried about the Iraqi threat than were European respondents. In the *Worldviews 2002* survey, only international terrorism was perceived by larger majorities of both Europeans and Americans as a critical threat. Clearly, Iraq was perceived as a matter of security concern on both sides of the Atlantic. Again, the main difference seems to one of strategy, rather than of perception. *What the World Thinks in 2002* supports the finding of *Worldviews 2002*. While Iraq is seen as a threat to regional and international security, American motives for using force against Iraq are viewed with suspicion.[32]

Since the 2003 war in Iraq, there has been a widening attitudinal gap between Europeans and Americans. While a clear of majority of Europeans and Americans agree that international terrorism is a threat to security, they disagree on the severity of the threat and the appropriate strategy; Americans generally express a much higher level of concern about threats than do European citizens. Differences in transatlantic attitudes that emerge most significantly in the 2004 Pew study include a stronger European predilection for obtaining UN approval for the use of force, a European belief that the war in Iraq hurt the war on terrorism, a European disbelief in American trust-worthiness, a perception that the United States acts unilaterally without taking into account the interest of other countries, and a European preference to have the UN help the Iraqis form a stable government rather than the United States. When respondents were asked if it would be a good thing for the EU to become as powerful as the US, half or more of the public in each of the five European countries surveyed answered affirmatively (90 per cent in France; 70 per cent in Germany; 67 per cent in Russia; 67 per cent in Turkey and 50 per cent in Britain).[33] EU public support for a more powerful EU is also followed by a dedicated interest in the EU pursuing more independence in security and foreign policy affairs (75 per cent in France; 60 per cent in Turkey; 56 per cent in Russia; 63 per cent in Germany and 56 per cent in Britain).[34]

Taken as a whole, these surveys suggest that there is a common transatlantic perception about the threat of terrorism, but markedly different European and American perspectives on the application of force, the role of the United Nations, and the unilateral approach favored by the Bush administration. While European governments expressed strategic divergence about Iraq in 2003, there seems to be a meeting of minds between European elites and public opinion. Currently, the major divergence is not so much between European govern-ments and their citizens but between European and American citizens, and to a lesser extent, between European governments and the Bush administration.

Conclusion

In 1956, in the early years of the Cold War, NATO acknowledged that,

> ... security is today far more than a military matter. The strengthening of political consultation and economic cooperation, the development of resources, progress in education and public understanding, all these can be as important, or even more important, for the protection of the secur-ity of a nation, or an alliance, as the building of a battleship or the

equipping of an army. These two aspects of security – civil and military – can no longer be considered in watertight compartments, either within or between nations. Perhaps NATO has not yet fully recognized their essential interrelationship, or done enough to bring about that close and continuous contact between its civil and military sides which is essential if it is to be strong and enduring.

In a post-Cold War, post-11 September context, those words seem prescient. It has become common wisdom to discuss the ways in which attaining security in a post-Cold War, post-9/11 world requires a sophisticated blend of military and civilian strategies. Despite its wisdom in 1956, NATO did not transform its strategic vision until the end of the Cold War. What about the EU? For the EU, security was provided by NATO and regional integration. Because the EU was a civilian power, it took the collapse of the Cold War and changes in international security to globalize the EU focus and to augment to the EU vision an explicit commitment to developing a common security policy. For the United States, it was 11 September that revolutionized its strategic doctrine. For both the EU and the United States, 11 September was a turning point – in threat assessment, in strategic focus, and in transatlantic relations. No less dramatic a moment was the decision by the United States, United Kingdom and other key allies to embark on regime change in Iraq on 19 March 2003.

Who then is the enemy? Both the EU and US agree on the 'triple threat' but European officials, both national and EU, highlight more comprehensive threat concerns more often than do American officials, who seem more singularly focused on the triple threat. In the post-9/11 period, the US seems to have returned to a more traditional geopolitical understanding of territorial defense whereas the EU shares a broad consensus that security threats are diffuse and mutually reinforcing and that only a comprehensive strategy of civil-military tools makes sense in response to them. The strategic divide between the EU and US (and among EU members in 2003) is not as significant and irreversible so as to end transatlantic cooperation or halt European integration in foreign and security policy. But both processes are being transformed and require more creativity, sensitivity and commitment to dialogue and consensus building. Perhaps the real challenge is for the EU and US to realize that they share a similar view of the enemy, and to build on the common values and interests that both actors embrace in a renewed effort to increase transatlantic cooperation, a critical component in realizing international peace and security.

Notes

1. See G. Marks, L. Hooghe and K. Blank, 'European Integration from the 1980s: State-Centric v. Multi-Level Governance', *Journal of Common Market Studies*, 34, 3 (1996) 341–78.

2. More than 100 interviews have been conducted by the author since 1996. This chapter uses interview data from over 60 interviews during the period 2002–04. Due to requests for anonymity, specific names and titles of interview respondents have been omitted. A future study will provide a more comprehensive content analysis of the interview data.
3. These explanations are derived from individual interviews with British, French, German and EU Officials in March 2004.
4. 'Die Rekonstruktion des Westens', *Frankfurter Allgemeine Zeitung*, 6 March 2004, personal translation.
5. 'A Secure Europe in a Better World', *European Security Strategy*, Brussels, 12 December 2003, p.3.
6. *ibid.*, p.5.
7. *EU Strategy Against the Proliferation of Weapons of Mass Destruction*, Brussels, 10 December 2003, p.2.
8. C. Patten and R. Perle, 'Patten vs. Perle: Is the U.S. a Unilateralist Hegemon?' *European Affairs* (Winter 2003), and J. Solana, 'The Voice of Europe on Security Matters', Royal Institute for International Relations, 26 November 2003.
9. *EU Strategy*, p.5.
10. For a classic statement elaborating on an expanded definition of security, see B. Buzan, *People, States, and Fear: An Agenda for International Security Studies in the Post-Cold War Era* (CO: Lynne Rienner Publishers, 1991).
11. UK Non-Paper, *EU Civil–Military Co-ordination*, 15 July 2002.
12. This perspective was echoed by nearly all of the British officials interviewed during the period of 2002–04.
13. G. Burghardt, *EU Civilian Crisis Management Capabilities and the Emerging EU Security Strategy*, Address (3–5 October 2003), http://www.eurunion.org/news/speeches/2003
14. S. Penksa and W. Mason, 'EU Security Cooperation and the Transatlantic Relationship', *Cooperation and Conflict*, 38, 3 (2003).
15. *ESS*, p.9.
16. C. Powell, 'A Strategy of Partnerships', *Foreign Affairs* (January/February 2004), 22.
17. *The National Security Strategy of the United States of America*, 17 September 2002.
18. Interview, US Official, October 2002.
19. 'A Secure Europe in a Better World', European Security Strategy, Brussels, 12 December 2003, p.12.
20. President Bush Addresses United Nations General Assembly, 23 September 2003, p.4.
21. R. Jervis, 'Understanding the Bush Doctrine', *Political Science Quarterly*, 118 (2003), 365.
22. Jervis, 371.
23. *ESS*, p.7.
24. An excellent discussion of the legal complexities of the application of force in anti-terrorism efforts is provided in A. Cassese, 'The Current Legal Vacuum in Relation to the Fight Against Terrorism', Executive Summary, Committee on Foreign Affairs, Human Rights and Common Security and Defense Policy of the European Parliament (January 2004).
25. *NSS*, p.12.
26. J. Solana, 'Three Ways for Europe to Prevail Against the Terrorists', *The Financial Times*, 25 March 2004, p.19.
27. See the full survey results in *Worldviews 2002*, Chicago Council on Foreign Relations and the German Marshall Fund of the United States, 2002; *Transatlantic Trends*

2003, The German Marshall Fund and the Compagnia Di San Paolo, 2003; *What the World Thinks in 2002*, The Pew Global Attitudes Project, Washington, DC, 4 December 2002; and *A Year After Iraq War: Mistrust of America in Europe Ever Higher, Muslim Anger Persists*, The Pew Global Attitudes Project, 16 March 2004.
28. *Transatlantic Trends 2003*, pp.12–13.
29. *ibid.*, p.13.
30. *Worldviews 2002*, p.12.
31. *ibid.*, p.9–10.
32. *What the World Thinks in 2002*, p.2.
33. *A Year After Iraq War*, p.9.
34. *ibid.*, p.8.

2

A Revolution in Strategy? Conducting War in an Age of Rogues

Jan Willem Honig

To bring out the issues involved in understanding and designing Western strategy in the post-Cold War world in this chapter, a simple conceptual approach is followed. The reader is asked to distinguish between the aims *of* war and aims *in* war.[1] This distinction neatly reflects the hierarchically linked, yet bureaucratically distinct spheres of the government and the military. The aims of war are politically defined and constitute the ultimate objectives that war as both an instrument and a means must serve. The aims in war are the translation of political aims into subordinate aims that can be directly attained by the use of force. First, I will first examine the nature of the West's political objectives in conflicts and the question of how and why they have changed since the end of the Cold War. Second, the subordinate level of the West's strategic objectives will be considered. Third, since war is an interactive (dialectic, if you will) process, the objectives and methods of the 'enemy' must also to be considered. Who are we up against? What are his motives? How does he fight?

Strategy, as conventionally understood, is about achieving political aims with the use of force.[2] In other words, strategy is the interface between politics and war; its task is to use the destructive process of war to achieve the desired political results.

If a revolution in strategy is taking place it will find expression in the definition of aims of war and the aims in war. The key issue is whether we have definitely left behind the era of total war, an age in which wars were struggles of survival which required huge military efforts. Liberal democratic regimes see war as a morally hazardous endeavor that should only be undertaken as a last resort. In practice, they tend to want to fight wars with limited aims.[3] In turn, that means that wars must be fought with limited means for limited strategic ends – which goes against the modern military understanding of what warfighting requires. Whether or not the revolution will be carried through depends on three big 'ifs': first, if the escalatory pressures emanating from an uncompromising realist and radical liberal world view abates; second, if no opponent emerges who both desires and is capable of threatening the survival of the West; and third, if the military adopt a radically different understanding of the nature of war. Analyzing the nature of revolutions is notoriously contentious, and trying to pinpoint the nature of one that may, or may not be, happening even more so. Still, whatever the outcome, an analytical focus on political and strategic aims should be a key aspect of any debate on contemporary war.

Aims of war: 'to act as a force for good in the world'

The legitimacy of war as a political instrument was seriously narrowed during the course of the twentieth century. At the century's start, the sanctity of national interest determined the question of war's legitimacy. The generally accepted notion was that if a state deemed a vital national interest to be at stake (or, interestingly, its 'honor'), it had the right to resort to force.[4] The right to go to war, in other words, was an inalienable attribute of state sovereignty. The most important restrictive change to this right came with the 1945 UN Charter.[5] States only possessed the 'inherent right' to use force in case of 'individual or collective self-defense' and then, according to article 51, merely:

> ... until the Security Council has taken the measures necessary to maintain international peace and security. Measures taken by Members in the exercise of this right of self-defense shall be immediately reported to the Security Council and shall not in any way affect the authority and responsibility of the Security Council under the present Charter to take at any time such action as it deems necessary in order to maintain or restore international peace and security.

In essence, therefore, the power to decide on the legitimate use of force was moved from the individual state to an international body which, in this crucial respect, acquired supranational powers that were to be exercised in the pursuit of the maintenance of international peace and security.

It is remarkably rare nowadays for a state using force not to claim to be acting out of self-defense. Even those rulers who probably do not accept the norm still publicly justify their forceful acts in these terms. In fomenting the crisis that led to his invasion of Kuwait in 1990, Saddam Hussein, for example, claimed that he must defend himself against the economic war being waged on him by those 'Arab brethren' who kept the oil price low and thus prevented Iraq from rebuilding its economy that had been shattered by the long war against Iran.[6] Likewise, but more sincerely, the United States consistently justified its intervention against Iraq in 1990–91 in terms of taking action against an unwarranted act of aggression. It avoided the use of oil as a vital national interest argument.[7] In 2002, facing war with India over Kashmir, Pakistan's leader General Pervez Musharraf claimed that 'we have good military deterrence. We not only have a good defensive capability but a good *offensive defensive* capability'.[8] Musharraf's choice of words reflected a clear concern with avoiding any impression of aggressive intent, even while hinting that, in self defense, legitimate and punishing attacks should not be discounted. US President George W. Bush was less restrained when he told West Point graduates on 1 June 2002 that 'the war on terrorism will not be won on the defensive'.[9] The statement expresses a US desire to re-assert sovereign control over the use of force and acquire greater freedom of action to allow for pre-emption. However, though the Bush Administration is clearly uncomfortable with the restrictions imposed by the UN-system on the use of force by states, even it accepts that unilateral and pre-emptive force is legitimized only in a context of self-defense. In Bush's words, the US aims to 'defend the peace against threats from terrorists and tyrants'.[10] Of course, there is a serious danger that these ideas will re-open the door to the more anarchic world of the past, in which force was a sovereign right of states. Nonetheless, at the moment, one can maintain that self-defense has become an accepted fundamental norm in international society.[11]

Invoking the right of legitimate self-defense, however, does not lead to a straightforward definition of war aims at the political level. Should the act of aggression be undone and the *status quo ante* restored, or should the root cause of aggression be tackled? In the case of the first Gulf War, was it enough to liberate Kuwait, or should Saddam Hussein have been removed from power? In the second war against Saddam, was the destruction of the weapons of mass destruction sufficient to end the threat of Saddam or must his regime finally be changed? In the war on terrorism, should terrorism merely be contained through 'homeland defense', or should all terrorists everywhere be hunted down and destroyed? This suggests strongly that the principle of self-defense cannot easily be restricted in its effects to merely its impact on the international system, nor can it be made to function properly in a world which fully respects state sovereignty. The principle of self-defense must inevitably intrude on an aggressor state's internal affairs. In Western democracies, where the normative principle of self-defense has greatest appeal, and where policy choices are in essence seen and presented as ethical choices, the rhetoric favors goal inflation and interventionism. Both Bush Administrations succumbed to the lure of grandiose political statements in their respective wars. The public emphasis on the evil of Saddam Hussein and the comparisons with Hitler, suggested that the Bush Sr Administration was aiming at the complete overthrow of the Iraqi regime. When it came to the crunch, President Bush Sr famously hesitated to deliver the *coup de grace* and instead left the removal of Saddam Hussein to internal forces – whose various attempts all failed. The Bush Jr Administration seems to have drawn from this episode the lesson that one should confront and destroy evil, unilaterally and pre-emptively, or else it can come back to haunt you again and again. President Bush Jr public statements regarding terrorism and Saddam Hussein have consistently been uncompromising. Nonetheless, behind closed (and half-open) doors, debates raged about how far the war (or wars) should actually be taken. Overthrowing the 'Axis of Evil' regimes and destroying terrorism may be a sincere desire on the part of the Bush Jr Administration because it offers a clear end to the problems, but (as we will see below) it raises serious political and moral challenges, not to mention questions of strategic practicality.

Since the end of the Cold War a variation on the idea of self-defense has come into its own as an effective legitimation of intervention, which, even more than the traditional idea, undermines the concept of national sovereignty. The defense of human rights has become, by itself, a necessary cause and justification for the majority of Western military interventions in the past decade. The interventions in the former Yugoslavia, from Croatia and Bosnia to Kosovo and Macedonia, and also in Somalia, Haiti and Sierra Leone would all have been impossible without the necessary justification of the abuse of human rights (even though I should quickly add that it may not, in fact, have been a sufficient justification). And, interestingly, after the failure to find weapons of mass destruction in Iraq, the evil of Saddam Hussein's regime has become a critical *ex-post facto* justification for the war that toppled him in 2003. This development reflects a deepening concern with the internal behavior of states, one that has begun to override the previously sacrosanct principle of national sovereignty. Ways have been sought to fit in the defense of human rights with the *jus ad bellum* as contained in the UN Charter. The brutal Iraqi suppression of the Kurdish and marsh Arab uprisings in the wake of the first Gulf War resulted in a Security Council interpretation that this constituted a 'threat to international peace and security' and the use of 'all necessary means' by the international community was authorized. Technically, it was argued that Saddam's domestic behavior fell under the remit of the Security Council because refugee flows had an international impact. The same principle was applied to Bosnia and Kosovo. In Kosovo, the Security Council did not in the end approve the use of force. But displaying the strength of their human rights concerns (as well as fears over their own political credibility), NATO countries nonetheless decided to use force against Yugoslavia. The Kosovo case illustrates at the same time both the strength and the weakness of legitimizing intervention on the basis of human rights. Paradoxically, human rights' concerns overrode Security Council reservations, but not NATO states' own reservations. They needed the additional, very traditional legitimation of a threat to NATO and UN credibility. The defense of human rights may have been a necessary cause for interventions other than those legitimated by self-defense, but, in contrast to self-defense, they have not generally constituted a sufficient cause as well to use force. As in Kosovo, in Bosnia ultimately other more traditional motives mattered as well. When, after four years of war and after the largest crime of the war at Srebrenica,

Western powers finally decided to use force, a critical reason was also the perception that the conflict began fundamentally to undermine NATO's and the UN's credibility.

But, as with self-defense, the defense of human rights does not easily translate into a ready-made set of immediate political objectives. Is it sufficient to stop human rights abuses, or should the effects of the abuses be reversed, such as the population shifts that were the result ethnic cleansing in Bosnia and Kosovo? Should the perpetrators of the abuses be removed from society and punished? And, if committed by governments, should such regimes be overthrown? The logic here, even more than in the case of punishing aggressors, favors the pursuit of absolute justice. Not only should the abusers of human rights be punished, but the territories in which they operated should be rebuilt on democratic and market economic principles. Yet political pragmatism counsels caution. The greater the degree of justice to be achieved, the greater the human, financial, and thus political, cost to be borne by the forces of intervention. In the face of this cost, there is clearly still a serious lack of conviction regarding the necessity to use force for humanitarian reasons alone. Governments, and perhaps electorates, need the reassurance of more traditional reasons of national interest. The net effect of these factors has been to put restraints on the political aims to be achieved, as well as on the military means employed.

The escalatory pressures inherent in the idea of defense of human rights are further restrained in the West by another more fundamental factor, which also applies to self-defense: the grave moral reservations regarding the actual use of force. The example of the 2003 war against Saddam Hussein is instructive in this regard. The case for war was made by a curious alliance of realists, neo-conservatives and radical liberals. Their arguments ranged from claiming that the best defense against a potential threat was its pre-emptive destruction, to the proven evil of the Saddam regime, which warranted its overthrow and the creation of a world of democratic, free market states would provide the best hedge against future wars. Their opponents – who in Europe appeared to constitute a clear majority – resisted the call for war and demanded containment. They were not convinced of the war's moral legitimacy. The aftermath of the war, with the failure to find weapons of mass destruction and the difficulties of democratic state-building, seems only to have reinforced their stance. The war may therefore prove to be a critical victory for them in their future pursuit of less ambitious, limited political aims.

Aims in war: 'sis miles pacificus'

In surveying the long decade since the demise of the West's major adversary, the Soviet Union, the casual observer may well be struck by how well the West has adapted militarily to the new security environment. The major military operations appear overwhelmingly successful. In 1991, Kuwait was liberated from Iraqi aggression after a five-week air offensive culminating in a 100-hour ground war. The war in Bosnia (and Croatia) was terminated with armed intervention in a matter of weeks in 1995 and 78 days in Kosovo in 1999. Afghanistan was freed from its oppressive 'terrorist' Taleban regime, again within just a few months, in 2001. To cap it all, a lightning, three-week offensive toppled Saddam in 2003. One could add the minor interventions in Haiti in 1994 and Sierra Leone in 2000 to the list. The only apparent outright military failure was Somalia. Once the West bit the political bullet to use force, military success was generally achieved quickly. On a military operational level, the West appears to have cracked the art of the major new post-Cold War military requirement, that of intervention.

That said, however, even the casual observer will note that, on a political level, things seem more troubled. Even the successful operations named above suffered from tortuous political decision-making processes. And in one notable instance – Rwanda – intervention failed to materialize for political reasons. Furthermore, military success was infrequently followed by comparable political success. One might therefore conclude that the key problem of contemporary war for the West is primarily of a political, and not a strategic, nature.

The common complaint from the military about interventions concerns the lack of clear political direction. Particularly in human rights interventions, the military bewail the political confusion on what should be achieved. One of the commanders of the UN Protection Force in Bosnia, Belgian general Francis Briquemont, summed up the attitude in the title of his memoirs: 'Do something, General!' Briquemont found his political guidance – particularly as exemplified in UN Security Council Resolutions – marked by an unworkable level of ambiguity.[12] Interventions legitimated by self-defense may appear to suffer less from this problem. Yet, it is not absent. As we shall see, in the wars over Kuwait, Afghanistan and Iraq, the process of correlating political objectives to strategic objectives was not a straightforward matter either.

Briquemont's complaint is, to an extent, justified and, as I have suggested, it is actually part and parcel of the political nature of interventions. However, often this complaint masks a somewhat different one, namely that the politicians do not understand the true nature of war. The prevailing paradigm among Western militaries, especially in the United States, holds that war is about rendering your opponent defenseless. The aim in war, therefore, is to destroy the enemy's means of resistance. This is best achieved by the use of overwhelming force. Politicians invariably hesitate in the face of the considerable demands that implementing such a strategy places upon them. First, overwhelming force requires a massive mobilization of military resources. Few exigencies, except for a direct attack on one's homeland that threatens the survival of state, unambigiously warrant such a huge effort.

Second, once employed, overwhelming force creates a normative challenge. If the intervention is legitimated by a normative understanding of war in the first place – to do good or to defend oneself – how can the process and the effects of the use of force – causing death and destruction – avoid invalidating the original normative considerations? Can one defend human rights with force without committing further violations to human rights? Can an act of defense justify an attack? The Western tradition of war has sought to reduce the impact of these ethical conundra by restricting the legitimate use of force to fights between narrowly defined, legitimate actors. Combat should only take place between uniformed armed forces, who are the responsible agents, on a strategic and tactical level, for the ultimate (politically) responsible actors, their governments. Civilian society can thus be left untouched and ethical problems minimized.

Two key recent technological developments, precision guided munitions (PGMs) and information acquisition and processing, aid in the execution of a discriminatory strategy that in theory limits targeting to the percieved evildoers and their agents. Even though so far their promise is only partially fulfilled, these technologies could be the central element in enabling the use of limited force and wielding it as a precisely calibrated instrument in the pursuit of justice. Yet, despite being ardent advocates of these new technologies, military officers have found it difficult to accept the ethical–political logic that is beginning to govern their use. This is not simply a function of the type of actors the West is up against, the majority of whom are either non-state or state-based 'rogues' who actively seek to exploit Western concern over collateral damage and who do all in their power to make it difficult to identify who or what to attack (a problem to which I will turn in the third section of this chapter). It is also a function of the prevailing strategic doctrine behind the use of armed force which, as said, focuses on the use of overwhelming force and making the enemy defenseless. Indeed, the development of PGMs and information warfare began in a politico-strategic context that favored this strategic doctrine. To offset its inferiority in conventional weaponry vis-à-vis the Soviet Union, NATO and the US in particular designed these new technologies to act as force equalisers. By being able to identify high-value targets and destroying them in a single strike, NATO hoped to be able to deter, or if necessary, halt any Soviet offensive in Western Europe and score the first, critical military victory in a war that was about saving the West and overthrowing Communism.

The example of air power doctrine and Kosovo illustrates well the tensions between the changed political landscape and the less novel strategic aims that are pursued with novel military means. Governments have found the use of air power over land forces attractive because it offers a less manpower intensive and (for their own side) represents a less casualty intensive war. Such an approach appears to fit in well with the West's usually limited aims – which, in the case of Kosovo, were not the overthrow of the Milosevic regime, but rather the establishment of a constitutional order in Serbia that respected the basic human rights of Kosovars. However, consider the words of NATO's Joint Air Force Component commander in the war over Kosovo, USAF Lieutenant-General Michael C. Short:

> we need to go in with overwhelming force, quite frankly, extraordinary violence that the speed of it, the lethality of it ... the weight of it has to make an incredible impression on the adversary, to such a degree that he is stunned and shocked and his people are immediately asking, 'Why in the world are we doing this? If this is just the first night, then what in the world is the rest of it going to be like? How long can we endure it, and more importantly, why are we having to endure it? Let's ask our leaders why this is happening.' ... You go after the head of the snake, put a dagger in the heart of the adversary, and you bring to bear all the force that you have at your command.[13]

This sort of rhetoric suggests that the objective is to affect the will-power of the enemy's civilian population, who will then force the national leadership to give in. This poses the obvious question about identifying key physical targets, the destruction of which will most affect popular will to resist and fight. Will purely military targets suffice? There is more than a hint here that this is not quite the case. (It also raises the question, a staple of the strategic bombing literature, of how popular will can affect governmental decision-making, which the literature concludes is not such a straightforward process in authoritarian regimes. Although, as we shall see, there is more of a link in the case of Serbia.) General Short, elsewhere in the interview quoted above, suggests that the objective of the bombing campaign was not so much the Serb people as 'the leadership in Belgrade'. The confusion between which actor one is trying to influence seems to have a lot to do with the fuzziness of the connections between cause and effect in air power doctrine (a handicap with a long history), as well as clear convictions on what constitutes the correct target set. The thinking is that if a chosen target set is destroyed from the air, preferably as quickly as possible, then the achievement of one's political aims will then naturally follow. For air power enthusiasts, however, this specifically does not mean attacking front-line troops. Short maintained that the target set was composed of strategic infrastructure, 'between 250 and 300 valid, solid military targets', located particularly in 'downtown Belgrade'. When invited to describe them, he stated:

> The first step in any air campaign is knocking down what we call the Integrated Air Defense System, the IADS. After that, we recommended that we go after what we believed to be the strategic target set in Belgrade – the power grid, lines of communication, as they effected [sic] Belgrade,

the river bridges, the traffic patterns into and out of Belgrade, ... and at least six to eight military command centers in Belgrade.[14]

It is not difficult to understand the nervousness of General Short's political masters when presented with such a plan. The war was explicitly not against the Serb people, but rather against their leaders and their policies in Kosovo. Would not the destruction of Serbia's power grid and the disruption of 'traffic patterns in and out of Belgrade', or indeed the general intent to cause what is now known as 'shock and awe', cause Serb civilians to direct their anger more against NATO and contribute little to preventing the Serb military from ethnically cleansing Kosovo far to the south of Belgrade? Short was not a general with exceptional ideas. His planned air offensive against Serbia followed the same pattern as the air campaigns against Iraq and also initially at least) against Afghanistan. The thinking behind the operation in Bosnia in 1995 (if not quite the practice) was also similar. Air power doctrine is thus rather rigid and formulaic. It offers only a generic solution, one that does not take sufficient account of the specific political objectives it is supposed to help achieve.

Interestingly, attacks on none of the targets mentioned (except possibly one) by General Short actually appear to have influenced Milosevic's decision to concede after 78 days of bombing. Milosevic was a political leader who relied critically on support from the Serb people (as his downfall in October 2000 graphically illustrated). Once he became unsure of popular support, he got ready to give in. The key developments were mounting Serb military casualties in Kosovo and the attacks on television and radio infrastructure, most graphically illustrated by the bombing of the television tower in Belgrade. Although NATO aimed for military hardware in Kosovo as ethically acceptable targets ('tank plinking' as a disgusted Short called it), it also killed, almost inadvertently, soldiers and paramilitaries. This led to demonstrations by the casualties relatives during May which rattled the regime. These worries were further reinforced by the growing inability of the regime to get the right message out to the Serb population as radio and television stations began to suffer destruction and blackouts (whether truly effective or not, propaganda was believed to be a key element in the ex-Communist Milosevic's political inventory). Coupled with the fear that electricity blackouts would possibly adversely affect popular morale, Milosevic began to dread losing his grip over his own people, this despite the fact that initial attacks aimed at 'dropping the bridges' actually helped him in mobilizing popular support against NATO. This still does not explain the exact timing of his surrender at the end of May. The most likely final push, if only because that is the only salient event very close to the moment of his giving up, was the indictment of Milosevic as a war criminal by the International Criminal Tribunal in The Hague. The fear of ground invasion, which in any case the US still opposed at that time, must be discounted, as such an attack could only have materialized at least three months later. Why give up in late May and not the day before the start of invasion? The most popular alternative explanation, that the Russians abandoned Milosevic, also does not appear to be compelling: their negotiator Viktor Chernomyrdin displayed genuine surprise at Milosevic's decision. In any event, General Short's assertion that 'body bags coming home from Kosovo didn't bother Milosevic' seems as mistaken as virtually all of the rest of his plan.[15]

It may be thought that air power doctrine is particularly insensitive to political demands. However, army doctrine also suffers from the same problem (I will ignore naval strategic thought since ships play a rather minimal role in contemporary war, other than in logistic support, and the commanders of American naval air power seems to share US Air Force's ideas). Planning focuses invariably on destroying the enemy's armed forces and thus can raise the strategic stakes beyond the politically desired ones. The 1991 war against Iraq is an example. The Bush Administration, mindful of the perception of harmful White House political interference during the Vietnam war, left the theater commander, General H. Norman Schwarzkopf, to devise his own campaign plan and approved it without major reservations. Schwarzkopf saw his task as being to render Iraq defenseless. If an air offensive along the lines described above would not achieve this goal, he would execute a ground offensive that took its inspiration (just as Germany's famous Schlieffen Plan) from the flanking movement carried our by Hannibal against the Romans in 216 BC at the Battle of Cannae. A heavily reinforced allied left wing would sweep round the Iraqi right flank and encircle the whole Iraqi army stationed in and around Kuwait and destroy it. The Joint Chiefs of Staff Chairman Colin Powell succinctly described the fate of the Iraqi army: 'First we're going to cut it off, then we're going kill it'. Politics stepped in again to end the war. The military in the theater were uneasy about the war being stopped early, before they had completed the destruction of the Iraqi army. It must be noted, however, that they accepted the order of their civilian superiors without quibbling. So, in a sense, proper civil–military relations were maintained. But, more significantly, neither party was mindful of the momentous political implications of this act. It allowed Saddam Hussein to use the military units which had been spared from destruction to put down subsequent rebellions in Iraq and survive in power. What the episode reveals is the disconnect that exists in the strategic thought ground force commanders, just as with the air forces, between political and strategic objectives. It also illustrates the difficulties political leaders have in judging the political implications of their armed forces' strategies.

The prevailing strategic paradigm makes strategy independent of policy. Moltke's celebrated dictum still applies with regard to the military, that politics stops as the war begins and only lets its voice be heard after the conclusion of hostilities.[16] Such a view of the independent nature of war and strategic objectives is particularly inappropriate to the ethically-driven interventions of the contemporary world. They demand close consultations between governments and military. A second problem is that the paradigm fails to take into consideration the nature of the enemy. It attempts to make the enemy, as it also does in politics, an independent variable. Although a strategy that makes enemy intentions irrelevant has obvious attractions, again it is inappropriate in the contemporary context. The requirement for the military is once again to become 'milites pacifici', soldiers who are mindful in their conduct of the greater purpose they are serving. If they do this, then we will witness a revolution in strategy.

The rogues

It may appear a daunting task to try and bring the threats that the West faces under a single heading. However, a key element that unifies all of the new threats is that they all emanate from 'rogues', that is from people – whether they be state-based or stateless – who do not play by the (or rather by the West's) rules. They are deemed to use force neither to defend themselves nor to protect human rights. Yet, when one looks at the cast of rogues, whether they be the members of the 'Axis of Evil', terrorists, or retired rogues, like Milosevic, one must note that none of them (not even Osama bin Laden) pose a fundamental threat to the West's survival. Not only can none of them hope to overthrow the West (or even any of its individual member states) because of a lack of capabilities, but also, critically, none of them appear to have the intent. Their quarrels with the West are subordinate to or derive from their primarily regional or even merely national agendas. These agendas, on the whole, are also quite limited. Milosevic, simply put, wanted to redraw the internal borders of Yugoslavia and he was quite willing to compromise on where the borders actually ran. This was an aim the West could have accepted, provided that it was peacefully negotiated. Where Milosevic made his big mistake (bigger than he needed to) was to pursue this limited political aim with an uncompromising strategy of ethnic cleansing. As a result of this strategic (mis)calculation he more or less forced the West to intervene. Saddam Hussein made a comparable miscalculation in 1990. His (reasonable) limited aim of economic relief led him into the strategic error of annexing a neighboring country. Again, it was the strategy, not the political objective, that got him into trouble. And again, a more limited strategic aim might have given him more success.

The surviving 'Axis of Evil' states must now be primarily concerned with their own survival. The growing US interest and aggressive condemnation must have served to have curtailed their regional ambitions and put them on the defensive. On the negative side, their concern about regime survival may make them very interested in obtaining weapons of mass destruction, not least because they offer the most readily available way to even out the military asymmetry. Paradoxically, that reinforces US interest and concern – which in turn raises the rogues' concerns and their interest in weapons of mass destruction. Despite the escalatory dynamic, the key challenge for the rogue states is that they ultimately do not want to hand the US any legitimation for taking action against them, which means they cannot use their weapons of mass destruction, either against neighbors or against the West. Unless the rogue states really want to put their survival at risk, WMD are only of deterrent value, not an offensive lever. If they do use them, military action against them is relatively straightforward, because they are states and states provide a point of attack. On the positive side, some rogue states have realized that WMD might make them more vulnerable, rather than less, and have taken steps to prove that they do not want to possess them any longer. Libya has gone the furthest, but Iran shows signs that it is aware of the problem as well. Even Saddam Hussein may have realized that his WMD were a liability. In short, one can argue that, given the asymmetry of forces between them and the West, rogue states are forced to play by a set of minimal rules.

States can be located on a map and disciplined. Non-state actors, like Osama bin Laden, seem to offer a greater challenge. This is true especially if we are really concerned about eliminating him and all other terrorists. If this is what the 'war on terrorism' is about, then al Qaeda's main strength is its lack of a geographical center. However, considered from the angle of the terrorist's objectives, his strategy and his capabilities, he may not pose that great a challenge. Bin Laden is certainly one of the more ambitious of terrorists, but even so it is doubtful that he seeks to overthrow the US. Rather, his aim is a regeneration of the Islamic faith which would express itself in the establishment of proper regimes in the Islamic world (and which requires the US to abandon its meddling in the region). The 11 September attacks were meant to provide a rallying cry for the process of religious regeneration to begin. In this respect, he glaringly failed (though the unnecessary war against Saddam may have given him a second chance) and in the process he made a great error in choosing the wrong strategy. By inflicting so much damage on the US (really at the top range of his capabilities), he ensured a response that would seek to end his and his organization's existence. In a sense, bin Laden is not a terrorist, in that he violated one of the essential principles of terrorism, the one that dictates that the terrorist should use a level of force that keeps him below the critical threshold where he avoids damaging his opponent so much that it hands the target the legitimacy to respond with overwhelming force and destroy the terrorist. Indeed, herein lies the challenge for the terrorist (and really for all non-state based aggressors): either they accept their weakness and fight a true terrorist campaign with limited force, which can never hope to dislodge its, by definition stronger, opponents, or he transforms himself into something else that offers more access to mobilizing resources that can help him pursue his political objectives. That 'something else' is invariably a state. But if he succeeds in forming or capturing a state or even control of territory within an existing state, the increase in resources comes at the price of becoming a 'stationary bandit' which can be more easily targeted.

There exists, in short, room for armed negotiation with at least some rogues. Given their limited aims and limited capabilities, and given the West's far greater capabilities, we have the option to fight wars our way. If that way is about the pursuit of limited political aims with the use of limited force, then that can be pursued.

Conclusion

To summarize the main points: first, contemporary international society severely restricts the legitimacy of fighting wars to objectives of self-defense and/or the defense of human rights. The principle of self-defense implies politically defensive wars, which suggests, in the main, wars fought for limited aims. Wars over human rights raise the problem of compromising human rights in order to protect them, which suggest, if not necessarily limited aims, certainly an element of restraint and the likelihood of confusion over war aims. The result is that contemporary wars waged by liberal democracies tend to be about limited political aims. Second, such aims only justify the use of limited force. Third, strategy is seen by the military as a variable that, by aiming to make the enemy defenseless by utilizing overwhelming force, is independent of both one's own political objectives and the intentions of the opponent. Fourth, this ambitious aim *in* war clashes with the limited aim *of* war. It leads to wars that are fought inefficiently and result in unhappy outcomes. Fifth, our opponents are rogues (that is, people who refuse to play by our rules) and whether state-based or non-state based, they are relatively weak actors with limited objectives. (Limited) force can therefore be used to reason with them. In the case of states that is easier than in the case of non-state-based rogues. However, the latter are by definition even weaker than states and pose even less of a threat. Moreover, to increase their chances of success, such rogues overwhelmingly want to become or usurp states, which, paradoxically, makes them stronger but at the same time more vulnerable to outside intervention. Finally, the logical outcome of a combination of limited political aims, limited war strategies and limited threats amounts to a revolution in strategy. The wars of the West will then no longer require uncompromising strategies that leave their enemies defenseless victims.

Notes

1. The phrases I take from Clausewitz, via Raymond Aron's *Penser la guerre, Clausewitz,* Vol. I: *L'âge européen* (Paris: Gallimard, 1976).
2. I deliberately do not write 'the use *or threat* of force' because, as Clausewitz pointed out, the threat to use force is meaningless without a willingness actually to use it. So, logically, within our context, the latter cannot be distinguished from the former.

3. I will build on the argument presented in A. Gat, 'Isolationism, Appeasement, Containment, and Limited War: Western Strategic Policy from the Modern to the 'Postmodern' Era', in Z. Maoz and A. Gat, eds, *War in a Changing World* (A. Arbor, Mich.: University of Michigan Press, 2001), pp.77–91.

4. In a typical phrase: 'niemals könne ein Staat darauf verzichten, Fragen, die seine Ehre und Lebensinteressen betreffen, selbständig zu regeln …' Quoted in J. W. Honig, 'Totalitarianism and Realism: H. Morgenthau's German Years', *Security Studies* 5, no. 2 (Winter 1995/1996), 286. An example that confirms the older practice by explicitly rejecting it is Article 9 of the post-Second World War Japanese Constitution: 'Aspiring sincerely to an international peace based on justice and order, the Japanese people forever renounce war as a sovereign right of the nation and the threat or use of force as a means for settling international disputes.' Quoted in 'Japan considers changes to preparations for war', *Financial Times*, 18 April 2002.

5. Of course, the UN Charter built upon tradition. The most important earlier international agreements governing the right to resort to war include 1899 and 1907 Hague Conventions I on the pacific settlement of disputes; the 1907 Hague Convention II on the limitation of force in recovering contract debt; the 1907 Hague Convention III on the opening of hostilities; the 1919 Covenant of the League of Nations and the 1928 General Treaty for the Renunciation of War as an Instrument of National Policy (the Kellogg–Briand Pact).

6. L. Freedman and E. Karsh, *The Gulf Conflict, 1990–1991: Diplomacy and War in the New World Order* (Princeton, N.J.: Princeton University Press, 1993), p. 46. See also the transcript of the 25 July 1990 meeting between Saddam Hussein and the US Ambassador to Iraq, April Glaspie, of which the Iraqi version was published in *New York Times*, 23 September 1990 (with a correction published in *ibid.*, 30 September 1990) and the US version in *ibid.*, 13 July 1991.

7. US Secretary of State James Baker used this argument publicly – but only once. The subsequent domestic outcry was so great that the Bush Sr Administration carefully avoided repeating the claim. Interestingly, in the run-up to the second war against Saddam, 67% of US respondents in a Pew Research Center poll believed that US use of force was explained by the threat Saddam posed and only 22% accepted that the US wanted to control Iraqi oil. In Europe the numbers were reversed (France: 75/21; Germany 54/39 and Russia 76/15), except in Britain where they were 44% to 45%. 'A Rising Anti-American Tide', *International Herald Tribune*, 5 December 2002.

8. Quoted in 'Musharraf Warns He Is Not Scared Of War Over Kashmir', *Financial Times*, 28 May 2002. Italics added.

9. 'Bush Charts First-Strike Policy On Terror Cells', *International Herald Tribune*, 3 June 2002.

10. *ibid.* See also: 'Defining a Preemptive Defense', *International Herald Tribune*, 18 June 2002 and the perceptive column by P. Stephens, 'The American Way of Defence', *Financial Times*, 14 June 2002.

11. The difficulties Bush and Blair faced after the war were caused precisely by their failure to substantiate the necessity for pre-emptive self-defense, a result of their failing to find any weapons of mass destruction.

12. F. Briquemont, *Do Something, General, Kroniek van Bosnië-Herzegovina* (Antwerp: Icarus, 1998), pp.30–1. Compare, however, the imaginative attempt by one of his successors, British general Rupert Smith, to devise a strategy based on the UNSC resolutions: J. W. Honig and N. Both, *Srebrenica: Record of a War Crime* (New York: Penguin, 1997), pp.141–58.

13. Interview with Lt. Gen. Michael C. Short for 'Frontline: War in Europe': www.pbs.org/wgbh/page...ntline/shows/kosovo/interviews/short.html.
14. *ibid.*
15. Quoted in W. M. Arkin, 'Operation Allied Force: "The Most Precise Application of Air Power in History"', in A. J. Bacevich and E. A. Cohen, eds, *War Over Kosovo: Politics and Strategy in a Global Age* (New York: Columbia University Press, 2001), p.5.
16.   Policy makes use of war to gain its objects, it acts with decisive influence at the opening and at the end of the war in such a way as either to increase its claims during the progress of war or be satisfied with lesser gains. With this uncertainty strategy cannot but always direct its efforts towards the highest goal attainable with the means at disposal. It thereby serves policy best, and only works for the object of policy, but completely independent of policy in its actions.
   Quoted in Von Caemmerer, *The Development of Strategical Science During the 19th Century*, tr. K. von Donat (London: Hugh Rees, 1905), p.85.

3
Strategic Terrorism: Threats and Risk Assessment

Friedrich Steinhäusler

What is strategic terrorism?

Conventional terrorism (CT) aims to intimidate the public by demonstrating that a government is powerless and unable to protect either its citizens or even its own representatives and thus, conventional terrorism tries to coerce decision-makers by using violence against non-combatant members of the target population. The ultimate goal of conventional terrorism is to blackmail decision-makers into giving in to the terrorists' demands, such as making changes to the existing political systems. This approach has been used for decades by terrorist organizations in Northern Ireland and the United Kingdom (IRA), in France (Action Direct), in Germany (Baader-Meinhof Group), Italy (Red Brigades), and in the Middle East (PLO). A conventional terror attack is commonly associated with the use of conventional weapons against a relatively small group of individuals, for example, a hand grenade thrown into a crowd of people in a market place; an assassin killing a politician with a pistol; or a mine detonated as a convoy of security forces passes by. Such types of action usually do not require lengthy planning or sophisticated weaponry and they are well within the capability of the several dozen terrorist groups currently operating around the world.

Strategic terrorism (ST), on the other hand, differs in its objectives, as well as in the degree of sophistication, the comprehensiveness of its logistical preparations and requirements, the attack mode and weapons deployed, the scale of harm inflicted on the targeted population, and the socio-economic and political impact resulting from such an attack. The terror attacks used against the US on 11 September 2001 represented a prime example of strategic terrorism. These attacks showed clearly that there were no constraints on the terrorist's desire to inflict mass casualties. Such an attitude is contrary to the normal approach of conventional terrorism, which usually aims to keep the number of casualties relative low, due to concerns about losing public support as a result of acts that result in mass casualties. A further difference between conventional terrorism and strategic terrorism is the fact that – upon successfully committing an act of terror – the perpetrators of a strategic terrorist attack neither seek to negotiate nor rush to claim responsibility for the attack.

An improved understanding of strategic terrorism and related global terrorist activities since 9/11 can thus be used to extrapolate which threats Western societies will likely face in the future. Such an assessment is an essential basis for any political, logistical and technical decisions on the countermeasures needed to prevent and mitigate future acts of strategic terrorism, in particular those that have the potential to inflict catastrophic harm to society.

Objectives of strategic terrorism and its impact on society

Strategic terrorism is not oriented towards a local goal, but towards regional, possibly even global objectives. The terror network al Qaeda has stated such ambitions in several of its communications, such as the Fatwa it issued on 23 February 1998.[1] This document, and others that preceded and followed it, include rather specific demands, directed at well-defined target groups, for example:

* the expulsion of US personnel and closure of American military bases in Saudi Arabia;
* regime change in those Muslim countries viewed as collaborators of the US;
* independence for Palestine.

Such announcements also include the instruction to al Qaeda's supporters to inflict the maximum harm possible on a targeted society, for example, by killing as many civilians and members of the US armed forces, and those of all of the nations considered supporting them, as possible. The agenda of al Qaeda, as the prime practitioner of strategic terrorism, reflects these objectives: attack American interests worldwide, from the Far East, to the Gulf Emirates, to the US Homeland. The unvarying message is hatred towards the US, communicated skilfully through mass media, such as television or radio stations (for example, *Al Jazeera*), and through dedicated websites on the Internet. It is suspected that at least some of al Qaeda communiqués that are broadcast also contain coded instructions for its followers, giving them instructions about future acts of terror against specific targets. It is a key feature of strategic terrorism to target not only the political system, but *all* of the aspects of the society viewed as its enemy, and in particular all the components of its vital infrastructure (the transportation industry in general and aviation industry in particular; energy sector; communication systems; financial markets; first responders networks). Since many of these components also often represent valuable financial assets, a successful terror attack can inflict severe economic consequences on the targeted society. For example, the direct damage inflicted as a result of the collapse of the Word Trade Center twin towers was of the order of US$64 billion; however, the indirect economic impact of 9/11on New York State alone is estimated to have been around US$600 billion.[2]

Furthermore, strategic terrorism is intended to cause a *chain reaction* among the allies of the targeted society. For example, al Qaeda places the United Kingdom, Australia, Spain, the Netherlands, Japan, Italy and Israel in the same category of enemies as it places the US.[3] This is a major security issue for the international community acting in Afghanistan and in Iraq, where members of the security forces of the UK, Italy, Poland, Spain, Germany, as well as staff members of the United Nations and the International Red Cross, have already been subject to terrorist attacks. Moreover, the terrorist bombings on four commuter trains in Madrid on 11 March 2004 were claimed by Ansar al-Islam, a radical Islamic group associated with al Qaeda that is thought to have been responsible for a string of terrorist attacks in Iraq, Jordan, Turkey and Morocco. The group said that the attacks were intended as an act of revenge against Spain's involvement in the war in Iraq and Afghanistan. International tourists are also a target, as demonstrated by the attacks on German tourists in Djerba, Tunisia (April 2002), on Australian tourists in Bali, Indonesia (October 2002), and on Israeli tourists in Mombassa, Kenya (November 2002). The attacks on 9/11 are a prime example of the successful application of the strategy of strategic terrorism, as they caused a ripple effect far beyond the sites of the actual terror attack themselves, significantly impacting, for example, on security-related expenditures. The effects of the war on terror, since it was declared by US President George W. Bush on 12 September 2001, have cascaded throughout the world, resulting in large investments in security upgrades at airports, harbors and borders in all regions and the vast majority of individual countries. These expenditures were either implemented or requested by the US Government, or decided upon by national governments, as a result of fears that their territory may be target of an equivalent terrorist attack. Such major investments in security have the disadvantage that they only have a negative impact on the overall financial situation of a country, as they do not offer a positive, visible gain, when compared to investments that result in increased industrial productivity.

Since strategic terrorism aims primarily at instilling fear, its practitioners have the potential to cripple a society financially simply by intensifying their internal communication, the so-called *electronic chatter*, hinting at imminent terror attacks without actually having to implement them.[4] For example, airlines and the public incurred severe financial damage during the period December 2003 to February 2004, when several scheduled flights by Air France, British Airways and Continental Airways from Europe to the US were subject to last-minute cancellations for security reasons. This situation is aggravated if some of the security concerns are based on faulty information or misjudgements by intelligence personnel.[5] Security costs at Los Angeles International Airport alone, where several flights were canceled due to security concerns, totaled more than US$3.8 million from 21 December 2003 to 8 January 2004.[6] Even simply increasing the level of public awareness of a potential terrorist threat is costly to society: raising the threat level in the US from yellow to orange, the second highest of five threat levels, is estimated to cost American taxpayers US$1 billion a week.[7] Besides a crippling financial impact on society, strategic terrorism also has a significant direct and indirect impact on civil liberties both nationally and internationally. In the United States, stringent counter-terrorism laws were passed in record time, within six weeks of 9/11. The *USA Patriot Act* enables authorities to infringe on the civil liberties of US citizens, resident aliens and visiting foreigners alike, and has been the subject of an intensive international debate.[8] Fear of future strategic terrorist attacks on the US homeland has resulted in multiple restrictive actions by the US Government against persons and goods entering the country, such as:

- US customs officials are checking freight destined for the US at selected foreign seaports, categorizing transport companies into 'trusted' and 'others';
- Airlines have had to provide advance provision of data on their passengers, covering 34 different categories of information, to US authorities, for flights into the US, if their landing rights at US airports were to be maintained. The required data includes: number and name of all persons travelling with an individual; address; telephone number; email address; number of seat and its location in the plane; total number of miles flown and destinations; mode of payment; if payment by credit card, card issuing company, card number, expiration date; information whether passenger has been a 'no-show' in the past; requests for special meals, special flight tariffs, or whether customer 'has shown aggressive behaviour', and up to 127 other bits of general data from the airline's customer profile. Such data remains stored in a US government database for at least three and a half years from the time it was collected;[9]
- US immigration requires that most visitors to the US have their finger prints and photos taken upon arrival, and mandates the inclusion of biometric data in all foreign passports in the near future;
- Exchange students or visiting researchers invited by US academic or research institutions are subject to stringent control on their American residential addresses, short-term foreign travel itineraries, as well as the duration of their stays and professional activities during their stay at the host institution.

In addition, many countries have reviewed their own legislation and have followed the US to either a greater or lesser degree, revising multiple regulations ranging from checking international financial transactions to authorizing increased electronic surveillance on their populations. In this way, strategic terrorism has demonstrated that it can inflict *inter alia* high costs and severe restrictions on civil liberties, that is, damage on society as a whole, even without actually staging an act of terror. In this manner, its international impact exceeds that of conventional terrorism in an unprecedented manner. It can be concluded that strategic terrorism has already successfully demonstrated its ability to reach one goal: to trigger multiple, detrimental impacts on a regional and even global scale following the attacks on 9/11.

Recruitment and training methods

It is clear that strategic terrorism recruits internationally. Prior to the attacks on 9/11, it had been known that al Qaeda 'sleeper cells' had been covertly established in over 60 countries, ranging from Australia, to South America, to Europe and in Africa. Initial contacts with potential recruits are made through dedicated organizations, such as *Al-Muhajiroun*, which openly admits to its recruitment activities.[10] Such contacts frequently occur at mosques, particularly in lower income rural areas in Arab countries. Upon receiving a basic set of instructions, contact addresses are supplied that enable the newly recruited trainee to use the services of al Qaeda supporters living abroad. This network of supporters provides the logistical support to the new recruits to take them across international borders until they arrive at their final destination: the training camp. Al Qaeda safely and openly operated such installations in Afghanistan under the ruling Taliban regime until the American invasion in 2001. It is estimated that altogether 18,000 trainees undertook training courses in basic terror skills in these Afghan training camps, with each course lasting several weeks.[11] Trainees came mostly from Saudi Arabia, Egypt, Algeria, Chechnya, Lebanon, Sudan, and the Philippines, but at least some were citizens of the United Kingdom and USA.

Current knowledge of the content of such training is largely due to a wide array of material discovered in Afghanistan after the fall of the Taliban, which significantly supplemented earlier information gleaned after the arrest of 16 men suspected of plotting attacks against Israel and Jordan around the time of the Millennium celebrations in 1999.[12] When these men were captured, books were discovered entitled *Encyclopaedia of the Afghan Jihad*, which turned out to be a training manual describing, in six volumes totalling about 1,000 pages, procedures on how to build explosive devices and detonate them, and how to conduct terrorist operations. The technical level of the books resembles that of military training manuals, and draws on information that is widely available on the Internet, such as instructions on the installation of anti-personnel mines and sniper training. Relatively simple, but technically correct drawings describe, *inter alia*, the use of small amounts of explosives in a cigarette lighter or pipe in order to maim a person, as well as radio-controlled devices that can be used for setting off a truck bomb. In contrast to such useful and reliable instructions, however, the level of sophistication of information concerning weapons of mass destruction (WMD) is comparatively low and, in some instances, even erroneous. Training videos found along with the WMD written materials included a demonstration of the effectiveness of al Qaeda's home-made chemical weapons, by showing tests of them killing animals.

After the destruction of its major training camps in Afghanistan, members of al Qaeda began searching for locations to establish new bases, including in the border area between Bangladesh and Myanmar, in Pakistan, Yemen, Somalia, the Pankisi Gorge in Georgia, Chechnya, and Mindanao in the Philippines.[13]

Strategic terrorism's international network

Strategic terrorism has established an international network of collaborators. A number of the key components groups of the loose association that comprises the strategic terrorism network are the terror organizations described below. It must be emphasized that strategic terrorism should not be viewed as a tightly organized international network, consisting of a traditionally structured hierarchy with 'command centre' at the top and sub-units in different countries below, waiting to receive their detailed instructions. Instead, strategic terrorism operates rather with a diffuse network of useful *ad hoc* allies, in which al Qaeda acts mainly as an ideological focal point for the other terror organizations, such as those in Indonesia or Spain, and provides occasional logistical or financial support. Such partnerships last for the duration of the planning and execution of a terror act and they should not be interpreted as long lasting alliances because, beyond the needs of a particular operation, the motives and capabilities of the partners can differ widely.

The international network of strategic terrorism

Al Qaeda (*'The Base'*) was founded in the late 1980s by Osama Bin Laden, to bring together and organize Moslems, mainly Arabs, who had gained military experience in the guerrilla war against the Soviet Army during its occupation of Afghanistan. In February 1998, it issued a Fatwa calling on Muslims worldwide to attack and the kill American military personnel and civilians, as well as those of its allies.

Major attacks: Attempted the synchronized mid-air bombing of 12 separate US airliners in 1993; synchronized car bomb attacks on US Embassies in Dar es Salaam and Nairobi in August 1998 (301 people dead and over 5,000 injured); attack on the *USS Cole* in the harbour of Aden, in Yemen; 17 sailors dead);[14] synchronized attacks with four hijacked US-civilian airliners on the World Trade Center and the Pentagon in 2001 (3,254 people killed).

Membership: estimated to have several thousand active members worldwide, with many more passive supporters. The central leadership consists of about 20 individuals.

Al Jama'a al-Islamiyya (*Islamic Group*), has grown to become the largest terror group in Egypt since it was founded in the late 1970s. Its aim is the replacement of the current Government with an Islamic fundamentalist society. It's most prominent member, Rifa'I Taha Musa, was an early supporter of the fatwa issued by Osama Bin Laden.

Major attacks: involved in the planning of the truck bomb attack on the New York World Trade Center in 1993, through its spiritual leader Umar Abd al-Rahman, who, at the time, was in exile and living in New York City; (six people killed and over 1,000 injured); attempted to assassinate President Mubarak in 1995; killed 58 tourists at Luxor in 1997.

Membership: several hundred.

Hezbollah (also *Islamic Jihad*, Party of God) was founded in Lebanon by Shia Muslims. The objective is the destruction of the State of Israel. Its main area of operation is Southern Lebanon, and it has its logistical base in the Bekaa Valley, as well as a presence in Beirut.

Major attacks: truck bomb attack against the US Embassy in Beirut in 1983 (63 people dead); bomb attack against the Israeli Embassy in Buenos Aires in 1992 (29 people dead).

Membership: estimated several thousand.

Abu Sayyaf Group; operating in the southern Philippines, it is renowned for its Islamic radicalism and high standard of military-style training. The main objective is the promotion of an independent Islamic state, one that would embrace several of the Philippine islands where Moslems live.

Major attacks: multiple assassinations, bomb attacks and kidnappings of locals and foreign tourists.

Membership: estimated 2,000 supporters, with about 200 core members.

Harakat ul Mujaheddin (also *Harakt al-Ansar*), founded by Fazlur Rehman Khalil. Its main area of activity is Pakistan/Kaschmir. In 1998, Khalil supported the fatwa issued by Osama Bin Laden.

Major attack: successful hijacking of a jet from Air India airlines, resulting in the release of three terrorists previously arrested by the Indian security forces for kidnapping British tourists.

Membership: estimated several thousand.

Islamic Movement of Uzbekistan is based in Eastern Uzbekistan in the Fergana Valley. The main objective is the overthrow of the current secular government under Islom Karimov and its replacement with an Islamic regime.

Major attacks: five coordinated car bomb attacks in Tashkent in 1999; multiple hostage takings, including those of foreign tourists in 1999 and 2000.

Membership: estimated several thousand.

Hamas (*Islamic Resistance Movement*), originally the branch of the *Muslim Brotherhood* in Palestine (founded in 1987). Heavily engaged as a social welfare agency for ordinary Palestinians, as well as covert terror attacks.

Major attacks: mainly suicide bombings against military and civilian targets in Israel (over 900 deaths since the declaration of the al-Aqsa Intifada in September 2000).

Membership: estimated at several thousand in the Gaza Strip and on the West Bank.

In its dedication to wage a jihad in Europe and elsewhere, an extended international network of recruiters has been set up by those who initiated strategic terrorism on 11 September 2001. The United Kingdom has become their European nerve centre, where British, Albanians and Swiss nationals have been recruited so far. Major emphasis is being placed on recruiting 'intelligent and highly educated' individuals.[15] France is the main recruiting area for foreign terrorists deployed in Chechnya. In Poland, Bulgaria, Romania, and the Czech Republic, newly recruited members are currently establishing Islamic terror cells. In Bosnia-Herzegovina and Kosovo, young Muslims have been recruited as members of the Saudi-financed Wahahbi Islamic fundamentalist movement, indicative of a tendency to change the ethnicity of terrorists to a so-called 'white al-Qaeda'. This is in line with indications that major recruiting efforts are also underway among prison inmates in the United States, an activity that is on-going and has been facilitated by a number of radical Muslim clergy who enjoyed, until recently, easy and unscreened access to US Federal and State prisons.[16] Over the past two years, Italy has had a major success in breaking up an international recruitment ring consisting of five men and women from Algeria and Morocco, who had been trying to find individuals who would be suitable for training as suicide bombers. In 2004, a website existed in the Czech Republic, which offered US$150 per day to new recruits willing to volunteer for combat in Chechnya, provided they sign up for a three-year minimum contract.[17]

Logistics and modes of attack

In order to understand the logistics and preferred modes of attack of strategic terrorists, it is necessary to recall their primary objective, that is, to engage in indiscriminate killing that is not necessarily aimed at one particular population group. For example, the attacks on 9/11 resulted in 3,254 dead, originating from 62 nations.[18]

The time period used for planning purposes for a major strategic terrorism attack can cover many years. For example, the car bomb explosion set off by al Qaeda network associates during their first attack on the World Trade Center in 1993 caused major damage but, due to a planning error, it failed to achieve the planned toppling of the tower. Several years of detailed further preparation then followed, that resulted in a fundamental change in the attack strategy, which, on 9/11, finally achieved the results that Islamic fundamentalist terrorists had been trying to achieve for at least a decade. In this case, success for the terrorist rested on an operational logistics network that was coordinated over numerous international borders, and that saw mainly Saudi Arabian nationals, who had lived as students in Germany and/or underwent flight training in Florida, maintained rented property in California, and hijacked planes in New England, come together from all over the United States and the rest of the world, at the last moment, in order to attack targets in New York and Washington, DC.

The strategic terrorism network carries out the implementation of individual terror acts in the following manner:[19]

- *Support cells* consisting of local residents, are responsible for fund raising, for providing documents, credit cards and lodging and for procuring the materials needed for the actual attack;
- *Sleeper cells* representing legal residents in the target country without any criminal record, remain inactive for extended periods of time. They can be activated upon external command for information and intelligence gathering, and to provide additional help for the more exposed support cell. It is estimated that there are several hundred such cells in the US;[20]

- *Execution cells* only arrive at the scene of the planned terrorist attack during its final stages; they utilize the information and materials previously assembled by the support and sleeper cells;
- *Operation commanders* coordinate the work of all of the cells, although they may only assist the execution cells shortly before the attack is launched, and they themselves are not necessarily involved in the actual attack itself. The commanders of the first WTC bombing in 1993 and the US Embassy bombing in Kenya were multilingual, computer literate college graduates.

In the case of the attacks on 9/11, the plan was hatched in 1999 by a small group of Islamic extremists who were living in Hamburg, and the script for the attack was developed in a series of meetings held across Europe.[21] To prepare themselves for the operation, teams of future hijackers learned to live in American society by staying there for years, while others started preparing for the attack in April 2001, by identifying flights from prospective airports that involved fully fuelled aircraft and carried a small load of passengers. Their activities led to the decision to hijack transcontinental flights leaving from US airports and departing on a Tuesday – known to be the lightest travel day of the week.

Targets and attack scenarios

For the targets of strategic terrorism, regardless of the extent of their planning and the sophistication of their threat analysis, the risks associated with and the impact of an act of strategic terrorism are not quantifiable with any degree of certainty. However, it is to some extent possible to narrow down the seemingly endless list of potential targets by identifying and analyzing the common characteristics of targets considered attractive by strategic terrorism.[22] The target of a strategic terrorism attack is selected with careful attention paid to its relative political, strategic, economic and symbolic value. Thus, in the attacks on 11 September 2001, the WTC represented the financial center of the largest Western economy, and the Pentagon stood for the nerve center of the sole global military superpower.

Locations at elevated risk for an attack are therefore: national monuments; major international tourist attractions; military/political/financial centers; key components of a nation's vital infrastructure; places of mass entertainment; embassies; bridges and tunnels leading into and out of major cities; strategic buildings; military bases; important ministries (such as defense and interior); transportation hubs, such as large airports, seaports and train stations; major land border crossings; and radio and television stations with a large national audience.

Among the major target groups, the shipping industry, in particular, remains extremely vulnerable to the threats posed by strategic terrorism. For example, it has been reported that the nationalist terror group that has long been battling for independence for their region with the government of Sri Lanka, (the *Tamil Tigers*), is training a cadre of about 3,000 so-called *Sea Tigers*, who will be capable of producing sea mines and building high-speed fibreglass boats equipped with machine guns.[23] To show this is no idle threat, since 1989 the Tigers have managed to destroy about one-third of the Navy of Sri Lanka. Some of their highly successful attack modes have reportedly also been part of the training given to members selected by al Qaeda, for example, how to hijack ships, the kidnapping of crews, and using scuba diving techniques to launch underwater attacks on harbours.

Maritime terrorism threats include:

- the use of a hijacked freighter loaded with explosives to ram a large cruise liner and sink it;
- hijacking a liquefied petroleum gas (LPG) loaded supertanker and crashing it into a harbour with an adjacent oil terminal or refinery complex;[24]
- using a shipping container stored deep in the hold of a large container ship to deliver a WMD into the harbour of a large city and detonating it by remote control;
- attacking a passenger ferry with kamikaze-style speedboats, loaded with explosives.[25]

Due to the international phenomenon of *phantom-ships*,[26] proper monitoring of all shipping is no longer possible and it is conceivable that a previously hijacked ship could be loaded with either large amounts of conventional explosives or WMD without such a cargo being detected by port authorities. Such poor monitoring of maritime traffic increases the risk that strategic terrorists may use such an attack mode in the future to target major harbors in Europe or the US, or to sink supertankers, luxury liners, or naval ships.

The civilian aviation industry is also known to be high on the list of targets for strategic terrorism. This industry faces a major security dilemma: on the one hand, ensuring the smooth flow of the heavy traffic of passengers and goods that pass through daily at major airports requires the airlines to cause only a minimum of security-related inconvenience to an already delay-weary public. On the other hand, the known security loopholes in air cargo handling, the largely unmonitored shipment of hazardous materials and airmail packages, combined with the proven availability of shoulder-fired surface-to-air missiles to terrorists, represent a continued elevated risk to both passengers and aircraft.[27]

Possible attacks on the civilian nuclear infrastructure of a targeted country is another area fitting the concept of strategic terrorism.[28] For example, the vulnerabilities of the civil power nuclear generating sector are well known. The nuclear installations most at risk are: research reactors using weapons grade nuclear fuel; spent fuel storage buildings; the control and containment buildings of nuclear powered generating plants; and the transportation system that takes spent nuclear fuel to reprocessing plants. Depending on the circumstances at the time of the attack and the specific characteristics of the nuclear facility, such an attack could result in a wide range of damage scenarios, from a minor uncontrolled release of radioactivity to a catastrophic loss of control that results in widespread contamination.

Strategic terrorism has also further refined conventional attack modes. For example, it has adapted the suicide bombing attack modes – an explosive strapped to a suicide bomber's body is detonated amidst a carefully targeted group of people – for example, at a group of political or business leaders, or well known and popular entertainment personalities. But it is not only the powerful or the famous that are at risk. The targets of a suicide bomber are often the random individuals who are together due to no more than the boundary conditions prevailing at the time of the attack. For example:

- the passengers of a plane carrying a covert suicide bomber (for example, explosives hidden in the shoe of a passenger in December 2001);
- the crew of a ship attacked in a high-speed suicide boat bombing (for example, the attack against US Navy warship *USS Cole* in October 2000);
- the occupants of a building rammed by a large suicide vehicle bomb (for example, the attacks against UN and Red Cross Headquarters in Baghdad, August–October 2003);
- passers-by who are in the area when synchronized suicide attackers with explosives wired to their bodies detonate them while walking past targeted buildings or vehicles (for example, the near-simultaneous bombing attacks on the offices of the of US-backed Kurdish parties in Arbil, Iraq, February 2004);
- torpedoes guided by suicide bombers and launched against navy warships (for example, '*Sea Tigers*' attacks against the Sri Lankan Navy).[29]

Strategic terrorism also seeks to optimize the use of *conventional weapons* in any act of terrorism. For example:

- the deployment of rocket-propelled artillery rounds, attached to timers, positioned around an airport;[30]
- the development of homemade rockets (with range of up to 12.5 km);[31]
- the construction, covert deployment and remotely-controlled detonation of large bombs with an explosive load of 100 kg, capable of destroying a main battle tank;[32]
- the detonation of a radiological dispersal device (an RDD or dirty bomb), delivered into a large city in the hold of a cargo ship, that then remains moored at a dock, awaiting the optimum meteorological conditions for maximum dispersion of radioactive fallout;[33]

- the simultaneous detonation of multiple bombs placed on board trains in backpacks and equipped with remote-controlled detonators linked to cell phones.[34]

Strategic terrorists select their weapons with the objective of inflicting damage on a scale that exceeds that which is usually the outcome of conventional terrorism. For example, the innovative concept of using hijacked, fully-fuelled civilian airliners as guided missiles, resulted in a devastating effect, comparable to the explosive yield of a small tactical nuclear weapon. The combined kinetic and chemical energy of a fully-fuelled airliner crashing into a building is in the order of 1,000 tons of TNT.

However, the most important difference between conventional and strategic terrorism is the fact that the latter openly declares the use of nuclear, biological and chemical weapons of mass destruction (WMD) as a desirable goal. The impact on the targeted society would be catastrophic in terms of casualties, as well as with respect to causing an unprecedented social, financial and political disturbance to the country that was the victim of such an attack. Al Qaeda has tried several times to obtain both fully-fledged nuclear weapons, stolen from existing nuclear weapons states stockpiles, as well as weapons grade fissile material. It has also experimented with other radioactive material, with the objective of constructing an RDD. Al Qaeda also documented animal experiments with chemical and biological weapons that it carried out, and these records were captured in Afghanistan. The Aum Shinrikyo sect, a Japanese religious cult, has also carried out extensive experimental programmes on nuclear, biological and chemical WMD. However, it is somewhat symptomatic of the problems associated with both constructing and using WMD that neither of these two terror groups – despite significant financial resources and manpower – were able to deliver a well-functioning device that performed even remotely like a WMD. For example, Aum Shinryko's sarin nerve gas attacks in the Tokyo subway were amateurish in the way they were carried out, by piercing thin-foil containers in an uncontrolled manner, and the result was that only a very small number of deaths occurred among the packed commuters.

Strategic terrorist attacks

Table 3.1 lists major terror attacks associated to some degree with al Qaeda in the period October 2002 to 2004. The list includes the following targets: two skyscrapers (the WTC's North and South Towers, USA); a national military command, control and communication centre (the Pentagon, USA); a modern warship (Aden); luxury residential compounds (Riyadh); tourist-frequented nightclubs (Bali); a restaurant/social club, community centre and tourist complexes (Casablanca and Mombassa); synagogues (Istanbul and Casablanca); the headquarters of international non-governmental

Table 3.1   Major international terror attacks with suspected links to al Qaeda

Date	Target	Location	Victims	Suspects
March 2004	Commuter trains	Madrid, Spain	202 dead	Islamic terrorist cell, likely linked to al Qaeda
March 2004	Shiite religious worshippers	Baghdad and Karbala, Iraq	271 dead	Islamic extremists, possibly under Abu Musab Al-Zarqawi
February 2004	Offices of Kurdish Parties	Arbil, Iraq	56 dead	Ansar al-Islam suicide attackers
November 2003	British Consulate, bank, synagogues	Istanbul, Turkey	62 dead	Turkish Islamic group, possibly linked to Abu Musab Zarqawi
November 2003	Military compound	Baghdad, Iraq	19 dead	European suicide bombers, recruited by Mullah Fouad
August–October 2003	Hotel, UN & Red Cross Headquarters	Baghdad, Iraq	50 dead	European suicide bombers, recruited by Mullah Fouad
August 2003	Mosque	Najaf, Iraq	Over 100 dead	Islamic extremists
May 2003	Luxury compound	Riyadh, Saudi Arabia	34 dead	Logistics cell arrested in Switzerland
May 2003	Social club & community centre	Casablanca, Morocco	33 dead	Moroccan Islamic group, possibly under Mohammed al-Garbuzi
November 2002	'Paradise' Hotel	Mombassa, Kenya	16 dead	Kenyan Islamic group under Al-Zarqawi
October 2002	Nightclubs	Bali, Indonesia	202 dead	Islamic radical group Jamaah Islamiyah

organizations (Baghdad); a consulate (Istanbul); the branch of a foreign bank (Istanbul); and military compounds (Nasiriyah).

Future outlook

Twenty-one months after 9/11, the presidents of the United States and Pakistan announced that the al Qaeda network – held responsible for these terror attacks – had been successfully dismantled.[35] This assessment was supported *inter alia* by the fact that over 500 persons, suspected of being al Qaeda members, had been arrested or killed worldwide. Among them were the following top leaders (place of arrest): Khalid Sheik Mohammed (Rawalpindi); Abu Zubaydah (Karachi); Abu Yasir (Lahore); Adil Al Jazeeri (Peshawar); Ali Qaed Senyan al-Harthi (Yemen); Zacarias Moussaoui (USA); Mohammed Haydar Zammar (Morocco); Abdur Rahim (undisclosed location); Anas al-Liby (Afghanistan); and Sawafan Ul Hashim (Fasilabad). For comparison, Table 3.2 lists the major successes of the European security

Table 3.2 European successes in law courts in the 'War on Terror'

Date	Country	Action	Crime
March 2004	Spain (Madrid)	Arrest of 10 Moroccan and Indian suspects	Attacks on commuter trains
November 2003	Germany (Düsseldorf)	Shadi Abdellah jailed	Attacks planned against Jewish targets
March 2003	Germany	Four terrorists jailed	Attacks planned against Christmas market in Strasbourg (France)
January 2003	United Kingdom (London, Manchester)	Arrests of several North Africans	Discovery of the toxin Ricin
April 2002	Spain	Arrest of Mohammed Galeb Kalaje Zouaydi (alias 'Abu Talha')	Key financial supporter of al Qaeda
April 2002	Spain	Arrest of Ahmed Brahim	Chief accountant of al Qaeda in Spain
Spring 2002	Italy (Milan)	Conviction of four terrorists	Planning attacks and transporting explosives and chemicals
2002	Italy (Milan)	Nine terrorists arrested	Provision of logistical support and false documents to al Qaeda
November 2001	Spain	Arrest of eight terrorists	Planning terror attacks and recruiting trainees for al Qaeda camps
September 2001	Germany (Wiesbaden)	Arrest of three al Qaeda members	Possession of weapons and forged travel documents

forces in their counter-terrorism efforts. But other key leaders of al Qaeda are still at large, such as: Osama bin Laden, mentor and acknowledged leader of the group; Saif al Adel, his chief body guard; Sulaiman Abu Ghaith, spokesman; Abu Mohammed al Masri, chief trainer; Sarwat Salah, strategist; and Ayman al-Zawahri, chief strategist.

Reviewing developments since 9/11, it is not evident that strategic terrorism has changed its objectives; nor are there any signs that it may have abandoned its tactics, including attempts to acquire and use WMD. The worldwide counter-terrorism actions taken against the network of strategic terrorism have introduced a new emphasis by al Queda leaders on 'subcontracting' the actual implementation of acts of terror to members of the international network of allied terror organizations. In this manner, the organizational structure of terror groups like al Qaeda become ever more diffuse. The military interventions in Afghanistan and Iraq have further fuelled the fanaticism of religiously and politically motivated Islamic radical groups, facilitating even further the recruitment efforts of strategic terrorism.

In the countries most at risk, that is, the US and UK, the continuously required vigilance necessary to guard against attack requires the allocation of significant financial and human resources. The politically declared *Global War on Terror* – lacking any definition as to what might constitute victory and its end – means that neither in the short-term, nor in the mid-term will there be any significant changes in the resulting burden on the national economies.

Furthermore, in Europe, the growing numbers of the Islamic population may also represent an expanding pool for recruiting new members potentially sympathetic to the goals of strategic terrorism:

- in Europe (including Russia) 52 million residents are identified as Muslims (3.2 million of them are resident in Germany);
- the annual growth rate in the number of Muslims living in Europe is about 6.5 per cent;
- in Austria, Muslims currently represent 4.2 per cent of the population, a doubling in their presence since 1991.

The continuously growing illicit trafficking of people across European borders should also be viewed as a significant loophole in the security of the region, enabling potential members of the international strategic terrorism network to infiltrate into the European Union.

In view of the continuing success of terrorists in carrying out major acts of terror on a global scale (despite all the major efforts to step up security), the unbroken networking among different local terror organizations (irrespective of increased international cooperation), the risk posed by the threat of strategic terrorism cannot be considered as having been significantly reduced over the past two years. The synchronized terror attacks in Madrid on 11 March 2004 signal a turning point for the security of Europe: strategic terrorism may have started a series of terrorist attacks against the members of the coalition of countries openly engaged in the US-led global war on terror. This could raise the threat level for other countries providing strong political support of the US, such as Poland, Italy and the United Kingdom. Therefore, the following efforts have to be increased on a global scale:

- to improve intelligence gathering on the logistical activities and technical progress being made by terrorist organizations worldwide, in order to assist in assessing the operational capabilities of terrorist groups potentially capable of committing an act of catastrophic terrorism;
- the need to step up efforts to strengthen the physical protection of sensitive sites, representing important components of the national infrastructure, against the deployment of conventional weapons;
- there must be increased R&D efforts in technical countermeasures, both in the area of detection of WMD-related clandestine activities, as well as

in the protection of first responders against the effects of an act of terror deploying such a weapon;

- a program to prepare the public in a realistic manner for the fact that there are only limited possibilities to prevent a large-scale terror attack or mitigate its effects, without sounding alarmist, needs to be undertaken by all governments.

Notes

1. Al Qaeda's Fatwa, February 23, 1998, URL: http://www.pbs.org/newshour/terrorism/international/fatwa_1998/
2. N. R. Kingsbury, 'Review of the Studies of the Economic Impact of the September 11, 2001, Terrorist Attacks on the World Trade Center', GAO Report No. 02–700R, Washington, DC, 29 May 2002.
3. *'We reserve the right to respond at the appropriate time and place against all the countries participating in this unjust war, particularly Britain, Spain, Australia, Holland, Japan, and Italy'* (taped broadcast allegedly from Osama Bin Laden, Al Jazeera TV), *The Times* (London), 21 November 2003.
4. A. Hudson and J. Seper, '"Chatter" led to increase in threat level', *The Washington Times*, 23 December 2003.
5. For example, the spelling of the name of a child has been mixed up with that of a terrorist suspect.
6. S. K. Goo, 'Threat Level May Fall to Yellow; Concerns Could Keep Some Cities and Airports on High Alert,' *The Washington Post*, 9 January 2004, p. A02.
7. Hudson and Speer op.cit.
8. USA Patriot Act (H.R. 3162), 24 October 2004, in Electronic Privacy Information Center, URL: http://www.epic.org/privacy/terrorism/hr3162.html
9. H. Stark, 'Rasterfahndung über den Wolken', *Der Spiegel*, No. 4 (2004), 92.
10. N. Fielding, 'Linked and dangerous: Terror Inc,' *The Sunday Times*, 23 September 2001.
11. *ibid.*
12. D. Ruppe, 'Terror Manual', *ABC News*, 18 September 2001.
13. R. Gunaratna, 'Der Terrorismus Al Qaida's ist nicht gebrochen', *Terrorismus*, No. 2 (December 2003), 1–8.
14. The attack on one of the most modern US warships, the *USS Cole* on 12 October 2000, in the harbor of Aden not only resulted in 17 dead and 42 injured sailors, but it almost sank the ship.
15. A. Barnett, J. Burke, and Z. Smith, 'Terror cells regroup – and now their target is Europe', *The Observer*, 11 January 2004.
16. R. Scherer and A. Marks, 'Gangs, prison: Al Qaeda breeding grounds?' *Christian Science Monitor*, 14 June 2002, URL: http://www.csmonitor.com/2002/0614/p02s01-usju.html.
17. 'Nayomnikam v Chekhii predlagayut $150 za den' voiny v Chechne' [Recruits in Czech Republic are offered $150 for a day of war in Chechnya], Information Channel 'Chechen Republic' (in Russian), URL: http://kavkaz.strana.ru/print/206627.html
18. J. Rodrigues, 'Those killed came from 62 nations', *Houston Chronicle*, 18 September 2001.

19. D. Lithwick, 'How Do Terrorist "Cells" Work?' *Slate*, 17 September 2001, URL: http://slate.msn.com/id/1008311/
20. S. Emerson, 'American Jihad', *The Free Press*, New York, 2003.
21. R. Willing and K. Johnson, 'Plot likely involved few', *USA Today*, 5 October 2001, 4A.
22. 181-page al Qaeda manual (*G2 Bulletin*, 7 December 2003).
23. D. Stockfisch, 'Bedrohung auf See: Terrorismus und Piraterie', in J. Schröfl and T. Pankratz (eds) *Asymmetrische Kriegsfuehrung – ein neues Phaenomen der Internationalen Politik?* (Baden-Baden, Germany: Nomos Verlagsgesellschaft, 2004).
24. In October 2002, a terror attack succeeded in setting the French supertanker *Limburg* on fire off the coast of Yemen.
25. On 23 October 2000, the terror organization the Tamil Tigers sank one such ferry in Sri Lanka; another one was severely damaged.
26. Kidnapped ship, where a ship is hi-jacked and its valuable freight unloaded and re-sold with forged documents.
27. F. Steinhäusler, *et al.*, 'Upgrading aviation security: A German proposal for a global initiative', *Aviation Security International* (December 2002) 19–22.
28. F. Steinhäusler, C. Braun and L. Zaitseva, 'International Terrorists Threat to Nuclear Facilities', *Österreichische Militärische Zeitschrift* (ÖMZ), Special Edition 'Nuclear Material Protection' (2003) 15–23.
29. D. Stockfisch, 'Bedrohung auf See: Terrorismus und Piraterie', in J. Schröfl and T. Pankratz (eds) *Asymmetrische Kriegsfuehrung – ein neues Phaenomen der Internationalen Politik?* (Baden-Baden, Germany: Nomos Verlagsgesellschaft, 2004).
30. An apparent malfunctioning of the timers prevented the rockets from being launched. See D. Jehl, 'New threats in Pakistan', *International Herald Tribune*, 28 February 2002.
31. Rocket *Kassam II*, developed by Hamas engineers in 2001. See J. Hammer, 'Another Lebanon', *Newsweek*, 4 March 2002.
32. Joint engineering by Fatah and Hamas resulted in the production of these bombs, capable of destroying Israeli-made *Merkava* tanks. See J. Hammer, 'Another Lebanon,' *Newsweek*, 4 March 2002.
33. In 2001, the British elite unit the *Special Boat Squadron* stormed a ship suspected of carrying an RDD, but actually frightened off the real al Qaeda ship bound for Britain. See J. Farah, 'Al-Qaeda's plan to nuke London: Dirty bomb plot foiled 2 years ago, says official', *G2 Bulletin*, 7 December 2003.
34. Ten backpacks loaded with dynamite were detonated on four commuter trains in Madrid on 11 March 2004. See 'Scores die in Madrid bomb carnage', BBC News, 11 March 2004.
35. Press Conference by George W. Bush and Pervez Musharraf, Camp David, USA, 24 June 2003.

4
Peering into the Abyss: Understanding and Combating NBC Terrorism

Ian M. Cuthbertson

Introduction

The attacks on 11 September 2001 against New York and Washington and in Madrid on 3 March 2004, coupled with a wide range of other terrorist attacks, in locations ranging from Turkey to Bali, have all served to highlight a new and unambiguous trend in the use of political violence, one that now makes terrorism a much greater danger than the world has traditionally had to cope with from ethno-nationalistic or ideologically motivated terrorist groups. In contrast to earlier terrorist organizations, radical Islamic fundamentalist groups seek not only to inspire terror in the target population, but also have the overweening ambition of totally undermining the key pillars of the West's political, social, economic, infrastructural and moral make-up. By attacking carefully selected targets, exemplified by the assault on the office workers in the World Trade Center, tourists in Bali and rail commuters in Madrid, the terrorists are seeking to inflict previously unthinkable levels of destruction and disruption. They want to use the power of the carnage itself to convey their message, rather than depending on media coverage and the spin doctoring by spokespersons and pundits that inevitably accompanies such attacks. The level of harm inflicted is in and of itself intended to send their uncompromising message of total war to the audience, both among the targeted population and to their own supporters. The aim is to demonstrate that the terrorist's power to inflict harm is virtually limitless. And in pursuit of the terrorist's objectives, the use of weapons of mass destruction to attack a major urban target must be regarded as a logical and to be expected escalation in the terrorist's arsenal of outrages.

The term 'weapons of mass destruction' (WMD) was long synonymous with nuclear, biological and chemical (NBC) weapons. This grouping included nuclear weapons; both lethal and highly debilitating chemical weapons; and a wide variety of lethal biological agents, embracing both pathogens and toxins. These various classes of weapons acquired the title 'weapons of mass destruction' because NBC agents, if used properly to take full advantage of the their considerable potential to inflict both heavy casualties and widespread destruction, were the most obvious candidates for a category whose very name inspires fear and whose actual use would bring terror in its wake. It was also thought that they could be further differentiated from more 'normal' weapons by their lethality and the relatively small amount of agent or weaponry necessary to inflict high death tolls and/or widespread devastation. But the use of mundane, conventional, everyday objects – in the case of the 9/11 hijackers, fully-fueled wide body jet aircraft – showed that there needed to be a serious rethink of what type of things should be thought of and could be used as a weapon of mass destruction. A good example that the definition can be widened is that, in recent years, the term WMD has also been used to characterize radiological weapons, so-called 'dirty bombs,' because of the likely psychological impact their use would have. This despite the fact that the limited damage and deaths such weapons are likely to inflict even if used successfully, make their place in the pantheon somewhat questionable.[1]

Yet any broader definition of WMD should not blind us to the unique characteristics possessed by NBC weapons themselves. While it is certainly true that NBC weapons can be seen as the quintessential weapons of mass destruction, like their conventional brethren, their use can be calibrated to inflict a wide range of casualties and destruction, depending on which method of detonation or dispersion is employed. In the case of a nuclear device, for example, lower damage and casualties can be obtained by using a low yield weapon in a less densely populated area or, in the case of chemical and biological agents, higher casualties can be inflicted by improved dispersal measures for the agent, such as by utilizing crop duster aircraft rather than motor vehicle-borne dispersal sprays. However, it is this same range of threat scenarios that can be generated by NBC weapons that makes them so attractive to terrorists who wish to threaten or inflict mass disruption or casualties. If a terrorist calls attention to the possibilities of a non-NBC weapon as a WMD, or such a use is even suspected, then the target will do all in its power to neutralize the threat. Witness increased security attending all forms of air transportation since 9/11 and surface transport, in particular trains and subway systems, since 3/11. In contrast, the power of NBC weapons to coerce, terrorize and inflict harm and destruction on a target is inherent and much more difficult to neutralize or even effectively mitigate.

Since 9/11, the general characteristics of NBC weapons have become well known as government officials, experts and pundits have deluged both the print and electronic media with details of their construction, likely availability and potential lethality. For a terrorist, the first and most important characteristic, and this especially applies in the case of nuclear weapons, is their enormous destructive power and their immense lethality: a single nuclear weapon can destroy a town and kill tens, perhaps hundreds of thousands of people. Radiological, biological and chemical weapons are less immediately destructive but may be equally deadly; in the case of a biological or chemical weapon, they inspire particular fear because their use would likely be unseen, silent and selective. They might, if used correctly, be able to attack a city, a town or perhaps even a single building. The second appealing characteristics of such weapons for terrorists are their compactness and portability, factors that allows them to be easily concealed, transported and delivered against defenseless civilian populations and inadequately prepared military forces. And the third significant commonality they possess is the increasing proliferation of the weapons themselves, the equipment required for their manufacture and their precursor components. The greater ubiquity of all of these elements in turn means that they can be more easily obtained by a terrorist with the necessary motivation and financing.

It is the unique combination of these three crucial characteristics that together make NBC weapons, in the hands of millennialist terrorist groups, perhaps the single most dangerous and destructive security threats faced by advanced Western democracies, both now and for the foreseeable future.[2] All societies, but because of their high level of integration, interdependence and connectivity, advanced industrial nations in particular, are vulnerable to the severe damage and heavy casualties that may result from some forms of NBC attack. In addition, it is these same societies that provide a welcoming and passively supportive environment for the terrorist as she or he plans and instigates their operations. The vulnerabilities inherent in a democratic, open and thoroughly integrated society are well known: porous borders; excellent and secure internal and external communications capabilities, both physical and electronic; free and open sources of information, including information on the construction and use of a wide range of WMD; ready access to at least some of the elements and components needed to build and deliver NBC weapons; thanks in part to the Internet and eBay, the ready availability of prophylactic drugs and protective gear against the contamination created by all forms of NBC weaponry; a wide choice of targets, especially a wide selection of compact and heavily populated cities with little or no active defenses against any form of NBC attack; and finally, a large and aggressive media that stands ready to broadcast the news and act as a megaphone for the harm done by any NBC attack to all corners of the globe.[3]

NBC targets

Terrorists using NBC weapons are likely to target both combatants and noncombatants, both in the adversary's homeland or anywhere in the world. Despite the long list of possibilities, however, it is arguable, given the unique shock characteristics of WMD, that terrorists are most likely to target populations or assets that are vital to their adversary's essential functions or are highly regarded by the general public. Given the difficulties involved in obtaining nuclear devices, and the limited impact of radiological weapons, the flexibility and potency of biological weapons, and to a lesser extent their chemical cousins, are significant. Various comparison studies on the relative effectiveness of nuclear and biological weapons have been completed in a variety of potential terrorist scenarios. In 1993, the US Office of Technology Assessment (OTA) published a comparative study in which the possible effects of nuclear and biological attacks were contrasted. The target area was assumed to contain between three thousand to ten thousand people per square kilometer or represented an area of just slightly less than half-a-mile. As presented in this study, the detonation of a 12.5-kiloton (KT) nuclear weapon would create a blast area of approximately three square miles. The explosion would leave between 23,000 to 80,000 people dead. However, in the event of the use of a biological weapon, in this case the dispersal of 65 pounds of anthrax spores on an overcast day or on a night where there was only a light wind, the result would be between 30,000 to 100,000 deaths, with casualties occurring within a cigar-shaped plume covering an area of 3.85 square miles.[4]

While the lethality of nuclear weapons is well known, the impact of the use of CBW is more difficult to assess. As the above study illustrates, under optimal conditions, they may be as lethal as, or perhaps even more lethal than a nuclear weapon. And even under adverse conditions, where the terrorists are unable to obtain wholly favorable circumstances for dissemination, the use of a CBW will likely still cause deaths, along with an enormous amount of social, political and economic disruption. And while the production of the vast majority of CBW presents a variety of scientific and engineering difficulties, some, such as ricin, can easily be extracted from their precursor elements. Indeed, as the activities of the Aum Shinrikyo cult, with their extensive and sophisticated NBC research and development effort[5] or the more primitive activities of al Qaeda in Afghanistan show,[6] with sustained will and sufficient financial resources, coupled to a modicum of trained technical personnel, CBW is not beyond the reach of sub-state groups.

This is especially the case if terrorists restrict their efforts to the simpler options, such as the production of mustard gas or the weaponization of anthrax. The multiple delivery options available for the use of CBW, from missiles, to contamination of the food and water supply, by truck, boat, aircraft and, in the case of a number of biological agents, even from person to person, also makes them ideal terrorist weapons. While such agents can be difficult to weaponize and disseminate, they are also likely to be more easily acquired than a nuclear capability.

Trends in NBC terrorism

Long before 9/11, it was a major concern shared by security specialists, in both government and elsewhere, that emerging trends in terrorism were seemingly inexorably evolving towards the use of greater and greater violence, with the oft-stated objective of inflicting the maximum possible amount of death and destruction. There were clear indications of an ever more intense interest on the part of a number of terrorist organizations in obtaining and using NBC weapons. This evolution in the thinking of terrorists has taken place at a time when there has been a significant increase in the availability of NBC weapons and their precursor technologies on the international weapons black market. Despite the considerable efforts that North Korean and Pakistani nuclear scientists seem to have put into aiding the cause of proliferation, this situation was largely due to the slow motion collapse of the Soviet Union and the continued disintegration of its successor states during much of 1990s.[7] This greater availability of NBC weapons and technology coincided with a series of striking transformations in the underlying motivations, structures and operational techniques of both long-standing terrorist organizations and a variety of emerging networks of political and religious extremists.

Many of these new terrorist organizations, best exemplified but far from restricted to al Qaeda and its growing network of franchised, loosely affiliated radical Islamic fundamentalist terror groups, are built on a foundation of absolutist ideologies, a belief system that embraces a totally uncompromising view of the world, both how it stands now and how it should, and would, look in the future, once their religion, ideology or cause emerged triumphant from the struggle. It is a missionary, messianic outlook, one that seeks not merely to triumph over the opposition but to annihilate it. These new terrorist networks were well positioned to take advantage of the proliferation of basic NBC technologies, in particular the explosion in the availability of information available on fabricating a wide range of WMD brought about by the revolution in information technologies made possible by personal computers and the Internet. The absolutist viewpoints and grandiose objectives of such terrorist organizations leave them with no interest in waging any kind of limited war. To them, even NBC terrorism is simply one more option to be employed to advance the 'cause'.

Motivating factors

The motivation even to consider the use of weapon of mass destruction is of a completely different order of magnitude to that required to plant a car bomb or carry out an assassination. In a violent world, such actions are often regarded as little more than the normal background noise of a planet in which murder and mayhem seem to form the perpetual backdrop to everyday existence. But WMD do not fit into this picture. As the events of 9/11 all too clearly demonstrated, use of a WMD retains its capacity to shock. The use of an NBC weapon in such a scenario would only increase the impact of such a WMD attack and the attention paid to it by media, public opinion and the political elite.

Every terrorist group has its own unique motivating factors. Such motivations may have grown out of ethnic discrimination, political oppression, economic hardship, a quest for social justice, nationalistic aspirations, a desire to save the planet from those who would pollute it, or a desire to cleanse this same planet as a precursor to building a new and more perfect society, based on any number of models for the future happiness and well-being of humanity. All of these diverse and often self-contradictory ideas have served to motivate terrorists in the past, but most groups shared a thread of core aspirations that were negotiable with their opponents. With few exceptions, until very recently, to misquote the great Prussian military theorist, Karl von Clausewitz, terrorism was simply a continuation of politics by other means.[8] The objective of the terrorists was to gain attention and open a dialogue with the putative target so that their anger could be appeased, their demands met and their goals achieved. The fact that this scenario rarely played out in practice and, even when it did, only in the most truncated and bastardized form, in no way invalidated the model in the minds of those who had dedicated their lives in pursuit of just such a progression.

The growing preeminence of religion, often in its most fundamentalist, extreme and exclusionary form, has largely destroyed this age-old paradigm. Today, it is religious extremism that serves as the most basic catalyst for the world's most radical and dangerous terrorists. Indeed, the US government believed, well before 9/11 confirmed its worst fears, that in the foreseeable future the vast majority of terrorist attacks aimed against Western interests were not going to be motivated by the familiar political or social discontents of the world's revolutionary vanguard, nor the ethnic or nationalist aspirations of the dispossessed of the planet, a motivator which has stood in good stead for starting wars in the past two centuries, but rather in an upsurge in religious zealotry. Careful analysis showed clearly that it was religious fervor that was inspiring a new generation of more radical, more absolutist, indeed apocalyptic terrorists. It was widely believed amongst terrorism experts that religious extremists not only had the greatest potential to be the users of weapons of mass destruction, in particular NBC devices, in most circumstances they were the only types of terrorist groups, as opposed to individual members, who would seriously contemplate such a step.

Religiously inspired terrorists, be they Christian, Hindu, Moslem or from the growing range of cults springing up all over the world, put their own warped interpretation on scripture, using this to sanctify a belief that violence committed in pursuit of their objective is more than justified; it is required. Doing violence against God's enemies thus becomes a religious obligation. In the eyes of radical Islamic fundamentalists it is both a duty and a sacrament, one that is required by their particular reading of the Koran. Jihad, the Struggle or Holy War against non-believers and apostates is, from this perspective, an instruction passed down, through the Prophet

Mohammed, by God. As a result, even mass and indiscriminate violence is justified, as it is a vehicle for implementing God's will. Long before 9/11, this outlook had crystallized in the mind of such religious zealots as Osama bin Laden. He and his supporters clearly and repeatedly stated as one of their major goals the possession and use of weapons of mass destruction. Bin Laden stated publicly that he regarded such weapons as holy instruments to be used to destroy the enemies of Islam, in particular the United States and Israel. Such a step was believed by him to be an essential prerequisite for his goal of creating a new Islamic caliphate that would embrace all the nations and peoples of the world.[9] Indeed, in March 2003, bin Laden's most senior deputy, Ayman al-Zawahri, publically boasted that al Qaeda had obtained on the Central Asian weapons' black market a 'suitcase' nuclear device stolen from the Russian stockpile.[10]

For such reasons, the resources in terms both of finance and personnel being committed to obtaining NBC weapons makes perfect sense from the terrorist point of view. The possession and use of an NBC weapon would give such groups greatly enhanced prestige and legitimacy in the eyes of their own key constituencies of supporters, while firmly establishing their importance and power in the eyes of their adversaries. In the case of groups such as al Qaeda and Christian identity groups, there is well-documented evidence of long-standing research, experiments and development efforts all designed to construct some form of biological or chemical weapons capability. And in the case of al Qaeda, there have also been repeated but so far unsuccessful attempts to procure a nuclear weapon from the international black market in weapons.

It seems not only possible but inevitable that someone is going to try and use some form of NBC weapon in the foreseeable future, given the widespread fear that the use of any such device would generate, not least because of constant media and governmental warnings about their potency and destructiveness. Possession and use of NBC systems as weapons of mass destruction have thus been elevated to the level of potent status symbols for any terrorist group, especially one such as al Qaeda, which is constantly anxious to assert its continuing strength and viability.

Responses to the WMD threat

The United States has been aggressively and often indiscriminately pursuing across the board counter-terrorism actions, from launching a war in Iraq to confiscating nail clippers from airline passengers. Even after the Madrid rail attacks, however, European governments have remained more circumspect in both their individual and collective responses to the terrorist threat. While a significant number of counter-terrorist measures have been implemented individually by European states, concerted action is still in its infancy. As the on-going debate amongst European nations large and small demonstrates, this is not least because of the sensitive issues of national sovereignty that so many of the most effective counter-terrorist activities raise. The very nature of counter-terrorism intelligence gathering and operations, activities that require the close integration of many fields of activity – political will, law enforcement efforts, legislative initiatives, financial implications and social adjustments – are steps that many European governments still remain hesitant to consider, let alone implement. Despite the appointment of an European Union (EU) terrorism 'czar' and the adoption of more robust language in communiqués, the EU as an institution still does not seem to be wholeheartedly embracing the idea of the introduction of specially designed measures, either by creating new bodies or better mechanisms for cooperation, to combat terrorism in general and the use by terrorists of WMD in particular. It is clear that European states have still to summon up fully the will to undertake the kind of fundamental rethink of their approach to terrorism, either organizationally or even rhetorically, that the creation of the Homeland Security Department represents for the United States.

As a result of this approach, at present only NATO would appear to have the capability to provide the type of coordination that is required. NATO's then Secretary General, Lord Robertson's June 2002 announcement that the war on terror was in future to be the organization's primary focus was an important first step in assuming a more activist role in the struggle to contain the threat posed by WMD in the hands of terrorists. In its declaration NATO emphasized that one of its key tasks would be 'improving NATO's ability to assist national authorities in protecting both civilian populations and critical infrastructure against the consequences of terrorist attacks, and particularly attacks involving chemical, biological, radiological or nuclear weapons.'[11]

This policy was crystallized in five complementary initiatives:

- building the prototype of a deployable analytical laboratory for nuclear–biological–chemical (NBC) detection;
- creating the prototype of a response team for NBC events;
- designing a virtual 'Center of Excellence' for NBC defense;
- building a NATO stockpile of biological and chemical defense measures;
- implementing a disease surveillance system, to provide early warning of a biological or chemical attack.

The emphasis on NATO, which already has a WMD Center working on NBC-related issues, has come about largely because at present it remains difficult to envision how the other major European wide organization, the European Union, can in the near future go about adequately preparing itself and its member states against the threat of radiological, nuclear, biological, or chemical terrorism. The mixture of nations involved and EU difficulties in developing common security policies would seem to preclude such a role in the short to medium term. Therefore, NATO's initiative is a worthwhile, if partial, contribution to Europe's preparedness in the face of NBC terrorism.

NATO has recognized that the array of responses is wide, ranging from pre-emptive actions to prevent or degrade terrorist attacks involving WMD, to extensive defensive measures designed to mitigate the consequences of such an attack. Pre-emptive operations will inevitably, given the likely disastrous consequences of WMD use, focus on thwarting any terrorist action as far back as possible along the food chain leading to an attack. Preparing for the results of the use of WMD needs to focus on ensuring the most effective deployment of detection and first responder capabilities, ensuring law and order are maintained; hardening and building redundancy into medical facilities to ensure their continued functioning; rapid casualty evacuation and treatment; and building strategic stockpiles in multiple locations of emergency medical supplies and antidotes. All of these elements should embrace the joint training of military personnel and public protection bodies such as law enforcement, fire and medical services, using frequent large-scale and realistic exercises to prepare first responders to cope with both man-made emergencies and natural disasters. And finally, governments and electronic media need to work together to prevent panic by having in place a carefully thought out and jointly agreed information policy that can be immediately implemented by governments through hardened communications links that can quickly disseminate to both press and the general public reliable information on the event that has occurred and how people in both affected and unaffected areas are expected to react and behave.

While the main responsibility in each of these areas is bound to lie initially with the individual governments in European countries, it is also abundantly clear that the simple geography of Europe, as in North America, as well as the dynamics of political, social and economic integration means that continent-wide cooperation is both essential and inevitable in order to deal effectively with any major terrorist attack, especially if it involves the use of NBC. In the event of a major WMD attack, national medical resources would quickly be inundated with both victims and those seeking prophylactic medications. There would be issues and dangers from the spread of chemical, biological and radioactive/radiological contamination, phenomena that, as the spread of fallout from Chernobyl or Mad Cow disease from the UK have amply demonstrated, do not respect national borders. The dangers posed by the inevitable after-effects of a WMD attack require the establishment of continent-wide joint planning and on-going close cooperation between the various national civil defense and disaster relief services, as well as those parts of the armed forces deployed to provide assistance to the civil power. A worthwhile first step to get this process started would be the setting up of a European-wide agency to coordinate contingency planning and resource allocations for civil defense, as well as the development of disaster protocols and specific resources earmarked to meet both natural and man-made events.

Currently in all of these areas European governments have done too little, too slowly to prepare their institutions and populations for the threats they face. It is not clear if and when Europe as a whole will accept that, like the United States, the continent is a target for international terrorists. Generally speaking, it seems that Europeans have not yet internalized the entire scope and nature of the 'new' terrorism, the desire to inflict mass casualties via the most destructive measures possible. As a result, Europe is finding it hard to face the costs and disruptions to everyday life entailed by the hard choices that need to be made when faced by the imminent threat of WMD use. Perhaps once the full implications of the Madrid attacks sink in to the political and popular consciousness of the continent and its citizens, opinion formers and decision-makers fully absorb the realization that a European state has suffered an attack of the same type and magnitude as those already inflicted on the United States, there will be a feeling of shared danger and risk.

By contrast, the United States, seeing a clear and present danger from the use of WMD in the aftermath of 9/11, has moved aggressively to address the issue of homeland security. The major public step, one that was specifically intended to signal seriousness of intent, was the creation of the Homeland Security Department. This new cabinet level organization absorbed a number of existing agencies dealing with border security and disaster preparedness, and assumed responsibility for intelligence coordination in the area of domestic security. Although the new department has faced its share of teething troubles, major financial and personnel resources have been allocated to it. For example, successive Federal budgets have allocated billions of dollars for improved intelligence gathering, enhanced law enforcement capabilities, improved border security and tracking of visitors, the procurement, stockpiling and distribution systems for vaccines and antibiotics, and better aviation security, along with a wide range of other counter-terrorism programs.

Overall US Federal government spending on homeland security in the fiscal year 2004/5 is expected to be US$47.4 billion.[12] The reason why all of this spending and the initiatives it pays for are important and worthwhile is that while the dangers that the use by terrorists of WMD represents are considerable, they are as much psychological as physical. The potential destructiveness of an NBC weapon, or any other WMD, may be catastrophic, as has been described earlier in this chapter. However, it needs to be borne in mind that the likelihood of every part of the terrorist plot running smoothly progressively degrades as more and more obstacles are put in their way. Initiatives taken to degrade the terrorists' freedom of action, impede their ability to deploy fully and covertly their offensive capabilities and mitigating the effects of their attacks will always be worthwhile. Visible defensive preparations are also a way of showing the citizens of a state that they are not helpless in the face of terrorism and boosting their self-confidence in the face of terrorist propaganda and threats.

The relative failure of the Aum Shinrikyo's Tokyo subway nerve gas attack illustrates how even well prepared and equipped terrorists can be spectacularly unsuccessful in carrying out their mission.[13] In addition, the inherent technological characteristics of NBC weapons means that all too often they fail to work as their designers and builders intended. Nuclear weapons are the most complicated machines ever created by humanity: devices that are stuffed with mutually incompatible components, sensitive electronics packed into small spaces with highly radioactive and destructive fissile material. Without continuous and expert maintenance by highly skilled technicians they are more likely to fizzle than detonate. Chemical and biological weapons, by their very nature, are highly unstable and their effective use requires the kind of extensive practical training that is unlikely to be available to a terrorist in a world on heightened alert to this danger. Demystifying the actual dangers posed by WMD will allow people who are trapped in an attack to be better prepared to take the steps necessary to increase their chances of survival. And it will reassure those outside of the targeted area that their continued survival is not at immediate risk and make them easier to mobilize to assist those in more immediate peril. WMD are as much weapons of despair and distraction as they are of destruction. Controlling the fear of such weapons robs the terrorists of one of their most effective force multipliers. For all of these reasons, any investment in passive defensives and the education and preparation of first responders, media and the general public to combat and mitigate the terror, panic and dislocation that will inevitably follow the even partially successful use of an NBC weapon by terrorists will repay tangible and substantial dividends.

The future

In today's world, there is a clear trend towards the use of greater and more indiscriminate violence by a whole host of religiously and ethnically motivated terrorists. At a time when purely political ideology has largely disappeared as a motivator for terrorism, it is these simpler, indeed often atavistic ideologies, which have filled the vacuum. It is a threat governments throughout the world, and in the United States in particular, are at last treating with the seriousness it has long deserved. In the United States, the new passive counter-terrorism measures in the field of CBW preparedness in particular that have been implemented since September 2001 have been extensive and expensive. However, it needs to be recognized and accepted that even if fully implemented and wholly effective, such passive defenses can only serve to mitigate a CBW attack, not prevent it. For prevention, we need to look elsewhere, to more pro-active measures.

There are a number of ways in which enhancements and alterations in a wide variety of Western policies would serve to develop the attitudes, tools and plans that would allow Western nations to tackle more effectively the threats that arise from both the possibilities and realities of NBC terrorism. First and foremost, if the legitimacy and stability of the international system is to be maintained and if there is to be any hope for its enhanced effectiveness, pre-emption cannot and must not be the unilateral prerogative of the United States. The unilateralist policy of the Bush Administration undermined the standards that had been established to govern the behavior of all states since the establishment of the UN. As the experience of the war in Iraq amply demonstrates, it also fatally undermines Western political and popular cohesion and resolve in the face of a wide array of threats. To counter this trend, and to set clear guidelines for the use of pre-emptive force in the war on terrorism, NATO needs quickly to develop comprehensive and effective pre-emptive capabilities to respond to any and all incipient acts of NBC terrorism as soon as they are detected and confirmed. It is clear that what is required is a much wider range of unconventional military and law enforcement capabilities and options, ones that are seen as innovative, proportionate, and discriminate responses to real threats. If such capabilities are seen as capable, useable and proportionate to the threat then Western publics and their political representatives are much more likely to be supportive of their aggressive use. If they are interpreted as unethical and ineffective half-measures, they will receive less support and it will be difficult to marshal the political will to deploy them in action.

For the United States, unilateral actions need to be the court of last, not first resort. Instead, a NATO core capability to carry out anti-terrorist operations anywhere in the world, using ad hoc groupings of both member and non-member nations, is for now the most effective multilateral answer to the scourge of terrorism in general, and the threat of NBC terrorism in particular. And European states can no longer shirk their responsibilities and get a free ride on the back of American power. They can and must fully contribute to building such a capability for NATO. Their defense budgets must be increased and refocused to give them the capability to fight the new war on terrorism properly. Despite on-going attempts at reform and restructuring, a lack of political will and public interest, reflected in crushing shortfalls in budget requirements, means that most European military establishments have remained structured and equipped to fight the long-defunct Warsaw Pact or participate in UN peacekeeping operations. Neither of these can now be viewed as acceptable as core combat missions. As long as Western states are the prime targets for WMD attacks, even when they may not be a direct party to the dispute, it is up to them to build a flexible, capable and useable anti-terrorist capability for their still considerable military might and to show collective leadership and solidarity to the rest of the international community in its deployment and use.[14]

The West also needs to face up to the morally and politically sensitive idea that there needs to be a fundamental re-examination and possible revision of the range of civil liberty protections afforded by Western nations to suspected terrorist groups and their individual members and supporters. To date, Western governments have only begun fully and properly to explore their options with regard to the most imaginative methods available for the prevention of terrorist attacks and so far they have tended towards adopting only the most publicly acceptable and politically palatable methods for use when investigating terrorist suspects. As the lessons of 3/11 and the inevitable attacks that will come in their wake are absorbed, it seems certain that one of the main conclusions that will need to be drawn is that the circumspect approach on the part of many European governments, in particular the patchwork of different laws and regulations in force in different European nations, means it has long been too easy for terrorists in general, and their more passive support infrastructure in particular, to find undisturbed havens in areas where law enforcement is lax or under resourced. The wide variety of strategies taken by law enforcement and intelligence agencies have, to date, not adequately addressed the seriousness of the consequences of failure should they not detect and prevent a terrorist attack that employs an NBC weapon. While it is totally appropriate to applaud law enforcement after it solves terrorist crimes, this should not blind us to the fact that it is, after all, the primary objective of any law-enforcement or intelligence agency to prevent crime or hostile acts, to thwart the destruction of property and, most importantly, to stop the murder of those whose well-being is the principal raison d'être of any government.

In confronting the fear of overreaching and abuse by those we entrust with the task of law-enforcement and domestic intelligence gathering, we would do well to understand that the liberties and freedoms we presently enjoy need not be lost by employing more forceful methods to attack the crime of terrorism. An in-depth dialogue needs to be started and sustained between governments and their citizens to identify, develop and introduce reasonable and practicable approaches to counter-terrorism that would both enhance surveillance and intelligence gathering capabilities and at the same time curb any potential excesses on the part of law-enforcement and intelligence gathering bodies. But such a dialogue needs to be carried out with a clear understanding that the West as a whole is at war. Even if an attack on a particular state has not yet taken place, even if individual citizens do not perceive any particular risk to their own well-being, we are all still at war. Why? Because regardless of whether or not we wish to participate in the war on terrorism, the terrorists are waging war on us. Refusal to acknowledge this simple reality does nothing to negate it.

No country can be fully or perhaps even adequately prepared to withstand an attack by WMD, especially if it involved the use of a nuclear weapon or the widespread dissemination of a chemical or biological agent. But that does not mean that steps cannot and should not be taken to mitigate the effects and overall impact of such an attack. In response to the lessons of 9/11, and the extensive reassessment of the level of general threat that the attacks on the World Trade Center and the Pentagon represented, the United States embarked on a massive program of passive measures to prepare for the next attack. First responders were trained, procedures developed and adopted, new equipment procured and distributed and large-scale exercises were held to test the system. While the results are not always positive, there is clear momentum and progress is being made. In the aftermath of 3/11, it is clear that European governments and their citizens are beginning to understand that they are at equal risk and how vital it is that they respond proportionately. A valuable first step would be setting up a European-wide agency to coordinate contingency planning and resource allocations for civil defense, as well as the development of disaster protocols and specific resources to meet both natural and man-made events.

While the use of a weapon of mass destruction is certain to be deadly, in the hands of terrorists, they are also weapons of mass despair and distraction. The psychological blow that the terrorist plans to land as a result of the use of such weapons is at least as important as any physical harm inflicted. Indeed, in many ways the attack on a nation's psyche is more prolonged and disruptive. The financial damage done to stock markets and the international economy far outweighed the cost of physical damage inflicted on 9/11. To prepare people for the psychological trauma that will likely accompany any future use of a WMD, much greater attention needs to be paid to the area of public education on issues related to both the threats and possible responses, active and passive, to the dangers posed by NBC terrorism. Beyond the information and perceptions that are derived from popular culture and the entertainment industry, many of them simplistic, partial or hopelessly incorrect, Western publics have no reliable information or even realistic impressions of the risks posed by NBC terrorism.

The reaction to the anthrax scare that followed 9/11 or to the radiological weapons warning circulated in May 2002 shows how starved the general public remains of simple and accurate information on relative threat levels and precautions, even after the media deluge that purported to address these very issues. Vague warnings and media punditry are no substitute for a concerted and thorough campaign of public education. Experience has also demonstrated, however, that because no such event has yet taken place, it remains difficult to engage and sustain public interest or media attention on the matter. Yet a sustained campaign of public information and education remains a vital necessity if we are to combat both ennui at the constant parade of threats and warnings of terrorist attacks or, in the alternative, mass hysteria when an NBC attack is either credibly threatened or occurs. While it would be both impossible and indeed undesirable to repeat the Cold War propaganda surrounding civil defense against nuclear attack seen in many countries during the 1950s and 1960s, information on the likely scale and impact of the types of NBC weapons available to terrorists, and simple defensive and preparatory measures against them, should be widely disseminated. It is an international public service campaign that needs to involve the best and the brightest minds in advertising and marketing to develop a full range of education and informational resources and activities that can give the average citizen the information he or she needs to prepare for, react to and survive an NBC terrorist attack.

These are broad and ambitious proposals, but terrorist attacks using NBC weapons are coming, either sooner or later. The ability of Western countries to survive such assaults, both individually and collectively, will be determined by the steps that are taken now.

Notes

1. R. L. Garwin and G. Charpak, *Megawatts and Megatons: A Turning Point in the Nuclear Age?* (New York: Knopf Publishing, 2001) pp.339–43.
2. B. Hoffman, *Inside Terrorism* (New York: Columbia University Press, 1998). pp.199–205.
3. For a discussion of the so-called 'CNN Effect' and the tensions that inherently exist between the agenda of government and a free press, see the views expressed by both working journalists and public officials in: S. Hess and M. Kalb (eds) *The Media and the War on Terrorism* (Washington DC: The Brookings Institution, 2003).
4. *Proliferation of Weapons of Mass Destruction: Assessing the Risks*, Office of Technology Assessment (Washington, DC: Government Printing Office, 1993), pp.53–4.
5. D. E. Kaplan and A. Marshall, *The Cult at the End of the World* (New York: Crown Publishers Inc, 1996), pp.119–22.
6. Unclassified Report to Congress on the Acquisition of Technology Relating to Weapons of Mass Destruction and Advanced Conventional Munitions (Washington, DC: Weapons Intelligence, Nonproliferation, and Arms Control Center, Central Intelligence Agency, 2002), p.12.
7. For a detailed description of the proliferation of both NBC and conventional weapons from the former Soviet space, and the erratic efforts at interdiction, see: G. K. Bertsch and W. C. Potter (eds), *Dangerous Weapons, Desperate States: Russia, Belarus, Kazakstan, and Ukraine* (New York: Routledge, 1999).
8. K. Von Clausewitz, *On War* (New York, Viking Press, 1982).
9. L. Harris, 'Al Queda's Fantasy Ideology: War without Clausewitz', *Policy Review* (August & September 2002), No. 114.
10. *Al-Qaida says it has briefcase nukes, writer warns* (Associated Press, 22 March 2004 07:00 AM) http://www.azcentral.com/news/articles/0322AlQaida22-ON.html
11. 'Tackling Terror: NATO'S New Mission' Speech by NATO Secretary General, Lord Robertson, American Enterprise Institute (Washington, DC: 20 June, 2002). http://www.nato.int/docu/speech/2002/s020620a.htm
12. *President's Budget Includes $274 Million to Further Improve Nation's Bio-Surveillance*, Capabilities Office of the Press Secretary, Homeland Security Department, (Washington, DC, 29 January 2004). http://2004www.governmentguide.com/govsite.adp?bread = *Main&url = http%3A//www.governmentguide.com/ams/

clickThruRedirect.adp%3F55076483%2C16920155%2Chttp%3A//www.dhs.gov/
dhspublic/
13. D. E. Kaplan and A. Marshall, op. cit. pp.248–51.
14. T. Delpech, *International Terrorism and Europe, Chaillot Paper No 56* (Paris, European Union Institute for Security Studies, 2003), pp.48–50.

5
The European Response to International Terrorism

Georg Witschel[1]

Today Europe enjoys more freedom, security and prosperity than at any time in its history. Aggression, as traditionally understood, particularly in the form of a large-scale attack mounted by one state against another, is extremely unlikely in the foreseeable future. The European Security Strategy (ESS), adopted by EU heads of government on 12 December 2003 correctly reflects the situation in its introductory remarks: 'Europe has never been so prosperous, so secure nor so free. The violence of the first half of the 20th Century has given way to a period of peace and stability unprecedented in European history.'[2]

On the other hand it is obvious that Europe's history has been marked by a long and tragic history of terrorist acts. Europe has not only been the stage for 'European' terrorists (the nationals of a European state and/or those having political aims linked to political or social changes in Europe), but the region has also served as the 'theatre of war' for non-European groups whose political aims relate to the Middle East or other regions in the world.[3] The terrible bomb attacks in Madrid on 11 March 2004 were only the most recent and tragic proof of this phenomenon.

In Europe itself, a number of terrorist groups, mostly with leftist revolutionary backgrounds, have either been destroyed or have disbanded over the last decades. Among them are the 'Brigate Rosse' in Italy, the 'GRAPO' in Spain, the 'Rote Armee Fraktion' in Germany and the '17 November' in Greece.[4] But others, more ethno-nationalist groups, have remained active, such as ETA in Spain or IRA groups like the 'Real IRA' in the United Kingdom. Despite the continued operations of such terrorist organizations, however, it has only been more recent developments in international terrorism that have led the EU to consider terrorism as a strategic threat (together with the proliferation of weapons of mass destruction, regional conflicts, state failure and organized crime).[5] The EU strategy briefly touches upon these developments, describing the 'most recent wave of terrorism' as 'global in scope' and 'linked to violent religious extremism'. For a better understanding of what has changed in the last decade and what the threat for Europe actually is, it is helpful to examine these recent trends more closely.

Eleventh September 2001 and many of the outrageous terrorist acts that have been committed since then – for example in Madrid, Istanbul, Jakarta, Jerusalem, Casablanca, Ryadh, Moscow, Bali, Karachi, Al Ghriba/Tunisia – are indicative of some of the more recent trends in the development of international terrorism. As a result of these trends, new challenges have emerged for the world community in general and Europe in particular and new answers have had to be found to tackle them.

Recent developments in international terrorism: the increasing dominance of religiously-motivated terrorism

Worldwide, the last two years have seen a decrease in the overall number of terrorist acts committed, a trend that has resulted in the lowest total of such acts since 1998 (1998: 274; 1999: 395; 2000: 426; 2001: 355; 2002: 199 terrorist acts)[6]. However the number of victims of such attacks has remained relatively high, a fact which can only be explained by the increasing dominance of religiously-motivated terrorism. In stark contrast to other groups, the number of religiously-motivated terrorist groups has increased exponentially since the 1980s.

Religiously-motivated terrorists – far more so than all others types of terrorist – remain largely indifferent to the number and identity of their victims. While most social-revolutionary groups went at great length to select the 'right target' for their operations – for example, a high ranking political, military or economic leader – and did all they could to avoid collateral damage among ordinary civilians, religiously-motivated groups seem hardly to differentiate. This attitude is not restricted only to cult-like groups, such as Aum Shinrikyo in Japan, which considered killing people in its attacks as being in itself a holy act. It is unfortunately also true for other religiously-motivated terrorists, who consider their victims as no more than a useful means for conveying their politico-religious message. Religiously-motivated terrorists, unlike social-revolutionary and even ethno-nationalist groups, are far less interested in trying to convince the broader public of the correctness of their cause. The multiple attacks on commuter trains in Madrid are a highly pertinent example of this attitude: the victims were average citizens from more than 20 countries, none of them in an important or prominent social, political or economic position. Obviously it was not their individual backgrounds that made them terrorist targets, but their sheer numbers, their mere presence in the Spanish capital and the impossibility of properly protecting them. By killing more than 200 civilians, by maiming and wounding more than 1,600, the perpetrators succeeded in conveying a terrible message of terror, one that the attackers claimed was connected with Spanish participation in the occupation of Iraq.

The lack of differentiation among targets is also a reason why religiously-motivated terrorists (and currently this applies only to them) are striving to achieve control over weapons of mass destruction or at least radiological devices (dirty bombs).[7] It is not, therefore, surprising that it was a religious group that used, for the first time in modern history, a chemical weapon in a terrorist attack (Aum Shinrikyo release of sarin nerve gas against subway passengers in Tokyo). The discovery of the toxin ricin and of ingredients for preparing other poisons and/or chemical weapons in locations used by suspected Islamist terrorists also points in the same direction.

Geographic shift

This shift from a more traditional ideological (social-revolutionary) or ethno-national terrorism to religiously-motivated forms coincides with a certain geographical shift from Europe and Latin America to Northern Africa, the Middle East and Asia as the locations from which terrorists operate and draw their support. We find that most of the hot spots of Islamist terrorism are either in countries with Muslim majorities or in countries with very substantial Muslim minorities (it is still too early to judge whether the attacks in Madrid imply a reversal of this geographical phenomena). Poverty, bad governance, corruption and human rights violations may provide a fertile ground for the recruitment of terrorists and for gathering support from slightly larger parts of the population. But there is no direct nexus between these factors and the emergence of terrorism in general or radical Islamist terrorism in particular. On the other hand, there are serious indications that the spread of extremist, fundamentalist Islamicist ideas through religious schools, such as the Ngruki-network in Indonesia[8] or certain Madrasses in Pakistan and elsewhere, are a significant 'root-cause' for terrorism. It also goes without saying, however, that other forms of terrorism still exist in various parts of the world and that various motivations (ethno-national, social-revolutionary and religious) often overlap.

The globalization of terrorism

Religiously-motivated terrorism (or religion as a unifying factor for different terrorist groups) is certainly not limited to any one religion. However, at least for the time being, only terrorism motivated by radical Islamic fundamentalism has reached beyond national and regional borders to become a major global threat for the international community.[9] Al Qaeda, the most striking example of a more general trend, is a truly global network, which cooperates more or less closely with national or regional groups like the GSPC in Algeria or the Jemaah Islamiyah in Asia. This globalization of terror, not the mere internationalization witnessed from the late 1960s onwards, is probably the most unwanted child of the third millennium.

Asymmetric warfare and communication strategy

The twin attacks on 9/11 were a perfect example of asymmetric warfare. Nineteen perpetrators were directly involved, 3,000 people were killed, and more than US $25 billion in direct damage, and far more in indirect losses, were inflicted as a result of the negative impact on the global economy. Even if the adverse economic effects of 9/11 were only temporary, they were immediate and costly. For the US, real GDP growth forecasts were downgraded by 0.5 per cent for 2001 and 1.2 per cent for 2002. Some estimates implied a projected cumulative loss in US national income through the end of 2003 amounting to five percentage points of annual GDP, equalling half a trillion US$.[10] There were major disruptions in air traffic, the insurance industry raised its premiums and rejected coverage of certain high-risk areas (such as airlines), and stock markets tumbled, all of which added further to the negative economic impact of 9/11. In retrospect, however, it seems that the direct economic effects of the attacks vanished quite quickly, as equity prices swiftly bounced back and consumer confidence and consumption, along with general economic activity, showed more resilience than expected. The swift reaction of governments and central banks, by ensuring sufficient liquidity and stepping in to ensure that insurance coverage remained available, played a key role in avoiding a major economic depression.

Attacks like those in Jakarta and Bali, but also in Istanbul, Riyadh, Tunisia and elsewhere may be less dramatic and effective. But they all had serious negative economic consequences for the targeted countries. In some cases, such as the single incident in Tunisia, the effect is only temporary. But in others, for example Saudi Arabia, there will probably be a much longer-lasting impact. One can only presume that these longer-term impacts will only further add to the negative economic effects that follow from imposing tighter border controls and from increased public spending for security and military operations. Terrorists are thus able to inflict major damage on an enemy that was and is, in terms of manpower, military equipment and financial resources, vastly superior. But it's not only the largely tactical asymmetry of means available to terrorists on the one hand and attacked states on the other that is significant. It is the asymmetry of warfare in a more strategic sense. Osama bin Laden explained, in a videotape of 27 September 2001, that 'it is very important to concentrate on hitting the US economy through all possible means'.[11] Unlike in earlier terrorist campaigns, which aimed at achieving independence for a specific group or at the overthrow of a regime, modern terrorism is no longer conceived as an initial (due to military weakness) 'prelude' to first guerrilla warfare and finally open, conventional warfare aimed at achieving a political objective against the will of an adversary.[12] Instead, modern terrorism tries to leap directly from terrorism to the final stage of inflicting complete defeat on the enemy, in the sense of achieving certain objectives.

As a result of the hardening of targets, especially in the United States, terrorist attacks against so-called 'soft targets' like tourist or international trade facilities, international traffic or foreign experts and aid workers, have become a regular pattern. Since there are so many possible targets, all over the world, it is impossible to protect all of them properly. Furthermore, a successful attack on a soft, but economically relevant target might well achieve the same, if not 'better' overall results as an attack against a harder target, such as an embassy or military compound. Such attacks can generate shock waves that receive global amplification by dint of the ample coverage they receive from the international media. Thus the intimidation caused by the attack is felt not only by the local population, but also by people thousands of miles away, deterring them from visiting, investing or delivering aid to the country where the actual incident took place. In fact, for religiously-motivated terrorists, the victims no longer have any particular importance, except as part of the communications strategy they are trying to orchestrate through the media. Thus terrorists increase the psychological burden (terror in its original meaning: instilling great fear) as well as the economic costs of combating terrorism, with the aim of forcing the target states and societies to surrender to their demands.

Inseparability of external and internal security

9/11 and the many terrorist attacks committed since have taught the world and Europe a terrible lesson, that no country is immune from the scourge of modern terrorism. Even a favourable geographic security environment, a mighty army and friendly relations with neighbouring states cannot protect either average citizens or their undefended cities from major terrorist attacks. The threat to any country is no longer exclusively in the hands of hostile foreign governments, even though state-sponsored terrorism still exists, albeit on a much lower level than in the 1960s and 1970s, but instead lies increasingly in the dangers posed by non-state actors, who have no affiliation to any particular state or even geographical location.

Lessons to be learned

There are a number of lessons to be absorbed from 9/11 and the terrorist attacks since then, in particular that internal and external security have become inseparable and that it is these non-state terroristic actors that have become the major threat to international peace and security, as well as to the personal security of the average individual. These lessons include that:

- Terrorism needs an international, if not global response, and will do so for many years to come;
- Terrorism needs a firm response, based on the rule of law;

- Combating terrorism requires a comprehensive, multifaceted and systematic approach by the international community, that comprises political, diplomatic, legal, economic, if necessary military means;[13]
- Prevention, anti-and counter-terrorism must all operate hand in hand;
- Resilience, both on the macro and on the microeconomic level, has to be increased.

The attitude of the European Union and its member states vis-à-vis international terrorism

The EU, well before 9/11, had repeatedly condemned all acts of terrorism as criminal and unjustifiable, irrespective their motivation, forms and manifestations. 9/11, however, triggered a large number of specific EU actions in the various areas relevant to preventing and combating terrorism, and elevated the war against terrorism so that it became a priority issue in all EU policies. The Madrid bombings reinvigorated the EU's anti-terrorism efforts, as demonstrated by the European Council's declaration of 25 March 2004.[14] Among all of the measures taken by the EU, the most important areas were set out in the following order: (1) the overall political attitude of the EU; (2) winning hearts and minds; (3) suppression of terrorism financing and implementation of UN Security Council (SC) resolutions; (4) international law and treaties; (5) legal and police co-operation; and (6) other areas.

Before going into detail, however, it seems advisable to describe how the EU defines terrorism or, more precisely, terrorist acts. Unfortunately, there is as yet no globally binding definition of terrorism or terrorist acts. Therefore, for purposes of clarity, the EU adopted on 13 June 2002 a Justice and Home Affairs Council framework decision on combating terrorism.[15] In article 1 of this framework decision, a number of offences are set out that are drawn from the so-called UN 'sectorial' conventions, that is, those relevant to terrorism, such as

- attacks upon a person's life, which may cause death;
- kidnapping or hostage taking;
- causing extensive destruction to a government or public facility;
- seizure of aircraft, ships, etc.;
- possession, supply or use of weapons, explosives or nuclear/biological/chemical (NBC) weapons

were considered to be terrorist offences if committed with the aim of:

- seriously intimidating a population;
- unduly compelling a government or international organization to perform or abstain from performing any act;

- seriously destabilizing or destroying the fundamental political, constitutional, economic or social structures of a country or an international organization.

By accepting this list of criteria, the EU (unlike the UN) has adopted not only a common definition of terrorist acts, building partly on the 12 'sectorial conventions' of the UN, but also a definition that remains compatible with the draft Comprehensive Convention on International Terrorism that is currently being negotiated by the UN General Assembly.[16]

The overall political attitude of the EU towards terrorism

The EU considers terrorism as a threat to both internal and international security, to the conduct of peaceful relations between States and to the development and functioning of democratic institutions throughout the world. The fight against terrorism is seen as a long haul task, and the challenges stemming from terrorism are viewed as being global in nature. The EU is against making concessions to terrorist demands and is determined to bring to justice the perpetrators, organizers and sponsors of terrorism. The EU does not recognize the concept of state terrorism, as it considers that illegitimate acts committed by states are adequately covered by other rules of international law. The EU also firmly believes that national as well as international efforts to combat terrorism must fully respect human rights and fundamental freedoms.

The EU and its member states represent important and stable elements of the global coalition against terrorism that was forged after 9/11. As early as 21 September 2001, the European Council 'decided that the fight against terrorism will, more than ever, be a priority objective of the European Union'.[17] The Council furthermore declared that the attacks against the United States represented 'an assault on our open, democratic, tolerant and multicultural societies' and stated that actions against terrorists 'must be targeted and may also be directed against states abetting, supporting or harbouring terrorists'. In the same European Council meeting a plan of action was approved that was designed to enhance police and judicial cooperation, develop international legal instruments, put an end to the funding of terrorism, strengthen air security and co-ordinate the EU's global action. Less than a month later, on 19 October, the Council again unequivocally stated its 'full support for the action taken against terrorism in all its aspects within the framework defined by the United Nations'. The Council underlined its determination to combat terrorism in every form throughout the world. The Council furthermore vowed to further strengthen the coalition being built by the international community to combat terrorism and requested that certain measures and operations already envisaged on 21 September, such as the implementation of a European arrest warrant,[18] be speeded up.

At its Laeken meeting on 14–15 December 2001, the Council[19] reaffirmed the 'total solidarity with the American people and the international community in combating terrorism with full regard for individual rights and freedoms.' It was the first time after 9/11 that the heads of state and government of the EU balanced their resolve to combat terrorism with the demand to respect human rights. Since then the EU has, on all levels, reiterated that human rights must be respected in the fight against terrorism. In the presidency conclusions of the EU-Summit in Seville (June 2002)[20] the contribution of the EU common foreign and security policy in countering the terrorist threat was highlighted, reinforcing the Council's decision of September 2001 to fight terrorism through 'a co-ordinated and interdisciplinary approach embracing all Union policies'.

On 12 December 2003, the European Council adopted the European Security Strategy,[21] which places the overall political attitude towards terrorism within the broader framework of the EU security environment. Terrorism is considered a key threat to Europe's security, together with the proliferation of weapons of mass destruction, regional conflicts, state failure and organized crime. The ESS rightly emphasizes the links between the various key threats. Thus the acquisition of weapons of mass destruction by terrorist groups is considered to be 'the most frightening scenario', according to the ESS, while regional conflicts 'can lead to extremism, terrorism', and state failure is 'associated with obvious threats, such as organised crime or terrorism'. The ESS concludes this threat analysis with a kind of synopsis ('taking these different elements together...we could be confronted with a very radical threat indeed'). Addressing the threats, the ESS states that 'the first line of defence will often be abroad' and 'that dealing with terrorism may require a mixture of intelligence, police, judicial, military and other means' and that this strategy demands that the EU 'develop a strategic culture that fosters early, rapid and when necessary robust intervention in co-operation with other partners'. Finally, in the aftermath of the Madrid Bombings, the European Council adopted on 25 March 2004 a 'Declaration on Combating Terrorism',[22] which re-emphasized the EU's resolve to counter terrorism through solidarity and collective action.

The main focus of the Terrorism Declaration is on the implementation of legislative and administrative measures already decided by the EU, such as the European arrest warrant. The other main elements are the political commitment to act in the spirit of the Solidarity Clause enshrined in the draft European Convention and the reinforcing of operational cooperation between law enforcement agencies and EU bodies such as Europol and Eurojust. The position of a Counter-Terrorism Co-ordinator was established and a revised plan of action adopted, listing seven strategic objectives. Among them are the further enhancement of international efforts to combat terrorism, reducing the access of terrorists to financial resources, better protection of international transportation links, ensuring effective systems of border control, enhancing capabilities for the consequent management of border crossing issues and addressing the factors that contribute to creating support for terrorism.

These strategic objectives revise the EU action plan of 21 September 2001[23] and will result in an overhaul of the so called 'road map' designed to help implementing it as a functioning, relevant and continually updated document, one that now consists of roughly 70 objectives and measures. These cover areas such as foreign relations, justice and interior issues, traffic and transportation matters and financial policies. Among the objectives are the strengthening of the anti-terrorist coalition and the partnership with the US, the support for a political and reconstruction process in Afghanistan, the systematic evaluation of the Union's relations with third countries in light of their possible support for terrorism, the inclusion of a terrorism clause in agreements with third countries, adjusting EU policies on non-proliferation and disarmament, the adoption of a European arrest warrant, and the entry into force of various Conventions on Extradition and on Mutual Assistance in Criminal Matters and in respect of money laundering, along with a large number of operational measures designed to implement these broad policies.

Winning hearts and minds – partnership for progress and reform

Winning the hearts and minds of people, especially in the regions or hotspots where religiously-motivated terrorism seems to be particularly important and appealing, is a particularly important objective for the EU. After all, preventing people from becoming terrorists is more efficient than preventing terrorist acts. The EU has realized that even major successes in detaining al Qaeda members and their associates do not suffice to destroy or disband terrorist groups or prevent them from successfully recruiting new members. It is equally difficult totally to prevent committed terrorists from getting access to weapons, counterfeit documents, safe houses and financial resources, especially if their supporting logistical infrastructures remain intact and sympathizers are abundant. Therefore, supporting those who promote a moderate vision of Islam, assuring Muslims that Western values are not necessarily at odds with Islam, avoiding radicalization and the misperception of a Western crusade against Islam are of the utmost importance. But international initiatives that address this context of the war on terrorism are relatively rare. One remarkable exception is the work of the so-called 'Extreme Fundamentalist and Terrorism group,' mandated by EU-foreign ministers, which submitted a report on 5 May 2003 to the European Council in Thessaloniki, asking for a partnership for progress and reform with the countries of the Middle East and Northern Africa. In this report, four key areas (relevant also for fora such as the Barcelona Process and for civil societies) are described, namely:

- promoting political dialogue to encourage democracy, the rule of law, good governance and human rights;
- promoting economic and social development;
- promoting freedom of the press, plurality of media; and
- promoting cultural and religious dialogue with the Muslim world, in particular Muslim communities within the EU.

As yet, however, there has been no decision taken by European leaders on a follow up to the report, so that final approval and implementation of the Partnership for Progress and Reform is still pending.

The fight against the financing of terrorism; implementation of UN Security Council Resolutions 1373 and 1267/1333/1290/1455

Fighting the sources of financing for terrorism is one of the top priorities of the EU in the war against terrorism, as cutting off, or at least reducing, the financial resources available to terrorists is one of the most effective tools for preventing their activities. Indeed, the Conclusions and Plan of Action of the Extraordinary European Council of 21 September 2001 considered 'combating the funding of terrorism ... a decisive aspect'.[24] The relevant EU councils and institutions were requested to take all necessary measures to combat any form of financing to terrorists and member states were called upon to sign and ratify the UN Convention for the Suppression of the Financing of Terrorism[25] as a matter of urgency. Since then, most EU members have become parties to that Convention and all have made major progress in implementing the eight 'Special Recommendations on Terrorist Financing' made by the Financial Action Task Force.[26]

More importantly in this context is, however, the fact that the EU has found a quite unique approach to implement the obligations flowing from the aforementioned UN Financing Convention and SC-Resolution 1373. The resolution is itself a short version of the Convention, and calls for implementation of the Convention's provisions under Chapter VII of the UN charter, thus making the Convention binding under international law. The Convention's aims are:

- to prevent and suppress the financing of terrorist acts;
- to bring to justice any person who participates in the financing, planning, preparation or perpetration of terrorist acts or in supporting terrorist acts;
- for states to co-operate closely and afford one another assistance;
- to prevent the movement of terrorists by effective border controls and controls of the issuance of identity papers and travel documents.

EU member states would probably be unable to live up to the obligations under the UN Convention and SC-Resolution 1373 if they were acting unilaterally, both on legal grounds (member states no longer have any legal competencies over the flow of goods and assets across the EU external borders) and for reasons based on the realities of their circumstances (the free flow of persons, goods, services and finances within the EU). Individual member states could, for example, only cover monetary transfers within the EU or their own territory. A number of EU member states are also members of the Schengen System, so that there are no longer any effective border controls left within large areas of the EU.

In a Common Position statement issued on 27 December 2001, the European Council decided,[27] therefore, to punish the financing of terrorism and to freeze the funds of terrorists and their supporters. Further elements of this common position related to

- bringing terrorists and their supporters to justice and considering terrorist acts as serious crimes;
- ensuring close cooperation and assistance with regard to investigations;
- creating more efficient border controls and effective proceedures for the issuance of identity papers and travel documents, in order to prevent counterfeiting, forgery or fraudulent use of identity papers.

In another Common Position of 27 December 2001, the European Council[28] decided to create a list of persons and organizations involved in terrorist acts. A specific body – the so called 'Clearing House' – was established and mandated to examine proposals for the inclusion of individuals and organizations on this terrorist list. The Clearing House then recommends the listing of particular terrorist organizations and individuals (usually through the Committee of Permanent Representatives) to the European Council, which then takes the final decision for listing. Afterwards, this decision is implemented by a European Community (EC) regulation, which is directly and immediately binding on all EU members. All EU members have consequently to ensure that all accounts of listed terrorists are frozen and that other measures provided for in SC Resolution 1373 and the aforementioned Common Position of 27 December 2001 are undertaken.

By early 2004, more than 60 individual terrorists and organizations, only some of them based or active in Europe, had been listed. The Clearing House process, albeit sometimes slow and cumbersome, has thus become an important tool by which the EU can take joint measures against terrorists, particularly the freezing of their bank accounts. Even more important is the political signal implied by such a listing: a group of 25 leading states is sending the same political message, and declaring that a group or organization, for example Hezbollah, is unequivocally a terrorist organization. On the downside, one has to realize that in the entire EU to date, only a few accounts, in less than 10 EU member states, have been frozen and a considerable number of proposals made by third (that is non-EU) states have not yet been decided upon, mainly because the sponsoring governments are unable to meet the requirement of Article 1, Paragraph 4 of Common Position 931/2001.[29]

While both the aforementioned UN Convention and SC-Resolution 1373 leave it up to UN member states to decide how they will implement their obligations to combat terrorism, the UN Security Council has established, through a number of resolutions adopted under Chapter VII, a specific sanctions regime against Osama bin Laden, al Qaeda and the Taliban.[30] In relation to bin Laden and the two named entities, this sanctions regime requires all UN members, and thus all European States, to:

- freeze their funds and other financial assets or economic resources;
- prevent their entry into or the transit through their territories;
- prevent all indirect supply, sale and transfer of arms and related material to persons and organizations associated with Osama bin Laden, al Qaeda and the Taliban.

Unlike under SC resolution 1373, it is a committee of the Security Council itself that decides on such listings. EU members, therefore, (with the exception of those who are permanent or non-permanent members of the Security Council) can only indirectly influence the decision-making process (for example, by way of proposing to the President of the SC the name of a person or organization that should be included on the list). However, they are obliged to implement the aforementioned resolutions and ensure that all necessary measures are taken against individuals and/or organizations, once these are listed by the Security Council as terrorist organizations or individuals. Thus, through a number of EU Council Common Positions, as well as with EC regulation 881 of 27 May 2002[31] and later amendments, the European Union implemented this sanctions regime. These documents define, in considerable detail, the exact meaning of terms such as funds, financial assets and economic resources. Subsequent regulations also ensure an updating process that is triggered whenever the SC amends its list. The EC regulations were immediately and directly binding for all EU members. Furthermore, EC regulation 881 stipulates that member states would also make provisions for an efficient, proportionate and deterring punishment of any violations of the sanctions regime. In Germany, for example, intentional violations of sanctions regimes are crimes that entail prison terms of at least two years.

The main problems with the implementation of al Qaeda/Taliban sanctions regimes are to be found within the UN itself. Only a portion of those terrorists who are wanted or have been detained worldwide have been communicated by UN members to the SC for listing. Among those listed, some lack sufficient identification information, rendering their listing largely useless in enforcing the travel ban or in taking other measures. In addition, many countries, including some EU members, lack the legal basis for freezing or confiscating financial assets other than those held in bank accounts. Again, the bare numbers are not very impressive. EU-wide, less than a million Euros have so far been frozen under all of these sanctions regimes, a sum which represents only a small percentage of al Qaeda's and other terrorist groups' financial resources.

The treaties

The Comprehensive Convention on International Terrorism

The EU is on record as strongly favouring an early conclusion to the negotiations on the UN's Comprehensive Convention on International Terrorism. The draft[32] presented by India, which has been under negotiation for quite some time in both the UN General Assembly's 6th Committee and in an ad hoc committee, is seen by the EU as providing a valuable legal instrument, particularly since it contains a generic, viable definition of what constitutes a terrorist act. The EU has undertaken a number of demarches in the capitals of certain countries, particularly members of the Organisation of the Islamic Conference, whose main objective was to urge these countries to accept the definition of terrorism provided in the Indian draft without far-reaching exemption clauses. These exemptions would regard acts of 'peoples struggle against foreign occupation, aggression, colonialism, and hegemony' as not being terrorist crimes. For EU members such far-reaching exemptions, which do not distinguish between civilian and military targets, would serve to undermine the entire Convention. This is because such an approach would result in the re-introduction of motivation as a factor in qualifying an act as being either terroristic or a legitimate act of political expression, a differentiation that is incompatible not only with EU positions, but also with a great number of UN declarations and resolutions. Unfortunately, to date not much headway on this critical issue has been made and the negotiations in New York remain deadlocked.

The UN sectorial conventions

The EU believes that the sectorial approach to the negotiation and conclusion of UN anti-terrorism conventions has been successful and therefore continues to strive for the early adoption, by consensus, of the draft Convention on the Suppression of Acts of Nuclear Terrorism. From the EU's perspective, the aforementioned Comprehensive Convention is designed to be of a complementary nature, and is not designed or intended to replace the sectorial conventions. Speeding up the signing, ratification and rapid implementation of all 12 existing sectorial conventions is a declared objective of the EU. The performance of EU members in that context is fairly good and the EU also assists signing and ratification by non-EU states, by providing both financial support for implementation, as well as advice to them (see below).

Legal and judicial cooperation

The EU has also undertaken numerous activities in the field of police and judicial cooperation, including the drawing up of new regulations related to the acquisition, storage and transportation of explosives, as adopted by the Justice and Home Affairs Council in October 2003. Other operational and legislative matters relate to cooperation by national authorities with Europol and Eurojust, to better cooperation and exchanges of information between national intelligence services, as well as between individual national police forces themselves. Further decisions relate to the implementation of a European arrest warrant and to the setting up of a Union mechanism for the co-ordination of civil protection measures. Approximately 30 different measures have so far been adopted or implemented, partly falling within the responsibilities of EU institutions such as the Council or Commission, and partly within the realm of individual member states. Some of them are briefly described below.

Europol

With a decision on 18 July 1995, the European Council created the European Police Office (Europol). Its main task is to improve the effectiveness of policing authorities in member states and strengthen cooperation between them. Areas of cooperation include preventing and combating terrorism, unlawful drug trafficking, the illicit trafficking of radioactive and nuclear substances, money laundering and some other particularly serious crimes. Europol's principle tasks are to:

- facilitate the exchange of information between member states;
- obtain, collect and analyse information and intelligence;
- aid investigations in the member states;
- maintain a computerized system of the information it collects.

After 9/11, Europol's counter-terrorism capacities were further strengthened by establishing a Counter-Terrorism Task Force. On the other hand, Europol has no competence to undertake its own investigations or enforcement measures. It is certainly not a European FBI, Scotland Yard or Bundeskrimi-nalamt. However, it is an important catalyst for ever-closer cooperation between EU member states in policing matters, by providing liaison capabilities to relevant national authorities through the mechanism of Europol's national units contacts, whose interaction with each other are building a more effective and co-ordinated cooperative network.

Eurojust

A more recent, post 9/11 innovation is Eurojust, an EU body established by a Council decision on 28 February 2002.[33] Eurojust was established to enhance the effectiveness of the authorities within member states that deal with the investigation and prosecution of serious trans-border crime. All of the types of crimes that fall within the competence of Europol – such as terrorism – are also covered by the general competence of Eurojust. Its main tasks are to

- improve co-ordination between competent authorities in member states (magistrates, prosecutors, etc.);
- improve the co-ordination of investigations and prosecutions in the member states;
- facilitate the execution of international mutual legal assistance and the implementation of extradition requests.

On March 2004 the European Council called on EU member states to ensure that the optimum and most effective use is made of both Europol and Eurojust.

The European Arrest Warrant

The European Arrest Warrant is designed to replace the current national extradition systems in place between member states, and to simplify and speed up extradition procedures by requiring national judicial authorities to recognize, with a minimum of formalities, requests made by the judicial authority of another member for the arrest and surrender of a person. According to a Council Framework Decision of 13 June 2002,[34] arrest warrants can be issued to conduct criminal prosecution, to execute a sentence or a detention order for serious offences such as terrorism. Cooperation with the Schengen Information System and the European Judicial Network (EJN) is provided for. By the end of 2004, the EU's Commission will submit a report to the European Parliament on the operation of the European Arrest Warrant, analysing whether the system works and, if necessary, will recommend legislative measures to improve it further.

Assistance

A number of UN resolutions call upon UN members to assist each other in combating terrorism. The so-called 'Counter-Terrorism Committee', established under Security Council Resolution 1373, established a matrix listing all of the requests made by UN members for assistance, as well as offers of such assistance. The leaders of the G8 (which includes four EU member States and the EU Commission) decided at their summit in Evian in June 2003 to expand and co-ordinate their assistance to non-EU states. Against this background, it is a declared objective of both the EU and its member states to identify specific actions that can assist third countries in implementing their commitments under UNSCR 1373. Security Council resolution 1373 calls on states to become parties to all of the conventions and protocols relating to terrorism. To this end, the Commission has established a strategy for providing projects on technical assistance to a number of third countries to facilitate the implementation of UNSCR 1373 and other relevant international obligations. When identifying pilot countries for such assistance, the following criteria are being used: their relevance to the fight against terrorism, their overall significance to EU foreign policy, their technical assistance needs, their readiness to cooperate and the existence of a comparative advantage for the EU vis-à-vis other potential donors. Indonesia, Pakistan and the Philippines have all been identified as the first priorities. The EU has also supported the Palestinian Authority in its efforts to counter terrorist activities originating from the territories under its control.

Conclusions

Altogether, Europe's response to terrorism has been swift and multifaceted. Europe's profile in preventing and countering terrorism is unquestionably much higher than it was before 9/11. With the creation of the European Security Strategy, a comprehensive political framework has been established that correctly puts terrorism into a threat context that also includes weapons of mass destruction, organized crime and failing states, and recognizes them all as the major threats to Europe in the early twenty-first century. But does that mean that Europeans can relax, proud of what has been achieved over the last few years? Certainly not! While the achievements are impressive, and indeed cooperation between Europeans, and between the EU and others, has reached unprecedented levels, a great deal still remains to be done. On the political level, the rift over the war on Iraq has to be healed. The attitude towards state sponsors of terrorism also deserves closer attention or rather needs to be moved beyond mere words to actual deeds. The EU has never invoked the various counter-terrorism clauses that have been included in international treaties to give a clear warning signal to a third state that may be sponsoring terrorism. Even more than such signals, a sustained dialogue with the Muslim world and – for Europe a particularly important part of it, the Arab countries and societies that border the Mediterranean – is an imperative.

More has also to be done to reduce the access of terrorists to financial and other economic resources. Despite major improvements, European intelligence, police and judicial cooperation in bodies such as Europol, Eurojust, the Joint Situation Centre and other bodies can still be significantly improved. The establishment of joint data banks on visa and online access of Europol, as well as access by national magistrates to the data banks of the Schengen information system, are other necessary steps. In addition, the protection of international transportation links and the quality of border controls need further improvements, including the enhancement of capacities for the identification of terrorists and the detection of terrorist devices at land, sea and air border entry points. Cooperation within the EU and between EU and NATO with regard to mitigating the consequences of a terrorist attack also needs to be deepened. The full implementation of the EU's health security program and the improvement of member states capacities to communicate with their citizens in case of a terrorist attack belong with the priority tasks in this area.

It may well be that some of the many measures adopted over the last few years need to be overhauled, and a stocktaking process is already underway. The EU doesn't need more strategies or action plans in the field of counter-terrorism, but rather a revised and coherent version of the existing ones, together with the setting of clear objectives along the lines described above. This would be a sufficient basis for completing measures already under way and taking those measures which are still needed to fill existing gaps and reach the stated objectives. All of this is necessary because, after all, preventing and combating terrorism is a long-term task, one that will require systematic and sustained efforts for the foreseeable future.

Notes

1. The views in this chapter are expressed by the author in his personal capacity and do not necessarily reflect the views of the German government.
2. European Security Strategy (ESS), Brussels, 12 December 2003, p.1.
3. The attack against the Israeli Olympic team in Munich on 5 September 1972 is a pertinent example; see B. Hoffmann, *Terrorismus – der unerklärte Krieg* (Frankfurt: Fischer Verlag, 1999), p.90.
4. *ibid.*, p.103.
5. ESS, p.3: 'Terrorism... seeks to undermine the openness and tolerance of our societies, and it poses a growing strategic threat to the whole of Europe.'
6. US Department of State, *Patterns of Global Terrorism 2002*, Washington, 30 April 2003.
7. D. Benjamin and S. Simon, *The Age of Sacred Terror* (New York: Random House, 2002), pp.129, 147.
8. P. Bolte, K. Möller and O. Rzyttka, 'Politischer Islam, Separatismus und Terrorismus in Südostasien', *SWP Studie* (Stiftung Wissenschaft und Politik, Berlin, 2003) 39.
9. U. Schneckener, 'Netzwerke des Terrors', *SWP Studie* (Stiftung Wissenschaft und Politik, Berlin 2002), 19–39.
10. P. Lenain, M. Bonturi, V. Koen, 'The Economic Consequences of Terrorism', OECD Economics Department Working Paper ECO/WKP(2002) 20, www.oecd.org/eco

11. D. Benjamin and S. Simon, *The Age of Sacred Terror*, p.156.
12. H. Münkler, Grammatik der Gewalt, *Frankfurter Allgemeine Zeitung* (18.10.2002).
13. H. Müller, 'Terrorism, Proliferation: a European Threat Assessment', *Chaillot Papers No. 58* (March 2003).
14. European Council, *Declaration on Combating Terrorism*, Brussels, 25 March 2004.
15. Council Framework Decision of 13 June 2002 on Combating Terrorism (2002/475/JHA), *Official Journal of the European Communities* of 22 June 2002, L 164/3.
16. United Nations, *International Instruments related to the Prevention and Suppression of International Terrorism* (United Nations, New York 2001); UN Doc A/C.6/57/WG.2/CRP.1, 15 October 2002.
17. Conclusions and Plan of Action of the Extraordinary European Council Meeting on 21 September 2001, Doc. Nr. SN 140/01.
18. Declaration by the heads of State or Government of the European Union and the President of the Commission on 19 October 2001, Doc. Nr. SN 4296/2/01 REV 2.
19. Presidency Conclusions European Council Meeting in Laeken, 14 and 15 December 2001, Doc.Nr. SN 300/1/01 REV 1.
20. Presidency Conclusions Seville European Council, 21 and 22 June 2002, Doc. Nr. SN 200/1/02 REV 1.
21. see fn 2.
22. see fn 14.
23. see fn 17.
24. see fn 15.
25. see fn 15, p. 113.
26. www.fatf-gafi.org/SrecsTF_en.htm
27. Council Common Position of 27 December 2001 (2001/930/CSFP), Official Journal of the European Communities, L 344, p.90.
28. Council Common Position of 27 December 2001 (2001/931/CFSP), *ibid.*, L. 344, p.93.
29. see fn 17.
30. SC res 1267, 1333, 1390, 1455.
31. Council Common Position 402 of 27 May 2002 (2002/402/CFSP; Official Journal L 139, p. 35–38); EC regulation 881 of 27 May 2002, Official Journal L 139, p. 9–22
32. Report of the Working Group Measures to eliminate international terrorism of 15 October 2002, Doc. Nr. A/C.6/57/WG.2/CRP 1.
33. Council Decision of 28 February 2002 (2002/187/JHA); Official Journal L63, pp.1–13.
34. Council Framework Decision of 13 June 2002 (2002/584/JHA), Official Journal L 190, pp.1–20.

Part II
The Transatlantic Relationship

6
Transatlantic Relations after 9/11 and Iraq: Continuities and Discontinuities

Regina Karp

There is a palpable sense amongst Europeans that major questions on the future of international politics no longer involve them. European opinions and preferences do not seem to matter, as the United States appears determined to define its interests nationally, assertively, and unilaterally. Long-established practices of consultation are pushed aside, replaced with calls for cooperation that do not appear to be issued with any serious desire that they will be heeded or acted upon. There is no doubt that an assertive, unilateral America challenges the basis of the relationship with its closest allies. Transatlantic relations are as much about shared vision as they are about joint policies. In the absence of one, the other inevitably atrophies.

A common culture and shared values have been the traditional foundation of US–European relations. Under the Bush administration, however, deep divisions have emerged over how a common culture and shared values should shape political goals. By and large, European preferences aim at conciliation, multilateralism and institutional binding. Taking cues from their own recent past of overcoming political strife and extending stability and peace to the East, Europeans embrace the presumption of diplomacy as the most promising approach to managing a world of complex interdependence and rapid globalization.

The Bush administration does not share the presumption of the usefulness of diplomacy nor does it view international institutions as effective. Rather, this administration believes that international peace and stability is not the result of painstaking negotiation and compromise but can only be achieved through the preponderance of American power. It is the exercise of power that orders world politics, eliminates the possibility of challenges and ignores dissent among allies.[1] The collapse of the Soviet Union propelled the United States into a position of peerless power, unfettered by the ties of balances and institutional rules. For the first time in its history, the United States is able to exercise the promise of its creation. Conceived as the exceptional power, imbued with universal values and above the fray of petty rivalries and power balances, the US is finally free to bestow upon the world the benefits of liberal democracy.

Europeans worry about the connections the Bush administration makes between the power it can wield and the values it wants to spread. Hence it is over the connection between values and power in US foreign policy that the transatlantic relationship suffered most during 2003. Europeans do not share the perception that international peace and stability should be imposed upon the world. To them, peace and stability have, first and foremost, an organic quality, are the result of voluntary consent by states to abide by rules and standards. By contrast, the Bush administration asks 'why wait?' American power can improve the quality of international relations without the delays caused by lengthy persuasion and power brokering.

The most profound implication of American primacy is the choices it offers to US policymakers. It is also the most dangerous for the transatlantic relationship. In the absence of a peer competitor, multilateral diplomacy and alliance relations no longer define how American leaders perceive the country's role. Preponderant power turns multilateralism and alliance relations into options. The US can, if it so chooses, take recourse to the UN and work with NATO. Whether it does, however, will no longer be determined by an understanding that collectively conceived goals are best served by working with others. Instead, multilateral policies will be pursued in the belief that unilaterally conceived goals best serve collective interests. International institutions and alliance relations thus become instruments of an American vision of international order and how it is to be achieved.

The fact that the United States has the capacity and, under the Bush administration, has repeatedly demonstrated a willingness to impose its preferred solutions raises important questions. Is this combination of power and vision likely to survive the Bush administration? Is it a uniquely Bushian policy mix of zealous neo-conservatism, one that seized upon a singular opportunity, the public pain caused by carnage wrought by the terrorist attacks of 9/11, married it with the availability of the national power resources necessary to topple Saddam's odious regime and which for good measure, also seeks to refashion the politics of the Middle East? Will the US return to a more restrained, cooperative approach under a different president, Republican or Democrat? Or, are there more structural issues at stake? Do Bush administration policies reflect the primacy of a great power that exercises power at will? In that case, how the US *chooses* to act is a paramount issue for US allies in Europe. After all, great powers can choose *not* to exploit their unique position. However, any hopes Europeans harbor regarding a return to 'normal' US behavior would be misplaced. Instead, Europeans need to focus on the *conditions* US primacy creates for the transatlantic relationship. By definition, primacy reduces the need for allies. In turn, primacy increases the needs allies have to influence how primacy is exercised. It is precisely because Europeans share the values of liberal democracy that their stakes in how those values are spread across the globe are high.

American primacy à la George W. Bush

The past three years have shown that the merger of US values and interests can lead to a reckless version of *realpolitik*, one that potentially leaves behind more chaos than it found. These years have also exposed the unique vulnerabilities of the United States. America is not threatened as a state but is vulnerable as a society to threats that ignore the many trappings of state power. The Bush administration's conclusion was that only America's power could confront and defeat the threat of terrorism and stop the proliferation of weapons of mass destruction. As expressed in the *National Security Strategy* of 2002, 'The United States can no longer solely rely on a reactive posture as we have in the past ... We cannot let our enemies strike first'. From this assessment of the threat to national and international security and how it is to be countered, the Bush administration embarked on a revolution in foreign policy, developing a kind of 'muscular Wilsonianism'.[2] Accordingly, America's power and, when necessary, its military might, will spread the values of democracy and liberty to wherever these values are threatened or absent altogether. America and, by implication, the rest of the world can only be safe once people everywhere can freely choose how to lead their lives. American self-perception has always been imbued with a strong sense of values and mission. After the First World War, Woodrow Wilson saw an opportunity to translate these values into international policy. After the Second World War, the Truman administration had the opportunity to use its nuclear monopoly to put an end to the challenge of Soviet communism. With the end of the Cold War, the administrations of George H. Bush and Clinton were in a position to redesign America's role in the world and foster the spread of democracy.

Interestingly, these opportunities did not lead to the current confluence of interests and values. Wilson found that his international activism had little domestic support and that American ideals and interests diverged. The League of Nations and its goal of universal collective security foundered precisely because interests and values cannot be presumed to coincide. Truman's administration considered and then discarded the option of launching a preventive war against the Soviet Union. With the onset of the Cold War, it was clear that the Soviet Union would emerge as a peer challenger, would endanger American interests in Western Europe and elsewhere, and would inevitably develop nuclear weapons capable of striking the American homeland. Thus there were strong reasons to eliminate the Soviet threat before it reached its full potential. As Marc Trachtenberg has shown, the security strategy that emerged from this early debate over foreign policy and the use of force in the nuclear age was, nevertheless, one of containment, not confrontation and defeat.[3] The Truman administration did make a strong connection between values and interests through the Marshall Plan and a defense guarantee to Western Europe, but these efforts were clearly informed by a sense of limits to American power and the utility of force. For George H. Bush and Bill Clinton, the 1991 Gulf War did raise the prospect of a new world order where freedom-loving nations would band together to defeat blatant aggression; at the same time it was assumed that such blatant aggression would be rare and that other, less obvious forms of aggression would make it much harder to act collectively. The Clinton administration especially found it hard to decide where to bring to bare American power to bear and to what effect. Its *National Security Strategy of Engagement and Enlargement*[4] was ostensibly internationalist but a poor guide for defining on which problems America would focus. Though values figured prominently, their connection to US national interests remained blurred.

In sum, these historical examples reveal a continuous emphasis of American values in the formulation of foreign policy but, more importantly, they also identify a consistency in the manner in which the promotion of values was linked to the national interest. This consistency means that the United States, even when it clearly had the opportunity to assert a confluence of values and interests, took other factors into consideration. The bottom line was that values and interests would be best served if they were promoted through strategies that did not threaten the loss of either domestic or international support. America was *primus inter pares*, was willing to lead, take on a disproportionate share of collective defense, and sought to conciliate, not impose.

The Bush revolution in US foreign policy gives notice to these established traditions.[5] As a result, foreign policy is driven by righteous ideological fervor, ready to defeat all those who threaten America's security or challenge its ability to do so. Bush's national security advisor Condoleezza Rice sees the 1990s as a decade when policy lacked 'an overarching, explanatory theory or framework that would describe the new threats and the proper response to them'.[6] Globalization and information technology, she argued, had not made military force irrelevant. Neither had preventing or limiting ethnic conflicts and humanitarian interventions been able to provide a clear sense of purpose. Thus the end of the Cold War and the attack on the World Trade Center are 'bookends of a long transition period'.

9/11 emerged as the long awaited catalyst for the re-sorting of American foreign policy. The United States finally had a strategic goal that was worthy of its primacy. Not only would America pursue international terrorists and destroy their networks, 9/11 also gave opportunity to continue the transformation of tyrant states into peaceful democracies. Evoking the successes of democracy in post-Second World War Germany and Japan, the ultimate goal of American foreign policy became 'to create a balance of power that favors freedom'.[7] Henceforth, the United States would use its power to create such a balance, living up to its 'responsibility to build a world that is not only safer, but better'. Democratic values and respect for human rights are universal. Rice dismisses differentiation between values and interests. 'In real life,' she says, 'power and values are married completely'. Accordingly, great powers matter and the values of great powers matter, too. In other words, America alone is equipped and has the vision, the will, to do what must be done. Six months later, the United States went to war against Saddam Hussein.

Clearly, the revolutionary nature of Bush foreign policy is its emphasis on the historical opportunity that now exists for change in the international order. Speaking at the London International Institute for Strategic Studies in June 2003, Rice declared that 'confluence of common interests and common values creates a historic opportunity to break the destructive pattern of great power rivalry that has bedeviled the world since the rise of the nation state in the seventeenth century. This is, in fact, more than an opportunity. It is an obligation'.[8]

The Bush 'revolution' offers a coherent intellectual framework. It identifies the primary threats to international security in the twenty-first century namely, international terrorism and the spread of weapons of mass destruction; it attributes these threats to the absence of democracy in states that deny liberty to their own people and harbor terrorists; it intends to counter these threats by defeating terrorism and, where necessary, imposing democratic regimes. Above all, the Bush 'revolution' provides a coherent vision of how threats to free societies relate to American power.

What many in Europe view as overheated emotional rhetoric, is the grand strategy of the Bush team. It sees the United States as history's chosen instrument, able to accomplish now what it only partially succeeded in achieving in the past. More importantly, this strategy taps into a national reservoir of beliefs that the United States is a benign power and that all those who share the values of liberal democracy have an opportunity to work together to obtain for others these same benefits. The president and his senior advisors may not be using the same language Europeans are used to hearing in their own political discourses but when the President of the United States speaks of 'evil-doers' and 'an axis of evil', everyone in America intuitively knows what he means. Those who disagree with his choice of words and their substance are nonetheless fully aware of the unifying power they convey.

Far from continuing the drift it saw in the policies of the 1990s, the Bush administration found focus and purpose. Focus was provided by US vulnerability to terrorist attack and the global specter of WMD proliferation. Purpose was gained by asserting the confluence of values and interests and the skillful weaving of a security strategy that ties vulnerability to threat, and threat to the power that can defeat it. As grand strategies go, this is no small feat. For those who accept the Bush logic of American primacy, the opportunities offered by unipolarity, the possibilities offered by the diverse sources of American power, and the obligation to share the benefits of democracy, all come together in an irresistible combination.[9]

Whatever happened to the balance of power?

Since the end of the Cold War, no peer challenger to US power has emerged. 'Why,' John Ikenberry asks, 'despite the widening power gulf between the United States and the other major states, has a counterbalancing reaction not yet taken place?'[10] The question becomes even more intriguing in light of the Bush administration's interpretation of power preponderance that limits the autonomy of others. Rice makes a structural case that power balancing has lost its legitimacy. 'Why,' she asks, 'would anyone who shares the values of freedom seek to put a check on those values?' Instead, what great powers should aim for is the creation of 'a balance of power that favors freedom'. This structural version of primacy transforms the meaning of balancing, shifting it from balancing against power to balancing against values.

Structural realists maintain, however, that balancing behavior will eventually set in. Under Clinton, so the argument goes, the administration's indecisiveness diluted the effects of unipolarity on the international system. Without clear purpose, American primacy remained unfocussed and did not threaten major states. There simply was no need to counterbalance. Both Bush Sr and Clinton were committed internationalists and exhibited few inclinations to exploit American power preponderance. But logically, major states will begin to curb US primacy once they fully grasp the impact of the Bush revolution on international relations.

Steven Brooks and William Wohlforth argue that 'If today's American primacy does not constitute unipolarity, then nothing ever will'.[11] By any measure, they continue, America's primacy has already removed the country from the reaches of any would-be competitors. Whether one takes military spending, economic performance, technological innovation, or popular culture as yardsticks, the United States has created not gaps but chasms between itself and others. To match the United States in any one category would force others into extraordinary efforts. The task of balancing is compounded by the fact that the US is not an emerging power but already firmly entrenched in its unipolar status.[12] Since America's position provides unprecedented opportunity to maintain this status quo, the US can be expected to resist a deterioration of its position.[13] It may not always be as blunt about its capabilities as the Bush administration has been but that should not hide the structural fact of unipolarity.

US preponderance strengthens unipolarity in international relations and supports the conclusion that, irrespective of who sits in the White House, the new structure of international relations should not be expected to erode.

Constraints upon the exercise of US power are unlikely to arise from balancing efforts. For the time being, balance of power mechanisms appear moot.

Liberals make the argument that even an enormous power gap between the United States, its allies and the rest of the world does not necessarily have to result in balancing behavior. Much of the discomfort caused by power imbalances can be ameliorated by policies that service the needs of others. American hegemony, it is argued, can benefit others even under conditions of unipolarity. The *right* kind of hegemonic leadership obviates the need for balancing. Thomas Risse, for example, suggests that power asymmetry can be offset through institutional binding.[14] Transatlantic relations, Risse argues, constitute a security community where liberal, democratic and capitalist values and norms create expectations of appropriate behavior. These expectations are embedded in institutions and 'bind', that is regulate, state behavior according to what the community as a whole deems acceptable. 'Binding,' Risse believes, 'constitutes an institutionalist response to perceived unilateralism'.[15] The argument is based on the assumption that the established code of conduct amongst community members is by and large adhered to, especially by the community's most powerful member. The community serves as a check on the behavior of states where disapproval is voiced and states held accountable. In turn, the offending state must explain itself and be willing to uphold the rules and norms of the community.

Risse's argument is interesting and explains much about the transatlantic relationship before the Bush administration. Disagreements, even divisive ones, were resolved through the overriding goals that bound all members of the community. Balancing against superior American power was neither necessary nor useful. America provided security benefits and built international institutions. Even after the end of the Cold War, when unipolarity might have threatened the cohesion of the security community, the United States could be seen to remain engaged in Europe, managing the enlargement of NATO and conflict in the Balkans. But under the Bush administration, Risse's argument is no longer compelling.

The Bush version of primacy and the concept of a security community are no longer compatible. Europe and America continue to share the same values but these values no longer lead to an institutional binding of the hegemon. Nor do they create a forum of peers to which the hegemon feels accountable. Rather, the security community has become a 'tool box' to which the administration turns for selective support. 'Coalitions of the willing' have replaced the defining characteristics of the transatlantic relationship. Now the security community is defined by its functional utility to unilaterally determined American foreign policy goals. Most consequential for Europeans is the loss of institutional leverage. Bereft of mechanisms to hold the US accountable to common rules and norms, the power asymmetry across the Atlantic highlights power differences that previously remained subsumed within the security community.

Neither the realist argument that the balance of power is the source of international order and even under conditions of established unipolarity will eventually reassert itself, nor the liberal argument that institutional binding of the hegemon obviates the need for balancing, appear to capture fully the transformation of international relations and the transatlantic relationship. Realists may well be right but their long-term vision of a return of the balance of power is not helpful. The long-term is a long way off and a poor guide for strategy in the interim. The liberal case also cannot be credibly made at this time. Benign hegemony may reduce the need for balancing. Indeed, much is known about the benefits of benign hegemony over the half-century history of transatlantic relations. However, the foundations for the liberal case have eroded and its analysis of the functioning of the transatlantic security community no longer applies. Instead, the structure of international relations has been fundamentally reshaped. More than ever before, the United States is in a position to choose how it wants to relate to the world and how it exercises the responsibility that comes with great power. Unconstrained by calls for isolationism at home and unbalanced by foreign powers, America's historical test, Joseph Nye argues, 'will be to develop a consensus on principles and norms that will allow us to work with others to create political stability, economic growth, and democratic values'.[16] The transatlantic arena will provide a crucial measure for how well the United States will pass this test.

Can Europe respond?

Europeans are at the receiving end of America's choices. The Cold War is over, Europe is at peace, and world politics are no longer forged within the Atlantic Community. Europe now faces the task of coming to terms with these realities. It must adjust to a much-reduced role in US policy and, by implication, a greatly reduced voice in what the ordering principles of international relations are.

On the other hand, the new realities open up opportunities for Europe to tackle the many questions about its own future that have been steadily accumulating but have not been resolved. There is an urgent need to focus on the future of integration in all of its dimensions and on the role of the United States on the European continent. Just as the transatlantic relationship prospered under American leadership during the Cold War, integration was also conceived in a transatlantic context. As 'a subset of the Atlantic community',[17] integration was an integral part of a shared vision: European rivalries would be subsumed under a security leadership provided by the US; Europe could build new relationships on the continent without the competitive balancing of the past.[18] In light of the differences that have arisen between Europe and the US, it is vital for Europeans to consider what integration steps to take next. A key factor guiding these deliberations is the political role Europe wants the US to play in continental politics. Quite clearly, the Common Foreign and Security Policy (CFSP) and the European Security and Defense Policy (ESDP) performed miserably over the use of force issue in the spring of 2003. At the heart of Europe's weakness in the foreign policy and security sectors is disunity over how closely the US should be used as a yardstick for Europe's autonomy.

Most former Eastern European states that joined the EU in May 2004, as well as the UK, Spain, Italy and the Scandinavians, prefer a strong US role as the basis from which to define their own support for EU security goals. For these states, European integration must remain a function of transatlantic relations and therefore steps in the security field must not threaten NATO's primacy. Others, most notably Germany and Belgium, led by France, have shown greater commitment to building a EU security identity. The key difference between these two broadly defined camps is not that one wants to keep the US security commitment and the other wants to eliminate it. Rather, the division centers on the issue of whether a Europe *run* by Europeans should actually be built. The future of Europe and the future of the transatlantic relationship are therefore intricately linked and one must be decided in terms of how well it serves the viability of the other.

Besides the issue of America's role in Europe, there is an integration dynamics at work that creates its own imperatives. In recent years, strengthening ESDP has been fueled by the need to complete integration. The EU's poor performance in the Balkan wars in the early 1990s and the minor role of the European NATO members in the 1999 Kosovo war, all drove home the lesson that Europe needed to build military capabilities to buttress its diplomacy. The realization spread that, as integration progressed, the EU needed to focus on defense as a key component of integration.

After Iraq, the defense question took on a new urgency. How much of a defense capability does Europe *need* in order to complete integration and how much should it *aim* for in order to satisfy different perspectives on the role of the US in Europe? Quite clearly, the demands of integration and transatlantic relations face a compatibility problem. Continued European dependence on the US puts a break on integration; increasing European autonomy will reduce America's role on the continent. Despite numerous efforts over the past several years to harmonize the requirements of integration and the transatlantic relationship, little progress has been made. The Franco-British initiatives at St. Malo in 1998, followed by various initiatives at EU summit meetings in Cologne in June 1999 and Helsinki in December 1999, aimed to strengthen Europe's military capabilities within NATO and, separately, within the EU.[19] Lack of progress in this area is largely due to skirting the only issue that really matters, which is to decide whether Europe *as a whole* is willing to do what is necessary to adapt integration and, by implication, their Atlantic relationship to the realities of US primacy. No institutional fine-tuning and no elaborate calibrating of when the EU will act on its own and when it will not will obviate the need for this decision.

Europeans therefore need to resolve the integration conundrum. 9/11 and its aftermath staked out markers for the limits of Europe's traditional approach to integration. Most strikingly, Europe's divisions highlighted how quickly commonalities disappeared giving way to a revived prominence of the state and the national interest. Europe's failure in December 2003 to adopt a constitution provides further evidence of persistent differences over national and common priorities. These failures call into question the suitability of traditional integration approaches to the areas of security and defense. Previous integration accomplishments, though often hard to attain, were within the realm of 'low politics'. By contrast, CFSP and ESDP are 'high politics'; there is very little 'common' and 'European' about them. The fact that both of these concepts exist in some fashion is neither evidence of long-term viability nor does it demonstrate credible performance in the short term. Indeed, it can be argued that the failure to act in unison over the Iraq issue reflects the futility of attempts to treat security and defense as though they were 'low politics'.[20] A number of states unambiguously asserted their preference for keeping these issue areas under national authority. Further attempts to treat them as anything other than 'high politics' are thus intrinsically flawed. Therefore, the assumption that after economic and monetary integration, security and defense are the *natural* next candidates for integration is plainly wrong. More institutionalization will not bring deeper integration but deeper divisions. To be blunt, the CFSP and ESDP cannot be meaningfully created because they require, to an unprecedented degree, transfer of sovereignty. Within the existing conceptual framework of European integration, none of the major states is yet ready to contemplate such a move seriously. Following this logic, when the war with Iraq loomed large in March 2003, European security institutions failed to perform not because they were novel and insufficiently developed but because they *were* developed to their fullest possible extent.

In his now famous speech at Humboldt University in 2000,[21] German Foreign Minister Fischer claimed that the era of plausible integration steps was over and argued that for the European Union to move forward, bolder, more conclusive steps towards true political union needed to be taken. Fischer's remarks are of enormous political significance. They strip European debates of their institutional covers and expose the issue at the heart of integration: who runs Europe? Is it to be run by institutions or states? If run by institutions, what is the relative balance between them? And where, in this concept of governance, do states fit? If Europe is going to be run by states, which states? What are the sources of agreement between them? What goals do they share? Europe's leaders have been wrestling with these questions since the 1992 Maastricht Treaty. At meetings in Amsterdam in 1997, Nice in 2000 and, most recently, in Brussels in 2003, answers eluded them. In 2000, Fischer did not invent these questions; he did, however, assert their importance in an unprecedented way. No amount of *institutional* innovation can hide the fact that fundamental *political* issues need to be resolved if integration is to have a future.

The crisis in transatlantic relations thus also points to inherent vulnerabilities arising from incomplete integration. While American foreign policy was multilaterally oriented, the slow pace of integration could be accommodated. Under the umbrella of America's benign hegemony, Europe focused on process, not endgame. Now that Washington has opted for unilateral, assertive internationalism, its foreign policy splits Europe into those states that want to be led by the US and those that do not. European loyalties are still fluid, oscillating between desires to integrate and the need to maintain American leadership. Rather than complementing European integration, US foreign policy has taken on a disruptive role. Were the US to return to a multilateral approach, it would buy Europe some time, but ultimately such a situation would only postpone the issue of how integration is to proceed and towards what goal. Inevitably, the next transatlantic crisis would expose similar integration weaknesses and national divisions with renewed ferocity.

Clarifying EU and NATO roles: a plan for the future

Europe's future partnership with the US must reflect the new prominence of the United States in international relations while not weakening the completion of Europe's integration. The many international problems, ranging from proliferation, to terrorism, to failing states and economic development, demand coherent and effective transatlantic cooperation. As Simon Serfaty argues, 'the United States and the EU cannot be expected to do everything together, but together it must be expected that they can and will do everything'.[22] The question then is, how is it to be done?[23]

First and foremost, Europe needs to re-visit the issue of hierarchy in the form of a core group of states clearly identified with leadership of the Union as a whole. When first proposed in 1994 by German conservatives Wolfgang Schaeuble and Karl Lamers, it was quickly dismissed both in terms of German arrogance and the political necessity to hide the leadership taboo under the cloak of commonality.[24] When France and Germany tried to fashion a European response to the use of force in 2003, many saw it as asserting a Franco-German condominium. Christoph Bertram and François Heisbourg, however, urge that a Franco-German core take the lead as 'the only idea that can get Europe out of its trans-Atlantic predicament'.[25] The call for a core Europe is echoed by Werner Weidenfeld, who warns that 'if the opportunities of differentiated integration are not used as the architectural principles of an enlarged Europe, pressing problems cannot be efficiently resolved'.[26]

Because the idea of a core Europe is no more popular now than it was ten years ago, much depends on how such a core is formed. Europe's ultimate goal must be to cooperate with the United States. In order to alleviate American fears of a European counterweight that confronts rather than supports the US, the core must include the UK. With the UK on board, American concerns of French plans for multipolarity can be largely offset.[27] Britain could be relied upon to avoid the development of a EU defense capability that questions NATO's security primacy. Though French ambitions would be stifled, the UK presence would reassure the EU's Eastern members that the United States maintains a presence in European politics. For Sweden and Finland, who rely on the US for balance against Russia in the Baltic region and the EU's new 'near abroad', UK membership in the core would mean that the EU 's security capabilities would not threaten NATO's collective defense role.

What would 'doing more' in the security field mean for members of the core? Essentially, the goal of deeper cooperation will be to confine EU capabilities to conflict prevention and robust crisis management. A clear limitation to specific tasks will defuse much of the debate about *autonomous* EU capabilities and not challenge NATO's collective defense mission. Crisis management is likely to attain the highest consensus for establishing a core and for maintaining and enlarging it. It clearly defines EU goals, and enables the EU to cooperate with NATO, but without rivaling it. Indeed, close EU–NATO cooperation should be welcomed. The more closely the two institutions work together, the less the EU needs to strive for autonomy. Together, both institutions can cover the entire range of security contingencies. At the same time, effective crisis management will give the EU the foreign policy profile it needs internally to complete integration and the credibility it craves externally as a serious international actor. Moreover, crisis management elegantly bridges the divisions between 'low' and 'high' politics since it encompasses diplomatic, civilian, and military tasks.

If understood as the central organizing principle of what the EU should do in the field of security, crisis management has much to commend itself. It is the only available basis for consensus among members and the only task around which a core group can reasonably coalesce. Europe's problem has not been a lack of autonomy but a lack of shared purpose. Seeking autonomy under unipolar conditions puts the cart before the horse: the question is how to stay relevant, not how to distance themselves from the United States.

In NATO, Europeans can advance their proper role in the transatlantic relationship. Ivo Daalder and James Lindsay argue that despite the American goal to spread democracy, there is the temptation to get out of a difficult situation before the job is done. This very tension between US over- and under-involvement opens opportunities for NATO allies. However much Europeans oppose America's unilateralism, if America were to fail in Iraq, the situation there and in the region would be much worse. Europe's task in NATO is to assure that a viable, democratic Iraq emerges. A NATO presence in Iraq gives the allies a say in the actual shape of a future Iraq and the wider region. Europeans would have the opportunity to bring their nation-building preferences to bear, a task for which the US, as the invading power, is less well suited.

Besides taking key steps to distinguish between responsibilities in the EU and NATO, Europeans also need to determine what NATO is for in a unipolar environment. NATO was established to strengthen Europe during the bipolar Cold War era. American forces were stationed on the continent and more were to reinforce it as necessary. Under unipolarity, NATO only makes sense if Europeans are willing to follow the US. This role reversal is anything but trivial. As Howorth and Keeler show, 'a quest for greater European autonomy' from the United States has not yet produced an outcome that satisfies either the EU or NATO.[28] European autonomy has focused on how Europe can be militarily engaged *without* the US. Now Europe needs to decide how it can operate *with* the US. The lesson of Iraq for NATO is that loyalty to the United States is not evenly distributed among NATO's European members. From a US perspective, we have already seen that unipolarity lessens the need for allies. Divided allies reinforce NATO's unattractiveness to the US and increase Washington's tendency to go it alone. In the final analysis, Europe has to decide if it wants NATO to continue if securing its future requires support of American policies that Europe does not uniformly embrace. This is by far the most important decision Europe has had to face in the history of the Atlantic relationship. It will determine the extent to which it will be possible to limit the development of the EU's military capabilities and avoid rivalry between the two organizations. Absent a decision on NATO, the Union will be pushed towards military ambitions it can neither finance nor sustain consensus on.

Since NATO is the only institutional security connection between America and Europe, it remains the only avenue for European influence. Though inherently less relevant to the US under unipolarity, NATO's relevance to Europe is now greater than ever before. Divisions amongst European allies rob NATO of Europe's leverage. America is now less willing to consult but, without a European consensus in NATO, Europe effectively eliminates any opportunity for coherent dialogue across the Atlantic.

Unipolarity, Europe's integration needs and the future viability of NATO require an unprecedented re-visioning of transatlantic relations. A modest EU military capability with a focus on crisis management, an alliance that can carry a European consensus on American leadership in international relations, and a core group of European states taking the lead in bringing others on board, these must be the issues high on Europe's agenda.

Conclusion

At present, the very idea of unipolarity and the concomitant requirements of adjustment to American power are still abhorrent to liberal internationalists. They see it as America's responsibility as a unipolar power to subject its capabilities to the constraints of international institutions and the approval of allies. The underlying assumption is that power serves international peace and security best if constrained. On both sides of the Atlantic, many expect the solution to unipolarity to emerge entirely from America's voluntary rejection of the unique opportunities of unrivaled supremacy. America should be modest, not despite its great power but because of it.

Samuel Grafton wrote in the New York Post that 'Even after you give the squirrel a certificate which says he is quite as big as any elephant, he is still going to be smaller, and all the squirrels will know it and all the elephants will know it'.[29] In 1944, William T. R. Fox used Grafton's analogy to argue that power differentials matter. The task after the end of World War II, Fox argued, was to 'discover the conditions of security'[30] in a world where some states have greater power than others.

Fox's reminder has lost none of its poignancy. Unipolarity and American primacy introduce an unprecedented power differential into international relations creating a new hierarchy among states. Would-be balancers are a distant prospect and allies lose their appeal. The events of 11 September 2001 and the war against Iraq in the spring of 2003 have thrown this new hierarchy into stark relief.

For Europeans in the EU and in NATO, US primacy brings vast changes to their relationship with America *and* with one another. For America, too, the new international hierarchy has great implications. If future presidents are seriously committed to establishing 'a balance of power that favors freedom' they must understand that democracy cannot be imposed. The Iraq experience tells that the path from liberation to democracy is a rocky one. Here allies can undoubtedly help. Whether their help will be offered, and accepted when offered, critically depends on how well Europe and the United States manage to define what the European Union and NATO can contribute to international peace and stability.

Notes

1. The *National Security Strategy of the United States of America* (Washington, DC: The White House, 17 September 2002); also see *National Strategy to Combat Weapons of Mass Destruction* (Washington, DC: The White House, December 2002).
2. J. Chace, 'The Complex Metamorphosis of American Foreign Policy', *The New York Times* (16 December 2003).
3. M. Trachtenberg, 'A "Wasting Asset"', *International Security* 13 (Winter 1988/89) 5–49.
4. *A National Security Strategy of Engagement and Enlargement* (Washington, DC: Government Printing Office, February 1996).
5. I. H. Daalder and J. M. Lindsay, *America Unbound: The Bush Revolution in Foreign Policy* (Washington, DC: Brookings Institution Press, 2003).
6. Condoleezza Rice, The 2002 Wriston Lecture, Manhattan Institute for Policy Research, 1 October 2002, http://www.manhattan-institute.org/html/wl2002.htm
7. *ibid.* For a critical analysis of this point see M. P. Leffler, '9/11 and the past and future of American Foreign Policy,' *International Affairs* 79, 5 (2003) 1045–63.
8. Condoleezza Rice, Remarks at the International Institute for Strategic Studies, London, 26 June 2003, The White House, Office of the Press Secretary, Washington, DC.

9. C. Krauthammer, 'The Unipolar Moment Revisited,' *The National Interest* 70 (Winter 2002/03) 5–17.

10. G. J. Ikenberry, ed. *America Unrivaled – The Future of the Balance of Power* (Ithaca and London: Cornell University Press, 2002), p.3.

11. S. G. Brooks and W. C. Wohlforth, 'American Primacy in Perspective,' *Foreign Affairs* 81, 4 (July/August 2002) 21.

12. *ibid.* 25.

13. R. Jervis, 'Understanding the Bush Doctrine,' *Political Science Quarterly* 118, 3 (Fall 2003) 383.

14. T. Risse, 'US Power in a Liberal Security Community,' in Ikenberry, pp.260–83.

15. *ibid.* 275.

16. J. S. Nye, *The Paradox of American Power, Why the World's Only Superpower Can't go it Alone* (New York: Oxford University Press, 2002), p.xvi.

17. S. Hoffmann, 'US–European relations: past and future,' *International Affairs* 79, 5 (2003) 1030.

18. N. Gnesotto, 'EU, US: visions of the world, visions of the other,' in G. Lindstrom, ed., *Shift or Rift – Assessing US–EU relations after Iraq* (Paris: WEU-ISS, 2003), p.41.

19. For historical background on EU–NATO defense relations, see J. Howorth, *European Integration and Defence: The Ultimate Challenge?* (Paris: WEU-ISS, 2000), Chaillot Paper 43; J. Howorth and J. T. S. Keeler, eds, *Defending Europe: The EU, NATO and the Quest for European Autonomy* (New York: Palgrave, 2003), pp.3–21.

20. H. Ojanen, *Theories at a loss? EU–NATO fusion and the 'low-politicisation' of security and defense in European integration* (Helsinki: Finnish Institutue of International Affairs, 2003) http.upi-fiia.fi/julkaisut/UPI_WP/wp/wp35.pdf

21. J. Fischer, Vom Staatenbund zur Foerderation – Gedanken ueber die Finalitaet der europaeischen Integration, Speech at Humboldt University, Berlin, 12 May 2000.

22. S. Serfaty, 'EU–US Relations beyond Iraq: Setting the Terms of Complementarity,' *EURO-FOCUS* 9, 3 11 April 2003 Europe Program, Center for Strategic and International Studies, Washington, DC.

23. A first attempt at answering this question is the European Union's European Security Strategy – A Secure Europe in a Better World, Brussels, 12 December 2003. Also see J. Dempsey, 'Words of War: Europe's first security doctrine backs away from a commitment to US-style pre-emption,' *Financial Times*, 5 December 2003.

24. H. Hubel and B. May, *Ein 'normales' Deutschland? Die Souveraene Bundesrepublik in der auslaendischen Wahrnehmung* (Bonn: Forschungsinstitut der Deutschen Gesellschaft fuer Auswaertige Politik e.V., 1995), pp.107–11.

25. C. Bertram and F. Heisbourg, 'Europe's role: A new trans-Atlantic relationship', *IHT*, 18 March 2003, http://www.iht.com/articles/90058.html

26. W. Weidenfeld, *Europa's Alternativen, Aufgaben und Perspektiven der grossen Europaeischen Union*, Vorlage zum Internationalen Bertelsmann Forum (Berlin: January 2004), p. 8.

27. D. de Villepin, Address at International Institute for Strategic Studies, London, March 27, 2003, http://www.iiss.org/showdocument.php?docID = 114

28. Howorth and Keeler, pp.5–6.

29. Quoted in W. T. R. Fox, *The Super-Powers, The United States, Britain and the Soviet Union – Their Responsibility for Peace* (New York: Harcourt, Brace and Company, 1944), p.3.

30. *ibid.* 4.

7
Three Fictions of Transatlantic Relations

Daniel N. Nelson

Three fictions persist both in official documents and in pronouncements about transatlantic relations. The first of these, believed on both sides of the Atlantic, is in the existence of a post-Cold War American primacy and unparalleled global dominance. A second, dating from 1949, is that the North Atlantic Treaty Organization (NATO) operates by consensus and exhibits unity of purpose and efficacy in action. A third and more recent fiction, derived from the halcyon days of 1989–91, is an image of one Europe, 'whole and free'. From the Western shores of the Atlantic, much of this is comforting, and all of it is wrong.

Fictions are created quickly for a purpose; myths incrementally develop purpose and evolve culturally over time. Americans have many myths – for example, about the Founding Fathers, about the conquest of the West, and about American capitalism. But, contemporaneously, politicians andpublics, elites and masses, create fictions that serve multiple roles, and discursively construct much of the security world we identify around us. For today's American conservatives, a powerful nation is ideologically seminal, and identity creating. For the European left, a powerful America is likewise defining, and equally necessary as a foil for political positioning. And, the 'oneness' of NATO and Europe, for each different constituency, means what communities and groups see as themselves vis-à-vis others.

But this essay is far less about the genesis of these fictions – stipulated more than proven here – than their unraveling in the post-Cold War, post-September 11 milieu. If events and evidence conspire to render such fictions falsifiable to populations as well as policymakers, to voters as well as politicians, what will remain of transatlantic relations? Are the transmutations of transatlantic ties that were evident even before 9/11 now irrevocable?[1]

The first fiction: American primacy

Power is the common currency of traditional international relations. But ubiquity does not mean definitional certainty. Who is most powerful, why, and what such a capacity means for those who possess it or are subjected to it, are matters of endless debate. Yet, the 'overwhelming nature of US military power' was, to many observers, settled by the 2003 war against Iraq.[2] Indeed, in post-9/11 wars, the US secured rapid battlefield dominance in both Afghanistan and Iraq, even more convincingly than in the Gulf War of 1991. In aggregate terms, the manpower, personnel and expenditure levels of the US military vis-à-vis allies or adversaries seem unequivocal; American primacy is taken as 'fact.'[3] But does military power ensure victory? Or, could America be defeated? And, if so, is such power incomplete, ephemeral or both?

I suggest that defeat is not the number of dead and wounded, unless political will evaporates. Failure to consummate battlefield success with the capture or death of enemy leaders has little to do with long-term prognoses if resistance is based on broad and deep antagonisms. Neither is defeat implicit when destruction of enemy forces or infrastructure is incomplete; other purposes may dictate avoiding annihilation even if that aim were in reach. Defeat is not an event pinpointed in time, and cannot be reduced to a singular military disaster. Defeats don't happen; they develop. A Diěn Biěn Phu or Mogadishu, for instance, are painful moments in an otherwise continuous process of defeat that builds momentum towards calamitous occurrences. What, then, is defeat? At its most prosaic, defeat is being compelled to alter behavior to one's own detriment.[4] Rather than imposed by others' strength, defeat can occur without war or an opponent. Defeat ultimately is self-failure – the symptoms of which are an irreparable imbalance between perceived or real threats and socioeconomic, political and military capacities. In that regard, defeat is the utter breakdown of security.

Four traits fatally obstruct a balance between threats and capacities and make defeat possible and even likely. Ignorance is a precursor of gross policy errors that enlarge threats and squander capacities. Lack of knowledge of other cultures, their histories, or their socioeconomic environments is a guarantee of commitments that extend well beyond realistic expectations. From here to the horizon is scattered human debris from interventions in places Americans knew not at all. Vietnam's long battle against the French was unknown in the US in the early 1960s. Somalia was but an image of state collapse, absent detailed on-the-ground knowledge of warlords or their alliances. Iraq's Ba'athist regime was labeled part of an 'Axis of Evil' with an ideological brush, not through reliance upon reliable and corroborated intelligence and the label was attached even as policymakers ignored the antipathy between a secular Ba'athist elite and radical Islam.[5] Attempts to alter local and regional political directions and traditions cannot and should not be the bailiwick of those without detailed preparations.

Moreover, defeat comes through arrogance. Since the dawn of nation-states, said Michael Billig, '... powerful states, who (sic) have proved their power in war, have sought to impose their own vision of a settled order...'[6] Capacity-driven behaviors are preceded by an assumption that power is deserved, and that deserved power endows one with a mission to use such capacities for a greater goal. American exceptionalism is not only a conservative mantra but also a vaguely but widely accepted public belief.[7] At a popular level, in contrast with European publics, the US population evinces far more national pride, much greater religiosity, and a stronger expectation that the state will place individual rights above the public good.[8] These are the ingredients of a missionary vocation, one irrevocably intertwined with hubris – the conceit of power. After 9/11, President George W. Bush and most Americans exhibited a collective response that 'involved a heightened sense of "us" [versus] "them".[9] 'If you're not with us [in the war against terrorism], you're against us' said President Bush. And against 'us' meant consorting with an evil against which an exceptional America is alleged to be the last bastion.

Yet, such arrogance conceals fundamental weakness. Every utterance of arrogant power generates fear, alienation and, ultimately, the development of countervailing and often asymmetric force. To Chalmers Johnson, the spectre of 'blowback' was evoked – backlash from resentful junior partners whose revenge would lie in either turning aside US requests for assistance at a time of need, or else conspiracies to weaken the hegemon.[10] With each deception or evidently cosmetic spin, the power of trust and the legitimacy of the use of just force wither. America the indispensable power, the salvation of democracies and the righteously vengeful nation after 9/11 has, in Afghanistan and Iraq, found that creating postwar peace and reconstruction depends on far more than a US army of occupation. Far beyond occupation and nation-building in the Middle East and South Asia, the United States alone cannot ensure outcomes it wants on a wide range of economic or transnational issues, where there is neither American hegemony nor empire.[11]

Distrust of friends, and dread of presumed enemy plots, join to produce the self-flagellation of paranoia. Everything is apprehension, and fright lies only slightly beneath the surface. 'Report suspicious behavior' flashes the sign above Washington's Beltway road system – and George Orwell nods. Where one can trust no one, isolated strongholds are one plausible approach to world affairs. The alternative path, and the one adopted by the Bush Administration, is a foreign policy of global unilateralism – pre-emption using raw force whenever narrow national interests seem threatened, surrounding oneself with coalitions of the willing in lieu of genuine alliances. A pre-emptive strategy is one adopted by nations, groups or individuals for whom others harbor evil intentions, and whose presumed intentions warrant immediate countermeasures. It is but a short distance between such trepidation and an irrational paranoia.

Greed is also a quick route to self-defeat. Believing in nothing but today's material interests is another way of believing in nothing. War to end a regime of one leader or party, to capture resources, or to shift a strategic balance, while ignoring justice and other paramount values is a harbinger of defeat. Lie about motives, deceitfully spin information, conceal data or events – do all of these while wars and their aftermath generate huge unaccountable profits for the corporate allies of decision-makers and one is sure to lose the normative war and therefore become the victim of peace. Enronize foreign policy and defeat will be self-imposed. How much money a global war against terrorism means for certain corporations and contractors may never be known, although some have attempted estimates.[12] At the very least, whether it is Halliburton and Bechtel inside Iraq, or Lockheed Martin, Boeing and Northrop Grumman among defense contractors, the profit to corporate officers and stockholders has been enormous. If one follows the money in a case such as Halliburton's profiteering from a no-bid contract to supply gasoline inside Iraq – charging far above market prices for the gas and its transport – you will be led to a Kuwaiti supplier linked to the al-Sabah royal family. The al-Sabahs have long had Marvin Bush, the President's brother, as a business partner.[13] Is this malfeasance or coincidence? At the very least, the appearance of impropriety makes it easier to portray US motives for war in light of the avarice of some. Absent revelations that lead to public outrage and legal action, such private greed will continue to affect public policy, and will assuredly enlarge the probability of ultimate defeat.

To the degree that ignorance, arrogance, paranoia and greed are all present, those who make decisions about war and peace will pursue a capacity-driven strategy, conflate discourses of war and peace, and incessantly strive for security through strength. Such decision-makers will, thereby, create enemies from friends, replacing mutual trust with endemic suspicion and fear. Victory and defeat are thus misunderstood as, respectively, the consequence of more or less power. Yet, in a contest of wills, deriving a resolution that leads to behavioral change in others without violence is victory. Self-sacrifice and personal denial are required for such victory – a triumph over ignorance, subjugation of arrogance, rejection of paranoia, and conquest of greed. But where self-sacrifice and personal denial are not in evidence, global ignorance blindly guides a swaggering arrogance, as fear of others accelerates a normative collapse. With each pre-emptive step towards global unilateralism, enemies multiply, friendships wane, and the imbalance between threats and capacities approaches the critical.

The second fiction: NATO consensus

A decade and a half after the Warsaw Pact dissolved, NATO's physical presence in a Brussels suburb remains tangible; however, post-Cold War and post-9/11, NATO's presence is less visible in its military or political capacities than in its bureaucratic habits, diplomatic conveniences and military camaraderie. The 1991 Gulf War, the 1999 NATO attacks on Serbia and its armed forces, and wars in Afghanistan and Iraq in 2001 and 2003 have made disparities in military capabilities within NATO abundantly clear. While European allied armed forces have more personnel than the US, their principal categories of advanced weaponry and equipment are far less numerous, and only one half as much is spent to support them.[14] Empirically, the United States needs NATO less as a single, unified alliance than as a reservoir of potential components for coalitions of the willing. With real or perceived threats being global rather than situated on the European landmass, Western Europe's territory, resources, and armed forces are regarded as far less critical than was previously the case.

Approximately 25 per cent of all active duty US military personnel are, as of mid 2004, deployed in an arc from the Mediterranean to East and Southeast Asia.[15] As US military personnel are rotated out of Iraq, their units (over 130,000 individuals) will be unavailable for additional duty for an unspecified period. In the continental US, Western Europe and elsewhere, are stationed the command, control, intelligence, logistical and other units that support front-line forces in the Middle East and South Asia. However one assembles the numbers, it would not be an exaggeration to say that half of all American forces are committed to prosecuting the current conflict, including eight of ten active duty Army divisions that are either in Iraq and Afghanistan, preparing for deployment, or returning from combat. Western Europe plays a tertiary role in the staging or implementation of these wars.

The global redeployment of US ground and air forces has been announced by the Bush administration, and is planned as a multi-year process. Within NATO countries, the US will close numerous bases in Western Europe, return thousands of personnel to the United States, and move many of the residual forces abroad to locations in what were once Warsaw Pact countries. Official discussions about such force transfers are couched in language about 'reconfiguring' the US military presence in Europe, and care is taken not to advocate precipitous withdrawal. Still, some inside the American military recommend a permanent reduction in US land forces in Western Europe to no more than four brigades and related commands.[16] Parallel Air Force 'reconfigurations' have also been advocated. In Hungary, the Taszar air base was already being modernized and utilized beginning in the mid-1990s at the time of the NATO (but US-led) intervention in Bosnia-Herzegovina. Thinking about establishing training locations and bases in Romania, Bulgaria and Poland has moved from the exploration to the planning stage. For example, a US European Command (USEUCOM) delegation visited Romania in early February 2004 to inspect bases, including in Dobrogea near the mouth of the Danube. This delegation, accompanied by high level officials from the Romanian Ministry of Defense, examined air and naval facilities for the likely relocation of assets from Western Europe, according to individual in the Romanian Defense Ministry who spoke with this author in February 2004.[17]

Other long-term deployments have led to heavy infrastructural investment in the Central Asian states of Kyrgyzstan, Uzbekistan and Kazakhstan, as well as in zones of active combat themselves (Afghanistan, Iraq, the Gulf States, and elsewhere). The shift away from Western Europe is tangible at an

American airbase in Kyrgysztan that has grown to a permanent facility with several thousand military and civilian personnel since the end of 2001. Even more dramatic is the Khanabad base in Uzbekistan, which is much larger and rivals in size and sophistication bases in Western Europe.[18] While not entirely secret, and already the subject of press accounts and Congressional discussions, the scale of movement already underway is not fully recognized by European or the American publics. Some estimates of American aid to the Uzbek dictatorship of Islom Karimov are in range of half a billion dollars in 2002–03 alone. Absent a reversal of policy within this decade, Western Europe will see American military forces only at several naval bases and a few air bases – with other activities confined to those of logistics, medical and related support functions. America's capacities for military intervention and global reach will be housed increasingly outside the confines of Cold War-era NATO.

Global strategic rethinking within the American security establishment accompanied the relocation of assets – although it is unclear whether thinking guided or followed tactical changes of political and military requirements before and after 9/11. Fundamental changes in the location, strength, and purpose of US forces abroad, in Asia as well as Europe, are now regarded as matters for urgent analysis, and involve organizations and agencies outside the Pentagon (such as the Congressional Budget Office[19]). How NATO's bifurcation and reduced relevance contributed to this larger strategic discussion is impossible to untangle. That both NATO's diminution and strategic reconsiderations are coincident, however, is obvious. National Defense University analysts wrote, in November 2003, of an urgent need for a 'dual track transformation' of NATO – a new Harmel Report of military and political metamorphosis – to be launched at the summer 2004 Istanbul summit.[20] Meant by its authors to provide a new Atlantic Alliance raison d'être in 'Partnerships for Cooperation' with countries of the Middle East at a time of immense strain and dissension, their discussion is notable less for the vision it provides than the point of departure, i.e., that the Alliance is broken and needs to be fixed. But, these and other analysts sorely underestimate how 'broke' NATO actually is, and what it will take to fix it. For a dozen years, a fiction was propagated that NATO survived the Cold War. In the midst of the slide towards another war against Iraq in 2002–03, this façade unraveled. Talk of collaborative security, with NATO as the fulcrum, was supplanted by recognition that theories about the nature of alliances remain intact – absent common threat, disintegration is only a matter of time. That time is upon us.

Metaphorically, NATO now lies in the emergency room, its body still convulsing even after the cortex has been severed. The link of America to Europe, insofar as it was grounded in a venerable Cold War alliance, is on life support.[21] As if to exemplify the Alliance's desperate condition, the annual Wehrkunde conference in Munich during February 2004 again evinced Euro-American distance and acrimony, poorly concealed by superficial civility. German Foreign Minister Joschka Fischer warned, at Wehrkunde, of 'fatal consequences for NATO' if the US pushed for Alliance control of a Polish-led division in south-central Iraq. For his part, American Secretary of Defense Donald Rumsfeld offered a 'feisty and unyielding' performance that 'stunned' Europeans in the audience by its arrogant tone and the implicit view that 'We're right, they're wrong, and we'll continue to be right.'[22] While the public discourse at NATO's Istanbul summit during summer 2004 was more diplomatic, George Bush was forced to back away from any expectation of additional troops from European members in Iraq, and European distance from American strategy and policy grew no smaller.

NATO has been reformulated, redesigned, metamorphosed – with a new doctrine, new commands, new members, and new missions. It has been enlarged, but reduced, and is now little more than a reservoir from which to assemble coalitions – unable but willing, semi-able and semi-willing, or unwilling and unable but there nonetheless.[23] In Joseph Nye's view, this is 'alliance a la carte.'[24] But, like most à la carte menus, the price may be too high. Such sub-sets of NATO, combined with a ragtag collection of other transient partners, are formed during crises less to provide military capacities than logistical staging and the political cover of multilateralism for a largely US planned and implemented operation. This is, by the way, not new; the Organization of American States (OAS) was used countless times to provide quasi-legality, even post hoc, for American interventions in Latin American – in the Dominican Republic in 1965, in Grenada in 1981, in Panama in 1989, and against Nicaragua throughout the Reagan presidency. No one, however, confused the OAS with a vibrant or even semi-equal alliance structure.

The genesis of NATO's unraveling is not merely or primarily US power versus alleged European impotence,[25] but rather fundamentally distinct worldviews between most of America and most of Europe derived from contrasting understandings of who acts, how they act and why they act on the international stage. While generalizations err on the margins, I have argued elsewhere that US and European portraits of the global stage differ regarding actors, modalities and motives in international relations.[26] In the American political context, Democrats of the John Kerry mold and Republicans such as George W. Bush will contest the role of multilateral institutions versus states in global affairs. Even liberal Democrats, however, would not rely as much as relatively conservative Europeans (such as former Spanish Prime Minister Aznar) on multilateral institutions or the strength of discursive identity to produce non-conflictual communities on the international stage. As to modalities, Democrats including Bill Clinton did not eschew the use of force (Somalia, Haiti, Bosnia, Kosovo, air attacks on Iraq and suspected terrorist camps in Afghanistan and the Sudan) and his Secretary of State spoke admiringly of America as the 'indispensable power.' Cooperation via international institutions and diplomatic accords finds greater resonance among Democratic politicians than today's Republicans, but promotion of the value of such means of global action occurs with far less frequency in American political rhetoric than in European. And Europe's evolution in the 1990s and early 2000s to a global presence with its own institutions, discourse and means cannot be reversed.

At the level of decision-makers and publics, NATO is no longer a consensual actor. NATO's utility as an alliance is over. Official Bush Administration rhetoric, of course, denies this dénouement of the Atlantic Alliance. Indeed, it insists that NATO is more significant than ever as a 'training ground for democracy', stabilizing countries such as Bulgaria and Albania, and expanding its roles through peacekeeping and reconstruction efforts in southeastern Europe, Afghanistan and elsewhere.[27] The Bush Administration's notion of a 'Greater Middle East Initiative' raised in early 2004 found antipathy in the region; yet, the Administration and some US Senators were enthusiastic about NATO's expanded role in the Mediterranean and the Middle East.[28] The American choice as the new NATO Secretary General, former Dutch foreign minister Jaap de Hoop Scheffer, has dutifully carried the Bush message of more 'out of area' duties for NATO.[29] Yet, were NATO to 'go global', engagement in additional arenas of tension and conflict seems unlikely to encourage greater consensus within the Alliance.

A tacit post-mortem from within the US Defense Department for NATO's consensual decision-making process was offered in August 2003. Arguing that an alternative to the consensus rule should be found (and that there are Congressional demands to do so), while acknowledging the political complexity of effecting such a change, one US National Defense University essay suggests several alternatives. Yet, the same author notes that the consensus rule de facto has already been discarded. From the Bush Administration's perspective, one of the options to consensus is clearly favored – empowering coalitions within NATO and using NATO as a 'toolbox from which the United States selects a few partners to join U.S.-led coalitions of the willing.'[30]

A decade and a half after the collapse of European communism and the dissolution of its nemesis, the Warsaw Pact, NATO survives on bureaucratic momentum. American forces are moving from Western Europe, and doctrine is adjusting rapidly. Larger and wealthier West European countries in NATO are unwilling to provide (except for the United Kingdom) more than diplomatic support to US interventions abroad, and severely limit the deployment and roles of such of their forces as have been assigned, for example, to Afghanistan. If NATO remains as a Brussels façade in coming years, it will be a Potemkin alliance, best seen by a leader's entourage from their carriages at a distance.

The third fiction: European unity

A Europe whole and free, with NATO as its core security institution, appeared quickly in political rhetoric after the Berlin Wall was breached in 1989. It was never to be, and may now be a distant chimera.

For the Bush Administration, and the American Right, the splintering of Europe is a direct consequence of an 'old Europe' rejecting American leadership and objecting to the war against Iraq. From this perspective, a Europe disunited is one that cannot be galvanized to oppose US interests, and thus may not be unwelcome. Secretary of Defense Donald Rumsfeld made such an 'old/new' Europe distinction in early 2003, expressing approval of Poland and other former communist states for their support of the American-led invasion of Iraq, while attacking German, French, and Belgian opposition to the war at the UN. Myopia in concert with arrogance may lead the Bush Administration to err greatly by inferring that Europe's divisions are but a reflection of positions vis-à-vis the United States and its policies. Instead, anti-Americanism is neither the glue holding the EU together nor 'the factor that divides it.'[31] Even those NATO-aspirant countries that signed on to the manufactured diplomatic support of the 'Vilnius 10' document did so to follow Blair not Bush.[32] Significantly, Europe is against itself, and far from a socioeconomic or political whole.

Europe is divided between east and west today as it has been for centuries. These divisions are, in the contemporary era, most evident statistically in socioeconomic data, but are multifaceted and crosscutting. One analyst, in assessing intra-European cleavages, listed no fewer than 15 planes on which continental divisions can be identified.[33] Many of these divisional planes are the residues of decades of communist rule in the twentieth century; others predate the last century, and are embedded in historical/cultural distinctions. Of the latter, some recur in visceral reactions of today's leaders – as when Silvio Berlusconi differentiated between Western civilization and Islam or Jacques Chirac warned Balkan states as the Iraq invasion approached that their EU future would be imperiled if they aligned themselves with the US.

The ten new Central and East European members of the European Union, however, are profoundly less developed than the 15 members of the pre-enlargement EU. The degree to which the new members trail the 15 ranges from three-fourths of the EU average GDP per capita (Slovenia and Greek Cyprus) to about a third of the EU average (in the case of Latvia and Lithuania). Additional countries such as Bulgaria and Romania, aiming for accession in 2007, are even farther behind.[34] Unemployment and government deficits in acceding countries are likewise higher, on average, than in the EU-15.[35] It is inaccurate to group all new EU acceding countries together, except insofar as they are joining the same *Acquis*, that body of common rights and obligations which bind all the member states together within the Union and they will be subject to the same social and economic norms. Such data begins to suggest that Europe's divisions are not east/west but multifaceted. After the initial failure to agree an EU 'constitution' in December 2003, it became common to contemplate a multi-track, variable-speed Europe.[36] Such a discussion, however, did not grasp that Europe is not two, but at least several,[37] and arguably four. As denoted by norms, wealth and institutional integration, Europe is not high and low, old and new, fast and slow, but rather an inner and outer core and an inner and outer periphery defined empirically by multiple indicators.

A Europe of an inner core, an outer core, as well as an inner and outer periphery, is neither whole nor entirely free. It is, however, accurate. An EU–NATO–euro zone institutional core provides only one portrait of the four Europes. Another is offered by measures of public tolerance of varied lifestyles and free speech. A third gauge of Europe's divisions might, arguably, be found in attitudes toward and concepts of the state – whether the state should focus on ensuring social welfare or defending against threats. And yet another portrait of Europe's striations is seen on the basis of GDP and purchasing power parity. These (or other) empirical measures do not perfectly agree. Yet, there are reminders that, for example, the Norwegians and Swiss – in terms of wealth, views of the state, and tolerance – are inner-core European even if they lack institutional memberships. By contrast, institutional memberships will not make the Baltic states or Balkan countries inner core Europeans any time soon, if indeed ever.[38] An EU constitution might be cobbled together. It will not, however, absolve Europe of its divisions and might, indeed, exacerbate them.

Seen from a more theoretical perspective, integrative momentum derived from socioeconomic and cultural ties have reached a critical juncture – where the differences within the current and projected EU members are too great to maintain extant decision making rules. To change those rules, however, requires both that overwhelming interests prevail to force compromise and that advocates of competing 'ideas of Europe' find common ground.[39] While such an outcome is not impossible, it is not yet at hand notwithstanding agreements on EU voting.

European unity is vulnerable at the public level far more on economic grounds than on issues related to Iraq and other distant interventions – another point that Americans too often ignore. Whether it is the Euro's rising value, the failure of some members to implement Lisbon goals for internal market consistency, or the sheer cost of enlargement because of agricultural subsidies, economic matters are divisive, and might be the straw that breaks a European camel's back.[40] Still, security demands attention. Europe's capacity to act as one, vis-à-vis many, will depend less on the Euro than on the European Security and Defense Policy (ESDP) of the EU. On this matter, the jury is not merely still out, but has yet to be formed. The debate in Europe has been lively, open and tough. All major European think tanks, ministries, and universities have participated. That's the good news. As always, the bad news is considerable. Thus far, one sees no consensus, no fulcrum of public or elite opinion, and certainly no resolution. Ought Europe be a security provider, and if so how? What should be the model for a common foreign and security policy? Given citizen indifference, and far greater traction for economic and social issues, the security dimension is vital but not publicly or popularly decisive for the future of the European project. Still, Europe cannot move ahead or beyond until commonality in foreign, security and defense matters is found.[41]

Public skepticism and indifference have steadily mounted about a united European future,[42] and such questioning is fueled by fears of unemployment, immigration, and a host of related socioeconomic issues. Yet, European rifts at the level of policy-makers and elites quickly and inevitably concern security. An ESDP has failed to mature (notwithstanding summits and drafts of a European Security Strategy such as the Solana Paper[43]), because of Europe's fundamental divisions, not because of US policy. Iraq brought Europe's divisions out into the open – painfully. As Solana identified new threats, three strategic objectives, and objectives for a European foreign policy, it was apparent that he was carefully avoiding a specific delineation of EU and NATO responsibilities within European security. He also never grappled with the chicken/egg issue – i.e., do all member states decide autonomously what the Common Security and Foreign Policy is to be, or will a collective decision come first? And, if the latter, how? The final published version of the Solona paper clarified threats (as key threats) and adjusted the text to spell out the EU's role in addressing such threats. Yet, the Security Strategy document, as revised, offers little detail about precisely what must be done to make the EU more active and capable.[44]

To the degree that autonomous capacities do develop (and the Headline Goal of 60,000 quickly deployable troops is a long way from being operational because of equipment shortcomings not lack of personnel), the Bush Administration and many on the right to center of the US political spectrum would succumb first to rampant suspicion and then to antipathy. In addition to material shortcomings, there is also the reality that there is a seeming lack of urgency because, apart from Germany, France and Belgium, other EU states are unlikely to share the same need for operational autonomy for EU forces, and evince far less desire to break the constraints of Berlin Plus.

A Europe thus stratified, still in the throes of institutional metamorphosis and identity creation, seems to confront the definition and implementation of European defense and security with hesitancy and imprecision. Movement is evident, and momentum was accelerated because neither America's primacy nor NATO's consensual future are assured. Yet the veneer of unity within even the EU can easily be stripped away, revealing a continent far from developing true commonality about threats or capacities, the core variables in the calculus of security. Notwithstanding '…professions of unity and common expectation,' '…tens of mortally divisive issues [lie] within the EU.'[45] If such mortal wounds are not felt and redressed, the hemorrhaging public and political support will certainly be fatal to the European project.

Conclusion

There are still those who believe that American primacy has ushered in a new epoch – a Pax Americana resting on 'an order that was created and sustained by American power.' Given durability by 'the deep congruence between the internal American political system…and the long-term project of modernity' such an '…unipolar order [has] robustness.'[46] These are the political realists of international relations, often bastardized into neo-conservative ideology by others far less astute.

NATO's first five decades of consensual interaction, albeit beneath American hegemony, is still thought to be alive, or at least salvageable. During preparations for the Istanbul Summit in June 2004, the Alliance's leading bodies – the Defense Planning Committee, and the top political body, the North Atlantic Council – continued to plan, issue decision documents, and establish force and readiness targets as if little had changed. But, of course, the entire transatlantic relationship is in the midst of a transmutation that has no certain conclusion.[47] Europe's future, too, is regularly assessed in terms of its developing unity, its emerging identity, and autonomous strengths. As if the accumulated weight of the *Acquis* provides credence for an assertion of progress towards one Europe, there is rejection of public skepticism, policy impasses, and pervasive stratification that makes Europe not one or two, but many.

We are easily comforted, in Europe and America, by strength, continuity and progress. It is not easy to contemplate weakness, disjunction and retreat. Even when these traits are visible and reported – chaos in Iraq, massive casualties, and evident deceit regarding intelligence findings before the war – denial is powerful. To stare defeat in the face, and to pursue lasting security, requires painful rejection of reassuring fictions that are either long past, or were never there. And how will such a reassessment occur? New political leadership in Europe and North America could accelerate the search for an answer. That the dangers of terrorism, proliferation and other global threats cannot be surmounted by the power of one state or institution ought to drive Europe and America towards a recognition of their mutual dependence.[48] But only trauma – defeat and institutional failure – can induce the level of political change needed to re-build a Euroatlantic Community on a liberal, pluralist, multilateral basis. Such trauma now seems to be a terrible likelihood.

Notes

1. See D. N. Nelson, 'Transatlantic Transmutations,' *The Washington Quarterly* No. 25(4) (Autumn 2002) 51–66.
2. J. S. Nye, Jr, 'U.S. Power and Strategy After Iraq,' *Foreign Affairs* (July/August 2003) 60.
3. The Center for Defense Information's publication, 'The Defense Monitor', provided a useful juxtaposition of data drawn from the International Institute of Strategic Studies, in: *The Military Balance 2003–2004* Vol. XXXII, No. 5 (London: 2003) 13.

4. Nye writes (Nye, op. cit., p. 65) that 'power is the ability to obtain the outcomes one wants.' While this is too simple, since an absence of power does not preordain that negative outcomes are certain to be imposed, an absence of power heightens the probability of imposed outcomes. Where negative outcomes are imposed, defeat exists. My point, however, is that defeat need not be, and frequently is not, externally imposed as much as internally developed.

5. At this writing, both President Bush and Prime Minister Blair have named commissions to examine intelligence failures prior to the Iraq war, while a US task force studying intelligence gaps before 9/11 has been extended. Efforts to redress ignorance about potential threats around the world, however, continue to be palliative and of questionable efficacy. Six former intelligence 'practitioners', for example, argued in *The Economist* ('American Needs More Spies,' 12 July 2003, 30), that such initiatives as the Terrorist Threat Integration Center, while important, fail to address analytical and collection issues. In late 2003, a senior State Department analyst told me, bluntly, that the TTIC was staffed by incompetent, poorly trained individuals, with little background in the countries and movements they were to assess.

6. M. Billig, *Banal Nationalism* (London: Sage, 1995), p.21.

7. For the intellectual side of the argument, see S. M. Lipset, *American Exceptionalism* (New York: Norton, 1996).

8. See data from The Pew Research Center, the Allenbach Opinion Research Institution and the National Opinion Research Center reported by *The Economist* (8 November 2003) 4.

9. M. Billig, 'Language as Forms of Death,' Preface to M. Dedaic and D. N. Nelson, eds *At War With Words* (Berlin: Mouton de Gruyter, 2003), pp.xi–xii.

10. C. Johnson, *Blowback: The Costs and Consequences of American Empire* (New York: Metropolitan Books, 2000). Note that Johnson wrote this book two or more years before 9/11.

11. Nye (op. cit., p.65) speaks of the world stage as a three-dimensional chess game; only on the first 'board' (one of military power) does the US seem dominant. Yet, even on that dimension, America is dominant only when confronting other state actors; otherwise, the US has been, and will continue to be, subjected to asymmetric threats that exact huge cost, and ensure that military triumphs are phyrric. Carrying the flag of political realism, Zbigniew Brzezinski cautiously criticizes Bush foreign policy in *The Choice: Global Domination or Global Leadership* (New York: Basic Books, 2004). Brzezinski, however, concurs with Nye (another international relations professor qua national security personage) insofar as dominance won't suffice as US foreign policy.

12. W. D. Hartnung, *How Much Are You Making on the War, Daddy? A Quick and Dirty Guide to War Profiteering in the Bush Administration* (New York: Nation Books, 2004).

13. Kevin Phillips in his *American Dynasty: Aristocracy, Fortune, and the Politics of Deceit in the House of Bush* (New York: Viking, 2003) notes this tie and paints, in terms of the Bush family history, a pervasive rapacity and mendacity.

14. Raw data is available from the International Institute of Strategic Studies, *The Military Balance 2003–2004* (London: 2003). European assessments of their own need to strengthen security capabilities have been examined often and in detail. See, for example, Heinrich Borchert and Roland Eggenberger, *Rollenspezialisierung und Ressourcenzusammenlegung: Wie Europas sicherheitspolitische Fähigkeiten gestärkt werden können*, in H.G. Ehrhardt and B. Schmitt, eds, *EU-Sicherheitspolitik im 21. Jahrhundert* (Baden-Baden: Nomos, 2004).

15. The Congressional Budget Office reported that, at the end of 2002 (before the Iraq invasion), about 200,000 active-duty US forces were permanently stationed (excluding 'temporary' deployments such as Afghanistan) on shore in foreign countries, representing about 15% of active duty personnel. These data also excluded 'forces afloat' (Navy and Marine personnel). The CBO reported that varying levels of US forces were at sea, and at the end of FY 2002 that number was 22,000. Yet, CBO also reported levels as high as 11% of US Navy personnel and 6% of Marines were afloat overseas. Using those upper limits, and adding the roughly 9,000 US personnel on the ground in Afghanistan, the total (before Iraq) was at least 260,000 or 18% of active-duty forces. From CONUS active and reserve elements from all armed forces, excluding units that had already been based abroad (in Germany), about another 110,000 US personnel were added to this total, yielding at least 370,000 overseas on shore or afloat. While a sizeable number of National Guard and Reserve units are in Iraq, subtracting that number from the 370,000 still yields a total that approximates the 25% figure I cite. See, Congressional Budget Office, *Options for Changing the Army's Overseas Basing* (Washington, DC: Congressional Budget Office, May 2004), pp.1–4.
16. R. A. Millen (LTC, US Army), *Reconfiguring the American Military Presence in Europe* (Carisle, PA: US Army War College, Strategic Studies Institute, February 2004).
17. This visit was also reported by Radio Free Europe/Radio Liberty on 13–14 February, 2004.
18. An American who worked for the International Crisis Group in Central Asia told me that the Kyrgiz and Uzbek locations, together, involved 10,000 American military and civilian personnel. The same informant related that the social consequences of such massive deployments and financial 'contributions' were distorting local socioeconomic conditions and giving rise to the usual consequences of a large-scale military presence. An American Special Forces officer also conveyed to me, when he returned to Europe from a Central Asian deployment in mid-2002, that the US presence was quickly alienating the populations in these countries from America largely because Washington was seen as being allied with dictatorial governments. A similar point is made in a piece in *The Nation* (16 February 2004) 13.
19. Congressional Budget Office, *Options for Changing the Army's Overseas Basing*, op. cit.
20. H. Binnendijk and R. L. Kugler, 'Dual-Track Transformation for the Atlantic Alliance', *Defense Horizons No. 35* (Institute for National Strategic Studies, National Defense University, November 2003).
21. E. Pond used the death metaphor in her *Friendly Fire: The Near Death of the Transatlantic Alliance* (Washington, DC: Brookings Institution, 2004).
22. E. Schmitt, 'Rumsfeld Fervently Defends Iraq War to European Critics,' *The New York Times* (8 February 2004) 11.
23. A foreign minister of a small southeast European country that joined NATO in 2004 said to me in late 2002 that his country could offer 'no enthusiasm and no military help' regarding Iraq, but would stand by America's side. I asked what that meant precisely, to which the response was 'as much or as little as is diplomatically necessary.'
24. Nye, 'U.S. Power and Strategy After Iraq', p.67.
25. This, of course, was R. Kagan's media-friendly argument in *Of Paradise and Power: America and Europe in the New World Order* (New York: Knopf, 2003).
26. D. N. Nelson, 'Transatlantic Transmutations' (see fn. 1).
27. At the George C. Marshall Center, a US DoD-German Ministry of Defense institution in Garmisch-Partenkirchen, Germany, this theme of NATO the democratizer

was, throughout mid-2002, a drumbeat of the curriculum taught principally to mid-career military, MoD and MFA officials from post-communist Europe and Central Asia. The results were not impressive on several dimensions, as I've reported in 'Defense, Diagnosis, Therapy: A Civil-Military Critique,' *Defense and Security Analysis* 18 (2) June 2002 and 'Democracy and Security in Southeast Europe,' *Armed Forces & Society* 28 (3) Fall 2002, 421–48.

28. The US Mission to NATO sponsors an annual seminar on security issues. In January 22–23, 2004, the topic was 'NATO and the Greater Middle East.' According to one attendee, there was pronounced emphasis on NATO's activities in the region as an organization, not as individual states.

29. See E. Sciolino's report, 'NATO Role Expanding at Urging of the U.S.,' *International Herald Tribune* (21 February 2004), 1.

30. L. G. Michel, 'NATO Decisionmaking: Au Revoir to the Consensus Rule?', *Strategic Forum No. 202* (Institute for National Strategic Studies, National Defense University, August 2003). The cited quote is from p. 6 of Michel's essay. Michel's 'toolbox' metaphor may have been drawn from Nye, p.67.

31. *SEF NEWS No. 18* (December 2003), 'From Utopia to Reality,' 13.

32. Regarding the Bruce Jackson-written 'Vilnius 10' document issued to the press hours after Colin Powell's UN speech, see D. N. Nelson, 'American Jihad', *Information* (Copenhagen), 21 February 2003, later reprinted on-line by the British American Security Information Council. Ivan Krastev, a highly regarded Bulgarian analyst and head of a Sofia think tank, as quoted from a Stiftung Entwicklung und Frieden (SEF) conference in October 2003, in *SEF NEWS No. 18* (December 2003), 'From Utopia to Reality,' 14.

33. E. Hankiss, 'The East–West Divide in Europe: Does it Exist', *East European Studies* (Newsletter of the Woodrow Wilson Center, Washington, DC, January 2004), 5–7.

34. Eurostat, *Key Structural Data for the 10 Acceding Countries* (Brussels: 5 December 2002).

35. European Commission, *Economic Forecasts* (Brussels: Autumn 2002 and 2003).

36. Of many, many reports referencing such a trend, see I. Black, 'Two-speed EU Will Create Splits, Ahern tells Prodi,' *The Guardian* (5 January 2004), http:/www.guardian.co.uk/international/story/0,3604,1116258,00.html; see also J. Dempsey, 'Support for two-speed Europe Gathers Momentum,' *Financial Times* (15 December 2003). As of this writing, the European Union constitution is likely to be revisited during the Irish presidency during the first half of 2004. Of remaining disputes about the draft constitution, expectations are strong that most can be resolved via compromise, although voting based on a 'double majority' remains essential for French and German acceptance.

37. Economic and Social Research Council, *Newsletter, Issue Eight 'One Europe or Several?'* (Autumn–Winter 2002), which notes that not only is EU enlargement not a 'done deal' but that, in concert with NATO's extension to the east, there are ample challenges the resolutions to which are not certain.

38. Much of the empirical support to which this paragraph refers are in D. N. Nelson, *Four Europes*, manuscript in progress.

39. Regarding the role of ideas versus interests in Europe's future, see Craig Parsons, *A Certain Idea of Europe* (Ithaca: Cornell University Press, 2003).

40. A flavor of early 2004 discussion can be seen in 'Ireland Faces Difficult Six Months at EU Helm,' *EU Observer* (5 January 2004), Paul Meller, 'Report Says Europe is Behind on Single-Economy Goal,', *The New York Times* (22 January 2004), John Burgess, 'Rising Euro Tests European Unity,' *The Washington Post* (24 January 2004) and 'Budget for an Enlarged EU,' *The Irish Independent* (24 January 2004).

Perhaps most evocatively, Giles Merritt, director of Forum Europe, asked in early 2004 'Will the "Big Bang" Blow the EU Apart?', *International Herald Tribune* (18 February 2004), 6. Similarly, see William Pfaff, 'Expansion Jeopardizes EU's Founding Vision,' *International Herald Tribune* (21–22 February 2004), 7.

41. Examples of these traumatic debates are many. H. G. Ehrhart chews on the issue in his Chaillot Paper No. 55 (October 2002), *What Model for CFSP* (Paris: Institute d'etudes de Securité, 2002).

42. One early and strong indication was the *Eurobarometer 55* (Brussels, IP/01/1005, 17 July 2001).

43. J. Solana, EU High Representative for the Common Foreign and Security Policy, *A Secure Europe in a Better World* first presented at the Thessaloniki European Council, 19–20 June 2003 and subsequently made available on the EU website and many other sites.

44. *A Secure Europe in a Better World: European Security Strategy*. Paris: The European Union Institute for Security Studies, December 2003).

45. J. Vinocur, 'Europe's Old Axis has Lost Its Luster', *International Herald Tribune* (February 19 2004), 8.

46. G. J. Ikenberry, 'American Power and the Empire of Capitalist Democracy,' in M. Cox, *et al.*, eds, *Empires, Systems and States* (London: Cambridge, 2001), p.212.

47. www.cesd.org/natonotes/notes56b.htm

48. Simon Serfaty speaks of a defining moment for transatlantic relations – wherein such mutual dependence is, indeed, understood and a new normalcy in a post 9/11 world reinvigorates US–European ties. (see his essay 'A Defining Moment in Purpose and Commitment' in the US State Department's on-line journal at http://usinfo.state.gov/journals/itps/0604/ijpe/serfaty.htm By contrast, I see the potential for defeat and NATO/EU institutional peril as traumas that would generate change as no other event or process.

8
European Security and Transatlantic Relations after 9/11 and the Wars in Afghanistan and Iraq

Heinz Gärtner

Traditional security thinking dominated the dynamics of the Cold War. Reliance on military capabilities was the primary strategy adopted to achieve greater security. In the post-1989 world, and in particular post-9/11, by far the largest proportions of the operational efforts of NATO and the European Union (EU) have shifted away from collective defense. Instead, crisis management became the paradigm that forms the cornerstone of the post-Cold War security system.[1] As part of this reorientation of effort, NATO and the EU are exploring ways to develop cooperation in the fight against terrorism. What is the benefit for the US in this process?

This chapter examines both the impact of developments before and after 11 September on both NATO and European Security in particular, and on transatlantic relations in general.

NATO's transformation

Based on the assumption that alliances cannot survive without a clear and unifying threat, after the end of the East–West conflict some analysts predicted NATO's imminent demise. No alliance in history has long survived the disappearance of its enemy. NATO did not expire, but it had to adapt and transform itself more and more, and along the way it gradually jettisoned collective defense as a core rationale for its existence.

Since the end of the East–West conflict, NATO has undergone a significant transformation process, one that has been speeded up by the terror attacks of 11 September 2001. After 9/11, NATO was again at risk of becoming irrelevant in a world in which terrorism had become the principal strategic threat. Founded as a collective defense organization at the onset of the Cold War, NATO had to revise its strategic concepts to respond to a broader spectrum of the threats.[2] Two initial attempts to revive Article 5 failed. First, the invocation of its Article 5 collective security commitments on 12 September, for a war that was not taking place on NATO territory, changed the meaning of this article, together with that of Article 6, the provision that prescribes the Alliance's area of operation. It turned out, however, that the United States did not want to make use of NATO's offer of support and instead kept the planning and conducting of the war in Afghanistan directly with US Central Command, bypassing NATO's SHAPE staff in Brussels. The US thus largely ignored NATO. Secondly, likewise before the war against Iraq began, Germany, France and Belgium blocked the beginning of any NATO military planning, conducted under Article 5, intended to protect Turkey against the threat of an Iraqi missile attack. Subsequently, Turkey requested consultations under Article 4 of the North Atlantic Treaty, the provision that states that NATO's members will consult together whenever, in the opinion of any of them, the territorial integrity, political independence or security of any NATO country is threatened. These events, taken with NATO enlargement, a greater voice for Russia in Alliance affairs, and NATO's limited military role in the wars against both the Taliban and Saddam Hussein's regime but its more prominent role in the peace operations afterwards, made it seem likely that NATO was going to lose or at least change radically its traditional role of as an instrument of collective defense.

It has become clear that while European governments will support the United States in crisis management operations, even if they take place out of NATO's core area, such as in the Balkans, Afghanistan and under certain conditions even in Iraq, the episode over Turkey makes it obvious that Europeans may not be willing to follow Washington in every instance, especially where European interests are not clearly at stake.

9/11 also had another impact: NATO became an organization with global reach. Not only Article 5 was transformed after 11 September; NATO's role definitively became global and made the geographical restrictions of Article 6 of the Washington Treaty meaningless. The final document of the NATO–Prague 2002 meeting states that 'in order to carry out the full range of its missions, NATO must be able to field forces that can move quickly to wherever they are needed…to sustain operations over distance and time.' NATO's Secretary General[3] concluded that 'the "out-of-area" debate has been resolved once and for all.' In Afghanistan, where NATO leads the international stabilization force, and in Iraq, where it will provide limited support to the stabilization of post-Saddam Iraq, NATO not only acts 'out-of-area' but 'out-of-continent'. For the first time ever five NATO nations[4] also held aerial war games with non-members, India and Japan, under an exercise codename *Cooperative Copethunder* in Alaska in July 2004. NATO will not actually scrap Article 6, in the same way as it will not scrap Article 5. This is because treaty revision is difficult and Article 5 keeps some of the new members happy, especially the Baltic States. These nations still read them in the traditional way. Nonetheless, both have been overtaken by events.

At the Prague Summit, the heads of governments approved the formation of a NATO *Response Force* (NRF) of around 20,000 troops to deal with the new threats of the twenty-first Century. A brigade (usually a military unit of about 5,000 troops) should be deployable wherever it is needed within 5 to 30 days. The new NATO *Response Force* is intended to be a coherent, high readiness, joint, multinational force package, technologically advanced, flexible, deployable, interoperable and sustainable. It will not be a permanent or standing force. Rather its component units will be reconfigured as required to meet the needs of a specific operation. The NRF will be able to carry out certain missions on its own, or serve as part of a larger force to contribute to the full range of Alliance military operations. Within the framework of the *Prague Capabilities Commitment*, individual countries will have to commit themselves within pre-set deadlines to provide specific equipment and expertise. The NRF and the European Union's *Headline Goal Force* are intended to be fully compatible and mutually reinforcing initiatives.

In September 2002, President George Bush outlined America's new *National Security Strategy* (NSS). It included the concept that the United States would be willing to take pre-emptive action, if a country or organization were developing nuclear, chemical or biological weapons for use against it. This pre-emptive approach to threats was intended to replace, at least in part, the two Cold War doctrines of deterrence and containment. The *Response Force*, proposed for NATO by Donald Rumsfeld at the NATO Defense Ministers Meeting in Warsaw in September 2002, could easily become an instrument for pre-emption if there were political consensus among the members. Is it likely that NATO would accept the doctrine of preemption? Perhaps not, but there is a historical precedence for such a shift in doctrine. In the 1960's NATO adopted the US doctrine of *Flexible Response*, which replaced the strategy of *Massive Retaliation; Flexible Response* included the possible use of nuclear weapons to meet even a conventional attack. When giving reasons for the creation of the new *Response Force*, former NATO Secretary General George Robertson[5] stopped short of mentioning pre-emptive strikes. But he said that: 'a critical lesson from 11 September is that threats to our security may fester in faraway regions before they suddenly strike at our homes.'

In another speech of George Robertson,[6] *pre-emption* sounded like this:

> Today, NATO is a problem solver. It must go where the trouble is. In today's world, if we don't go to the trouble, the trouble will come to you.... The new threats can strike from anywhere, and with little warning. We need to react much quicker than we ever previously had to contemplate.

He added: 'Peter Struck [the German Defense Minister] is right: We must defend our security on the Hindu Kush.' If NATO were to incorporate the strategy of *pre-emption* into its doctrine, it would further undermine Cold War collective defense commitments. There can hardly be mutual assistance if no party to the Treaty has yet been attacked!

Secretary General Lord Robertson[7] also stressed that 'if operations such as ISAF in Afghanistan are to succeed, we must generate more usable soldiers and have the political will to deploy more of them on multinational operations.' He criticized the situation that whereas the non-American NATO members collectively had standing armies of 1.4 m soldiers and 1 m reserves, they were still not able to deploy more than the current 55,000 troops on multi-national operations without feeling overstretched. The problem in expanding NATO into Iraq is that it has already had to stretch its available resources to the limit to do enough in Afghanistan.

Europe's security and defense

The European Union launched a 60,000-strong *Rapid Reaction Force* in 2001 (*Helsinki Headline Goal*), that was supposed to be up and running by 2003. It failed to meet this deadline and the EU continues to struggle to achieve this objective amid budgetary restrictions, the effects of post-11 September events, and the wars in Afghanistan and Iraq. Therefore, it seems likely that the force will not be operational before 2010.

After the end of the East–West conflict, European deficiencies in military capabilities became more and more visible. One important reason lies in the legacy of the Cold War itself. During its duration, European armies prepared for a confrontation with the major threat from the East as part of a collective effort to defend their territories. The conflicts and challenges after the end of the military bipolarity do not require massive, heavy-metal European armies, unsuited for transportation and projection to distant places, but rather rapid reaction forces with flexible structures and light weapons, deployable over great distances, equipped with modern communications, surveillance and reconnaissance facilities to coordinate and enhance their actions. At the *Capabilities Improvement Conference* on 19 November 2001, EU member states agreed on a *European Capability Action Plan* (ECAP) that incorporated all of the efforts, investments, developments and coordination measures executed or planned, at both national and multinational levels, that were deemed necessary for the Union's future activities.

In 2004 the EU Heads of State will probably adopt the new European Constitution. Although the document is subject to a referenda in the individual member states, they did, however, agree on the *European Security and Defense Policy* (ESDP), with some adjustments. This document recognizes that the concept of security is very broad, and by nature indivisible. It is one that goes beyond the purely military aspects and covers not only the security of states but also the security of citizens. It gives the Union military options over and above the civil instruments of crisis prevention and management.

The document contains specific provisions for implementing the ESPD, including future steps towards framing of a common Union defense policy. These steps could lead to a common defense when the European Council, acting unanimously, decides it is in accordance with the member states' respective constitutional requirements.

- The tasks of the Union, which are the extended *Petersberg* missions, include joint disarmament operations, humanitarian and rescue tasks, military advice and assistance tasks, conflict prevention and peacekeeping tasks, tasks of combat forces in crisis management, including peacemaking, and post-conflict stabilization. All of these tasks may also contribute to the fight against terrorism, including by supporting third countries (e.g. the US) in combating terrorism in their territories.[8] According to the document, the *Council of Ministers* may ask the member states participating in such cooperation to carry out at Union level any of the tasks referred to above, in the course of which the Union may use both civilian and military means.
- The Council may entrust the execution of a task, within the Union framework, to *a group of member states* in order to maintain the Union's values and serve its interests.
- Those member states whose military capabilities fulfill higher criteria and that have made more binding commitments in this area with a view to being able to undertake the most demanding missions shall establish permanent *structured cooperation* within the Union framework.
- A European *Armaments, Research and Military Capabilities Agency* will assist the Council in evaluating the improvement of military capabilities.
- If a member state is the victim of armed aggression on its territory, the other member states shall have towards it an obligation of aid and assistance by all the means in their power, in accordance with the self-defense provisions of Article 51 of the United Nations Charter. This shall not, however, prejudice the specific character of the security and defense policy of certain member states.
- Some member states (at least one third) may also wish to establish *enhanced cooperation* amongst themselves to further the objectives of the Union, protect its interests and reinforce its integration process.
- A proposed *Solidarity Clause* is designed to help prevent terrorist threats. Should a Member State fall victim to a terrorist attack or a natural or man-made disaster, the other member states shall assist it at the request of its political authorities.[9]

The clause guaranteeing mutual assistance was not included because of any thorough analysis of the new challenges or threats. Terrorism, weapons of mass destruction, asymmetric conflicts, instability generated by failed states do not require mutual defense commitments. No military alliance can respond to these dangers. The true reason for this clause might be that it would be sensible to allow those member states who wish to intensify their cooperation, and in particular to define their defense identity within the framework of the Union rather than outside the Union, to go ahead and do so. In all probability, that is why the United Kingdom, in spite of its strong commitment to NATO, accepted the provision, after previously strong resistance. But the UK also insisted that a second paragraph be added to the clause reasserting obligations under NATO, which is to remain the foundation of the collective defense of its members: 'Commitments and cooperation in this area shall be consistent with commitments under NATO....'

The neutral and non-aligned states – Finland, Sweden, Ireland and Austria – have expressed reservations over this article, which establishes a mutual defense clause in the case that a member state is attacked. At their meeting in December 2003, the EU Head of States added that the measure concerning assistance in the case of an armed attack on EU land does not affect the individual nature of security and defense policies of certain member states.[10]

Building on a British–French proposal that member states should create rapid deployment forces or *battlegroup*s that, on behalf of the EU, could be sent on emergency missions, notably in Africa, then by 2007 the EU should have the capacity to supply, targeted combat units for the missions planned, structured at a tactical level as combat formations, with support elements including transport and logistics, capable of carrying out the tasks referred to above (extended *Petersberg Tasks*). These capabilities could operate at either the national level or as a component of multinational force groups, in particular in response to requests from the United Nations Organization under Chapters VI and VII of the UN Charter (although not exclusively and necessarily, however). These 13 formations would be composed of up to 1500 troops, ready to be deployed for combat within a period of 5 to 15 days, e.g. in jungle, desert and mountain operations. This *battlegroup* concept might well fit into the *structured cooperation* foreseen in the draft constitution.

To achieve these goals member states should[11] harmonize the identification of their military needs, by pooling and, where appropriate, specializing their defense means and capabilities, and by encouraging cooperation in the fields of training and logistics. They also should take concrete measures to enhance the availability, interoperability, flexibility and deployability of their forces, in particular by identifying common objectives regarding the commitment of forces; this may possibly include reviewing their national decision-making procedures.

It might well be that efforts to achieve the *Headline Goal* will slow down under the new provisions, because military capabilities will not stretch to the soldiers and equipment needed within this framework. They could also lead to duplication within the EU itself. To avoid duplication, some states that want to do so could set up such *battlegroup*s, which would cover the upper end of the *Petersberg Tasks*, while other states concentrate more on the middle and lower part.

The European Security Strategy

Javier Solana, the High Representative for Foreign Policy of the European Union, presented a *European Security Strategy*[12] that was adopted by the

European Council in December 2003. The document asserts a need and role for the European Union in global security and in any actions, including military force, deemed necessary to achieve that security. It calls for member nations to increase their military abilities and share military resources. It explicitly includes pre-emptive action:

'Preventive engagement[13] can avoid more serious problems in the future. . . . With the new threats the first line of defense will often be abroad.' This also requires 'early, rapid, and when necessary, robust intervention.' The *battle-group* concept could meet these criteria and would therefore perfectly able to meet the requirement to act militarily preventively.[14] The new strategy involves 'both military and civilian capabilities.'

This document clearly and deliberately concurs with the American assessment that the potential spread of weapons of mass destruction, especially in the hands of terrorists, represents a direct threat to global security. Despite criticism in Europe of the US Security Strategy on military pre-emption, the European Security Strategy is not all that different from the American one.

The approach of the European Union is a light version of the US doctrine. It puts the emphasis somewhat more on multilateral cooperation than the US document. Thus, it describes the United Nations as the 'fundamental framework of international relations.' But it does not require an explicit authorization by the UN Security Council for military operations. It also underlines the necessity of conflict prevention. It includes not only civilian but also military operations. As the ESDP moves toward pre-emption/prevention, its efforts to become a *collective defense organization* (in the shape of the *closer cooperation* or not) might – as in NATO – be undermined. A preventive military operation will by definition not wait until an attack occurs.[15]

Just war

Since the *European Security Strategy* does not explicitly require an authorization of the UN Security Council (UNSC) for 'preventive engagement' it will become necessary to formulate preconditions for its application. They may include civilian measures, and in grave situations they may also include military action. But what is a grave situation? Where should we draw the line in determining when military prevention is indispensable? Who makes the decision to use force preventively? One possibility could be applying the criteria of the just war, like *just cause* (if there is e.g. large-scale loss of life, large-scale ethnic cleansing, planned or acts of terror, actual or imminent), or *right intention* (to prevent terrorist attacks or human suffering). These criteria still leave open the question who is the competent authority to decide what is right or just.

Joseph Nye has argued that 'preemption that is legitimized by multilateral sanction is far less costly and sets a far less dangerous precedent than the

United States asserting that it alone can act as judge, jury, and executioner.'[16] Nye is correct that military prevention in particular should be based on a multilateral cooperation that is as broad as possible, to legitimize it and to avoid international isolation and criticism. The objection that there might be no time to negotiate in the UN Security Council, in NATO or the European Council what is just or right if a threat is imminent, is not convincing. The principle of self-defense in the UN-Charter applies perfectly to this situation. Reliable intelligence is critical here, however. Whether there is a threat and how imminent it is, are basically questions of good intelligence. However, even the best intelligence can turn out to be wrong, as was the case in Iraq. Using intelligence and risk assessment that are vague as the basis for pre-emptive war – and it is hard to say whether they are sketchy or not – can lead to wrong decisions about whether military prevention is justified or not. Given these uncertainties, a broad multilateral legitimacy is all the more indispensable and this is best provided by the United Nations. In addition, it is hard to imagine that the EU's civilian and military preventive engagement will be used for regime change. It will rather serve as conflict prevention and preventive deployment, an approach that worked well, for example, when 800 NATO troops prevented the spread of the Balkan wars to Macedonia in the 1990s.

NATO and EU: a common command structure?

In April 2003 France and Germany proposed the creation of a EU military command and planning structure, separate from that of NATO. The US expressed consternation about this proposal and stated its strong desire that the EU works within NATO. NATO's European members have long been searching for ways to enable themselves to undertake military actions independently from the United States without dividing the Alliance and needlessly duplicating existing capabilities. France and Britain had already agreed in St. Mal ó in 1998 to allow European Union members to undertake autonomous operations 'where NATO as a whole' was not 'engaged.'

To meet these requirements, however, the EU has to develop some independent capacities for the civil and military aspects of security at the lower to middle levels of intensity and for multilateral peace operations. This includes the need for an operational planning headquarters, a fundamental requirement if the EU is to carry out missions independent of NATO. So far, in the autonomous European interventions in the Congo, Sierra Leone, and Côte d'Ivoire, neither the United States had any interest in joining nor was 'NATO as a whole engaged.' After some debate, the EU and NATO agreed in December 2003 to locate a EU planning cell at NATO's military headquarters, rather than a new and separate 'headquarters' in Tervuren. This planning cell is used when the EU calls of NATO assets and capabilities in EU-led operations, in accordance with the *Berlin plus* agreement and to run crisis management operations when NATO is not involved. Some Europeans have complained that the US administration wants to reduce NATO to the role of a military *toolbox* for the United States to use as and when it desires.[17] However, the *Berlin plus* mechanism allows the Europeans to do the exactly the same thing.

The number of planners on the EU's existing strategic planning nucleus will be increased and NATO liaison officers are to be stationed at the EU. These decisions acknowledge that Europe requires and has its own limited capability to conduct military operations. According to the agreement, the EU would first turn to NATO, then to member states' national headquarters to plan and run a EU military operation. In cases where NATO is not involved, operations will be planned and run by this new planning cell. 'The Council (of EU foreign ministers) may decide, upon the advice of the Military Committee, to draw on the collective capacity of the EU military staff, in particular where a joint civil/military response is required and where no national Headquarters is identified,' the text[18] says. In other cases operations can be conducted by the command and control centers that several EU states already have. For example, in the case of *Operation Artemis* in Congo, the EU mission in cooperation with the so-called *framework nation*, France, acted under the authorization granted by United Nations Security Council Resolution 1484, which called for a multinational interim emergency force in Bunia.

Since NATO would still enjoy clear primacy, except where it is specifically transferred to wholly European auspices, the system – where only select technically more advanced and capable countries could go ahead in a common defense (*structured cooperation*) – does not hurt the transatlantic relationship.

These command arrangements, designed as a compromise among the three big European powers and the US, might turn out to be a complicated and bureaucratic system. To meet new challenges and threats, however, European forces need to be flexible, light and agile, and able to respond quickly to sudden changes. In the long run such a complex and ritualized system is not going to be appropriate if Europe is to react flexibly and rapidly adapt to changing events.

To avoid unnecessary duplication it would be more efficient to build a common command structure of NATO and EU for crisis management. The EU's and NATO's crisis management activities will have to be increasingly harmonized and coordinated. The aim could be to have a common command structure. The common exercises that are already taking place are a good starting point. They allow the EU to use expensive NATO assets instead of duplicating them.

As more exercises are to follow, standing arrangements for consultation and cooperation between the two organizations, mechanisms that can also be used in times of crisis, will be necessary. On an operational level, greater interoperability can progressively be achieved by synchronizing NATO's *Prague Capabilities Commitment* (PCC) and the EU's *European Capabilities Action Plan* (ECAP). Ensuring consistency, transparency and the mutually reinforcing development of capability requirements common to the two organizations is already the main objective of the *NATO–EU Capability Group*. It hopefully will foster mutual reinforcement between the NATO *Response Force* and the EU *structured cooperation* and its newly proposed *battlegroups*. Both are likely to adopt a preventive strategy to fight terrorism and the proliferation of weapons of mass destruction. Taking into account limited defense budgets, NATO and EU members will not be able to maintain two separate Rapid Reaction Forces. NRF and EU *battlegroups* will most likely consist of the same troops, merely wearing different hats. An important step towards better EU–NATO cooperation are meetings between the North Atlantic Council (NAC) and the Political and Security Committee (PSC) of the European Union, which are taking place already.

There is already an almost identical analysis of the threats and challenges by NATO and EU. Combating terrorism, curbing the proliferation of weapons of mass destruction, civil emergency planning, building new military capabilities are just some of the areas where they have in principle common interests and goals and also considerable expertise. At the Istanbul summit, a joint NATO–EU declaration on terrorism was decided upon.

The problem with this approach is, however, that since the end of the Cold War the strategic perspectives of the US and Europe do not always overlap. For the US, the existential, overarching threat has shifted from the Soviet Union to terrorism, the Gulf, the Middle East and northeast Asia.[19] For the Europeans these risks are important but less immediate and tangible. On the one hand, therefore, the US is more likely to use force in these conflicts than the Europeans. On the other hand, the US might not get involved in conflicts that are hardly existential but are essential for all or some Europeans, such as those in the Balkans or Africa. Therefore, the independent use of the command structure must be possible, whether in the framework of *Berlin plus* or without NATO involvement for the Europeans, and as 'coalition of the willing' for the US.

EU–US: duplication or division of labor?

For the US, a duplication of security commitments is not tolerable. However, one can only avoid duplication by clear divisions of labor. Effective coordination of EU and NATO military and command structures can avoid duplication and create a complementary division of labor, one where the EU concentrates on the whole spectrum of the *Petersberg Tasks*, with concentration on the lower half (disarmament operations, humanitarian and rescue tasks, military advice and assistance tasks, conflict prevention, peacekeeping tasks and post-conflict stabilization) but with some elements of higher level (combat forces in crisis management, including peacemaking). Meanwhile, US military forces will concentrate on the latter, although without giving up the skill for peacekeeping, peace- and nation-building, which was the approach the Bush administration favored before 9/11.

The wars in Kosovo, Afghanistan and Iraq clearly demonstrated that the overwhelming US contribution is its war-fighting capability – in comparison with the limited European capability in this area. This gap in purely military capabilities between the US and the rest of the world is huge and growing. EU and European NATO defense ministries are not even able to contemplate asking for resources reflected in the Pentagon's budget request for fiscal 2005 of US$402 billion. In contrast, European NATO members spend less than the half this amount and even this smaller sum produces war-fighting capacities that are disproportionately lower. Ironically, US requests for higher defense spending by the Europeans would inevitably lead to duplication of efforts and capabilities. And why should the Europeans catch up with the Americans? There is no arms race between Europe and the US and there are no direct threats to the EU territory.

However, a capability to act does not only imply war fighting alone. European military capabilities are more tailored towards projecting low-intensity power, peacekeeping, humanitarian action, disaster relief and post-conflict reconstruction rather than the rapid deployment of large combat forces over long distances. EU members provide up to ten times more soldiers than the US for policing and peacekeeping in places such as Bosnia, Kosovo and several countries in Africa, and European NATO nations have at all times contributed more than 90 per cent of ISAF's troops in Afghanistan.

There does need to be, however, some risk- and responsibility sharing. There should not be a clear-cut division of labor, where the Europeans do the peace and the Americans do the war. The US forces should not be reduced to war fighting alone, but need also to be capable of carrying out humanitarian, rescue and peacekeeping operations. Such a *qualified division of labor* only means that the Europeans concentrate more on the smaller-scale operations at the lower end of the conflict spectrum, but there should be some European contribution in crises where higher intensity enforcement capabilities are required (as the *battlegroup* concept proposes).

The United States will need to continue to project forces in high-intensity conflict. The NRF can be an example for a cooperation among allies 'at the sharp end of military operations, so there is no division of labor between those who do the dirty work and those who do the dishes,' as NATO Secretary General, Jaap de Hoop Scheffer points out.[20] In the NRF there still will be a qualified division of labor, with an advanced US in heavy lift and C4IR[21] capacities, with selected European allies contributing some of those capabilities.

Just as Europeans should keep and develop some war fighting capability, US troops should participate, at least at minimal levels, in lower end peace support operations, peacekeeping and nation-building. The US administration should give up its unwillingness to contribute troops for 'constabulary' duties, peacekeeping, and *nation-building*.[22] The wars in Iraq and in Afghanistan have shown that for *high-intensity* war with advanced combat technology, the US does not need support from allies. For post-conflict reconstruction, peacekeeping and state-building and *lower intensity* capabilities, European armed and police forces are better equipped and trained – a chastening lesson US troops[23] learned during the occupation in Iraq.[24] The US is already changing its attitude towards post-conflict reconstruction and *nation-building*. Based on its experiences in Iraq, the US has brought in more mobile and less obtrusive units, staffed by soldiers with some knowledge of the local language and customs based on undergoing 'cultural sensitive training', to replace heavy armored units.[25]

In Afghanistan, the 12,000-strong US-led force of mostly American troops, 'Enduring Freedom', which is part of the US war on terrorism, hunts the remnants of the Taliban and their al Qaeda allies, and operates separate from the NATO-led peacekeeping mission of the International Security Assistance Force (ISAF), which was set up in December 2001 after the defeat of the Taliban regime. As part of the proposed cooperation, NATO could begin closer cooperation with the forces engaged in *Enduring Freedom*, although a complete merger is unlikely and probably not workable. As the division of labor in Afghanistan shows, there should not only be coordination between the two forces but also elements of each force as part of the other.

The EU forces should concentrate on those capacities they can provide best, where they have a comparative advantage to the US and where they can make a difference. NATO's former Secretary General[26] admitted that NATO does not need 'to address each and every crisis.' And it does *not* mean there has to be US leadership in every case. 'Some problems might be better addressed by the EU, or perhaps by *coalitions of the willing*. In some cases, a division of labor will turn out to be the most practical solution.'[27]

Concluding remarks

NATO's strategic partnership with the European Union has been formalized in the *Berlin Plus* arrangements, which provides for 'separable but not separate' EU forces. These arrangements allowed the EU to mount its first military operation in Macedonia. Bosnia is the next case for the application of *Berlin plus*. NATO Secretary General, Jaap de Hoop Scheffer, calls it a 'litmus test for the relationship between NATO and the EU' and 'litmus test for *Berlin Plus* agreement.'[28]

A qualified division of labor, one where Europe and the US, EU and NATO concentrate on capabilities where each has a comparative advantage seems to be a feasible concept. Other types of division of labor are emerging, too. One is geographical. For NATO, Afghanistan is 'priority number one;'[29] the European Union concentrates more and more on the Balkans, Macedonia and Bosnia. While NATO, following in the wake of the United States, is getting more and more involved in the Middle East, the EU takes over missions in Africa. The other division is functional. An initiative for the 'Greater Middle East' provides that NATO would offer countries in the region new forms of military cooperation, including training for peacekeeping missions, border security and counter-terrorism, as well as reforms to encourage civilian control of the military – similar to the Partnership for Peace Program. The European Union, meanwhile, would expand its existing trade and development links along the Mediterranean periphery, with the goal of achieving free-trade arrangements by 2010.[30]

Despite the transatlantic differences, there is clearly a consensus among some of the EU member states and the US on the need to develop more coordinated and where possible common force planning and strategies for *ad-hoc coalitions of the willing*, an approach that will allow such coalitions to have access to NATO and EU economic, military and human assets. The compatibility of NATO's NRF and the EU's *structured cooperation* and *battlegroup* concept could set an example. Taking this possibility of cooperation into consideration, it is short sighted when Americans still see *structured cooperation* as a potential seed for decoupling Europe and the United States. The concept is rather to link the NSS to NATO's NRF and use both as a useful tool to fight terrorism – even preemptively.

Julian Lindley-French[31] observes that deepening effective and real cooperation in crisis management is vital as a first step in a new transatlantic relationship: 'Both the European Union and NATO bring distinct and complementary contributions to such management, which is strengthened by the legitimacy afforded by the political autonomy of decision-making in both organizations. No single state or institution can manage such complexity.'

How does the EU–US cooperation in the field of crisis management and the concept of *qualified division of labor* fit into the unilateralism-multilateralism debate? Unilateralists see multilateralism as a means of controlling US power; multilateralists see in US unilateralism the danger that the US would use force wherever and whenever it wants, without consulting its allies. Both sides can point to merits in their arguments. On the one hand, the decisive wars in Afghanistan and Iraq were only possible because of the exertion of unilateral US power. On the other hand, peace cannot be established without multilateral efforts. *Qualified division of labor* would leave the US the means to keep its *high-tech, high-intensity, high-speed* war fighting capability, but it would also give multilateral nation-state building, peacekeeping and reconstruction effort broader legitimacy. The Americans will do what they want and Europeans what they can. A limited participation in each other's efforts would also ensure risk and responsibility sharing. This is sharing not only the dangers of suffering casualties but also the responsibility for failure and success.

Notes

1. H. Gärtner, A. Hyde-Price and E. Reiter (eds), *European Security, the Transatlantic Link and Crisis Management: Europe's New Security Challenges* (Boulder/London: Lynne Rinner, 2001), pp. 125–48.
2. How broad NATO's mission has become is shown by the fact that NATO helped with security during the 2004 Olympics in Greece.

3. G. Robertson, *Europe's Transformation*, Secretary General's Speech at the Conference of the Aspen Institute Berlin and the NATO Host Committee for the Prague Summit, Prague, 20 November 2002.
4. Britain, Canada, Germany, Turkey and the United States.
5. Nato Secretary General Lord Robertson, at The OSCE Permanent Council, Vienna, Austria – 6 November 2003.
6. Lord Robertson, Speech at the 'Welt am Sonntag Forum,' The Role of NATO in the 21st Century, Berlin, 3 November 2003.
7. Lord G. Robertson, NATO Secretary General, Introductory Statement at a Press Conference, Colorado Springs, 9 October 2003.
8. These are the so-called *Petersberg* Tasks that have been proposed by the Western European Union at the Petersberg in Germany in 1992. Subsequently, they were incorporated into the Amsterdam Treaty of the European Union. The draft constitution extended them by including disarmament efforts, conflict prevention, and terrorism.
9. On March 26 the Heads of State and Government adopted the clause independently of the constitution. This clause must not confused with a mutual defense commitment, since it applies to non-state terrorism and is also not part of the chapter of the ESDP.
10. This formula already is already included in the text of the constitution, but it is now repeated in this specific context.
11. Addendum to the presidency note, Conference of the representatives of the governments of the member states, Brussels, 9 December 2003, Protocol on permanent structured cooperation, established by Articles I-40(6) and III-213 of the Constitution, Article 2.
12. Version adopted by the European Council, Javier Solana, *A Secure Europe In A Better World*, December 2003.
13. After some Member States stated concerns about the expression 'pre-emptive engagement' it has been replaced by 'preventive engagement' in a revised draft. This is mainly a semantic solution, since there is no real difference between pre-emptive and preventive military engagement.
14. The British Defence White Paper to Parliament published Ministry of Defence in December 2003 already makes this connection clear:
'So, as a result of the end of the Cold War new terrorist threats and the proliferation of weapons of mass destruction, our expeditionary stance will be the template for our future operations. We can no longer wait to defend ourselves against attack – it would be too late. We must take on our enemies before they can attack us, by denying terrorists safe havens, and by changing the economic and social environments in which terrorism can flourish.' Quoted by Geoff Hoon, UK Secretary of State for Defence, Speech to the City Forum, London, 27 November 2003, UK Ministry of Defence; issued 27 November 2003.
15. A EU-commissioned report of September 2004 entitled 'A Human Security Doctrine for Europe' for implementation of the European Security Strategy argues that security forces need to be configured in a new way to fit the challenges and threats of the 21st century. The overall idea is to put the protection of humans, i.e. civilians, not territories, at the centre of a new EU security strategy. It deals with the new triple threat of international terrorism, failed states and weapons of mass destruction. According to the report a military response is necessary but not enough to deal with the new threats and challenges faced by the international community. While urging Europe to increase its military capacity, the report also stresses the need to complement traditional firepower with a host of civilian

elements. The report wants to see the creation of a new 15,000-strong force to be made up of both soldiers and civilian experts such as police, lawyers and aid workers. The force should be deployable in Europe and beyond. – 'A Human Security Doctrine for Europe: The Barcelona Report of the Study Group on Europe's Security Capabilities,' September 2004.

16. J. S. Nye, Jr, 'U.S. Power and Strategy After Iraq', *Foreign Affairs* (July/August 2003).

17. For example, German Defense Minister Peter Struck, Deutsche Welle German radio; issued 4 November 2003.

18. Euro Active, Security & Defense, 16 December 2003.

19. J. Thomson, 'US Interests and the Fate of the Alliance', *Survival*, vol. 45, no. 4 (Winter 2003–04), 207–20.

20. General Jaap de Hoop Scheffer, NATO Secretary General, Speech at the National Defense University, Washington, 29 January 2004.

21. Command, Control, Communication, Intelligence, Reconnaissance.

22. James Dobbins in his Testimony before the Committee on Foreign Relations, US Senate (18 September 2003), rightly criticizes that, as to *nation-building*, 'if there is any lesson to be learned from our "post-conflict" involvement in Iraq …, it is that we have failed to adequately learn the lessons from previous such experiences. … [W]e have not institutionalized that knowledge; we have not integrated it into our doctrine, our training, and our planning for future operations. Neither have we regarded people with experience in this field as a national asset, to be retained, rewarded for good service, trained further and placed in positions from which they can be made available the next time such skills are called for.' http://foreign. senate.gov/testimony/2003/DobbinsTestimony030923.pdf

23. This does not mean that US troops are not capable of conducting non-combat tasks. Special Operations Forces (SOF) with specialized tactics, equipment, and training; foreign, language skills, and flexible unit deployment options, for example, are tailored to a wide range of tasks. Given their linguistic, cultural, and political training, SOF are well suited to both coordinate humanitarian assistance operations and perform combat search and rescue missions. – 2003 Secretary of Defense Annual Report to the President and the Congress (http://www.defense link.mil/execsec/adr2003/adr2003_toc.html)

24. See also A. Missiroli, *Mind the gaps – Across the Atlantic and the Union*, in: G. Lindstrom, *Shift or Rift: Assessing US–EU relations after Iraq* (Paris: EU Institute for Security Studies, 2003), pp. 77–90.

25. Interview with Col. Mike Formica, of the First Calvary, in New York Times, 10 February 2004.

26. G. Robertson, NATO Secretary General, Securing the Peace: The NATO Vision, Speech at the NATO Public Diplomacy Conference, Brussels, 16 October 2003 (highlighted in the original).

27. G. Robertson, NATO Secretary General, Closing Remarks at the 2nd European Parliament meetings on Defence, Brussels, 25 November 2003.

28. J. de Hoop Scheffer, NATO Secretary General, speech at the Munich Security Conference, 7 February 2004.

29. General J. de Hoop Scheffer, NATO Secretary General, Speech at the National Defense University, Washington, 29 January 2004.

30. W. Drozdiak, 'Looking For A Vision', *Newsweek* (23 February 2004).

31. J. Lindley-French, 'The Ties that Bind', in NATO-review (Autumn 2003).

9

NATO Cohesion from Afghanistan to Iraq[1]

Christian Tuschhoff

Introduction

NATO's decision to invoke its mutual defense clause (Article 5 of the Washington Treaty) after the terrorist attacks on the World Trade Center and the Pentagon surprised the world. No one expected that the NATO Alliance would take such a bold step without extensive debate among the allies, national governments, political parties and the public. Yet, it took the North Atlantic Council (NAC) meeting at the level of Permanent Representatives (not ministers) only two meetings and a few hours to determine that the attack on the United States was an attack on all of the NATO allies, provided that further evidence proved it was an attack from abroad. This step came at a time when most experts had lost faith in the value of the Alliance in light of the Kosovo experience, during which it seemed more sensible to abandon NATO in favor of other security institutions, such as the European Union or the Organization for Security and Cooperation in Europe (OSCE), institutions that appeared to be geared more towards the post-Cold War security environment. At a time when states had every reason to run for the exit because they risked becoming the next terrorist target, governments decided to honor the treaty commitments that they had agreed to under very different circumstances and expectations. This decision is strong evidence of the endurance, cohesion and vitality of the Alliance. Despite academic predictions that its years are numbered, the North Atlantic Treaty Organization persists and adapts.[2] It has been argued, however, that since the 12 September 2001 decision, NATO has appeared to be marginalized because the United States did not ask for substantial support nor did NATO substantially contribute to the war effort.[3]

I challenge these assessments by making a number of arguments. First, the 12 September 2001 decision to invoke Article 5 – the mutual defense clause – had been prepared for in advance, in decisions agreed on after the Washington Summit in April 1999. NATO's swift and decisive action not only demonstrated the managerial effectiveness of the Alliance but also the mutual commitment among allies. The mutual defense reflex proved strong enough to silence objections to the invocation of Article 5 in national capitals. Second, contrary to some newspaper reports since April 1999, NATO allies have been engaged in a process of reforming their military capabilities in accordance with the requirements of the new strategic concept. I do not argue that NATO has achieved all its force goals and capability objectives. Due to the limited financial resources individual national governments have allocated to defense, progress has been slow and often disappointing. However, the process of modernizing and adapting forces and command structures was and still is well under way. NATO may have moved with frustrating slowness, but it is on the right track. Third, NATO's various decisions on modernizing its armed forces have themselves guided individual national programs of military reform. Fourth, the decision to invoke the mutual defense clause triggered a number of responses in national capitals, demonstrating the strong impact of NATO on national policymaking. I particularly point to how governments, including the United States, proved willing to go along.

However, institutions guaranteeing NATO's cohesion and commitments in the post-Cold War era are not nearly as strong as their Cold War predecessors. I have argued elsewhere that previous NATO arrangements would have made responses to armed attack automatic.[4] The mutual defense of NATO allies was not left to political consideration but was written into military arrangements such as the layer cake deployment of military forces. As we have seen, current trip wires trigger political solidarity but no automatic military reaction. In order to maintain and strengthen Alliance cohesion, a future reform of NATO should re-establish military tripwires that respond to contemporary security threats by improving contingency planning and by pre-delegating authority.

The decision to activate the mutual defense clause

The history of the decision to activate Article 5 of the Washington Treaty is instructive. The initial idea did not originate in any national capital but at NATO headquarters in Brussels. NATO's Secretary General, Lord Robertson, claimed the idea was his. He drafted a resolution and broached the idea in a telephone conversation with US Secretary of State Colin Powell by asking, 'Have you considered invoking Article 5?' Mr. Powell said he had not. Robertson sent a copy of the resolution to the State Department in Washington and received an approval only eight minutes later. The short time frame did not allow for extensive consultation in Washington, at a time when political leaders were extremely busy and were struggling simultaneously with a wide range of issues. While concerned with the step, national governments in Belgium, the Netherlands, and Luxembourg chose not to oppose the decision. In addition, Robertson's draft resolution was not formally introduced by the United States but by Britain and Canada. It took only two meetings of the NAC and about 30 hours to approve the resolution invoking Article 5. The NAC changed only two words in Robertson's draft.

The Washington Summit 1999: preparing NATO for the terrorist challenge

The NAC statement of 12 September 2001 explicitly referred to the Washington Summit of NATO in April 1999 when it stated:

> When the Heads of State and Government of NATO met in Washington in 1999, ... they also recognized the existence of a wide variety of risks to security ... More specifically, they condemned terrorism as a serious threat to peace and stability and reaffirmed their determination to combat it in accordance with their commitments to one another, their international commitments and national legislation.[5]

Former Supreme Allied Commander in Europe, General Wesley Clark, explained that the Alliance was obligated to invoke Article 5. Indeed, the documents agreed at the Washington summit support the interpretation that it was inevitable that Article 5 would be invoked after 9/11. While the 'Washington Declaration'[6] itself remains rather vague and may have led to some confusion in the press about the serious nature of the commitment, the final communiqué and the strategic concept are much more explicit. The communiqué first reiterates the tasks of deterrence and defense 'against any threat of aggression against any NATO member state ...' and later states 'Terrorism constitutes a serious threat to peace, security and stability that can threaten the territorial integrity of States. We reiterate our condemnation of terrorism and reaffirm our determination to combat it in accordance with our international commitments and national legislation'.[7] This language became a standard wording that has been repeated in subsequent NATO documents and was a significant departure from previous treatments of the threat of terrorism,[8] indicating that the Alliance now considered it a threat against territorial integrity.

The precise meaning of the documents adopted in 1999 can be appreciated only when key terms such as territorial integrity are properly understood as cross references to statements of commitments, including those of the NATO Treaty. In addition, the proper interpretation is supported by comparing the new standard wording against previous statements treating terrorism as a criminal offense rather than as a threat to territorial integrity or as an armed attack. The interpretation that the strategic concept of 1999 entailed all the necessary components to activate Article 5 in order to counter terrorist attacks is also supported by the fact that while NATO has changed several key policies and procedures since 9/11, as explained below, it saw no need to amend the strategic concept.

Political preparations after the Washington Summit

Even in the absence of direct evidence, it is reasonable to assume that after the Washington summit NATO had fully defined the criteria by which Article 5 applied to terrorist attacks. The Article itself indicates that activation of the mutual defense clause requires an 'armed attack' on one or more member states. Apparently, it was also essential to make a distinction between attacks by domestic terrorist organizations and attacks directed from abroad. This distinction became necessary to reassure states such as Spain, the United Kingdom, and Turkey that domestic terrorism would not lead to NATO interference. Finally, the geographic limitation of the NATO treaty applied. Consequently, Article 5 was not activated after the attack on the warship USS Cole because the US navy ship was located in Aden, Yemen, outside the perimeter of the NATO area, when it was attacked on 12 October 2000.

However, there were two other important reasons to activate Article 5 on 12 September 2002. First, it put NATO firmly in charge of the allied response by eliminating the option of using the European Security and Defense Policy (ESDP). ESDP can be used for all but collective defense missions. Second, activating Article 5 allowed NATO and its members to use fast track procedures for mobilizing civilian support and resources. Secretary General Robertson explained:

> But the United States is a part of the NATO alliance, and invoking Article 5 gave you some useful options. Once the decision was made to launch the Afghanistan campaign, a switch clicked and the United States had only to ask for things like the use of alliance airspace, ports, and harbors, or the deployment of NATO AWACS to the United States. These things may look small, but they were actually fundamental building blocks to the campaign. In my opinion, NATO's invocation of Article 5 also allowed the United States to build its anti-terror coalition much faster because the full authority of the NATO alliance was behind the effort.[9]

It is important to understand the standards for the application of Article 5 as well as the fact that they had been discussed and decided upon before the 11 September attacks. The standards allowed the NAC to limit its considerations to whether or not the attack on the World Trade Center and the Pentagon building had met the necessary criteria. Without such standards, decision-makers would have had to engage in lengthy considerations of the circumstances under which they were willing to meet their mutual defense commitment and of the limits of their national constitutions and laws. These questions had already been decided when the terrorist attack occurred on 9/11, allowing the NAC to limit its discussion to the issue of whether or not the predefined standards for Article 5 activation applied. The limits on required deliberations and decisions enabled the Alliance to act as quickly and unanimously as it did. The agony of Alliance decision-making regarding its involvement in the Balkans shows how difficult it is to reach a consensus and make decisions in the absence of such simplifying standards. The more recent transatlantic conflict – particularly between the US and Germany – over the use of military force against Iraq adds further evidence to this argument.

Military preparations after the Washington Summit

Since the end of the Cold War, NATO has engaged in adapting its specific collective defense assets to more general ones for use in a wider range of contingencies. This process has also affected military capabilities. The new strategic concept with its supporting decisions and the subsequent changes in NATO's posture were significant steps within this fast-moving and important process of Alliance adaptation. It explains above and beyond previous realist and institutional accounts why NATO has persisted and continues to persist not only as an organization but also as an alliance. Based on this new mandate, NATO members individually and collectively continued to reform the command and force structures of the Alliance to generate the capabilities necessary to deal with a much broader range of threats and security risks.

The principal idea behind a series of reforms, including the command and the force structures, was written into the Defense Capability Initiative (DCI) and also adopted at the Washington Summit in 1999. The idea was to develop the Combined Joint Task Force (CJTF) concept approved at the Brussels summit in 1994 into multi-national tri-service headquarters based on deployable self-contained NATO elements. These improved headquarters would provide NATO with the capability to conduct two simultaneous corps size operations in and beyond the Alliance's territory. More specific actions after the Washington summit included streamlining the command structure and increasing its flexibility. It now consists of 20 headquarters at three different levels. While some experts have argued that NATO does not have the right kind of capabilities,[10] a closer examination reveals that they were mainly talking about Special Forces, which are in very short supply in all militaries, including that of the United States.

In light of its experiences after 9/11, NATO changed or is in the process of changing a number of key policies, culminating in the decisions taken at the summit meeting in Prague on 21 November 2002.[11] The main changes were the so-called Prague Capabilities Commitments streamlining the DCI, the planning of a NATO Response Force (NRF), and rationalizing of the Military Command Structure. The commitments are more focused than in the DCI and member states made firm commitments to ensuring their achievement, including a binding timetable. The PCC have also been included in the next five-year cycle of NATO defense planning, the Force Goals 2008. In addition, the PCC are related to the European Capabilities Action Plan that aims at implementing the Helsinki Headline Goals for a European Security and Defense Policy (ESDP) of the European Union. This is a clear indication that the efforts of NATO and EU members to improve the defense capabilities of both organizations are now no longer perceived as being in competition but rather are being seen as mutually reinforcing. Specific member states have also assumed responsibilities in providing leadership to and coordination for other participants in building up certain capabilities. Spain, with support from Denmark and the Netherlands, leads a group of members to improve aerial refueling capabilities. The Netherlands heads a four-partner consortium to organize purchases of precision-guided munitions. Norway takes the lead of members engaged in developing Special Forces; the Czech Republic steers a group gathered to improve defenses against nuclear, biological and chemical attacks. And Germany leads the group of members in charge of improving airlift capabilities. The next step of the PCC implementation process is to change national defense plans accordingly.

The movement from the DCI to the PCC confirms previously detected patterns of results in Alliance force planning. NATO allies do not meet commitments if the goals are too broad, unrealistic in light of existing defense budgets and are introduced outside of normal defense planning cycles. These experiences date back to the Lisbon Force goals of 1952 and the Long-Term Defense Program proposed by the Carter Administration in the late 1970s. However, after NATO adjusted its unrealistic goals and proposed more focused planning guidelines, allies have in the past met them in their essentials, if not always on time.

The NATO Response Force (NRF) was first proposed by US Secretary of Defense Donald Rumsfeld at an informal meeting of NATO defense ministers in Warsaw in September 2002. Its land component consists of 21,000 troops, made up of a brigade of some 5,000 troops, plus an air and a maritime component. The air element must be capable of a minimum of 200 sorties per day. The force will be on high readiness, which is defined as being available for out of area deployment within five to 30 days. It will be capable of fighting as a stand-alone force for 30 days or of securing, without host nation support, initial entry into a theater for follow-on forces. The timetable foresees an initial capacity by October 2004 and a full capability by October 2006.

The NRF is a nucleus around which a larger military force might be built. This bigger force will also be capable of fulfilling similar roles and missions to those of the NRF. NATO's new response force is helpful because it is based on a better understanding of contingencies and the types of missions that will be necessary in the future. The European allies accepted the principle of out of area missions that move military operations away from territorial defense. Despite initial skepticism,[12] the NRF concept has been accepted and more recent comments by European defense ministers indicate that it now serves as guidance for the restructuring of national militaries as well.

The Heads of State and Government also decided to further streamline NATO's command structure. SHAPE will remain the only strategic command headquarters in NATO. The other of the two operational strategic commands, SACLANT has been turned into a functional command in charge of transformation issues. It will facilitate interoperability of national forces and guide the national processes of force modernization.

These recent developments on the Prague Capabilities Commitments, the NATO Response Force and the streamlining of the command structure are all very much in line with the strategic concept first outlined in 1999. They represent reasonable and not unpredictable adjustments in light of the 9/11 attacks and the limited defense budgets of the European partners. They also confirm previously established patterns of force development and planning in NATO dating from the Cold War. They are evidence of the viability of NATO as an institution that has not become irrelevant but rather is a robust organization that is able to incrementally adjust to a changing international environment.

To accommodate new NATO requirements, national member states took steps to streamline, restructure, and reform their armed forces and command structures. Most importantly, they created multi-national units to allow for extremely deep forms of integration below the corps and, in some instances, the divisional level. Furthermore, they adjusted their individual armed forces to allow combined joint task forces, units similar to those used by the US Central Command for operations in Afghanistan. And finally, they created special operations forces that exercised and trained with their counterparts in other allied countries, including those of the United States and United Kingdom.

Shaping domestic politics: the impact of the mutual defense clause activation on Germany

The decision by NATO to invoke Article 5 also yielded a number of important effects in Alliance member states. Since it is impossible to provide a detailed analysis of the impact in all of the member states, I chose to concentrate on the case of Germany, not least because it has the most stringent domestic criteria for the authorization of the use of force. Most importantly, it shaped the discourse of the domestic debate. Initial concerns in some quarters that the war on terrorism might divide the Alliance, drive a wedge between the United States and its coalition partners, or evoke prohibitive opposition and protest in Western societies were shown to be unfounded. Supported by the main coalition and opposition parties, Chancellor Gerhard Schröder spoke of the terrorist attacks as a 'declaration of war' against the civilized world and assured President George Bush of the 'unrestricted solidarity' of Germany. In addition, the German commitment allowed Chancellor Schröder to discipline dissenting members of his governing coalition parties by forcing a vote of confidence authorizing the use of military force.

The debates in the German Parliament (Bundestag) accurately reflected the national discourse.[13] The content of the arguments, the strength of the support, and the focus of the discourse on Germany's international reputation rather than on its national interest pointed out the importance of honoring international commitments. NATO's Article 5 invocation helped German policy-makers change the focus of the discourse to concentrate on multilateral motives. No one engaged in a debate about how to define 'self-defense'. The risks involved in military operations were not considered. And nobody kept insisting on requesting limited, let alone comprehensive, information and consultation. Instead, the leader of the parliamentary opposition, Friedrich Merz, explained: 'NATO triggering the mutual assistance clause ... is the expression that it is in our own interest to participate without hesitation in the battle against international terrorism'. Gerhard Schröder emphasized: 'in short, the reliability of our policy is at stake....We must meet the expectations of our partners'. Peter Struck, the leader of the SPD parliamentary party, added that mutual defense in NATO is a constant. 'This constant may not be eliminated when our solidarity is required for the first time'. Using different words, all speakers argued that the invocation of Article 5 redefined German national interest by putting its reliability and reputation as an ally on the line. 'In such a situation,' Schröder explained, 'it is also indispensable that the chancellor and the government can count on the support of a majority by the coalition parties'. Therefore, he combined the vote to authorize the German military contribution to the war in Afghanistan with a vote of confidence (under Article 68 of the German Constitution). Schröder considered it necessary to demonstrate to Germany's allies that the German government would do whatever it takes to maintain its reliability, and that he personally was not afraid of risking his own political future. Maintaining the perception of being a reliable and predictable partner who meets responsibilities and commitments in times of crisis became the overriding priority of German foreign policy after NATO voted on Article 5. This concern dwarfed all other arguments and considerations in the debate and pushed the critics, both inside and outside of the governing coalition parties, to the fringes. The chancellor and party leaders twisted the arms of pacifist members of the coalition parties who grudgingly bowed to the pressure. The Bundestag voted 336 to 326 to express its confidence in the Chancellor.

However, without sustained support from NATO, the national discourses can easily shift back from international reputation to national interest, as two recent German decisions demonstrated. The Federal Government refused to participate in a war against Iraq because it considers it as against German interest. In addition, when it requested that the Bundestag extend the mandate for Germany's participation in ISAF and Enduring Freedom in Afghanistan, it argued that recent terrorist attacks in Djerba, Bali and against a French oil tanker demonstrated the continued threats against Germany. It is in the German interest to defend itself against such acts of aggression.

Yet, the important point is that absent a new NATO decision, the German government framed its justification in terms of the national interest discourse rather than international reputation. This recent shift has important implications for both Alliance cohesion and transatlantic relations.

Iraq, Turkey, and NATO's cohesion

When NATO invoked Article 5 by considering the attacks on 11 September 2001 as a threat to all member states after remarkably little debate in the NAC and in national capitals, the Alliance looked cohesive and strong. However, the conflict among allies over the war in Iraq and how best to defend Turkey in case of an Iraqi attack sent the opposite message, one of an divided and weak Alliance to member governments, potential enemies, and the general public. The key difference between these two cases is that the member states had previously committed to collective defense under Article 5 conditions, i.e. an armed attack from abroad. This peacetime commitment had enormously simplified and structured decision-making in NATO. The only issue to be discussed was whether or not the attacks of 11 September met the conditions of Article 5. Once this was established member states were asked to make available requested assets to meet collective defense missions. Failing to meet these requests would have undermined collective defense. Under the best of circumstances, the reluctant member would have been excluded from the collective defense arrangements. Under the worst of circumstances, the Alliance would have been dissolved. In light of these unattractive options, member governments had to make every effort necessary in accordance with Article 11 to meet NATO requests even, in some cases, against domestic opposition. The clear lesson is that when an existing peacetime commitment is activated, NATO, as an institution, structures and simplifies the multilateral and domestic decision-making processes to ensure Alliance cohesion.[14]

The war in Iraq, however, did not meet any contingencies for which the allies had made specific commitments during peacetime. The case covered much more uncharted territory, offering a huge number of problems and options for consideration at both the multilateral and domestic levels. Turkey, encouraged by the US, reduced some of this complexity when it invoked Article 4 of the NATO treaty. It requested that NATO headquarters start contingency planning for the defense of Turkey in case of an Iraqi attack and that its allies prepare to defend Turkey, e.g. by deploying AWACS and PATRIOT air defense missile systems. France, Germany, and Belgium perceived these requests as an American attempt at entrapment, as steps to move them towards support of a pending UN resolution authorizing the war in Iraq. Resisting considerable pressure in the North Atlantic Council (NAC), they blocked a multilateral decision authorizing NATO to meet Turkey's requests. They did, however, make the requested national assets available on a bilateral rather than a multilateral basis – an option that the North Atlantic treaty offers to all member states. By adopting this approach, they sought to avoid a potentially open-ended commitment to NATO involvement in the Iraq war and to voting in the UN Security Council, while simultaneously meeting Turkey's request for their national military assets in order to defend their ally in case of an Iraqi attack.

The events leading to the deployment of multilateral assets to protect Turkey, i.e. AWACS, are also extremely instructive. In light of Belgium's reluctance to give its approval for such a step in the Defense Planning Committee, Secretary General Lord Robertson told the Belgium representative that he already had the pre-delegated authority to deploy AWACS to Konya, Turkey, i.e. one of the Forward Operation Bases (FOB) for these systems. Robertson said he was prepared to do so with or without Belgium consent. This threat of NATO action against the veto of one of the member states effectively removed Belgium's resistance and restored Alliance cohesion. In this case the key mechanism was the pre-delegation of authority to the Secretary General or to SACEUR that ensured NATO's effectiveness against the potential veto of a reluctant ally. It is therefore important to understand how these two mechanisms – contingency planning and national collective defense commitments during peacetime, as well as the pre-delegation of authority – contribute to the cohesion of NATO.

Contingency planning for 'out of area' missions

Consensus building among 19 member states on non-Article 5 issues has proved to be the most difficult issue. Intergovernmental organizations such as NATO operate on the basis of unanimous rather than majority voting rule. Recently, the debate on NATO has moved towards changing this consensus rule.[15] Yet, once policy-makers understand the implication of such a drastic change, I doubt whether the proposal stands much of a chance of implementation. Therefore, I am proposing here a viable alternative. NATO should engage in more detailed political and military contingency planning on possible 'out of area' missions. If allies can agree on a set of contingencies that include conditions for out of area missions, crisis decision-making will be far more structured, focused, simplified, and – most importantly – efficient. I suggest the setting up of a tree of key decisions.

The first thing that needs to happen is for NATO allies to agree what constitutes the out of area cases in which NATO has an interest in becoming involved. It is important that these cases cover not only military contingencies, such as threats to allied forces operating outside the NATO territory, but also cases of conflict prevention that involve the use of polit-ical and economic means. The entire range of potential Petersberg and non-Petersberg tasks has to be considered. Second, contingencies must also be categorized according to the stakes involved for one or more allies or for

NATO as a whole. The higher the stakes are, the lower the number of conditions for collective action. Third, the risks of NATO engagement must be assessed. The higher the risks, the more stringent the conditions that will apply to gain approval for a mission will need to be. Fourth, NATO must determine what kind of political approval is necessary to carry out a mission. Finally, based on an approved mandate, a certain kind of mission can be carried out.

This proposed tree structure (Figure 9.1) could be amended as deemed necessary. For example, NATO can make distinctions about the degree of its involvement. Such distinction may include NATO controlled operations (Kosovo), NATO supported operations of one or more allies (Berlin-plus), NATO aided operations (Poland in Iraq), or NATO approved bilateral support of an ally's defense (AWACS, PATRIOTS to Turkey). Conditions for approval may also vary according to the degree of NATO involvement. The less involved NATO will be, the lesser the requirements for approval.

Such a structured decision-making tree – to demonstrate the principle Figure 9.1 is only a simplified example for a much more elaborate and complex structure – provides several advantages to an intergovernmental organization. First, it simplifies decision-making among allies and in national capitals because any crisis that arises can be matched to and categorized with a limited number of prepared cases. The first crisis decision

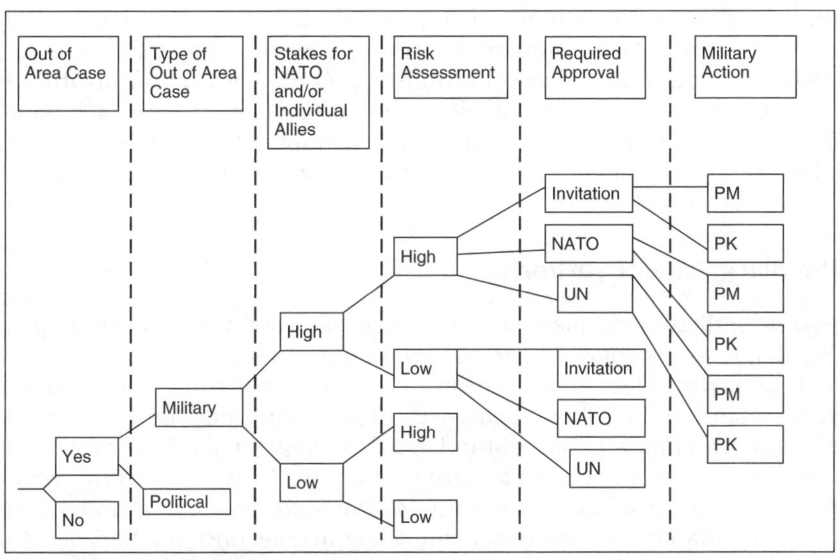

Figure 9.1 Out of area decision-making tree

will be to determine to which set of cases the unfolding crisis best fits. This decision would then set in motion a train of subsequent decisions. The choices at these intersections have already been prepared in peacetime, including some conditions determining which way the Alliance is likely to move if conditions are met. Second, this procedure increases the transparency of decision-making for all allies involved and thus serves to rationalize behavior.

Third, it increases the predictability of both the likely outcome of Alliance decision-making and the behavior of member states because they have already committed to a course of action under different sets of conditions.

All three advantages together provide for stronger Alliance cohesion and a more effective course of action. Pre-planned contingencies also guard against diverging policies in times of crisis, divisions that can lead to frustration and inertia. In addition, NATO could conduct planning exercises to test the viability of each type of contingencies, which would then enable each member state to assess the strength of the commitments of others.

I do not argue that setting up such a decision-making tree will be easy or uncontroversial. The opposite is the case. I would argue, however, that it would be easier and less consequential to determine whether or not allies can agree on certain contingencies in peacetime than it is during a crisis. NATO should not wait until it ends up looking bad in a crisis, but rather try to be prepared for such situations. The choice for the allies is not whether they wish to make these decisions but when they want to make them and under what time-constraints. Overall, such an exercise would also help each member state in determining for themselves in what contingencies and under what conditions NATO will be a useful institution for achieving security and for which contingencies it is not a suitable device. Depending on the results, each member state can then decide whether its investments and stake in NATO generates a reasonable rate of security provision return.

Pre-delegation of authority

NATO's military headquarters also have to prepare for military contingencies that involve deployment in out of area missions. The NAC has to review and approve these contingencies. However, the NAC and national governments should limit themselves to approving military contingency plans in peacetime and then authorizing their employment in a crisis, rather than trying to micromanage a 'war by committee'. Therefore, contingency plans need to spell out the authority of the Secretary General and – even more importantly – the military commander in chief once the NAC decided to employ a certain contingency plan.

The SHAPE system and the Military Committee mean that member governments should have confidence in the professional competence of

NATO commanders and trust their professional judgment. Most of them have representation in SHAPE and national officers participate in the military contingency planning processes of NATO headquarters. However, pre-delegation of authority requires that NATO headquarters, staffed with allied officers representing the member states, will actually take operational command in 'out of area' missions. Field commanders of NATO forces should report to SACEUR, SHAPE or its subordinated headquarters. Pre-delegation of authority is politically more problematic to the commander of a national headquarters of a member state if a representative cross-section of allied officers did not participate in the military contingency planning process.

Conclusions

Contrary to the often-heard argument that the 11 September terrorist attacks marginalized NATO, I have argued that the Alliance proved its purpose and functioning. It was able to respond quickly and effectively to the attack. NATO members did not run for the exit, but engaged in collective defense when they invoked Article 5. Swift decision-making provided strong evidence for the functionality of NATO's general assets, such as its decision-making procedures. NATO's institutions still provide the binding ties among allies that have significant 'second image reversed' effects on member states. Multilateralism by NATO reaches into member states and can change their policies and politics.

NATO's mutual defense reflex points out the political preparedness and value of the Alliance. The Washington Summit in April 1999 laid the ground for the 12 September 2001 decision, by committing the allies to mutual defense in case of a terrorist attack. The initiative for the invocation of Article 5 did not come from Washington, DC, but from NATO headquarters in Brussels. All allies, including the United States, went along with NATO's plan without hesitation. Washington did not choose to veto the invocation of Article 5 or ignore NATO's condition to submit evidence that the attack was directed from abroad. Also, it submitted a list of requests on how NATO could most effectively assist its war efforts. In addition to meeting multilateral and bilateral requests for assistance, other allies chose to take unilateral measures after Article 5 was invoked.

NATO had also prepared militarily for a wide range of Article 5 contingencies that were encompassed by terrorist attacks. It engaged in a fundamental restructuring of its armed forces and command structures. Furthermore, it guided the planning process of national military reforms in member states. While considerable defense deficiencies remain, it is important to note that NATO was on the right track even though the process was frustratingly slow. Even if anyone had anticipated the terrorist attack on 11 September 2001, NATO would not have prepared differently. Priorities and programs would still have been the same. However, the planned reforms might have been speeded up.

Finally, NATO's decision shaped domestic responses to the attack in individual member nations, by establishing a new balance in the debates between national interests on the one hand and international responsibilities and reliability on the other. Allies became aware that their reputation as a partner was on the line, and they had to prove how they could meet their commitments. The Article 5 decision shaped the discourse in political debates in member states. Political leaders, like Chancellor Gerhard Schröder, put their own political futures on the line to discipline domestic opponents and to demonstrate their unwavering commitment to NATO and the United States as the attacked ally.

In sum, NATO proved itself to be far from being irrelevant. It has repeatedly demonstrated its political and military value. It responded automatically to the attacks with the mutual defense reflex. Its response shaped national decisions and behavior in two distinct second image reversed effects. First, and long-term, it had guided national military reforms in accordance with its revised threat assessment based on a new strategic concept. Second, and short-term, its Article 5 decision shaped national responses and domestic debates to ensure that previous commitments to mutual defense were honored. However, NATO appeared weak, divided and indecisive when no contingency plans were in place prior to an important decision, such as the war in Iraq, and when authority was not pre-delegated to the military commanders under specified conditions. Future NATO reforms must address this weakness in addition to the ongoing process of improving its military capabilities.

Notes

1. I gratefully acknowledge comments by R. Art, F. Burwell, L. Gardner-Feldman, P. Katzenstein, R. Keohane, A. Moens, T. Oelstrom, T. Remington, S. Sloan, and C. Wallander as well as by the participants of the Conference on NATO and the Future: Risks and Relevance; Challenges and Opportunities, Bureau of Intelligence and Research, US Department of State, Arlington, VA, 28–29 October 2003 on an earlier drafts of this chapter. A version with more detailed references has been published in *International Politics*, Vol. 40, No. 1 (2003) 101–20.
2. See the academic debate: R. Wolf, 'Was hält siegreiche Verbündete zusammen? Machtpolitische, institutionelle und innenpolitische Faktoren im Vergleich,' *Zeitschrift für internationale Beziehungen*, Vol. 7, No. 1 (2000), 33–78; Reinhard Wolf, *Partnerschaft oder Rivalität?* (Baden-Baden: Nomos Verlagsgesellschaft, 2001); G. Hellmann and R. Wolf, 'Neorealism, Neoliberal Institutionalism, and the Future of NATO,' *Security Studies*, Vol. 3, No. 1 (1993), 3–43; G. Hellmann and R. Wolf, 'Wider die schleichende Erosion der NATO. Der Fortbestand des westlichen Bündnisses ist nicht selbstverständlich' in W. Link, E. Schuett-Wetschky and G. Schwan, eds, *Jahrbuch für Politik 1993, Halbband 2* (Baden-Baden: Nomos Verlagsgesellschaft,

1993), pp. 285–314; J. J. Mearsheimer, 'Back to the future: Instability in Europe after the cold war', pp. 78–129 in M. E. Brown, S. Lynn-Jonnes and S. E. Miller, eds, *The perils of Anarchy. Contemporary Realism and International Security* (Cambridge, MA: MIT Press 1995); C. A. Wallander, 'Institutional Assets and Adaptability. NATO after the Cold War,' *International Organisation*, Vol. 54, No. 4 (2000) 705–35; C. Tuschhoff, 'Alliance Cohesion and Peaceful Change in the NATO,' pp. 140–61 in H. Haftendorn, R. O. Keohane and C. A. Wallander, eds, *Imperfect Unions. Security Institutions over Time and Space* (Oxford, New York: Oxford University Press, 1999).

3. D. Puhl, 'Where's Germany's Grand Strategy?' http://www.aicgs.org/topics/911/ puhl.shtml (12 November 2002); D. Schuemer, 'Getrennt Abmarschieren: Europa in der neuen Weltordnung,' *Frankfurter Allgemeine Zeitung* (12 December 2001) 43; M. Inacker, 'Grosse Worte, kleine Muenze,' *Frankfurter Allgemeine Zeitung* (3 February 2002) 3. For a contending view see Clark 2002. More recently, observers added that the political coalitions formed after 11 September 2001 do not provide a solid and enduring basis of consensus on the political strategy against terrorism and crucial policies; Lothar Ruehl, 'Der Krieg gegen den Terror droht zu zersplittern' *Frankfurter Allgemeine Zeitung* (12 February 2002) 10; K-D. Frankenberger, 'Selbstberauschung und Larmoyanz.' *Frankfurter Allgemeine Zeitung*, Zeitgeschehen. (12 February 2002) 10.

4. Christian Tuschhoff, *Deutschland, Kernwaffen und die NATO 1949–1967. Eine Untersuchung zum Zusammenhalt von und friedlichem Wandel in Bündnissen* [Germany, Nuclear Weapons, and NATO. An Analysis of the Cohesion and Peaceful Change in Alliances]. Internationale Politik und Sicherheit (30/7), Stiftung Wissenschaft und Politik, Baden-Baden: Nomos Verlagsgesellschaft. 2002.

5. M. Kaminski, P. Hofheinz *et al.*, 'NATO allies back Bush in war on terrorist "evil" ', *Wall Street Journal Europe* (13 September 2001), UK1; P. H. Gordon, 'NATO after September 11,' *Survival*, Vol. 43, No. 4 (2001–02) 89–106.

6. NATO, 'The Washington Declaration', Press Release NAC-S (99)63 (23 April 1999), http://www.nato.int/docu/pr/1999/p99-063e.htm (12 November 2002).

7. NATO, Washington, Summit Communiqué, Press Release NAC-S (99) 64, 24 April 1999 (http:/www.nato.int/docu/pr/1999/p99-064e.htm); NATO, The Alliance's Strategic Concept, Press Release NAC-S (99) 63, 24 April 1999 (http://www.nato.int/ docu/pr/1999/p99-065e.htm).

8. Previous documents used similarly standardized language when treating acts of terrorism as criminal offenses that violated human dignity and rights. In coping with it NATO promised more cooperation in this field. See, for example, 'Declaration on Terrorism,' North Atlantic Council (10 December 1981).

9. J. Kitfield, 'NATO Is Too Busy to Be Irrelevant', *National Journal* (9 February 2002).

10. S. Daley, 'NATO, though supportive, has little to offer militarily,' *New York Times* (20 September 2001) B5.

11. NATO, Prague Summit Declaration, issued by the Heads of Staten and Government on 21 November 2002 Press Release (2002) 127, 2002 [cited 12 December 2002]. Available from http://www.nato.int/docu/pr/2002/p02-127e.htm, R. G. Kaiser and K. B. Richburg. 'NATO Looking Ahead to a Mission Makeover. New Members, Force and Philosophy.' *Washington Post* (5 November 2002) A 1.

12. G. Baker. 'NATO is not Dead but Missing in Action'. *Financial Times* (21 November 2002) 21; Judy Dempsey, 'If Bush does not make clear that NATO can be involved in critical issues, the Alliance will atrophy'. *Financial Times* (20 November 2002) 19.

13. The *Bundestag* debated the issue several times. Quotes and references are taken from the following meetings: session 186 of the 14th *Bundestag* (12 September

2001), 187 (19 September 2001); 192 (11 October 2001); 202 (16 November 2001). All translations are mine.

14. NATO's swift military reinforcements of its peacekeeping troops in Kosovo after the outbreak of ethnic violence in March 2004 is also evidence for Alliance cohesion and effectiveness when commitments are clear and agreed procedures are in place.

15. L. G. Michael, 'NATO Decisionmaking: Au Revoir to the Consensus Rule?' *Strategic Forum*, No. 202 (Institute for National Strategic Studies, National Defense University: August 2003) 1–8.

Part III

European Crisis Management and Conflict Prevention

10
The European 'Centaur': Power and Authority in Europe's Society of States

Adrian Hyde-Price

The puzzle of European order

The collapse of communism and the geopolitical transformation of European international society sparked a major debate on the nature of the post-Cold War European security system. This debate acquired a new momentum after the events of 11 September 2001 and the subsequent war in Iraq, which exposed deep divisions within the transatlantic relationship and within Europe itself. At the heart of this debate on the future of Europe is the question of order. What is the underlying ordering principle upon which contemporary European international society is based? How has the demise of bipolarity affected this ordering principle? Is European order still based on Westphalian principles such as state sovereignty? Above all, what is the mix between power politics and consensual authority, and what is the role of military force in the reshaping of European order?

These questions touch on issues at the very heart of the post-Cold War European security system. Is the European security system still characterized by the security dilemma and security competition, or has a more cooperative system of international order emerged? The question of the nature of international order is one of the most fundamental questions of International Relations as an academic discipline – indeed, it is one of *the* questions that is constitutive of international relations as a discipline.[1]

Machiavelli's Centaur and European order

In attempting to conceptualize the contradictory and complex nature of the European security order – with its mix of power politics and authority, coercion and consent – Machiavelli's allegory of the Centaur, 'half beast and half man', provides an excellent starting-point. Machiavelli believed that the foundation of any political order was 'good laws and good arms' – in other words, a judicious mix of force and authority, coercion and consent, power and hegemony.[2] Indeed, he believed that 'good arms' were an inescapable prerequisite for 'good laws', and that 'where there are good

[arms], good laws inevitably follow'. This line of thought was picked up by Antonio Gramsci, who spoke of the 'dual perspective' in political life 'corresponding to Machiavelli's Centaur – half animal and half-human'. Gramsci's concept of the dual perspective referred to 'the levels of force and consent, authority and hegemony, violence and civilisation, of the individual moment and the universal moment',[3] and so on.

The allegory of the centaur provides a good image of the nature of international order because it points to the existence of elements of both power and force on the one hand, and consent and legitimate authority on the other. The history of European international society since the emergence of the modern states system provides ample evidence for this dynamic, if not dialectical, understanding of the nature of international order. Whatever institutional architecture has been created, and whatever the normative understandings reached by the great powers, a stable international order has also been underpinned by a distinct set of power relationships – most usually, in the form of a bi- or multi-polar balance of power. All systems of international order thus rest on a mix of two distinct forms of conflict resolution, and involve elements both of force and consent, power and authority.

The dialectical unity between force and consent in international order – which Machiavelli's allegory of the Centaur captures so well – is best understood in terms of an enduring and ineluctable tension between the power and authority models of politics. As Ian Clark has argued, all international political practice can be encompassed within two distinct models of conflict resolution: the *power model* and the *authority model*. The former involves 'the unbridled interplay of opposing forces in which the capabilities of the contestants will determine the outcome', and involves a continuum of practices 'that begins with diplomacy and bargaining and ends with outright violence'. It also includes the 'many decisions, or non-decisions, that are made by those more powerful parties who do not actually have to employ their force but can keep it tacitly in the background'. The authority model, on the other hand, involves the creation of decision-making procedures that are widely regarded by each of the constituent units as legitimate. It describes 'the whole history of efforts to establish norms, procedures, techniques and institutions that might compensate for the absence of a supreme decision-making body within the international system'. Clark notes that historically, forms of international order have not corresponded directly to either of these two extremes, but have been combined in different degrees and ways. 'It is the tension, the conflict, the uneasy harmony between the power and the authority models of politics that provide the fascination in the study of international relations'.[4]

The 'English School' and international society approach

The approach to international relations that best captures the uneasy harmony between the power and authority models of politics, and which is most compatible with Machiavelli's allegory of the Centaur, is that of the 'English School'. The English School, whose leading exponents include Hedley Bull and Vincent Wright, argued that international order was best understood in terms of the concept of a 'society of states' (or 'international society'). This concept refers to the emergence of common interests and shared understandings between states through a process of continual diplomatic, political, economic, military and societal interaction over centuries. A 'society of states', Bull argued, 'exists when a group of states, conscious of certain common interests and common values, form a society in the sense that they conceive of themselves to be bound by a common set of rules in their relations with one another, and share the workings of common institutions'.[5] The most important of these common institutions are diplomacy, the balance of power, the management role of the great powers, international law and war. Their relative importance has changed over time, but taken together they form of normative and institutional framework for the emergence of order within the international system. Hedley Bull captured the essential tension and ambiguity at the heart of international society in the title of his seminal work, *The Anarchical Society*, a phrase that brilliantly encapsulates the nuances of the English School's Grotian approach to international relations.

The great strength of the international society approach is that it provides a *via media* between the Realist and Liberal traditions. It shares a number of classical realist assumptions (most notably, that concerning the importance of power in international relations), but also recognizes the importance of history and culture in generating shared norms, values and understandings. In contrast to neo-realism's parsimonious conception of international relations as a self-help system occupied by rational utility-maximizing unitary actors, whose interaction resembles balls on a billiard table, the English School emphasises the socially textured and historically evolving nature of Europe's society of states. International relations might be 'anarchic' in the sense that there is no sovereign authority able to enforce compliance and generate legally binding decisions, but it is an anarchic *society* composed of conscious and reflexive actors whose interactions with each other over time have led to the emergence of a framework of interaction structured by distinct institutions. 'International Relations', Ruggie has argued, 'like all social relations, exhibit *some* degree of institutionalization: at minimum, a mutual intelligibility of behaviour together with the communicative mechanisms and organizational routines which make that possible'.[6] The emergence and subsequent strengthening of this institutional framework for interaction is the result of a process of socialization. As David Armstrong has argued, international society 'is not just a juridical association but a framework within which multifaceted social interaction among states takes place – most intensively among the major liberal democracies'. In the course of such interaction, 'states are subject to a constant process of socialization in which they internalise each others' policies and practices across a wide sectrum, including economic, financial, educational and social policies'.[7]

The emergence of a society of states does not eradicate the struggle for power and influence in the international system, but it does refract, channel and moderate it. The institutions that characterize international society – the balance of power, management role of the great powers, diplomacy, war and international law – were specifically created to structure and regulate the struggle of power. Over time, they have acquired a strength and influence of their own, becoming embedded in the normative and material structures of international relations. At the same time, the struggle for power and influence between states has taken place in changing cultural and normative environments characterized by distinct sets of political norms and values. Together, the institutions of international society and the dominant norms and values of the historical period have functioned as intervening mechanisms that alter the structural dynamics of power politics in Europe's 'anarchic society'. The balance of power, for example, functioned most effectively during the eighteenth century 'Age of Reason', when decisions of war and peace were in the hands of absolutist rulers and diplomacy was largely divorced from ingrained patterns of enmity and amity. Once nationalism emerged as a potent political force and more sections of society began participating in government, however, the balance of power operated much less smoothly and mechanically.[8] The nature of war has also changed as political structures and normative values have evolved.[9] Thus while neo-realism's parsimonious theory can shed some light on the broad patterns of international relations, it misses the fine-grain of historical development. More importantly, neo-realism overlooks the element of learning inherent in a system consisting of sentient, reflexive actors. For this reason, neo-realism finds it hard to account for institutionalized multilateral and bilateral cooperation within the international system. This complex interplay of power and authority in Europe is evident from an analysis of the historical evolution and development of European international society.

Europe's society of states

The balance of power in Europe

Order in regional security complexes can take three forms: Balance of Power; hegemony; or constitutionalism.[10] These constitute 'ideal types' rather than mutually exclusive categories, and actual historical orders – as noted above – consist of mixtures of these ordering principles based on the power and authority models of conflict resolution.

Order in modern European history has primarily taken the form of the balance of power. Europe's variegated geography has encouraged a diversity and plurality of different political, economic and social institutions, often based on cultural, ethnic and linguistic differences. Much of European history can be read as a continual struggle by the leading states in the system to contain the hegemonic aspirations of the most powerful of their number. In contrast to China, India or Japan, the operation of the balance of power prevented the emergence of an alternative ordering principle based on hegemony. Thus the European state system that emerged from the Peace of Westphalia was characterized by ceaseless diplomatic activity and frequent wars among its member states, within a genuinely multi-polar structure. In the sixteenth century, Spain, France, Austria and England were the leading powers of Europe. In the early seventeenth century, they were briefly joined by Holland and Sweden, although these were later to be eclipsed by Russian and Prussia (Spain too was to lose its leading position in the mid-seventeenth century). By the early eighteenth century, the European international society had finally matured into a genuine multi-polar system in which there were five great powers (France, Britain, the Habsburg Empire, Russia and Brandenburg-Prussia) and a myriad of lesser powers. Within this multi-polar system, order was created primarily by the operation of the balance of power. Indeed, the eighteenth century has been described as the 'golden age of the balance of power'.[11] As one historian has noted, 'never before or since has it been the object of so much generally favourable discussion by so many different writers. Never before or since has a single idea been so clearly the organising principle in terms of which international relations in general were seen'.[12]

One distinctive feature of this multi-polar states system was the continued existence of almost all of the states of Europe (Poland being the only notable exception). This was by no means the case with other state systems, as the rise and fall of a plethora of mighty empires in the ancient world makes abundantly clear and was the outcome of a constantly shifting but generally maintained balance of power between the principal European states. For nearly four centuries, the pluralist and multi-polar state system in Europe that emerged at the end of the Middle Ages was able to contain successive bids for hegemony by the Spanish, Austrians and the French.

However, the internal equilibrium of the European state system was fatally undermined by the rise of German power at the end of the nineteenth century. The formation – by 'blood and iron' – of a centralized German state possessing substantial industrial, financial and human resources, and with enormous political and military potential, was to lead to the disintegration of the balance of power in Europe. Without American intervention in 1917, it is possible that Germany might have prevailed in the First World War, and it was the only the involvement of the Americans and the Soviets – Europe's two great flanking powers – which prevented German domination of the continent in 1939–45. The years from 1870 to 1945, therefore, are the years of the disintegration and collapse of the multi-polar European interstate system which – based primarily on the balance of power as its central ordering principle – had existed for over four centuries. The bipolar structure of international order that emerged in Europe after the end of the Cold War was characterized by the dominant role of the two superpowers in European affairs and the creation of two rival bloc systems. Within this bipolar framework, the United States played the role of an 'offshore balancer'. In providing a security guarantee to Western Europe to prevent Soviet hegemony, however, it also acted as Western Europe's 'pacifier'. Its military presence and political authority dampened down security competition throughout the Euro-Transatlantic area, thus facilitating a process of postwar reconciliation and institutionalized integration in Western Europe. It is important to note that this integration process and the subsequent emergence of what Karl Deutsch called a 'pluralistic security community' was made possible by a particular configuration of great power politics in the region. This meant that the strengthening of the 'authority model of international order occurred by working with the grain of power politics, not against it. As the allegory of the Centaur would suggest, the power and authority models coexisted in Cold War Western Europe, the strengthening of the authority model taking place under the protective umbrella of American military power.

The strengthening of the authority model

Whilst shifting patterns of power politics have provided much of the impetus behind the constitution of European order since the emergence of the modern states' system, they cannot account for some significant developments in the evolution of European international society. As the metaphor of the Centaur ('half-beast, half-man') suggests, all international orders involve combinations of power and authority, coercion and consent. One distinctive trend in modern European history, however, is the strengthening of the authority model of order. This is reflected in the growing use of various forms of institutionalized multilateral cooperation, first evident after the defeat of Napoleonic France in 1815, but attempted on a more ambitious scale following the defeat of Nazi Germany in 1945. 'Over time', John Ikenberry has argued, 'post-war settlements have moved in the direction of an institutionalised order, and have begun to take on constitutional characteristics';

> Power is exercised – at least to some extent – through agreed-upon institutional rules and practices, thereby limiting the capacities to states to exercise power in arbitrary and indiscriminate ways or use their power advantages to gain a permanent advantage over weaker states.[13]

One important reason why there has been a strengthening of the more consensual elements of order in Europe is that states are not simply insensate actors locked into the unyielding structural logic of an anarchic system.

Rather, they are complex institutional ensembles with a capacity for reflection and learning. The experience of war has encouraged the development of new and more sophisticated models of conflict management and resolution. Although states have not been able to escape the logic of anarchy, they have been able, to a greater or lesser extent, to moderate and tame its operation. This is best understood in terms of a shift away from what Oran Young has termed *spontaneous* or *self-generating systems* of order to either *imposed order* or *negotiated order*.

Spontaneous systems of order are not the product of human design, but emerge through the operation of the 'hidden hand' of international anarchy. They 'are distinguished by the facts that they do not involved conscious coordination among participants, do not require explicit consent on the part of subjects or prospective subjects, and are highly resistant to efforts at social engineering'.[14] In international society, spontaneous order primarily takes the form of the balance of power. *Imposed order* is 'fostered deliberately by dominant powers or consortia of dominant powers', and is exemplified by classical feudal arrangements as well as imperial systems. They involve the deployment of hard power resources in order to compel subordinate actors to conform if necessary. 'In short', Young argues, 'imposed regimes are established deliberately by dominant actors who succeed in getting orders to conform to the requirements of these arrangements through some combination of coercion, cooptation, and the manipulation of incentives'. A modern example of imposed order would be the Soviet bloc in postwar Eastern Europe. *Negotiated order*, on the other hand, is characterized by bargaining, consensus and the search for legitimate forms of international regulation. Systems of negotiated order involve 'conscious efforts to agree on their major provisions, explicit consent on the part of individual participants, and formal expression of the results'. Young distinguishes between 'comprehensive negotiated regimes' arising from careful and orderly negotiations, and 'those that can be described as partial or piecemeal'. 'Given the conflicts of interest prevalent in international society, however, it is to be expected that negotiated arrangements will often exhibit a piecemeal quality, leaving many issues to be settled through practice and precedent'.[15] The primary example of negotiated order would be postwar Western Europe and the European integration process.

The strengthening of the authority model of European order is manifested in the changing character of the five main institutions of international society, and in changes in their relative importance. In a nutshell, there has been a steady increase in the relative importance of diplomacy, international law and great power management of European international society, and a change in the character and relative importance of war and the balance of power. Changes in the character and structural importance of the institutions of international society have occurred primarily as a response to the experience of major wars, and has been reflected in the various peace settlements that have followed such conflicts.

The 1648 Peace of Westphalia was particularly significant in this respect. It formally institutionalized the modern states' system based on the legal equality of sovereign states, replacing the medieval structures of overlapping and interlocking authority and power institutionalized in the universalistic claims of the Catholic Church and the Holy Roman Empire. Within the Westphalian system, order was generated spontaneously by the operation of the balance of power between the major actors. With the 1713 Treaty of Utrecht, the balance of power was explicitly recognized as the formal basis of European order, and the role of Britain within it formally specified for the first time. This represented the shift from a *spontaneous* to a *negotiated* understanding of the operation of the balance of power between the great powers in Europe. The balance of power in Europe was to be regulated by a mix of diplomacy and periodic wars. For much of the eighteenth century, these wars were generally 'limited' in character, both in terms of their means and ends.[16] But with the French Revolution and wars of Napoleon, which unleashed the forces of nationalism across Europe, war once again became – in Clausewitz's words – 'the business of the people..., all of whom considered themselves to be citizens'. Fueled by the passions of nationalism, war thus became more brutal and more 'total' in character.[17]

With the end of the epochal wars of the French Revolution and Napoleon, the great powers attempted to reshape European order on a more consensual basis. The result of the 1815 Congress of Vienna was the 'Concert system', which sought to regularize the management of European affairs by the great powers. The concert system itself rested on a consciously constructed balance of power, and on the normative commitment to the status quo. For the great powers, therefore, this was a system of *negotiated order*, based on an explicit strengthening of the authority model. Henry Kissinger, who analyzed the Congress system in his classic 1957 study *A World Restored*, argued that

> [t]he foundation of a stable order is the *relative* security – and therefore the *relative* insecurity – of its members. Its stability reflects, not the absence of unsatisfied claims, but the absence of a grievance of such magnitude that redress will be sought in overturning the settlement rather than through an adjustment within its framework. An order whose structure is accepted by all major powers is 'legitimate'.... The security of a domestic order resides in the preponderant power of authority, that of an international order in the balance of forces and in its expression, the equilibrium.[18]

The great flaw of the Concert system was that it failed to recognize and address the potent force of nationalism. In the second half of the nineteenth century, the map of Europe was reshaped by the wars of Italian and German nationalism and unification. These transformed the distribution of power in the continent, above all in Central Europe, where the creation of a Prussian-dominated *Kleindeutschland* ('small Germany', i.e., without Austria) transformed Germany from the 'anvil' to the 'hammer' of the Westphalian states' system. The failure of European international society to accommodate the power of a united Germany was ultimately to lead to two world wars, each of which was followed by ambitious attempts to achieve a more consensual form of negotiated order based on a strengthening of the authority model of conflict management and resolution. The first followed the 1914–18 war and resulted from the Versailles peace settlement. This established the principle of national self-determination as a key ordering principle, and created the League of Nations as the institutional foundation for a new system of European order based on international law, collective security and multilateral diplomacy. Its failure was ultimately due to the lack of perceived legitimacy enjoyed by 'Versailles', and the increasingly revisionist foreign policies of the fascist powers and the USSR.

The post-1945 settlement of Yalta and Potsdam was an even more ambitious attempt to craft a negotiated order based on a strengthening of the authority model. Its center-point was the United Nations and the UN Charter, which, building on the foundations of the principle of state sovereignty, sought to make aggressive war illegal and fashion a new system of 'collective security'. It attempted to avoid the mistakes of the League of Nations by institutionalizing great power management of the international system in the form of the veto power enjoyed by the five permanent members of the Security Council. The Security Council was also given the principle authority for preserving international peace and security. At the same time, the UN included the potentially subversive notion of human rights as part of its constitutive values, thus laying the foundations for subsequent challenges to the principle of state sovereignty. The operation of the UN system was stymied for much of its history by the East–West conflict. Nonetheless, it provided a legal and normative framework within which a liberal international order was to emerge within the Western community of states. This liberal zone was based on institutionalized multilateral cooperation (in shape of the WTO, G7, OECD, EU), deepening economic interdependence and shared political norms and values.

Collective security in theory and practice

The principle of collective security, which was first raised in the context of the League of Nations and which lay at the heart of the UN system, was based on the idea that all members of the international community were jointly responsible for the security of each other. An attack on one would be regarded as an attack on all, and was to be met by the collective response of all. For some of its proponents, this was the antithesis of the balance of power, and represented a new and more morally acceptable principle of international order. Thus US President Woodrow Wilson declared that collective security would prevent wars and that what the international system needed was 'not a balance of power, but a community of power, not organized rivalry, but an organized common peace'.[19] As an 'ideal type', collective security does indeed constitute a significant break with the logic and rationale of the balance of power, which is based on competitive security and rival alliances. Collective security in its pure form represents an attempt to base international order on a 'universal' alliance involving a high degree of international cooperation, shared interests and a normative commitment to act on the basis of an enlightened self-interest to counter aggression against others, even if one's own national interests are not directly threatened.

In practice, however, the principle of collective security can be seen as representing a continuation and development of the balance of power, not its antithesis. As Martin Wight argued, President Wilson was only able to attempt the reshaping of international order because the United States had itself become part of the balance of power by entering the First World War in 1917. The League of Nations represented not so much a way of abolishing the balance of power, but as an attempt to institutionalize it, 'to make it work more automatically, more effectively and more rationally, to enable it to forestall more wars and to end the wars it could not forestall by a more decisive combination of power against the aggressor, wielded with a more coherent purpose'.[20] Both principles shared a common concern to manage power in the international system and to avoid hegemony, and both shared a general belief in the efficacy of deterrence. They also both assume that all states will look beyond their immediate national interests and consider the requirements of systemic, or international, security. Clausewitz, writing about the balance of power in the nineteenth century, argued that '[p]olitical relations, with their affinities and antipathies, had become so sensitive a nexus that no cannon could be fired in Europe without every government feeling its interest affected'.[21] Collective security similarly assumes that no cannon can be fired without all governments feeling their interests affected. Collective security in practice, therefore, can be seen as a logical outgrowth of the balance of power system of the eighteenth and nineteenth centuries, rather than a radically different ordering principle. In the same way as the Concert of Vienna system built on and refined the operation of the balance of power, collective security sought to provide the balance of power with legal underpinnings, thereby making it more rational, more reliable, and more efectively preventive.

The balance of power in contemporary Europe

It has been suggested that the main significance of the *annus mirabilis* of 1989 was that it spelt the end, not only of the Europe of Yalta, but also of the whole balance of power system in Europe. Thus the influential British diplomat Robert Cooper has argued that 'what happened in 1989 was not just the end of the Cold War, but also the end of the balance-of-power system in Europe'.[22] Similarly in 1997 US Secretary of State Madeline Albright argued that the fact that '[t]oday in Bosnia, virtually every nation in Europe is working together to bring stability to a region where conflict earlier this century tore the continent apart' represents 'a sharp departure from the spheres of influence or balance of power diplomacy of the past'.[23]

However, it can be argued that what ended in 1989 was not the balance of power *per se*, but a particular form or understanding of the balance of power associated with a Hobbesian world of *Realpolitik* and intense security competition. With the end of bipolarity, concerns about the relative power capabilities of other states continue to preoccupy Europe's major powers. After the collapse of the Soviet Union and the disintegration of the Warsaw Pact, NATO continued to justify its existence in terms of the need to balance the residual military power of Russia. Similarly, Russian security policy has increasingly been framed in terms of the perceived need to maintain multi-polarity and avoid hegemony in Europe. German unification was also accompanied by oft-voiced concerns about the potential power of an enlarged Germany, concerns that led to collaborative international efforts to embed Germany in multilateral structures and reduce its conventional military capabilities. Power political considerations thus remain of concern to European states. However, they do not manifest themselves in an atmosphere of tension and uncertainty, and do not lead to an unremitting struggle to survive and expand. Instead, the balance of power operates in the context of a society of states structured by a series of regularized patterns of behaviour and normative values. The operation of the balance of power in contemporary Europe can thus be understood in 'associative' rather than 'adversarial' terms. The concept of the balance of power is widely associated with realist theory and power politics, which is rooted in a Hobbesian view of the international system. However, as Richard Little has argued, there is also an 'associative' concept of the balance of power rooted in the Grotian tradition. Whereas the former 'depicts political actors in competitive and self-interested terms', the latter 'assumes that in a balance of power political actors an be cooperative and pursue policies which embrace the interests of others'.[24] An associative balance of power is based not simply on a military balance against expansionist or revisionist states, but on an international order which recognizes and harmonizes the interests of all states, and which is therefore perceived as just and legitimate by all of the major powers. The balance of power is thus not the incidental by-product of a selfish pursuit of national interests by individual states, but is rather the result of a deliberately fostered equilibrium.[25] The prime historical example of this is the diplomacy, centered on the Concert of Vienna, which was practiced by Metternich and Castlereagh.

This Grotian understanding of the balance of power informs the work of Hedley Bull, who saw the balance of power – in its associative rather than adversarial form – as a primary institutional expression of the emergence of a 'society of states'. According to this understanding, the balance of power was a mechanism for establishing an international 'equilibrium' between the major powers such that none could dominate the others, thereby enabling the 'social' aspects of the international system – like diplomacy and international law – to flourish. This Grotian approach to the balance of power is best understood by recognizing the problem for which the balance of power was a partial solution in the early period of the modern states' system. The balance of power was a way of reconciling two apparently contradictory requirements: the desire to sustain a society of states based on a multiplicity of competing sovereign states; and the wish to preserve the ideal of a European international community sharing common values, institutions and aspirations. In this way, the balance of power idea was an important catalyst for encouraging political leaders to think in terms of an interdependent international system, thereby stimulating a shared appreciation of the value of a 'society of states', in which coercive power would be mitigated by more consensual forms of authority. If the balance of power in contemporary Europe is to exercise a positive role in post-Cold War Europe, Michael Sheehan argues, it must be in its Grotian form. 'The sophistication of the mid-nineteenth-century notion of equilibrium needs to be combined with late-twentieth-century ideas on collective security, common security and arms control to produce an 'equilibrium' based upon the right of states and individuals to equal security'. The balance of power is not going to disappear, he argues, but 'it is the Grotin image which offers by far the greatest possibility for achieving a future in which the incidence of war and the threat of war are significantly diminished and a more mature version of 'anarchy' prevails which supports the continuing development of the societal elements of the international system'.[26]

The balance of power has therefore not disappeared as one of the institutional pillar of European international society, but its character and functioning has changed. Europe's great powers continue to keep a wary eye on the relative distribution of power and influence, and the continent's small and medium-sized states remain concerned about their place in the power structure created by the interaction of the great powers. But as even proponents of offensive realism acknowledge, this has not manifested itself in intense security competition and arms races. This is because residual Russian military power is balanced by the United States and NATO, and there is a rough parity in power between Europe's second order states – Germany, France and the United Kingdom. There are no major sources of tension; no great power perceives Europe's post-Cold War order as illegitimate; and no country is in a position to strive for hegemony. In this context of balanced multi-polarity, the European balance of power is manifested in its 'associative' form, and contains a strong element of cooperation and consensus. This is evident from the emergence of informal structures of great power management of European international society – a 'concert system' – most evident from the work of the 'Contact Group' in Bosnia.

From war to coercive diplomacy

The transformation of European international society in late modern Europe is also evident from the changed character and function of war. With the end of the Cold War, there was a widespread sense of optimism that military conflict could be effectively eradicated from Europe's 'zone of peace' and disputes settled by preventive diplomacy and conflict management. However, with the violent break-up of Yugoslavia and a series of bloody conflicts around the periphery of the former Soviet Union, this optimism quickly evaporated. The paradox of post-Cold War European security is that despite the end of the East–West conflict, with its associated threat of nuclear Armageddon, Europe's armed forces have been busier than at any time in their recent history. Major war between the great powers in Europe might have become obsolete, but Western democracies continue to use military force as an instrument of state-craft. This raises the question of what role – if any – military force will play in the reshaping of European order in the twentieth century.

War, it has been said, is a 'floating signifier'. It is certainly true that there is often little consensus about when the use of force constitutes 'war'. During Operation Allied Force, for example, many European leaders strenuously avoided describing NATO's offensive bombing campaign against rump Yugoslavia as 'war'. Yet by almost any generally accepted definition, this is what it was. Certainly in Clausewitzean terms, it was war, i.e., 'an act of violence intended to compel our opponent to fulfil our will'.

One reason for the terminological inexactitude surrounding the use of force in contemporary Europe is that, like the balance of power, 'war' as an institution of European international society has changed its character and function. First, Western armed forces are no longer primarily concerned with collective territorial defence but with conducting expeditionary warfare and humanitarian intervention. European democracies, in other words, are no longer faced with the prospect of fighting 'wars of necessity' for national survival, but with 'wars of choice' or 'wars of conscience'. Secondly, modern Western war-fighting consciously eschews escalation and 'total' war – the defining features of both World Wars in the first part of the twentieth century. Instead, European democracies seek to use force discriminately in the context of strategies of coercion rather than wielding what Thomas Schelling called 'brute force'.[27] Coercive strategies involve the threat of force, or the use of limited force, to alter the decision-making calculus of the target state or actor. Strategic coercion – or 'coercive diplomacy' – is different from deterrence that seeks to prevent a threatened action from taking place, and from 'brute force', which is an all-out military assault to achieve one's goals. Strategic coercion involves a mix of diplomacy backed up by 'just enough force of an appropriate kind to demonstrate resolution and to give credibility to the threat that greater force will be used if neces-sary'.[28] It involves being able to convince the target state of one's political resolve and military capabilities. 'Even more so than with deterrence strategy important signalling, bargaining, and negotiating dimensions are built into the strategy of coercive diplomacy'.[29]

Thus war remains one of the constitutive institutions of contemporary European international society, even though its character and function has changed. The prospect of great power war has greatly receded, and 'wars of necessity' have given way to 'wars of choice' and 'wars of conscience'. In addition, military force is increasingly used discriminately in the context of coercive strategies, rather than as an instrument of 'brute force'.

State sovereignty or human rights?

In this chapter, we have considered how the elements of power and authority have interacted in European international society since the emergence of the Westphalian states' system in the seventeenth century, giving rise to distinct patterns of international order. The years since the end of the Cold War suggest that a potentially profound transformation in the constitutive principles of international order is currently underway. This arises from the clash between the principle of state sovereignty – which has provided the fundamental building block of international order and international law since the 1648 Peace of Westphalia – and the principle of human rights. The lesson of the 1990s, from Operation Restore Hope in the wake of the 1991 Gulf War to the Kosovo war in 1999, is that respect for basic human rights now takes priority over territorial sovereignty.

In the early twenty-first century, therefore, two fundamental ordering principles now co-exist in an uneasy and ambiguous relationship. European order is no longer solidly based on Westphalian principles of territorial sovereignty, but neither is it clear who has the authority to respond to gross violations of human rights, and how. With the Kosovo war, therefore, Europe has entered uncharted territory between two competing principles of international order. In his conclusion to his book on the Kosovo war, German Defense Minister Rudolf Scharping wrote that 'a new balance between two principles of international law needs to be worked out, namely state sovereignty and the universal validity of human rights. The conflict over Kosovo, the intervention against genocide and major crimes against humanity, is hopefully the start of such an international learning process'.[30]

Conclusion

The central theme of this chapter has been that while contemporary European international society is no longer a realm of intense security competition and naked power politics, neither has it emerged as an oasis of Kantian 'perpetual peace' and multilateral cooperation. Rather, Europe remains an 'anarchic society' based on a mix of power and authority. Machiavelli's metaphor of the Centaur thus remains pertinent for the modern 'princes' of our time. Europe's democracies must learn to act cooperatively and consensually when possible, but be capable and willing to use military force coercively to back up their diplomacy when necessary. In acting like the beast, however, Machiavelli stresses that one should not be like a lion and rely simply on 'brute force':

> So, as a prince is forced to know how to act like a beast, he should learn from the fox and the lion; because the lion is defenceless against traps and a fox is defenceless against wolves. Therefore one must be a fox in order to recognize traps, and a lion to frighten off wolves. Those who simply act like lions are stupid.[31]

Notes

1. All disciplines must be 'about' something, and as Iver Neumann has argued, '[o]rder in world society is an "about" which must remain constitutive of the discipline of IR'. Iver Neumann and Ole Waever, eds, *The Future of International Relations: Masters in the Making* (London: Routledge, 1997), p.368.
2. Writing specifically about the state, he argued that 'the main foundations of every state, ... are good laws and good arms; and because you cannot have good laws without good arms, and where there are good ones, good laws inevitably follow, I shall not discuss laws but give my attention to arms'. For a useful discussion of Machiavelli's contribution to the international relations, see Howard Williams, *International Relations and Political Theory* (Milton Keynes: Open University Press, 1992), pp.45–55.
3. A. Gramsci, *Selections from Prison Notebooks* (London: Lawrence and Wishart, 1971), pp.169–70.
4. I. Clark, *The Hierarchy of States: Reform and Resistance in the International Order* (Cambridge: Cambridge University Press, 1989), pp.14–16
5. H. Bull, *The Anarchical Society* (London: Macmillan, 1977), p.13.
6. J. Ruggie, *Constructing the World Polity* (London: Routledge, 1998), p.2.
7. D. Armstrong, 'Law, Justice and the Idea of a World Society', *International Affairs*, vol.7, no.3 (July 1999), 547–61 (560).
8. See M. Sheehan, *The Balance of Power. History and Theory* (London: Routledge, 1996), pp.98–9.
9. As Clausewitz argued, 'every age had its own kind of war, its own limiting conditions, and its own peculiar preconceptions'. The changing nature of war could only be understood 'if we consider the nature of states and societies as they are determined by their times and prevailing conditions. ... The semi-barbarous Tartars, the republics of antiquity, the feudal lords and trading cities of the Middle Ages, eighteenth-century kings and the rulers and peoples of the nineteenth century – all conducted war in their own particular way, using different methods and pursuing different aims'. Clausewitz, *On War* [1832] (Princeton: Princeton University Press, 1989), pp.593, 586.
10. J. Ikenberry, *After Victory: Institutions, Strategic Restraint, and the Rebuilding of Order After Major Wars* (New Jersey: Princeton University Press, 2001), pp.23–5.
11. H. Morgenthau, *Politics Among Nations*, fifth edn (New York: Knopf, 1978), p.196.

12. M. S. Anderson, *The Rise of Modern Diplomacy 1450–1919* (London: Longman, 1993), p.163. See also Sheehan, *op.cit.*, pp.97–116.
13. Ikenberry, *op.cit.*, p.19.
14. O. Young, *International Cooperation* (Ithaca: Cornell University Press, 1989), p.85.
15. *ibid.*, pp.88–9.
16. Jeremy Black, *Eighteenth Century Europe* (London: Macmillan, 1999), and M. S. Anderson, *Europe in the Eighteenth Century* (London: Longman, 1991).
17. Clausewitz, *op.cit.*, pp.592–3.
18. H. Kissinger, *A World Restored: Europe After Napoleon* (Gloucester, Mass.: Peter Smith, 1973 [1957]), p.145.
19. M. Wight, *Power Politics* (London: Penguin, 1973), p.207.
20. M. Wight, p.207
21. Clausewitz, p.590.
22. Robert Cooper, *The Postmodern State and the World Order* (London: Demos, 1996), p.7.
23. M. Albright, 'Review of Foreign Policy Agenda', US Information Service, London: US Embassy, 9 January 1997.
24. R. Little, 'Deconstructing the Balance of Power: Two Traditions of Thought', *Review of International Studies*, vol.15, 1989, 87–100 (88).
25. Sheehan, *op.cit.*, p.168.
26. Sheehan, *op.cit.*, pp.204–5.
27. T. Schelling, *Arms and Influence* (New Haven: Yale University Press, 1966).
28. Alexander George quoted in *Strategic Coercion*, edited by Lawrence Freedman (Oxford: Oxford University Press, 1998), p.20.
29. G. Craig and A. George, *Force and Statecraft: Diplomatic Problems of Our Time* (Oxford: Oxford University Press, 1995), p.196.
30. R. Scharping, *Wir Dürfen Nicht Wegsehen: Der Kosovo-Krieg und Europa* (Berlin: Ullstein Buchverlage, 1999), pp.222–3.
31. Machiavelli, *The Prince* (London: Penguin, 1962), p.99.

11
The European Union and Crisis Management

Kari Möttölä

Crisis management in the European Security Strategy

Crisis management is an increasingly central feature of the European Union's identity and profile as an international actor. Moreover, the Union's activities in crisis management underpin its functional position and practical role in multilateral cooperation. Finally, the Union's capability for crisis management constitutes one of its most powerful assets for shaping the international security order.

The significance of crisis management in the Common Foreign and Security Policy (CFSP) and the European Security and Defence Policy (ESDP) is made clear in *A Secure Europe in a Better World: European Security Strategy*[1] adopted by the European Union in 2003. As the first comprehensive security strategy of the Union, this document provides an assessment of threats, determines the Union's strategic objectives and outlines an improved capability for defending its interests and promoting its values. The security strategy gained additional significance because it was launched in parallel with the intergovernmental conference that was negotiating a draft constitutional treaty for the European Union, including significant steps forward in the area of external relations and the CFSP/ESDP. Three requirements, related to culture, function and power, explain why the initiative for *European Security Strategy* was taken and why it can have lasting value for the development of the Union and its external influence.

Strategy as culture

First, there is the concept of strategy itself. While there are a multitude of definitions of strategy, it refers to a purposeful behavior, based on an ends-means structure, by an actor such as a nation-state. For an international institution such as the European Union, it is a challenge to demonstrate consistency in its behavior and to embody actor-like capabilities to make and implement joint decisions. Moreover, strategy is connected with the potential for and use of power, including military power, in international relations. While its impact on international developments and events through common policies has become more tangible, the EU has traditionally been a civilian power and it has been identified as such by its members and others.[2]

An actor's strategic behavior is determined by factors that are socially constructed like interests, identities or worldview. It requires a coherent set of ideas, which a state, as a centrally governed social system, can channel to make decisions. Consequently, as a strategic actor the EU needs to have a strategic culture between both its individual members and also as a united entity. The *European Security Strategy* spells out these requirement by calling for 'a strategic culture that fosters early, rapid, and when necessary, robust intervention.'

According to the traditional viewpoint, strategic culture can only be created with the convergence of the member-states' ideas about the role of force in international relations. On the other hand, with the enlargement of the concept of security and the emergence of new threats, the non-military agenda is increasingly relevant for the welfare and survival of the Union and its members, and, because of this, also calls for strategic thinking. Strategic cultures of the member states are shaped by their particular historical experiences and geopolitical worldviews. The search for a Union strategy must go deeply into the mental maps and social structures of member states. The Union's strategic culture will be more than the sum of its member states' cultures, but whether, for example, it is a synthesis of these or reflects a dominant culture, remains a task for analysis.[3]

Cultures embedded in member states may be a source of strategic coherence and incoherence. Strategic choices, individual or collective, may be rational or social. To fulfil the traditional or realist notion of strategy, the European Union should, as the international environment becomes more demanding and pressing, be able to make rational choices out of a combination of social and national choices. It may well be, however, that the collective choice will remain social as well, reflecting the deeply felt and experienced liberal ideologies that are dominant in highly developed welfare societies. The question to be asked is whether the member states separately and the Union as a whole possess a sufficient consensus on the nature of strategic relations, their inevitability or amenability, and on the use of force.[4]

The *European Security Strategy* offers no direct or definitive advice on the future orientation of the Union towards the use of force as a collective action or indeed its acceptability in general. However, with two key concepts, one pertaining to and calling for the reform of the international order, *effective multilateralism*, and the other focussing on *preventive engagement* as a basic operational activity, the document reflects a consensus on the established strengths of the Union. International security cooperation should aim at strengthening the orderliness of the international system around common norms and institutions. Furthermore, the point of gravity should be on preventing conflicts from arising by the employment of a broad array of instruments that impact their societal and other root causes and a well-functioning practice of cooperation and coordination among relevant international institutions and other actors.

Strategy as function

Secondly, the preparation of the *European Security Strategy* has been viewed as another response to the frustrations and failures the Union has experienced, due to its inefficiency and disunity, in addressing violent conflicts and managing crises in its neighborhood and beyond. The debacle over Iraq was but the latest in a series of events that included such post-Cold War crises as the unravelling of the former Yugoslavia and the humanitarian catastrophe in Rwanda. The Union responded to earlier cases of insufficiency and failure with new steps aimed at enhancing its competence and capability for implementing joint actions. Most notable among them are the inclusion, in the Amsterdam Treaty on European Union (1997), of the Petersberg crisis management tasks in the CFSP and the introduction, in the Cologne, Helsinki and Nice documents (1999–2000), of the Common European Security and Defence Policy, which contains the military resources, decision-making and planning organs and partnership arrangements required to implement such tasks.[5]

The ESDP, along with the first two EU-led military missions that were completed in 2003, moved the Union onto the level of international security making traditionally identified with great powers or military alliances such as NATO. The *European Security Strategy*, dealing with the prevention and management of conflicts and such radical new threats as terrorism and the proliferation of weapons of mass destruction, is another effort to bolster the ESDP. At the same time, reflecting a comprehensive concept of security, the strategy covers the CFSP as a whole and the external relations conducted in the Community pillar, the one that involves economic and humanitarian resources. To be more effective not only requires the usability of the Union's newly acquired military and civilian resources for crisis management but also the whole spectrum of its civilian instruments, those that are aimed at promoting economic reform, development, good governance, stabilization and conflict prevention.

In parallel with the employment of the wide selection of instruments for managing globalization, supporting stabilization and promoting political and economic transition, the EU has, as a matter of high priority, strengthened its capacity for conflict prevention. Institutional requirements for conflict prevention have become more demanding, as they call for early engagement, warning and action in situations and regions where difficulties loom for the security of the Union and the international community as a whole. Consequently, the program for the prevention of violent conflicts adopted in 2001 calls for mainstreaming conflict prevention into the external activities of the Union and enhancing its capability for intelligence gathering, analysis, planning and decision-making.[6]

In the field of civilian crisis management, capabilities to be committed and deployed for the tasks agreed upon can be generated and pooled from resources and institutions that are integral elements of EU societies (policing, the rule of law, civil protection, civilian administration). The requirement of a capability for military crisis management, which was introduced for post-1989 security challenges, has acquired a new dimension with the threat perceptions connected with the post-2001 agenda. The stronger military pillar of the ESDP calls for the definition of the high end of the Petersberg missions within the Union's competence, possibly including the use of military coercion. Another key task for a more active and functional ESDP will be to determine the division of labor between the EU and NATO in military crisis management.[7]

The development of the ESDP was initiated by the pooling and listing of resources and by the establishment of the relevant institutional bodies, while the scenarios and purposes of missions remained sketchy and ambiguous. The adoption of the *European Security Strategy* will provide the political and strategic framework needed for the enhancement of the Union's role in international military security. The enlargement of its established security role as a civilian power to include military tasks, as well as the expansion of its geopolitical emphasis from Europe to a global scope of activity, will place new demands on the political will and the structural and institutional capability of the Union, while also changing its profile and image.[8]

The task of a strategy is to make it possible for the actor to shape developments and affect outcomes in a dense and complex international system. Consequently, to have a strategic function, the EU will need to generate sufficient competence, capability and authority as an international institution to be taken seriously by other actors in international affairs.

Strategy as power

Thirdly, the *European Security Strategy* has been seen as a response to the challenges posed by the theses and doctrines contained in the *United States' National Security Strategy*,[9] in particular those related to the use of force and pre-emptive action, the dispensable nature of multilateralism, and the tendency towards unilateralism. The *European Security Strategy* could be seen as a countermove by the EU to the agenda-setting power of the United States and an effort to introduce a parallel – albeit largely similar – agenda for international security, threat assessment and prioritizing strategic objectives.

Through the dialogue on security strategies the EU has entered onto a playing field where actors of necessity must respond to the American pre-eminence in international relations. To the extent that the international security order is based on the distribution of power among a variety of actors, the European Union will need to emerge as a strategic power capable of shaping its structure. It has been envisaged by some that the European Union will rise to surpass the United States in the totality of the dimensions of its power. There are several factors involved in this, not only the growth of the aggregate power of the Union but also a decrease in the will and capability of the United States to sustain over time its current primacy. The possession of military power alone is not enough to prevent the end of the American era, when the dynamics of European integration strengthen the EU's external role in parallel with the waning of American domestic growth and an internationalism that is based on the doctrine of exceptionalism.[10] From another perspective, balance between the United States and the EU is not achieved as a result of a realist competition for hegemony but is rather embedded in the general primacy of liberal democracy and market economy in international relations.[11] A precondition for such win–win upward balancing is improved and sustained transatlantic cooperation in global security issues.[12]

In any scenario, the strategy of the European Union in any challenge to US pre-eminence would employ functionalist and institutionalist power to supplant American structural power. Its success would require consensus on, and mutual commitment to, the binding role of common rules and multilateral institutions as constituting elements of the international order by the transatlantic partners. Going beyond the politics of balance of power, the EU strategy would be aimed at restraining power and making primacy legitimate and asymmetries of power acceptable by embedding all the actors, including the most powerful states, in the institutional and binding framework of constitutionalism and multilateralism.[13]

In the *European Security Strategy*, the goal is 'an effective and balanced partnership' with the United States, which calls for both the enhancement of the Union's overall capability to deal with security problems and its capability to engage the United States in a bilateral and multilateral framework of cooperation. It needs to be understood that the EU is the only other global actor that matches the power of United States, albeit with a different set of capacities and approaches. The EU is not, however, seeking to ride on the bandwagon of American power. Instead, it seeks leverage over the United States' use of its power and means of persuasion to affect US intentions across the global security agenda.

Development of military and civilian capabilities for crisis management

Having reached the force goals set for 2003 in the Helsinki Headline Goal, as well as the goals that were set for civilian capabilities, made progress in improving qualitative and quantitative military capabilities and addressing remaining shortfalls, and having successfully undertaken its first civilian and military operations, the European Union could look forward at the Brussels 2003 summit to setting new goals for 2010 in the development of the ESDP.[14]

Military capabilities

For military capabilities, the EU declared in May 2003 that an operational capability would be developed to carry out the full range of the Petersberg tasks, albeit limited by constraints caused by shortfalls in deployment time and the fulfilment of upper end missions. Committed contributions have matched or surpassed the numbers laid down in the Headline Goal at the 1999 Helsinki Summit (60,000 men, to be deployed in 60 days and sustained for at least one year) with a pool of more than 100,000 men, around 400 combat aircraft and 100 ships.

Additional contributions are called for to improve both the quantitative and qualitative aspects of the inventory of troops, equipment and collective strategic capabilities. Enhancements are also called for to improve the qualitative aspects of individual national armed forces to meet the requirements of availability and deployability, as well as their survivability, sustainability and interoperability. Moreover, to meet new risks and more demanding tasks, concepts and procedures are being developed for identifying Rapid Response Elements, including the introduction of battle group formations, for more demanding tasks, particularly for humanitarian and rescue missions, those requiring accelerated decision-making and deployment within 5 to 30 days.

The process of generating common capabilities from the pool of national defense establishments and industries is driven at the working level by two institutionalized mechanisms, the European Capability Action Plan (ECAP), and the Capability Development Mechanism (CDM), which have been adopted as a review tool for the military core of the ESDP process. The work of the ECAP is linked with the development of armaments and procurement cooperation among members states. As a major move towards closer linkages, a decision was taken in 2003 to establish an agency in the field of defense capabilities development, research, acquisition and armaments during the course of 2004. While there exists a variable geometry of armaments cooperation among EU members, a common EU-level institution encompassing all of the members on an equal basis will provide added value by promoting and monitoring the harmonization of procurement plans, supporting research in defense and security technology and strengthening the defense industrial and technological basis as a whole in the EU area, even though concrete national, bilateral and multinational projects would still be constituted and managed in various combinations and configurations.

The deepening of integration and consolidation in the armaments sector – defined, in addition to crisis management, as the other main area of a common defense policy – is indispensable for a successful participation of European countries in enhanced transatlantic defense cooperation, which again is a prerequisite for any effort to close the transatlantic gap in defense technology and in the management of the revolution in military affairs. A key problem, however, remains protectionism on both sides of the Atlantic.[15]

The monitoring and evaluation mechanisms for military capabilities takes account of the corresponding and parallel work within NATO and the Partnership for Peace (PfP) Planning And Review Process. The CDM is aimed at ensuring coherent, transparent and mutually reinforcing development of the capability requirements common to both the EU and NATO. While both institutions maintain their political autonomy in setting goals and guiding capability development, there is an interest in avoiding unnecessary duplication or a divergence of criteria in force planning that is preparing a common pool of forces for contingencies under NATO's PfP, the EU or possibly for the UN. The ECAP process, national and multinational work on force development and deepening armaments cooperation are linked together and, from the ESDP perspective, served by the CDM. The intention is that the capabilities required for current and future ESDP missions are defined and evaluated through the capability development mechanism and introduced into service as efficiently and cost-effectively as possible.

The permanent arrangements (the Berlin plus) between the EU and NATO in crisis management, agreed by the Copenhagen Summit in 2002 and finalized in 2003, will enable the EU to utilize NATO assets and capabilities in EU-led military crisis-management operations. This arrangement conformed to the guiding principles and practical arrangements outlined by the Union at the Nice Summit in 2000, which was a response to the offer made by NATO at the Washington Summit in 1999. The Berlin plus arrangements created a strategic partnership between the EU and NATO by providing a permanent framework for joint action in crisis management, while respecting each institution's decision-making autonomy. It consists of:

- consultation, cooperation and transparency to be carried out by contacts at various levels between the two institutions, such as joint meetings between the Political and Security Committee (PSC) and the North Atlantic Council (NAC), both outside and in times of crisis;
- a formula on how NATO will provide the EU with guaranteed access to NATO's planning capabilities, the presumption of the availability of pre-identified NATO capabilities and common assets and the delineation of a range of command options that are available to the Union. Most EU-led operations are likely to be based on a recourse to at least some NATO assets and resources.

Moreover, as steps for the further development of planning capabilities, decisions were taken at the Brussels European Council in 2003 to establish a EU cell within NATO's SHAPE and a military–civilian planning cell within the EU Military Staff (EUMS), where NATO will have also liaison staff. The EU planning cell provides, for the first time, the option of common operational planning in autonomous EU operations, which are foreseen as being mainly limited operations with an inherent civilian-military component and purpose. Such a capability will also support the third option, an autonomous EU mission run by command structures provided by member states through a framework of nation or multinational arrangement. Thus, in 2003, the Berlin plus arrangements were applied to the EU Operation *Concordia*, which was the follow-up to NATO's *Allied Harmony* in Macedonia, whereas Operation *Artemis* in the Congo in 2003 was an autonomous EU operation led by France as a framework nation. During 2004, the EU is preparing to take over from NATO, again using the Berlin plus arrangements, the military stabilization operation (SFOR) in Bosnia and Herzegovina.

Civilian capabilities

In the field of civilian crisis management, the capability targets for the priority areas adopted at the Göteborg summit (200 officials in the field of the rule of law, civil protection intervention teams of up to 2000 persons, a pool of experts on civilian administration) have been achieved and even exceeded through commitments already made. A particular priority is set on the EU's capacity for providing policing support by way of the Police Action Plan: 5000 police officers with 1400 rapidly deployable within 30 days covering the full range of police missions (training, advisory, monitoring and executive). As a result of this political and structural readiness, the EU launched its first civilian crisis-management operation (EUPM) by taking over the UN International Police Task Force (IPTF) in Bosnia and Herzegovina from 1 January 2003. The EUPM, launched with 500 personnel from 33 countries, includes a number of third-country partners. In addition, the EU Special Representative in Bosnia and Herzegovina is doubling as the High Representative in the Office of the High Representative (OHR). In Bosnia and Herzegovina, the Union will employ all of its civilian and military instruments simultaneously in the same field once the military operation is launched. Another police mission (*Proxima*) was also launched in Macedonia in 2003.

The combination and coordination of military and civilian tools provides an asset that is being streamlined. A concerted effort to generate institutions and resources for civilian crisis management was launched in parallel with the military process in the framework of the ESDP. The coordination of civil and military instruments in EU-led crisis management operations is being planned and prepared as an integral element of the operational culture underlying the ESDP and the military–civilian planning cell in the EU Military Staff is aimed at such contingencies. Moreover, the concept of Civil–Military Co-operation (CIMIC) has been adopted for EU-led military crisis management operations, covering cooperation and coordination between EU-led forces and external civil actors, including national populations and local authorities, as well as international, national and non-governmental organizations active in the field. Much of what the EU has been doing in the framework of stability promotion and peace building can be interpreted as conflict prevention, addressing the indirect or root causes of conflicts. As part of comprehensive security, it is an activity aimed at contributing to internal or international developments that would reduce the danger of conflict or as reconstruction efforts that will prevent the renewal of confrontations in societies that have undergone conflict or in failed states.

The principle of mainstreaming makes conflict prevention an underlying consideration in all policies and instruments of the Union aimed at following, assessing and influencing the external environment. The programmatic approach is used to harness institutional resources within the EU (both the Council and Commission) and the member states, and thus create added value for the capability of the Union as an international actor. Added value is sought not only by having coherence between pillars and consistency among the member states, but also between them and the Union in the making and implementation of common policies and by applying the doctrine of conditionality to external policies (trade, development cooperation, governance assistance, etc.) that used to be conducted more on their own merits.

Mainstreaming conflict prevention and 'contributing to a global culture of prevention' is based on four elements:

1. setting priorities within the preventive strategies, as well as monitoring and assessing implementation regularly;
2. harnessing resources for information gathering and analysis in Brussels and in the field, within the Council, Commission, and member states;
3. strengthening and refining the extensive set of instruments available to the Union in development cooperation, trade, arms control, human rights, environmental policies and political dialogue for long-term action and diplomatic and humanitarian instruments for short-term action; and
4. intensifying cooperation and partnership with the UN, the OSCE and other international organizations.

The EU employs targeted measures (economic support, promotion of democracy, reforming the security sector, and so on) towards particular situations in particular countries or regions or addresses more general issues (such as drugs, small arms, natural resources, environmental degradation, communicable diseases, population flows) as factors that may cause tension and conflict. In the short-term, as a reaction to nascent conflicts, political and diplomatic measures, including dialogue, special representatives, international cooperation with other actors and using preventive or smart sanctions are at the forefront. For the long-term policy of conflict prevention, the

EU uses regular country reviews based on identifying indicators of potential conflict. The main purpose in the formulation of indicators is to detect the root causes of conflict as a basis for establishing watch lists, monitoring and early warning by EU bodies and structures in the field, in Brussels and in national capitals. Conflict prevention and civilian crisis management provide a combined effect: by mainstreaming conflict prevention, the EU will address the root causes of conflicts and by creating specific tools for civilian crisis management, the Union will generate a more rapid and targeted response to specific situations.

The issue of coherence and consistency

The comparative advantage of the EU as an international actor is predicated on meeting the combined requirements of coherence and consistency, as stressed in the conclusion of the *European Security Strategy*. Ultimately, the issue concerns the effectiveness and predictability of how the EU acts, which is predicated on decision-making as an expression of political will, making linkages between institutions and structures of the Union to give added value, and coordinating different sectors of external relations as a means for building a comprehensive policy.

Coherence is a key factor contributing to the capability of the EU to act in the field as an interwoven complex of institutions and bodies. Coherence determines how the means and assets at the disposal of the Union can be harnessed to provide added value to the decision-making and actions of the Union through synergy, complementarities and coordination among institutions and bodies across the structure of all three pillars, as well as the member states. Coherence concerns the process of policy-making and pertains to its institutional and functional aspects.

Consistency concerns policy as an outcome of policy-making. Consistency reflects the ability of the Commission and the Council's General Secretariat to coordinate the various areas of policy they govern in order that the Union can act in a unitary manner. In addition, consistency applies to the relationship between the different pillars and between the various issue-areas. The aim is mutual reinforcement between political, military, economic, humanitarian and other policies. Moreover, the requirement of consistency goes beyond the integration of Community (first pillar) and CFSP (second pillar) policies, as the national policies of the member states are channelled through Union institutions and partly conducted separately in bilateral relations with target countries and regions.

Consequences for transatlantic relations

Although the Common European Security and Defence Policy has been driven by practical challenges on the ground in Europe, it has become an integral part of the identity and profile of the European Union as an international actor. Consequently, the ESDP has been viewed by the United States as an increasingly crucial element for its interests in transatlantic relations and global security policy.

Authority of the EU as a security-policy actor

The basic model for ESDP-based military crisis management remains an operation with recourse to NATO assets and strategic resources in close consultation between the EU and NATO and thus also with the United States. There is a growing awareness among European analysts that the situation has changed, however, and the rationale for a stronger common security and defense policy is strengthening the autonomous role of the EU in crisis management. When the ESDP was launched, in addition to being driven by internal integration dynamics, it was a tool to engage the United States in European security by providing a more equitable sharing of the defense burden and, moreover, to strengthen NATO by providing enhanced European military capabilities for the use of both institutions. As it seems likely that the United States is transferring European crisis-management responsibilities increasingly to Europeans and NATO is becoming, for the United States, a source of ad-hoc coalitions for out-of-area missions, Europeans have come to view the ESDP in a new light. The focus has shifted from a careful consideration of political and institutional sensitivities regarding NATO's competence and capabilities to a concern about the marginalization of NATO and Europe in general. As a consequence, the ESDP has become more indispensable for European interests, since the ability to provide a military contribution has become an increasingly vital means of influencing US policies and pursuing an effective partnership policy.

The strengthening of the authority of the EU is not self-evident, as developments in the wider security environment affect not only consensus among the member states but also the policies of its potential partners. The ESDP is included in EU membership criteria and obligations, and new Union members from Central Europe have made significant commitments to the EU pool of forces. They are, however, also likely to continue to stress, doctrinally and politically, their particular regard for cooperation with the United States through NATO and its presence in European security, in parallel with their new Union membership responsibilities.[16] Likewise, the importance of the ESDP in EU–Russian relations remains open. Russia is investing in its relationship with the United States and the significance of the ESDP for Russia's security concerns remains ambiguous, although a closer partnership with the EU promotes Russia's internal reform and European identity. In the triangle of the EU–Russia–US relationship, Russia has retained a flexible position, despite its cooperation with France and Germany over the Iraq issue.[17]

The attitudes of the American foreign policy elites towards the ESDP vary.[18] Traditional Atlanticists, many of them Democrats, support the ESDP, with some reservations regarding its effects on NATO. They view the ESDP as a means of creating a more credible balance of burden-sharing, which is essential for continued public and Congressional support for the US contribution to European security. Moreover, they desire new and expanded roles for a unified and reformed NATO. Conservative Atlanticists are sceptics and question the rationale and wisdom of the ESDP, viewing it as a distraction from commitment to NATO. They doubt that the ESDP will ever fulfil its promise and worry about the duplication of resources.

Two new transformationist schools are close to, and feed into, the thinking of the Bush administration. Neo-conservatives regard the ESDP as an argument for freeing the United States from unnecessary European responsibilities, advocating burden-shedding and the voluntary strategic decoupling of the US from its commitments in Europe. Such strategic transformationists speak of a division of labour between the United States and the Europeans through *backfilling*, whereby the Europeans take over all remaining tasks in Europe and support the United States as it carries the main burden of facing new threats elsewhere. For defense experts that believe that fundamental military transformation is underway, the ESDP is nearly irrelevant, as the Americans and Europeans are not preparing themselves for the same kind of tasks, find themselves at different levels of qualitative weapons development and not following the same standards. Such military transformationists are resigned to transatlantic divergence caused by the technological and strategic gap in military capabilities and to a widening expectations-capabilities gap in the development of the ESDP.

The relevance of the ESDP, when measured by the military capability factor alone, is largely considered as minimal in American assessments. The European process is not seen as producing capabilities for high-end military missions that would make the EU forces – or the European NATO partners – capable of cooperating effectively or decisively with their American partners, except in auxiliary roles and mainly through national contributions by such medium powers as the United Kingdom, France or Italy.

Significance of the broad capability

The picture changes, however, when viewed against the relevance of the European Union's other capabilities and in the light of the roles that the United States and the EU serve globally and regionally in international security. The ESDP has further enhanced and broadened the Union's capabilities for post-conflict reconstruction, low-to-medium intensity military crisis management, civilian crisis management and multi-faceted conflict prevention. These are all roles that can support and complement the militarily focused US contributions to conflict management, whether in the Balkans, Afghanistan or potentially in Iraq and the wider Middle East. Moreover, the role of the EU in countering international terrorism equals or surpasses that of the United States in the field of domestic and justice affairs, where the Union is able to draw on its concerted capabilities and institutions across the third and first pillars in implementing the Plan of Action adopted after 9/11 and enhanced after the 11 March 2004 terrorist attack in Madrid.[19] The EU has also incorporated the fight against terrorism into its external relations. By inserting an element of conditionality, through its insistence on a counter-terrorism clause in its agreements with priority third countries, the EU is evaluating its relations with, and providing assistance to such nations based on their stance on international terrorism. The same approach is being introduced for policies on WMD proliferation. More widely, its policies for post-conflict stabilisation and conflict prevention address the root causes of terrorism in unstable and failing societies and deny terrorist networks the opportunity to take over such states and their societies or use them as bases for their activities.

The solidarity clause in the draft constitutional treaty reflects the need for close cooperation in civilian and military crisis management. The EU is involving the instruments of the ESDP in counter-terrorism by strengthening intelligence sharing, developing a common evaluation of terrorist threats and determining capabilities required to protect forces deployed in EU crisis-management operations. This is in parallel with exploring how civilian and military capabilities could be used to protect civilian populations against the effects of terrorist attacks. The member states are committed to assisting each other in the spirit of the solidarity clause, with all the instruments at their disposal, including military resources, when requested by a member state in the event of a terrorist attack on its territory. The choice of the most appropriate means is left to individual member states.[20]

Restraining power

Beyond the political–military agenda, the transatlantic relationship becomes more symmetrical in terms of capabilities and roles offered by the EU and the US. With its leading role in trade policy, unity buttressed by the Union's competence, as well as its expertise in international economics, development and environmental affairs that is driven by a mix of Union and national competences, the EU is a global actor whose only equal in the management of the implications of globalization for international security and stability is the United States.

Taking into consideration the comprehensive set of functional capabilities possessed by the EU and the potential capabilities of the United States in soft as well a hard power, the preconditions exist for an equal partnership and a transatlantic community of values and interests between them that reinforces global security and stability. Doctrinal asymmetries between the EU and the US as actors grow, however, in direct relationships to the extent to which military capabilities are prioritized and emphasized as policy responses and the use of force becomes part of the solution.

In addition to the dimension of military power, partnership between the EU and the United States is shaped by the degree and significance accrued to institutionalism and strategic restraint in the international security order. The EU is a strong proponent of norms and institutions in international relations and a leading actor across the board in multilateral institutions such as the UN, the Council of Europe, the Organization for Security and Co-operation in Europe, the World Trade Organization (WTO) and financial and development cooperation institutions. In addition, the EU is an embodiment of the benefits of binding institutionalism, going beyond inter-governmentalism to supranational integration and the sharing of sovereignty.

It has been argued that great powers can maintain their position and use their power most effectively by constructing and maintaining international institutions, and to bargain in them for a stable and mutually recognized relationship with weaker and smaller states. Such a positive impact for institutionalism is impeded by the application of unilateralism and the exceptionalist idea of sovereignty in US security policy, as well as its tendency to use ad-hoc coalitions instead of deferring to established multilateral fora, channels, institutions and partners. There is no attempt to counterbalance US power by the EU or any other great power, at least as long as the US behaves with restraint and a value community of liberal democracy binds Europeans and American together. Although the ESDP could be viewed as a step towards counterbalancing, it is not generating enough political or military power to create such an effect in practice. There are, however, increasing signs of competition on the doctrinal level in global strategies. In the longer term, a key factor in shaping the EU–US relationship will be the construction and development of the strategic identity and outlook of both sides. In the ongoing discussion, a stark contrast has been drawn between European and American thinking on the nature of international relations, in particular, on the significance of power and the use of force in addressing security challenges versus the multilateral and institutionalist approach. While partnership is the natural and widely sought relationship between the EU and the United States, a concern about an emerging division of labor, one that accepts political and strategic divergence by design or by default, dominates the discussion. It is not in the EU's interest to allow a geopolitical or functional division of labor to grow, be it in high/low-intensity missions, military/non-military missions or in Europe/beyond Europe. Nor would it be in line with the goals of the ESDP to freeze a gap in capabilities or a divergence in strategies. The goal of the comprehensive CFSP/ESDP remains to have an equal and more symmetrical relationship with the United States, both by developing the capabilities of the EU and by influencing the strategic approach of the United States towards the management of security challenges.

Concluding remarks

While the first civilian and military crisis-management missions signify the coming of age of the ESDP, the authority of the European Union as a security-policy actor is still in question because of differences among the member states and the challenge posed by the dominant position of the United States in global security. On the other hand, disputes related to the implications of the ESDP for NATO's competences and capabilities have been overcome by new collaborative arrangements. Moreover, the US interest in having the EU take over low-intensity stabilization tasks in Europe creates additional space for the ESDP.

In the shaping of the global security order, the roles of the EU and United States are evolving. For the Union to influence US policies, it will have to enhance its authority by building upon its comprehensive non-military capability and pursuing its newly adopted strategy of effective multilateralism, which highlights the significance of legitimacy. At the same time, the Union will have to adapt its doctrine and capability to an international environment where the use of force remains high on the agenda set by US preferences and interests and where US military capabilities continue to dominate.

The capacity for crisis management will be a crucial factor in moving the European Union towards an equal partnership with the United States. While a barren division of labor is rejected and a full symmetry in power assets is not achievable, the completion of broader capabilities will enable the Union to more effectively use the strategic advantages of its multi-faceted function in international relations. Moreover, the tasks of crisis management will make the Union more cognizant of the requirements of coherence and consistency in its own decision-making and actions. In the end, the outcome will depend on the evolution of the strategic culture among the member-states, which will determine the weight and direction of the European Union's common policies.

Notes

1. *A Secure Europe in a Better World. European Security Strategy* (Presidency Conclusions, Brussels European Council, 12 December 2003).
2. H. Larsen, 'The EU: A Global Military Actor?', *Cooperation and Conflict* No. 37(3) 283–302.
3. S. Heiselberg, Pacifism or Activism: Towards a Common Strategic Culture within the European Security and Defense Policy?, *IIS Working Paper* No. 4 (Copenhagen: Danish Institute for International Studies, 2003).
4. S. Rynning, 'The European Union: Towards a Strategic Culture', *Security Dialogue*, No. 34(4) (2003) 479–94.
5. Documents on the evolution and highlights of the ESDP are collected in *Chaillot Papers* No. 47 (May 2001), No. 51 (April 2002), and No. 57 (February 2003) as well as on armaments cooperation in No. 59 (April 2003) published by the EUISS.
6. *EU Programme for the Prevention of Violent Conflicts* (Stockholm: Ministry for Foreign Affairs, 2001).
7. J. Howorth, 'ESDP and NATO: Wedlock or Deadlock?', *Cooperation and Conflict* No. 38(3) (2003) 235–54; Ch.M. Schweiss, 'Sharing Hegemony. The Future of Transatlantic Security', *Cooperation and Conflict* No. 38(3) (2003) 211–34.

8. S. E. Penksa and W. L. Mason, 'EU Security Cooperation and the Transatlantic Relationship', *Cooperation and Conflict* No. 38(3) (2003) 255–80.

9. *The National Security Strategy of the United States of America* (Washington, DC: The White House, 2002).

10. Ch. Kupchan, *The End of the American Era: U.S. Foreign Policy and the Geopolitics of the Twenty-first Century* (New York: Alfred A. Knopf, 2002).

11. M. Mandelbaum, *The Ideas That Conquered the World: Peace, Democracy, and Free Markets in the Twenty-first Century* (New York: Public Affairs, 2002).

12. D. Hamilton, 'Three Strategic Challenges for a Global Transatlantic Partnership', *European Foreign Affairs Review* No. 8(4) (2003) 543–55; G. Lindstrom, ed., *Shift or Rift. Assessing US-EU relations after Iraq* (Paris: European Union Institute for Security Studies, 2003).

13. G. J. Ikenberry, *After Victory. Institutions, Strategic Restraint, and the Rebuilding of Order after Major Wars* (Princeton and Oxford: Princeton University Press, 2001).

14. *Presidency Conclusions*, Brussels European Council (12 December 2003), *ESDP Presidency Report* (Annex).

15. At issue is a military transformation gap, as outlined in D. S. Hamilton 'What is Transformation and What Does it Mean for NATO?', in D. S. Hamilton, ed., *Transatlantic Transformations: Equipping NATO for the 21st Century* (Washington, DC: Center for Transatlantic Relations, 2004).

16. M. Quinlan, 'ESDP and EU Enlargement', in: E. Brimmer, ed., *The EU's Search for a Strategic Role: ESDP and Its Implications for Transatlantic Relations*, 23–33 (Washington, DC: Center for Transatlantic Relations, 2002).

17. T. Forsberg, 'Russia's Role in ESDP', in: E. Brimmer, ed., *The EU's Search for a Strategic Role: ESDP and Its Implications for Transatlantic Relations*, 85–99 (Washington, DC: Center for Transatlantic Relations, 2002); F. Splidsboel-Hansen, 'Explaining Russian Endorsement of the CFSP and the ESDP', *Security Dialogue* No. 33(4) (2002) 443–56.

18. D. Hamilton, 'American Views of European Security and Defense Policy', in: E. Brimmer, ed., *The EU's Search for a Strategic Role: ESDP and Its Implications for Transatlantic Relations* (Washington, DC: Center for Transatlantic Relations, 2002) 147–57. On the origins of US policies towards the ESDP, see S. Sloan, *NATO, the European Union and the Atlantic Community* (Lanham/Boulder/New York/Oxford: Rowman & Littlefield, 2003) pp. 171–89.

19. D. Dubois, 'The Attacks of 11 September: EU–US Cooperation Against Terrorism in the Field of Justice and Home Affairs', *European Foreign Affairs Review* No. 7(3) (2002) 317–35; *Declaration on Combating Terrorism* (Brussels European Council, 25 March 2004).

20. *Declaration on Solidarity Against Terrorism* (Brussels European Council, 25 March 2004).

12
The OSCE Response to 9/11

P. Terrence Hopmann

The OSCE role in Eurasian security

The Organization for Security and Cooperation in Europe (OSCE) is a regional security organization, recognized as such under Chapter VIII of the United Nations Charter. Formed by the Helsinki Final Act, signed in Helsinki, Finland by 35 heads of state on 31 July 1975, it was known until 1995 as the Conference on Security and Cooperation in Europe (CSCE). From its inception, the CSCE defined 'Europe' very broadly. Its original 35 participating states (as well as its 55 current participants) come from across the entire northern hemisphere, including not only all political entities on the European continent, but also the United States and Canada as well as the new nations that arose on the territory of the former Soviet Union. Thus the area covered by the CSCE/OSCE extends through the Far Eastern portions of the Russian Federation and includes the Central Asian states that emerged after the breakup of the Soviet Union. Therefore, OSCE insiders often refer to 'Europe' as an area that extends 'from Vancouver to Vladivostok, the long way around.'

The CSCE was the only regional security organization to bridge the East–West divide during the Cold War, and this history has given it a unique role to play in the international relations of the European region since the Cold War came to an end in 1989. Since negotiations started in 1973, the CSCE has established a set of normative principles intended to guide security relations among European states. These principles played an important role in undermining the influence of authoritarian regimes in communist states during the Cold War,[1] and they have played an equally important role in defining the guiding principles of security in post-Cold War Eurasia.

In addition, the Helsinki Final Act focused on three substantive areas of activity:

- confidence-building measures in the realm of military policy;
- cooperation in economic, scientific and technical spheres;

- cooperation in activities involving the 'human dimension' of security, including individual human rights and the rights of persons belonging to minorities groups.

The OSCE is unique, therefore, because of its comprehensive definition of security. In practice, as the organization evolved, the economic dimension has declined in relative importance, as other institutions such as the European Union have assumed a primary role in this field. However, the OSCE is still the only major European security organization that links the military and human dimensions of security at the very core of its guiding principles. This linkage proved to be especially important in providing the OSCE a special role in dealing with the many ethnic and secessionist conflicts that appeared on the territory of former communist states after the end of the Cold War, and it has also defined its unique attributes in responding to the threat posed by terrorism in more recent years.

At the same time, the OSCE is often referred to as a 'soft' security organization, because it is based on a political agreement rather than a legally binding treaty and also because it does not have at its immediate disposal military forces to implement or enforce its decisions. It depends heavily, therefore, upon the persuasive powers of its participating states, on the diplomatic skills of its officials and the professional staff of its missions and field activities, and on cooperation with other institutions that do have access to instruments of force.[2] Thus, the OSCE's comparative advantage lies in the diplomatic, political, and humanitarian dimensions of security in addition to the military domain. It focuses more on education, modeling, and persuasion than on the use of force to accomplish its mission.

The bonds among OSCE participating states are based on a series of politically binding agreements rather than legal treaties. As a consequence, the OSCE must obtain political consensus among its participating states, and it operates largely with the consent of those states on whose territory it carries out its field activities. This requires its representatives to exercise subtle political discretion, as no state is legally required to have an OSCE mission operate on its territory, and missions may be removed if they fail to retain the support of the governments of the states where OSCE staff work. In spite of this limitation, the political weight of an organization of 55 states, including some of the wealthiest and most powerful in the world, has given the OSCE a greater capability to operate in regions of conflict than might have been reasonably expected on the basis of its limited mandate. The reality of a large, multilateral organization representing a wide range of values and viewpoints is also that the OSCE and its representatives must often speak and act cautiously in an effort to minimize conflict among its many diverse participating states. These limitations have been most serious when it comes to dealing with problems such as media freedom and political competition in those participating states, such as several in Central Asia and the

Caucasus, that frequently fall short of meeting OSCE standards regarding democratic processes. This does not mean, however, that the OSCE operates on the basis of a set of 'minimum common denominator' principles. Consistent with its founding political principles, the OSCE has enlarged its normative foundation and changed its functions significantly since the Cold War ended. Not only has the organization become more deeply institutionalized over time, but it has also extended its normative base beyond the original three Helsinki 'baskets' to embrace the basic principles of liberal democracy and the rule of law. In addition, the OSCE has assumed a wide variety of new functions in many of the troubled regions that have emerged in Europe and Eurasia after the collapse of communist regimes and the breakup of the Soviet Union and the Federal Republic of Yugoslavia. These have included in particular a number of institutions charged with tasks involving the linkage between political/economic issues and security:

- The Conflict Prevention Center in Vienna coordinates the work of Missions of Long Duration and other offices and assistance groups in 18 countries and regions as of January 2004 (as well as seven prior missions that have been closed down) where violence has threatened to break out or where it has actually occurred.[3] These missions have included a focus on
  - long-term conflict prevention through building democracy;
  - short-term conflict prevention in the face of imminent threats of violence;
  - mediation of cease-fires in ongoing violent conflicts;
  - mediation after conflicts to resolve underlying causes; and
  - post-conflict security-building.[4]

  The political functions associated with long-term conflict prevention and post-conflict reconstruction have assumed particular importance in the aftermath of the terrorist attacks against the United States in 2001.
- The High Commissioner on National Minorities (HCNM) in The Hague works extensively with relations between national minorities and governments to prevent inter-ethnic tensions from reaching the stage of violence. The HCNM operates largely through personal diplomacy and on short notice, and intervenes when events or specific actions of governments or minority groups threaten to produce violence.
- The Office of Democratic Institutions and Human Rights (ODIHR) specializes in democracy building and establishing the rule of law. It supports elections and monitors for human rights violations, while providing advice and consultation in strengthening democratic institutions and the rule of law.
- The Office of Freedom of the Media in Vienna emphasizes media pluralism, especially preventing abuses of media freedom during political campaigns.

- The Office of the Coordinator of Economic and Environmental Affairs focuses on issues involving economic competition and environmental degradation that may provoke conflicts.
- The Secretariat provides overall administration for the OSCE, and it has recently added two units of special significance since 9/11, namely the Action against Terrorism Unit (ATU) and the Strategic Police Matters Unit (SPMU).
- The Forum for Security Cooperation focuses on the negotiation of new instruments to combat new security threats that may arise within the OSCE region, and its Support Unit works to implement these new provisions.

Although each of these units is relative small in terms of personnel, this compact size generally facilitates cooperation across these units in responding to new security threats, especially where different dimensions of security are interlinked. It cannot be stressed enough that this comprehensive approach to security is what provides the OSCE with its unique strengths in responding to the newest security challenges in the Eurasian region. The United States is, of course, the most powerful of the OSCE participating states, attaining a position of primacy within the international system, totally out of proportion to the dominance of the world's great powers at any previous time in history.[5] Furthermore, at least in the immediate aftermath of the 9/11 attacks, virtually all of the other OSCE participating states shared a common sense of injury, as evidenced in Europe by NATO's decision to invoke Article V of the North Atlantic Treaty for the first time since the Alliance's creation in 1949. Even when intervening events served to reduce the direct perception of threat from terrorism among Eurasian participating states, there could be no doubt that after 9/11 the foreign policy priorities of the United States would shift dramatically. This, in turn, inevitably also had an impact on US participation in and support for the activities of the OSCE. As a major financial contributor, especially to OSCE special missions, it became apparent that the United States would try to push the OSCE to take up the new challenges presented by global terrorism and that the OSCE would have to respond in some way if it was to retain any viable role in the security environment of the early twenty-first Century.

Changes in the OSCE after 9/11: can the OSCE assist in the struggle against terrorism?

After 9/11, the United States immediately placed its primary foreign policy emphasis on responding to the global threat of terrorism, and in almost all areas US foreign policy became preoccupied with the 'war on terrorism'. During its first eight months in office, the Bush administration had generally disengaged from many international involvements. The administration openly looked with disdain on previous efforts at 'nation-building' in 'failed states' and upon all forms of 'humanitarian intervention' in regions where massacre and genocide were occurring. This presumably implied a diminution in the importance with which the new administration regarded the OSCE. At first the change in attitudes and policy on the part of the Bush team was barely noticeable from that of the previous administration. Under domestic pressure and in response to the failure of the OSCE to contain the crisis in Kosovo, the Clinton administration had already de-emphasized the role of the OSCE in the conduct of American foreign policy. In contrast to its earlier decision to assign principal responsibility for the political administration in Bosnia-Herzegovina to the OSCE as an integral part of the Dayton Accords in 1995, or even to support creation of the Kosovo Verification Mission under OSCE auspices in 1998, by early 1999 the Clinton administration placed its European security emphasis on NATO, signaled by its opening of the air campaign in Kosovo without endorsement by either the OSCE or the UN. In spite of this reduction in the high profile issues dealt with by OSCE, the US had remained engaged, using the OSCE as a vehicle for dealing with Russian military action in Chechnya, Russian troops stationed in the Transdniestria region of Moldova, and the efforts of the Minsk Group to broker a settlement of the conflict between Azerbaijan and Armenia over the enclave of Nagorno-Karabakh.

All of these efforts continued in the early months of the new Bush administration, but there was little priority assigned to them. By 2001 the major OSCE activities focused on conflict resolution and post-conflict nation-building in post-communist Eurasia, coupled with prophylactic efforts at building democracy, respect for human and minority rights, and the rule of the law in those regions of former communist states where political transformation was slow or nonexistent. Thus, the OSCE focused exactly on those kinds of activities that the newly elected president had deprecated. The OSCE thereby became even more marginalized in Washington's foreign policy priorities, even though the US maintained its usual low-profile participation in the routine work of the organization in Vienna and in its missions and other field activities. This was not inconsistent, however, with the overall drift in the early Bush II administration, which emphasized minimal international involvement.

All of this, of course, came to a sudden end on 9/11, when US foreign policy essentially made a dramatic 'about face'. In many ways, the 'war on terrorism' further marginalized the OSCE in the eyes of the Bush administration, since its relevance to this new struggle seem, at best, remote. However, insofar as US policy-makers at the mid-level continued to deal with the OSCE, they did so almost exclusively in terms of the new global 'war'. Only three weeks after the terrorist attacks on New York and Washington, Assistant Secretary of State for European Affairs, Ambassador A. Elizabeth Jones, declared in testimony before the United States 'Helsinki Commission,' composed of leading members of Congress and several members of the executive branch:

> The immediate challenge is to enlist OSCE in the fight against terrorism. This will be a sustained campaign. Applying OSCE commitments and principles in our common struggle against global terrorism will be crucial to the success of this effort.[6]

At the same time, the administration asserted its desire to continue diplomacy as usual, including the traditional US emphasis upon human rights and the other 'human dimension' issues that were so central to the Helsinki Final Act, the Charter of Paris, and the Copenhagen Document – the normative core of the OSCE regime. The war on terrorism, administration spokespersons emphasized, would not undermine the principles embraced by the OSCE and the UN. At the same Congressional Hearing on 3 October 2001, Lorne Craner, Assistant Secretary of State for Democracy, Human Rights and Labor, cited senior administration officials to reinforce this point:

> Since September 11, Secretary Powell communicated to our posts that 'we must continue the normal business of diplomacy.' Dr. Condoleezza Rice said only a week after the horrific September 11 attacks, 'Civil liberties matter to this President very much, and our values matter to us abroad. We are not going to stop talking about the things that matter to us, human rights, religious freedom and so forth and so on. We're going to continue to press those things; we would not be America if we did not'.[7]

He continued to assert that this would apply, especially to US dealing with Russia and other regions in Eurasia:

> Even as we move to greatly increase our cooperation on counter terrorism with many NIS states, we must continue to push for improvements on such areas as rule of law, religious tolerance, and other basic human freedoms, since democracy and respect for human rights will help enhance the stability of the region.[8]

These general principles thus guided the initial US efforts to transform the OSCE into an institution that would support US efforts to counter terrorist threats. These new initiatives also arose at a time when previous OSCE efforts in all five of its major conflict management functions seemed to be reaching a turning point. First, some of the early long-term conflict-prevention cases had begun to see success, with the OSCE withdrawing from active participation in Estonia and Latvia, while transforming its field activities in Tajikistan and Ukraine into lower profile operations. Second, shorter term conflict prevention also seemed less urgent as the string of crises that had followed the breakup of the Soviet Union and Yugoslavia began to fade, and fears of new conflicts arising diminished, with the significant exception of the situation in Macedonia; fears of a new round of ethno-national violence and separatist conflicts thus largely disappeared as a major focus for OSCE conflict management activities. Third, efforts to broker cease-fires largely fell by the wayside, with the re-ignition of violence in Chechnya in 1999 and the failure of the OSCE to obtain a significant role as a mediator in the renewed conflict, in spite of hopeful signs that emerged from the November 1999 OSCE Summit in Istanbul. Thus the major ongoing, violent conflict in the region remained largely out of the reach of OSCE influence. Fourth, the efforts at conflict resolution in the aftermath of violent conflicts also seemed to stall. One relatively successful effort in Tajikistan moved off the central agenda, while the other situations in Nagorno-Karabakh, Georgia (Abkhazia and South Ossetia), and Moldova (Transdniestria) became largely frozen. By 2003, renewed efforts in Moldova spearheaded by the OSCE mission had begun to produce some prospect of progress. However, in the immediate aftermath of 9/11, all of these conflicts seemed hopelessly deadlocked and showed few signs that this situation might change rapidly. Fifth, following the war in Kosovo in 1999 and the electoral defeat of Slobodan Milosevic in Serbia in 2000, the efforts at post-conflict reconstruction within the OSCE region became generally hopeful and increasingly routinized. Large missions in Bosnia-Herzegovina, Kosovo, and Croatia, along with a smaller presence in Albania, all continued their previous efforts at building security and democratic political structures, but in an environment where the threat of renewed violence appeared to have receded.

Therefore, the OSCE's focus on the prevention of violent conflict, a mission that originally was sparked mostly by the collapse of multinational states, became a less central concern, again with the significant exception of the situation in Macedonia. The mission of combating the global terrorist threat thus landed in the lap of the OSCE at a time when it was searching for new activities that would keep the organization relevant within the overall European security scene. However, it also was immediately apparent that the OSCE had relatively little to offer when it came to directly combating terrorism, especially in terms of the immediate effort to break up the networks of international terrorism represented by al Qaeda and other terrorist organizations. Indeed, the OSCE has identified its special niche in the struggle against terrorism primarily as doing what it has been doing all along – namely strengthening security through human dimension activities such as promoting political participation, rule of law, human rights and minority rights.

Although the initial focus of the US government, and many other governments and institutions, has been on the immediate efforts to limit terrorist violence, there is also a growing comprehension that the real struggle against terrorism requires a long-term effort to remove the conditions that give rise to terrorism in the first place: widespread disparities in material well-being within and among societies around the world; religious and ideological intolerance; environmental degradation; widespread corruption and the absence of government based on law; lack of respect for all forms of diversity (racial, national, religious, political, linguistic). In sum, the very conditions that promote violence and that had been the focus of OSCE conflict prevention activities are also associated with the appearance and diffusion of terrorist organizations. Thus, while the OSCE has made some modest contributions in the direct effort to combat terrorism, especially enhancing cooperation among national police forces and border guards in tracking terrorist movements and among financial institutions in tracking terrorist financing, the major OSCE contributions have not been, and are unlikely in the future to emphasize immediate, operational responses to the threat of terrorism. Rather they are likely to emerge from a continuation, deepening, and occasional refocusing of the original OSCE efforts represented by the three baskets of the Helsinki Final Act: the linkages among national and human security, the human dimension, and economic and environmental well-being. The OSCE's potential contribution to combating terrorism is thus likely to stem from the fact that it is the only institution functioning in the large Eurasian region that integrates these broad goals within its central mission.

It follows, therefore, that the major changes that can be noted in the OSCE region since 9/11 emphasize two primary sets of priorities, one based on a subtle shift in issues and the other on its regional focus. In particular, the OSCE since 9/11 has increasingly emphasized the long-term conflict prevention activities associated with good governance and social integration, as opposed to more immediate conflict prevention, management, and resolution activities that constituted its central focus throughout the decade of the 1990s. Similarly, its focus has turned to those regions in Eurasia where democratic institutions are least visible, where economic and environmental conditions are most impoverished, and where the worlds of Islam and Orthodox Christianity have often collided throughout centuries, namely Central Asia and the Caucuses.

The 'new' post-9/11 issues

The United States was quick to press the OSCE to place the issue of terrorism high on its list of priorities and to institutionalize its importance for the organization. As a result of this pressure, in December 2001 the OSCE created an 'Action against Terrorism Unit' (ATU) within the OSCE Secretariat in Vienna, which began operations in May 2002. In early 2004 this unit consists of nine professional and support staff headed by Brian Woo, a senior US diplomat.[9] Its primary purpose was to enhance the capacity of OSCE states for combating terrorist threats within their own countries or to the region as a whole by assisting states in implementing a wide range of international protocols that have been adopted by numerous institutions in response to the terrorist threat. It provides information and training to officials in participating states about best practices, and it may arrange external experts to consult with participating governments about how best to implement the relevant international protocols.

The ATU was established especially to implement the Bucharest Plan of Action, adopted at the OSCE Ministerial Meeting in December 2001. This document calls on the new terrorism unit to cooperate closely with ODIHR to further assist participating states in building democratic institutions, strengthening their administrative capacity, local and central governmental institutions, judiciaries, and civil society, all with the goal of reducing the conditions that may help give rise to terrorism. UN Security Council Resolution 1373, adopted on 28 September 2001, encouraged all member states to become parties as soon as possible to all previous UN conventions dealing with terrorism. At the Bucharest OSCE Ministerial meeting in December 2001, all 55 participating states agreed to sign and ratify twelve conventions by the end of 2002 if possible. A major function of the OSCE's ATU has been to encourage states to sign and ratify these documents, an endeavor in which it has enjoyed considerable success, and to provide them with technical assistance in drafting national legislation to implement these conventions and to create the additional national infrastructure that would be necessary to carry out these UN protocols.

Also in December 2001, the Bishkek International Conference on Enhancing Security and Stability in Central Asia issued the Bishkek Programme of Action, which serves as a foundation for international cooperation in combating terrorist influences in Central Asia. Special focus here was placed on enhancing the capacity of national judicial and other governmental institutions to respond to the threat of terrorism within a democratic framework. At the OSCE Ministerial held in Porto, Portugal in December 2002, the OSCE also adopted two additional documents dealing with terrorism: the OSCE Charter on Preventing and Combating Terrorism and a decision on implementing these actions. These documents identified four priority operational areas in the struggle against terrorism: policing, border security, anti-trafficking, and suppressing terrorist financing. A special focus of the OSCE anti-terrorism activities has been to work closely with other international institutions that also have a mandate in this area. Cooperation has been especially close with the UN Counter-Terrorism Committee in fulfilling obligations under UN Security Council Resolution 1373. Similarly, cooperative relations have been established with the UN Office on Drugs and Crime to combat money laundering and transnational organized crime. Finally, an informal group of 'Friends' was established in February 2003 to improve inter-organizational cooperation on anti-terrorism issues along with other institutions including the Council of Europe, the European Union, and the UN.

Also included are efforts by the OSCE Office of the Coordinator for Economic and Environmental Activities to assist participating states in passing relevant legislation against money-laundering and to create structures to enforce such legislation, as an enhancement to the regional capacity to trace and suppress the financing of terrorism. Similarly law enforcement institutions in general need to be strengthened to fight transnational organized crime, which is sometimes associated with terrorist organizations. In addition, border guards need to be trained to police borders more effectively against the flow of known terrorists without at the same time impeding legitimate travel and commerce from moving across international boundaries, and while also protecting fundamental human rights. One area of special attention has included coordination of the production of travel documents to reduce forgeries and to enhance the capacity to monitor cross-border activities.

Additional measures were adopted at the 2003 Ministerial Conference in Maastricht, the Netherlands. Of central importance was the adoption of the OSCE 'Strategy to Address Threats to Security and Stability in the Twenty-First Century.' This document placed considerable emphasis on improving the training and coordination of national police forces in combating terrorism, and substantial improvements in border security that would not only make the flow of terrorists across borders more difficult but would also cut down on other flows of contraband, trafficking in women and children, and other illegal cross border activities. Similarly, an increased emphasis has been evident in OSCE documents in recent years dealing with efforts to reduce racism, xenophobia, anti-Semitism and other forms of discrimination based on race, religion, and ethnicity. In short, strengthening the 'human dimension' in the OSCE portfolio has been a major emphasis of the effort to respond to the threats posed by 9/11 and other occurrences of terrorism in the OSCE region.

The OSCE has also undertaken several specific efforts directed at enhancing the operational capacity of participating states to combat terrorism. First, in 2002 the OSCE adopted a Document on Small Arms and Light Weapons, which was intended to slow the flow of small arms across national borders, a traffic that often fuels local and regional conflicts. This was followed by the production of a handbook: 'The Best Practices Guide of Small and Light Weapons.' Although this measure was more directed at preventing outbreaks of ethno-national or other similar forms of violence, it may also have a modest effect on terrorist access to weapons and on their ability to transport them across borders.

Second, and of more immediate significance, however, was the adoption by the Forum for Security Cooperation of measures to control the export of Man-Portable Air Defense Systems (MANPADS). The ready availability of such weapons on world markets provides easy access for terrorists to weapons that can easily threaten civil aviation. In January 2004, 44 participating states attended a workshop, organized by the ATU, that provided technical advice on tightening security around airports against MANPADS that might be used to attack civilian aircraft and on improving emergency response procedures in event of such an attack.

Third, the ATU has assisted participating states in enhancing border controls, especially in the area of improving the security of passports and other travel documentation. The goal is to enable all participating states to issue machine-readable passports with digitized photos and, if possible, with at least one biometric identifier. Other advice is provided to combat the counterfeiting of travel documents, and also in monitoring borders for the transfer of radiological materials that might be used in the manufacture of 'dirty bombs' or radiological dispersion devices. This effort has been conducted in cooperation with the International Atomic Energy Agency (IAEA), also based in Vienna.

Fourth, in cooperation with the OSCE Office of the Coordinator for Economic and Environmental Affairs and the UN Office of Drugs and Crime (UN ODC), the ATU has organized national workshops in Armenia, Azerbaijan, Kazakhstan, Kyrgyzstan, Uzbekistan, and Tajikistan as of January 2004 on combating money laundering and tracking and suppressing terrorist financing. Technical assistance has been provided to Albania's Financial Intelligence Unit to improve its capacity to counter money laundering.

At the same time, the OSCE, especially through ODIHR, has emphasized the importance of conducting efforts against terrorism while simultaneously respecting fundamental human rights. Specifically, it has warned states against using anti-terrorism measures as 'an opportunity to restrict certain fundamental freedoms by targeting, for example, minority or religious groups, NGOs and journalists.'[10] It has worked with the Council of Europe, which adopted on 11 July 2002 'Guidelines on Human Rights and the Fight against Terrorism.' These guidelines include provisions against arbitrary arrest, invasions of privacy, police custody and pre-trial detention without warrant or provision of access to legal council, and extradition to states that may engage in torture or inflict the death penalty. In this regard, it should be noted that the OSCE Parliamentary Assembly, at its meeting in Rotterdam in July 2003, adopted a resolution deploring the actions of the United States for its treatment of prisoners held at Guantanamo Bay, Cuba, and calling upon the US to fulfill its OSCE and other international obligations by providing for the rights of prisoners not to be held indefinitely without legal council or trial, and the United States was criticized especially for incarcerating children in contravention of international law.[11]

In short, the OSCE has tried very hard to establish its bona fides with respect to adopting measures intended to combat the threat arising from global terrorist networks. On the other hand, the absence of significant resources, and the reluctance of some participating states to cooperate fully, has frequently made it difficult for the OSCE to advance much beyond rhetoric and a few limited actions when it comes to implementing anti-terrorism measures that can effectively combat terrorist threats at the operational level.

The post-9/11 regional focus: priority on Central Asia and the Caucasus

In addition to the shift in issues of attention since 9/11, there has also been a partial shift in the regional focus of the OSCE. While the Caucasus has been an area of concern to the OSCE since 1991, the overall significance of the area has grown since 2001. More noteworthy has been the substantial emphasis placed by OSCE institutions and officials on Central Asia. Although these regions have hardly replaced the Balkans as a primary focus of attention, the relative proportion of time and attention devoted to these two regions compared to the prior preoccupation with events in the Balkans is notable.

The five Central Asian republics that emerged from the wreckage of the Soviet Union have been among the slowest to develop even rudimentary democratic institutions. All five gained their independence with strong national leaders in charge, often with close connections to the Soviet past. The OSCE has established centers in each of these countries to encourage, mostly through gentle persuasion, greater openness to participation by the populace in governance with the eventual goal of full democratization. The focus of OSCE efforts in Central Asia has been on stimulating education about democratic practices, governance, rule of law and other human dimension issues. This is part of an institutional division of labor in the region in which the International Monetary Fund and the European Bank for Reconstruction and Development have taken the lead in economic development initiatives, the European Union has emphasized technical assistance programs to promote governmental capacity-building, NATO has brought the four countries (except Tajikistan) into its Partnership for Peace and the Euro-Atlantic Partnership Council in the realm of military security and the UN took the lead in conflict resolution and peacekeeping in Tajikistan, supported by the OSCE mission, after a peace accord was signed in May 1997.[12] The OSCE has taken the lead in organizing seminars with local political elites and NGOs in which outside specialists on various human dimension issues are brought into the country to discuss the obstacles that must be overcome to begin to build democratic institutions in the region. Its activities have included supporting and protecting NGOs, often threatened by governmental repression, and the protection of human rights, with special efforts directed against the use of torture.[13] The OSCE has devoted special attention to preventing a re-ignition of the conflict between ethnic Kyrgyz and Uzbek citizens in the Ferghana Valley region that strtches across

Uzbekistan, Kyrgyzstan, and Tajikistan, where violence was experienced in the early 1990s. Of particular concern here has been the Islamic Movement of Uzbekistan, which draws its main strength from this region and has engaged in violence against both the government and Western institutions and officials there.[14] Similarly, political conflicts along regional lines or between regions and the central governments have threatened to break out in the Osh region of Kyrgyzstan and in the Khojand region of Tajikistan. The OSCE has also been concerned with the potential rise of fundamentalist political Islam in this region, a relatively new phenomenon in states where religion had been largely suppressed during Soviet rule. A special issue as well in Tajikistan and Uzbekistan has been the long common border with Afghanistan, combined with elements of ethnic Uzbeks and Tajiks residing in Afghanistan, who became the core of the Northern Alliance that fought with the US and other international forces in the overthrow of the Taliban. Prior to the outbreak of the war against the Taliban, border security rested largely in the hands of a small group of Commonwealth of Independent State (CIS) troops, primarily composed of Russian along with a few Central Asian units, which patrolled this border region. The fear of terrorist infiltration, or even of fundamentalist ideologies spreading across borders, has preoccupied the post-Soviet regional governments, providing them with an additional incentive to cooperate in the struggle against terrorist influences in border regions. Most of the OSCE focus, however, has been on a more indirect threat, namely trying to alleviate the root causes that might provide fertile ground for radical ideas, messianic beliefs, and terrorist organizations to gain a foothold. This has also led to a renewed emphasis on the economic dimension of OSCE activities. Unfortunately, local corruption and a lack of stable governance remain the primary obstacles to economic development in the region. As a result, appeals for greater assistance, based in part upon defusing terrorist threats, have thus far gone largely unheeded.

The human rights situation has deteriorated most severely in Turkmenistan. The situation grew so serious in late 2002 that the OSCE invoked the 'Moscow Mechanism' for the first time, when ten states requested information about serious and pervasive threats to human rights following a government crackdown in the aftermath of an assassination attempt against President Niyazov. The OSCE appointed a Rapporteur, jurist Emmanuel Decaux of France, to investigate. However, he was denied access to the country by its government and had to prepare his report from information available outside of Turkmenistan.

In 2003 the Chairman-in-Office (CiO), Netherlands Foreign Minister Jaap de Hoop Scheffer, appointed former Finnish President Martti Ahtisaari as his personal representative to Central Asia. Ahtasaari made several trips to the region to meet with government authorities, political leaders, and representatives of civil society and nongovernmental organizations. The aim of his visit was to discuss strengthening democratic institutions, rule of law, and observance of fundamental human rights throughout the region. He also focused on efforts against terrorism and the trafficking in drugs and other contraband. In March 2003 the CiO, Foreign Minister de Hoop Scheffer arranged a meeting with President Niyazov to express the OSCE's deep concern about the severe human rights crisis in his country, although the ultimate impact of his warnings remains unclear.[15] In July 2003, the CiO again made a personal tour of the region, except for Turkmenistan. In Kyrgyzstan he worked on arrangements for a new OSCE comprehensive police assistance program that began in August 2003. In Kazakhstan he helped to initiate a new OSCE-supported Summer School for Prison Staff, designed to train prison administrators from all of the Central Asian states, again except for Turkmenistan.

The Caucasus region has also constituted a central emphasis of the OSCE since 9/11. In addition to continuing efforts to resolve the secessionist conflicts in Chechnya, Abkhazia, South Ossetia and Nagorno-Karabakh, attention has also focused on monitoring the border between Georgia and the breakaway region of Chechnya within the Russian Federation. The goal has been to prevent the spillover of the conflict from Chechnya into northern Georgia, and also to restrict the flow of men, arms, and contraband across the border at the crest of the Caucasus mountain range. Especially given Russian reports of the involvement of terrorists from outside the region in the fighting in Chechnya, and possible links between some factions in Chechnya and other breakaway regions with terrorist networks, perhaps including al Qaeda, this effort also fits in with the post-9/11 emphasis on combating terrorism. Although this operation began in late 1999, it has expanded considerably since 9/11 to also include the border between Georgia and the Ingush and Dagestan Republics of the Russian Federation, which border Chechnya on the west and east respectively. Observation posts have been established along the border at the highest ridges of the Caucasus Mountains staffed by unarmed OSCE monitors, numbering 144 in the summer months and 111 during the long winter in 2003. Units of the Georgian army have provided security for the observers.

The OSCE also played a modest role in facilitating the transition following the 'rose revolution' in Georgia in December 2003 and January 2004. An OSCE election-monitoring mission run by ODIHR had been strongly critical of the conduct of the November 2003 parliamentary elections, and it assisted in setting up and monitoring the presidential elections that ensued in January 2004 following the resignation of President Shevardnadze, in which Mikhail Saakashvili was overwhelmingly elected as the new president.

In addition, the OSCE has worked diligently to try to encourage the Russian Federation to close its military bases and withdraw its troops and equipment from both Georgia and Moldova. At the same time, however, criticism of the behavior of Russian troops in Chechnya, especially actions that potentially violate the 1994 OSCE Code of Conduct on Politico-Military

Affairs, has become muted since 9/11. Contrary to the proclamations immediately after 9/11 by Condoleezza Rice and others that the US human rights efforts would be as vigorous as ever within the OSCE context, in general criticism has become low-key and carries few, if any, consequences. Clearly Moscow's cooperation in the struggle against terrorism, based in part on the claim (partly supported by available evidence) that at least some elements in the Chechen organization have connections with transnational terrorist networks, has been sufficient to convince Washington and other capitals not to criticize the Russians too strongly lest such criticism be turned against the US for its behavior in Iraq or Afghanistan, especially with regard to the sensitive issues of prisoners held at US bases in Iraq, Guantanamo Bay, Cuba and elsewhere.

Conclusions

The OSCE has clearly adapted its priorities and actions to the realities of the post-9/11 world, but largely in modest, low profile ways. The OSCE has always been starved for resources to carry out its lofty aims, and this problem has not been solved after 9/11. Furthermore, in the grand scheme of security policy in both Europe and especially in the US, the OSCE has been further marginalized as an instrument for carrying out the primary goals of foreign and security policy. The expanding role of the EU's Common Foreign and Security Policy, along with the increasing unilateralism displayed by the United States since 9/11, has provided only marginal and limited space and very few resources for the OSCE to be able to respond effectively to the challenges posed by international terrorism. It should not be surprising, therefore, that in the first two years since 9/11 the OSCE's response has been more evident in declarations and resolutions than in concrete actions on the ground. At the same time, it would be unfair and inappropriate to ignore the fact that even the modest steps taken by the OSCE, when viewed cumulatively, have strengthened the capacity of some countries, those where terrorism is most likely to take hold, breed, and find sustenance, to mount modest efforts to resist terrorist advances. The OSCE accomplishments with regard to terrorism, as in many other issues, tend to be many, but modest, and almost always occur outside of the glare of public attention.

Therefore, while acknowledging the OSCE's limitations as a major institutional focus for combating international terrorism since 9/11, it would be a mistake to ignore its modest accomplishments and its potential to play a more significant role in the future. Once the world ceases to focus on the immediate stop-gap measures to combat what are perceived, whether rightly or wrongly, as imminent threats and takes the longer view about the nature of the challenge in responding to terrorism, it may become apparent that the OSCE's linkage of security, economic justice, and the human dimension gives it greater strengths in combating the overall challenge presented by international terrorism than institutions whose roles and functions are more narrowly defined. In the final analysis, a broad conceptualization of the underpinnings of terrorism may yield a greater awareness of the capacity of multifaceted, multilateral institutions like the OSCE to play an important role in enhancing the security of individuals, peoples, and states throughout the vast Eurasian and North American regions.

Notes

1. See D. C. Thomas, *The Helsinki Effect: International Norms, Human Rights, and the Demise of Communism* (Princeton, NJ: Princeton University Press, 2001).
2. See E. Adler, 'The OSCE's Community-Building Model,' in E. Adler and M. Barnett (eds), *Security Communities* (Cambridge, UK: Cambridge University Press, 1998), pp. 132–8.
3. See http://www.osce.org/field_activities/; seven mission and field activities have been closed down in the past several years after fulfilling their mandates or after the host states refused to have their mandates renewed.
4. For further explication of these functions see P. T. Hopmann, 'An Evaluation of the OSCE's Role in Conflict Management,' in H. Gärtner, A. Hyde-Price and E. Reiter (eds), *Europe's New Security Challenges* (Boulder, CO: Lynne Rienner, 2001), pp. 219–54.
5. See Z. Brzezinski, *The Grand Chessboard: American Primacy and its Geostrategic Imperatives* (New York: Basic Books, 1997), p. 23.
6. http://www.csce.gov/witness.cfm?briefing_id = 200&testimony_id = 213, p. 7.
7. http://www.csce.gov/witness.cfm?briefing_id = 200&testimony_id = 214, p. 1.
8. *ibid*, p. 2.
9. I am grateful to Brian Woo for much of the information contained in the remainder of this paper, based largely on an interview in Vienna on 18 February 2004, and on the OSCE's 'Field Reference for OSCE Anti-Terrorism Efforts' updated in January 2004 by the Action against Terrorism Unit.
10. *ibid*, p. 22.
11. http://www.oscepa.org/admin/getbinary.asp?FileID = 98
12. N. MacFarlane, 'International Organizations in Central Asia: Understanding the Limits,' *Helsinki Monitor*, XIV, (2003) 291–5.
13. W. Höynck, 'The OSCE in Central Asia – On the Right Track?' *Helsinki Monitor*, XIV (2003) 303–5.
14. *ibid*, 309.
15. *ibid*, 310.

13
Multilateral Arms Control as a Response to NBC Proliferation: a New Transatlantic Divide?

Alexander Kelle

Different approaches to arms control

While Europe and the United States have been involved together in various arms control[1] negotiations since the 1950s, they have not always seen eye to eye with regard to the objectives to be pursued through such negotiations, the means by which to achieve goals, or the role of arms control in the overall strategic landscape. More often than not, it was the US that was the engine that drove forward arms control proposals, with at least some Europeans only following on reluctantly. The Nuclear Non-Proliferation Treaty (NPT), for example, was an agreement over which certain European countries, such as Germany and Italy, faced bitter domestic debates about ratification. Yet continuous exposure to arms control negotiations, together with the on-site verification measures carried out in European states – some of which originated in the 1950s, as in the case of the Western European Union's Agency for the Control of Armaments[2] – led over time to a widespread European acceptance of arms control as a legitimate tool of security policy. In the nuclear realm, cooperative arms control measures have, through EURATOM, become part of the overall European effort at overcoming the past divisions of the continent through a number of integrative efforts, including multilateral control measures.[3] As a result, for most Europeans, arms control has over time acquired a normative quality that goes well beyond the narrow scope that 'traditional' US arms controllers have come to attribute to the concept.[4] When taken to extremes, therefore, normatists can end up asking 'what can we do for arms control', instead of the more traditional, or utilitarian approach, which is more interested in the question of 'what can arms control do for us' in the pursuit of national security interests.[5]

In the early 1990s normatists seemed to have won the day, as prospects for both bilateral and multilateral arms control looked better than ever before. Indeed, a number of agreements were concluded at this time: the bilateral

START I and II treaties on the reduction of strategic nuclear weapons, and on the multilateral level, the Chemical Weapons Convention (CWC) and the Comprehensive Test Ban Treaty (CTBT). However, after the 1995 NPT Review and Extension Conference the still American-led arms control train seemed to quickly lose steam. New negotiations for a Fissile Material Cut-Off Treaty (FMCT), for example, did not, as expected, get under way at the Geneva-based Conference on Disarmament (CD) and the ratification and implementation by the US of already treaties that had already been concluded turned out to be far more cumbersome than anticipated.

Many observers attributed this lost of impetus in US arms control policy to the Clinton Administration's focus on domestic policy and the lesser attention that was consequently paid to security policy issues. In addition, the effects of a divided government, in which a Senate controlled by conservative Republicans held arms control treaties hostage to the realization of their own political agenda, also had a significant impact. This situation is exemplified in the conditions attached by the Senate to the ratification of the CWC in April 1997 and its rejection of the CTBT in the autumn of 1998.[6]

In 2001, the new Bush administration made it clear from the very beginning that two of the major tenets of US arms control policy were to undergo radical change: first, arms control was no longer to be enshrined in bi- or multilateral treaties. Instead, it would to take the form of unilateral reductions plus – where feasible – concomitant or subsequent negotiations. In addition, previously agreed upon arms control treaties would no longer be regarded as untouchable. The US administration would not hesitate to withdraw from arms control agreements it considered outdated and/or no longer to be in the interests of the United States. This represents the utilitarian approach in its purest form, and almost bordered on an outright rejectionist policy in some parts of the administration. It is embedded in strategic reasoning which places a premium on stopping 'rogue states and their terrorist clients before they are able to threaten or use weapons of mass destruction against the United States and our allies and friends.'[7]

The approach adopted by European governments stands in marked contrast to the current US positions. As the British Foreign Secretary Jack Straw pointed out during a speech given at Kings College in London in February 2002:

> International arms control means setting and defending international standards. The value of existing measures, strengthened where necessary, should not be underestimated.
>
> So the international community should not talk down arms control and non-proliferation measures, nor lightly seek their amendment....[8]

Similarly, German Foreign Minister Fischer summed up the his government's approach to arms control during his speech at the Second Conference to Facilitate the CTBT's entry into force in November 2001:

We have emerged from the shadow of the Cold War, have cast off confrontational modes of thought and now face a new, no less dangerous challenge. A new impetus for global disarmament and arms control must be part of the response of the community of states in order to live up to the core task of maintaining international peace and security, as laid down in the UN Charter. In Germany's opinion, it is particularly important:

- to avoid new, mainly regional arms races;
- to maintain and enhance the comprehensive system of disarmament and non-proliferation treaties; and
- to contain more effectively than hitherto the proliferation of weapons of mass destruction and their means of delivery to state and non-state actors, using political means as well as treaties.[9]

As the European Security Strategy of December 2003 clearly shows, this strong support for multilateral arms control regimes is based on the positive experiences Europeans have had with their normatist approach. These experiences have resulted in the belief that 'security can be increased through confidence building and arms control regimes. Such instruments can also make an important contribution to security and stability in our neighborhood and beyond.'[10]

Multilateral nuclear arms control in the strengthened NPT review process

The strengthened NPT review process that was agreed upon during the 1995 NPT Review and Extension Conference contains both a procedural and a substantive element. In terms of procedure, the parties to the NPT agreed to considerably expanded preparatory meetings between any two treaty review conferences. With regard to substance, a set of principles and objectives to enhance the implementation of the NPT was agreed upon. Paragraph 4 of the principles and objectives explicitly addresses three nuclear disarmament related issues: It calls for the conclusion of negotiations on the Comprehensive Test Ban Treaty (CTBT), which was achieved in 1996, the commencement of negotiations on a Fissile Material Cut-Off Treaty (FMCT), and, what is more, the nuclear weapon states (NWS) who are parties to the treaty agreed for the first time that the total elimination of their nuclear arsenals represents the eventual end-point of the disarmament process.[11]

This latter commitment was reinforced during the 2000 NPT Review Conference, which ended with the 'unequivocal undertaking by the nuclear weapon states to accomplish the total elimination of their nuclear arsenals'. In addition, the final declaration of the Conference contained a number of practical steps which add up to a 'multi-stranded approach of unilateral, bilateral, plurilateral and multilateral measures, which all need to be addressed in parallel as part of the overall process of reducing the legitimacy and reliance on nuclear weapons.'[12] Again, the urgency of the entry into force of the CTBT and the early conclusion on a FMCT were singled out as important immediate steps to be taken. Furthermore, the final declaration, for the first time ever, mentioned non-strategic nuclear weapons. It also called for the irreversibility of all nuclear disarmament steps.

Yet, not all EU states held identical views on all of the disarmament-related issues that were addressed by the review conference. On the contrary, the two EU nuclear weapon states, Britain and France, found themselves confronted in negotiations about nuclear disarmament-related language for the conference's final declaration with the so-called New Agenda Coalition (NAC), two of whose seven members are also EU member states – Ireland and Sweden.[13] In these initially confidential negotiations, France was reportedly much more reluctant to agree to wording calling for the elimination of nuclear arsenals in the final declaration. When these negotiations became public, other EU states, most notably Germany and Belgium – who are two of five so-called NATO-5 states[14] – complained about the secretive nature of the meetings, which seem to be taking place at the expense of long-time allies. Despite, therefore, a joint statement in the general debate of the review conference, EU states were divided into three separate interest groups, reflecting their nuclear (or non-nuclear) status and the degree to which their position on the normatist-utilitarian spectrum overrides considerations of EU cohesion.

The 2002 meeting of the Preparatory Committee for the 2005 NPT review conference saw similar subdivisions of EU member states with respect to nuclear disarmament issues. Again, the joint EU statement delivered by the Spanish presidency of the Union covered general themes, including those related to disarmament.[15] In the subsequent deliberations of the Preparatory Committee differences in interpretation and emphasis among the EU states once again came to the fore.[16] France, for its part, complained about the reporting requirements of the disarmament obligations under the NPT, because comparable requirements do not exist for other obligations states had assumed under the treaty. Britain drew some criticism for the remarks by her ambassador that '[h]aving reduced our nuclear weapons to a single system at the minimum level necessary for the UK's national security, further unilateral steps we can now take without compromising that security are limited.' He went on to point out that '[w]hen we are satisfied that sufficient progress has been made to allow us to include British nuclear weapons in multilateral negotiations without endangering our security interests, we will do so.'[17] The New Agenda Coalition (NAC), with its two EU members, welcomed the prospects of bilateral US–Russian disarmament steps, emphasizing, however, that reducing the operational status of strategic nuclear weapons cannot replace legally binding, verified, and irreversible steps towards complete nuclear disarmament.[18] This ultimate goal also featured prominently in one of two working papers submitted by Germany: starting from the assumption that the goal of the total elimination of nuclear weapons was undisputed, the paper laid out a set of prerequisites that are regarded by the German government as being of particular significance for achieving this goal. Most prominent among the prerequiites mentioned in the paper are the establishment of a fissile material inventory, that can serve as a baseline against which the final stages of disarmament steps towards a nuclear weapon free world can be judged. Secondly, the paper emphasized the need for effective verification of all disarmament steps, with the aim of reassuring all states that no one retains a capability to covertly breakout from any future nuclear prohibition regime.[19]

In the second German working paper on non-strategic nuclear weapons, the efforts to include these weapon systems in the disarmament process – ranging from the 1991/1992 US–Russian presidential initiatives to the inclusion of tactical nuclear weapons in the final declaration of the 2000 NPT review conference – were acknowledged. However, the paper also recognized that the elimination of tactical nuclear weapons 'will not be possible in one leap' and therefore a 'gradual approach' might yield the greatest benefits. The steps proposed include, *inter alia*, the reporting by the US and Russia on the 1991/1992 initiatives and the formalization of the initiatives into a legally binding document, one that would include 'appropriate verification measures which would give assurance of compliance with them.'[20]

Despite differences in emphasis among the Europeans in nuclear disarmament matters, for the time being, the European non-nuclear weapon states seem content with the fact that British and French nuclear weapons are not part of the nuclear disarmament process. That is, as long as the two states participate actively in other aspects of the arms control agenda and do not rule out their future participation in this process once the arsenals of the US and Russia have been reduced to numbers much closer to the British and French nuclear arsenals than they currently are. As summarized by one observer, the 2003 NPT Preparatory Committee:

> may represent a 'return-to-the-past' turning point for the non-proliferation regime, echoing the Cold War emphasis on preventing 'undesirables' from acquiring nuclear weapons, while nuclear disarmament is consigned once again to the periphery, as a distant, rhetorical objective that does not really impinge on the ringfenced privileges of the 'already haves'.[21]

In other words, the nuclear weapon states, led by the US, are more and more able to shield their utilitarian calculations concerning the need for their continued reliance on nuclear weapons from normatist demands for nuclear disarmament.

BW arms control

The Biological Weapons Convention (BWC) was concluded in 1972 and entered into force in 1975. Its main deficiency came to the fore rather quickly after the treaty came into effect: the absence of a verification or compliance monitoring mechanism. As early as the second half of the 1970s, suspicions were voiced that the Soviet Union possessed a clandestine, offensive BW program. After the anthrax outbreak in the Soviet city of Sverdlovsk in 1979, the BWC review conference in 1986 agreed on a first set of confidence building measures (CBMs). Additional CBMs were agreed upon during the 1991 review conference. Yet, despite the exemplary performance of the EU states – all of which are members of the BWC – as well as a number of other states, the overall number of required annual declarations detailing compliance with the treaty has been more than disappointing.[22] As a result, the BWC states parties decided at a Special Conference in September 1994 to begin negotiations to strengthen the BWC through a legally binding compliance protocol.

The Ad Hoc Group Negotiating process

Negotiations in the Ad Hoc Group (AHG) commenced in January 1995 and came to an unexpected close in July 2001 when the Bush administration declared that it could no longer support the AHG negotiating process and was unwilling to accept any compliance protocol emanating from this process. Throughout the negotiations Europe had made a significant contribution to the strengthening of the BWC through the AHG, both in terms of leadership it exercised and the significant number and high quality of the personnel involved in the negotiations.

A number of European Union Common Positions, which embrace the 15 EU states and to which 14 other states usually commit themselves, made a valuable contribution to the AHG process. In March 1998 the European Union issued such a Common Position in order to 'actively promote decisive progress in the work of the Ad Hoc Group, with a view to concluding the substantive negotiations by the end of 1998, so that the Protocol can be adopted by a Special Conference of States Parties early in 1999.'[23] After all, a situation in which 29 States have agreed to certain negotiating objectives would seem to represent a significant step towards consensus in negotiations which have frequently involved only some 50 or so states parties to the BWC. In another Common Position, adopted by the Council of the Union on 17 May 1999 the EU spelled out the elements of a compliance protocol it deemed essential for an effective protocol. These include declarations relevant to the BWC, so as to enhance transparency, 'effective follow-up to these declarations in the form of visits', 'appropriate clarification procedures', 'provision for rapid and effective investigations into concerns over non-compliance', 'establishment of a cost-effective organization', and measures 'to further international cooperation and exchanges in the field of biotechnology.'[24]

Finally, there were a large number of European working papers submitted to the AHG with a total of 108 – out of 363 national papers – submitted by

May 2001 by the European Union states or the EU as a whole.[25] In comparison, the United States submitted 16 working papers, Ukraine 14, Russia 27, and South Africa 77. In terms of substantive issues, the EU states can be said to have been among the most progressive, creative and determined to bring the AHG process to a successful conclusion. The issues addressed by various EU states cover all the issues identified in the 1999 EU common position as being central to the effective functioning of the future BWC compliance regime. The US, in contrast, tried to limit the scope and the intrusiveness of the compliance measures in particular, i.e. declarations, investigations and visits, and of the measures to promote cooperation in the peaceful uses of the biosciences. Against the background of this negotiating position, the US criticism that the Protocol would be too weak to accomplish the goals set for it cannot come as anything but a surprise.

The 5th BWC review conference and the 'New Process'

After the categorical US rejection of the AHG efforts to negotiate a legally binding compliance protocol whose implementation would have been overseen by a new international organization set up for this purpose, the EU shifted gears and tried to write as many proposals as possible into the final declaration, measures that would necessitate follow-up action after the review conference and thus at least allow for a discussion forum on BW-matters to exist independent of the AHG.

With respect to Article I of the convention, which outlines the scope of the BWC and contains the core normative guidelines for state behavior, that is not to produce or use biological weapons, the scientific and technological developments in some areas of the life-sciences represent an issue of growing concern to BWC states parties. Many states parties hold the view that the five-yearly review conferences are no longer an adequate means of keeping track of all of the scientific and technological developments relevant to the BWC. Following this line of reasoning, the EU proposed 'to establish a Scientific Advisory Panel (SAP) for an annual update of scientific and technological developments relevant to the Convention to report to States Parties.'[26] Likewise, the EU called upon 'States Parties to explore a possible set of common principles in the field of export controls to be applied on a voluntary basis' in order to continue a dialogue between the two camps of export control advocates and its critics.

In the context of the CBMs agreed upon during the 1986 and 1991 Review Conferences, the EU's working paper proposed to make the annual declarations submitted by BWC states parties more accessible: 'With a view to increasing the transparency of CBM declarations, the Conference calls upon the UN Secretary General to set up a database, easy to consult, of States Parties' annual declarations.' In addition, the EU suggested that 'the scope for declaration could be extended under some specific measures in order to provide a broader range of relevant information, consistent with the approach agreed in 1991.' The most far reaching proposal related to CBMs, however, was the suggestion to 'consider as mandatory the requirement to provide information' under two of the CBMs. So-called measure E requires the declaration of the export and import of microorganisms and toxins – which according to the EU paper should also include the mandatory declaration of criminal legislation. Measure G, that is the declaration of vaccine production facilities, should equally be made mandatory and should 'be extended to cover animal vaccines, microbially based pesticides and biocontrol agents.'

Because of the adjournment of the review conference, which was caused by a last-minute American demand to definitively terminate the AHG's mandate, no final declaration that could have reflected the EU's proposals was agreed upon.[27] When the conference re-convened in November 2002 the only proposal that was put forward by the chairman of the conference envisaged a weak follow-up mechanism, along the lines suggested by the US government's earlier proposal. The chairman's proposal, which was cleared in advance with most delegations, did not make an explicit reference to the fate of the AHG, nor was it subject to further discussion during the resumed session of the conference. When the proposal was agreed upon, the conference established a 'New Process' to be implemented between 2003 and the next BWC review conference in 2006.[28]

The substantive issues with which BWC states parties are allowed to concern themselves are a far cry from the comprehensive approach of the Protocol negotiations. To a large degree, the measures agreed upon are national in character, not multilateral, and where there is an international dimension to the issues to be discussed, it is usually for the coordination of national measures.[29] From a European perspective, this approach is much less pro-active that the positions taken during the first part of the 2001 Review Conference. Obviously, engaging the United States in any process, however watered-down it might be, had a higher priority for European states than working on a substantive strengthening of the BW control regime.

CW arms control

The States of the European Union, working within the Western European and Others Group, played a strong role in the negotiations in the Conference on Disarmament (CD) and subsequently in the Preparatory Commission of the CWC. The larger states maintained large delegations in Geneva and subsequently in The Hague, including both diplomatic representation and experts from chemical defense laboratories. All member states of the EU became original parties by ratifying the CWC before its entry into force.[30]

The Chairmanship of the CD Ad Hoc Committee rotated on an annual basis between the three political groups – Western, Eastern and the Group of

21 (Neutral and Non-Aligned). As a result, over the course of the negotiations, a number of EU delegations from the Western Group held the chair and were thus in a position to put their stamp on the negotiating process. This applies especially to the German Ambassador Adolf von Wagner, who was Chairman in 1992 and brought the work of the Committee to a successful conclusion. European delegations also provided practical input into the negotiations, particularly through their involvement of their domestic chemical industries, work on analytical questions, and practical inspection exercises.

European states have also been at the forefront with respect to the ratification and implementation of the CWC. Sweden was the first EU country to ratify the CWC in June 1993 and Luxembourg completed EU ratifications in April 1997. The CWC contains a set of elaborate rules and procedures that require state parties to enact implementing legislation at the national level. It seems that here again, EU states did not encounter great difficulties, including countries with large chemical industries. France, for example, ratified the CWC as early as March 1995. This ratification did not cause any particular problems, with the 19 December 1994 Law (94–1098) authorizing ratification passing almost unanimously. The implementing legislation was only voted on in June 1998, but it was preceded by several legal provisions providing for the implementation of all French obligations under the CWC.

Germany ratified the CWC on 12 August 1994, and was one of the first states with a large chemical industry to do so. While the ratification process did not encounter any difficulties during its passage through lower house of parliament, the *Bundestag*, the implementing legislation was delayed in the *Bundesrat*, the upper house of German parliament, in which the 16 federal German states are represented. In particular, the states that comprise the territory of the former German Democratic Republic objected to the legislation because of uncertainties relating to the cost of implementation. They demanded an unequivocal statement from the federal government that it would cover all of the costs involved with compliance with the CWC, in the event that chemical weapons left by the Soviet Union or other old CW were found on their territory. After the federal government gave this assurance, the implementing legislation was passed. None of the EU countries attached any unilateral reservations or conditions to the ratification or implementation laws that would have limited the CWC's applicability in their states. However, the exact opposite happened in case of the US legislation implementing the CWC.[31]

In addition to unilateral exemptions to the CWC's scope and the applicability, the US government also did not submit the required industry declarations in time. According to the CWC, initial declarations of any relevant industry facilities had to be filed within 30 days after the entry into force of the Convention for a state party, which for the US would have been by the end of May 1997. In fact, the US declaration was not forthcoming for another four and a half years. US officials explained that because of a delay in enacting the implementation legislation, which was necessary if information was to be collected from private chemical companies, the US industry declaration could not be submitted earlier. This extended delay, however, led to a seriously imbalance in the distribution of industry inspections among States Parties with large chemical industries. In 1998, the member states of the European Union hosted more than 60 per cent of Schedule 2 and more than half of all Schedule 3 inspections worldwide, which is far more than they would have had to bear if the US had submitted its declaration on time. In an effort to redress this imbalance and under some pressure from their own chemical industries, members of the European Union utilized the budget negotiations of the Organisation for the Prohibition of Chemical Weapons (OPCW), the CWC's monitoring authority, to limit the number of industry inspections. In this way, the US delay had not only the effect of disrupting the smooth operation of the CWC's industry verification regime, but was also the underlying cause for two of the review conferences of states parties to become bogged down in endless debates over a few line items in the organization's budget.

During preparations for the First Review Conference on the implementation of the CWC, which was held in April/May 2003, some observers wondered whether states parties to this multilateral control regime should expect US actions similar to those displayed during the 5th BWC Review Conference, i.e. the naming of non-compliant states parties and the tabling of unacceptable last-minute proposals. Although the former strategy was employed by the US vis-à-vis Iran and a few other states parties, it did not disrupt the conference.[32] With respect to an issue the US did not want to have discussed during the Review Conference – so-called non-lethal chemical weapons, or toxic incapacitants[33] – the US approach was only slightly more diplomatic. It successfully influenced the conference agenda so as to prevent the International Committee of the Red Cross (ICRC) from speaking during the general debate of the Conference. The focus of the ICRC presentation was to have been the danger presented by the development and potential use of toxic incapacitants for the overall objectives of the CWC.[34]

Conclusion: normatists, utilitarians, rejectionists, and the future of multilateral NBC arms control

At the beginning of this chapter the point was made that the concept of arms control, as conceptualized by the US in the early 1960s, had been regarded as a useful policy tool for US security up until the mid-1990s. Taking a transatlantic perspective, when arms control was put into practice in the 1960s and

1970s by successive US administrations, Europe was either the target of the arms control efforts of that time or presented an additional obstacle in bilateral US-Soviet arms control talks. These 'traditional roles' have been reversed. Today, Europe is the stronger supporter of NBC arms control measures, while the US is, at best, reluctantly following.[35] In that sense, the differences across the Atlantic are not new, but the traditional roles have been reversed.

There is a clear trend in both the US political system and the academic debate towards viewing multilateral NBC arms control through the prism of American dominance in world politics. Underneath this line of reasoning, however, there is more than one approach that is being followed. Clearly the Bush administration consists largely of people who completely reject any idea that arms control can be a useful policy tool in international relations. According to this view, the enormous US advantage in military power must not be equalized through legally binding multilateral arms control agreements. The Bush administration does not seem to see much utility in supporting the notion of legalistic equality that is inherent in many such agreements and seeks instead to maintain or even expand its technological superiority in a whole range of weapon systems.

However, given the arms control performance of the Clinton administration, even a future Democratic administration is unlikely to engender immediate transatlantic harmony in the area of arms control. On the contrary, a clear policy shift occurred across the political spectrum in the US during the second half of the 1990s and, as a result, it seems likely that the best option that will be available in the near future would be a return by the United States to a utilitarian arms control policy, one which re-integrates and upgrades multilateral arms control within the overall range of security policy tools being utilized to protect US national interests. Intellectual support for such a policy can be identified in the scholarly debate on arms control.[36] Yet, contributions to this debate seem to suffer from two shortcomings: first, arms control is still seen as a bilateral exercise; the move to multilateral arms control via global control regimes and the importance attached to them in large parts of the world seems to have slipped below the radar screen of some analysts.[37] Secondly, and related to this, some scholars who do see a future for arms control also seem all too keen to apply the concept to issue areas like cyberspace.[38] This not only risks applying arms control to issue areas for which it was not originally designed, and thereby overburdening it with expectations it cannot fulfill, but also ignores the shortcomings of current arms control regimes that need to be addressed.[39]

Europe, overall, seems to emerge as the 'model student' of multilateral NBC arms control. Although this might be attributed to the fact that a comparable unilateral temptation does not exist for Europeans, and thus does not stand in the way of their embracing multilateral arms control arrangements as the primary response to security risks emanating from NBC weapons proliferation, the mere absence of a unilateral temptation caused by military incapacity is a somewhat limited explanation for the European normatist stance towards multilateral arms control regimes.

Rather, three interrelated causes are at the root of this phenomenon. First, the Europeans have been socialized into recognizing arms control not only as an acceptable and useful tool of security policy, but have integrated the normative standards of multilateral regimes into the definition of their national security interests. As Müller has shown, the internalization of normative standards for behavior, especially in the area of security policy, involves debates over the acceptance of these norms.[40] Particularly heated debates could, for example, be observed in Germany and Italy when the NPT was up for ratification in the early 1970s.

Having been socialized into multilateral arms control in this way, it is reinforced by a second factor: the fact that Europeans are used to the internalization of normative guidelines issued from a 'higher EU authority'. Officials in national capitals may not always like the guidelines they receive from the EU bureaucracy in Brussels, but in most instances they comply with them. In principle, the same process is at work with the internalization of the principles and norms that constitute the basis of NBC arms control regimes. In both areas European states were able to contribute to the design of the 'higher authority' and therefore compliance with the normative structure thus erected and its maintenance is the default, rather than the exception in their behavior.

Thirdly, the strong European support for multilateral arms control regimes is informed by the externalization of the institution building processes that were used to create transparency, predictability and security within Europe in the first place. This institution building comes in two forms: first, it took place in the CSCE/OSCE context, which at least initially was pursued with a group of states perceived as adversaries. The success of this process taught the Europeans that institution building has a chance to succeed even when the states that are regarded as part of the problem and not of the solution are taking part in the exercise. It can be assumed that the success of this process influences European thinking on multilateral NBC regimes, where again the 'problem states' are part of the process and will inevitably influence the outcome. Secondly, institution building has taken place within the EU in order to harmonize policy on issues such as dual-use export controls or the formulation of common positions and joint actions. Exposure to these processes gives Europeans a higher degree of confidence than the US appears to have in the actual functioning of multilateral institutions and the international bureaucracies backing them up.

These causal mechanisms underlying European NBC arms control policies are embedded in the context of broader 'changing ordering principles of European international society'.[41] Along the lines of Hyde-Price's reasoning we can assume that an approach based on balance of power thinking has been superceded as a mechanism for ensuring security within Europe by a negotiated, liberal order, one that has continuously evolved since the end of the Second World War. The opportunity to create and benefit from this order has endowed many Europeans with a belief in the possibility of progressive change in the international system – resting to a large degree on an increased communication and interaction density, and eventually leading to a regulative order which determines the proper behavior of states.

Yet, if this reading of the evolving European international order is correct, the strong and continuous European support for multilateral NBC arms control regimes should not come as a surprise. These international regimes are exactly about overcoming balance of power reasoning and creating a regulative order, providing the normative standards of behavior with respect to certain categories of weapons. Seen from this point of view, in the eyes of many Europeans, the United States more and more fails the 'normative test'[42] of behaving like a civilized state in the area of NBC arms control.

Taking causal mechanisms like these into account also helps better explain the visceral reactions of European governments to American attempts either to gain preferential treatment for itself – as in the case of CWC implementing legislation and the submission of industry declarations – or to abandon a process of increasing the density of rules and procedures in a given regime, as with the case of the BWC compliance protocol.

For multilateral NBC arms control to have a future under these conditions requires first of all an intensified transatlantic dialogue about what constitutes arms control, and its relative importance for utilitarian and normative arms controllers. Utilitarians in the US need to appreciate more fully that the strong European support for multilateral NBC arms control reflects both the internalization of the multilateral regimes' principles and norms and the externalization of processes that Europe has successfully experienced internally. Consequently, this approach is unlikely to change in the foreseeable future. At the same time European normatists need to realize that hopes of the US to embrace their normative approach are bound to be disappointed. At best a backing off from the rejectionist policies of the Bush administration and the adoption of a utilitarian approach, one which upgrades the importance of multilateral arms control measures in the arsenal of US security policy tools, can be expected. On the basis of these realizations utilitarians and normatists have to define the common ground on which they can agree for the maintenance and strengthening of multilateral NBC arms control regimes.

Notes

1. Arms control in this chapter is understood to encompass both disarmament and non-proliferation measures.

2. H. Müller, 'The Evolution of Verification: Lessons From the Past for the Future', *Arms Control*, 14 (1993) 333–56.

3. D. Howlett, *EURATOM and Nuclear Safeguards* (Basingstoke: Macmillan, 1990).

4. J. Goldblat, *Arms Control: The New Guide to Negotiations and Agreements*, 2nd edn (London: Sage, 2002).

5. A. Kelle, 'Utilitarian and Normative Approaches to Arms Control', *International Studies Review*, 47 (2003) 386–9.

6. On the CWC see A. Smithson, 'Bungling a No-Brainer: How Washington Barely Ratified the Chemical Weapons Convention, *The Battle to Obtain Ratification of the CWC*, Report No.35, Washington, DC: Stimson Center, 1998, and B. W. Kubbig, M. Dembinski and A. Kelle, *Unilateralism as Sole Foreign Policy Strategy? American Policy towards the UN, NATO, and the OPCW in the Clinton Era*, PRIF-Reports No.57, November 2000, Frankfurt; on the CTBT see D. Kimball, 'How the U.S. Senate Rejected CTBT Ratification', *Disarmament Diplomacy*, Issue No.40, October 1999, 8–15.

7. The President of the United States, *National Security Strategy of the United States*, Washington, DC: The White House, September 2002, p.14.

8. 'The future of arms control and non-proliferation', speech given by the Foreign Secretary, Jack Straw, at King's College, London, Wednesday 6 February 2002, available at http://www.fco.gov.uk/text_only/news/speechtext.asp?5869, last accessed on 19 February 2002.

9. Address by Joschka Fischer, Minister for Foreign Affairs of the Federal Republic of Germany, at the Second Conference on Facilitating the Entry into Force of the Comprehensive Nuclear Test-Ban Treaty, New York, 11 November 2001, last accessed on 19 March 2002 at www.auswaertiges-mt.de/www/en/aussenpolitik/ friedenspolitik/ausgabe_archiv?archiv_id = 2287 &type_id = 3&bereich_id = 12

10. *A Secure Europe in a Better World*, European Security Strategy, Brussels, 12 December 2003, available at http://ue.eu.int/solana/securityStrategy.asp, last accessed 6 March 2004, p.10.

11. See the 'Principles and Objectives for Nuclear Non-Proliferation and Disarmament', issued as conference document NPT/CONF.1995/32/DEC.2, adopted on 10 May 1995, reproduced in *PPNN Newsbrief*, No.30, 2nd Quarter 1995, 23f.

12. R. Johnson, 'NPT 2000: Implementing the Disarmament Pledges', *Disarmament Diplomacy*, Issue No.48, July (2000) 3–9.

13. The remaining five members of the NAC are Brazil, Egypt, Mexico, New Zealand, and South Africa. The following account is based on Rebecca Johnson: 'The 2000 NPT Review Conference: A Delicate, Hard-Won Compromise', *Disarmament Diplomacy*, Issue No.46 (May 2000) 2–21.

14. The other three being Italy, Netherlands and Norway, the latter one a NATO- but not a EU-member.

15. See Statement by H. E. Carlos Miranda, Ambassador of Spain, on behalf of the European Union, at the First Session of the Preparatory Committee of the 2005 Review Conference of the Parties to the Treaty on the Non-Proliferation of Nuclear Weapons, New York, 8 April 2002, available at: www.basicint.org/ nuclear/prepcom2002/Spain_EU.htm

16. See R. Johnson, 'NPT Report – The 2002 PrepCom: Papering Over the Cracks', *Disarmament Diplomacy*, Issue No.64 (May–June 2002), available at www.acronym. org.uk/dd/dd64/64npt.htm

17. Statement of Ambassador Peter Jenkins, Acting head of UK delegation, New York, 9 April 2002 as quoted in Johnson, note 16.

18. See Working Paper submitted by Egypt on behalf of the New Agenda Coalition (Brazil, Egypt, Ireland, Mexico, New Zealand, South Africa and Sweden), Document NPT/CONF.2005/PC.1/WP.1, available at www.basicint.org/nuclear/prepcom2002/WP-NAC.htm.

19. See the paper submitted by the German Delegation, *Attaining a Nuclear-Weapon Free World*, New York, 11 April 2002, available at www.basicint.org/nuclear/prepcom2002/C1-Germany2.htm.

20. See the paper submitted by the German Delegation, *Non-Strategic Nuclear Weapons*, New York, 11 April 2002, available at www.basicint.org/nuclear/prepcom2002/C1-Germany.htm

21. R. Johnson, 'Rogues and Rhetoric: The 2003 NPT PrepCom Slides Backwards', *Disarmament Diplomacy*, No.71 (June–July 2003), available at http://www.acronym.org.uk/dd/dd71/71npt.htm

22. For a detailed assessment of the CBM's see I. Hunger, 'Article V: Confidence Building Measures', in G. Pearson/M. Dando (eds) *Strengthening the Biological Weapons Convention: Key Points for the Fourth Review Conference*, Geneva: QUNO, 1996, pp.77–92, and M. I. Chevrier/I. Hunger: 'Confidence-Building Measures for the BTWC: Performance and Potential', in *The Nonproliferation Review*, 7 (2000) 24–42.

23. United Nations, *Working Paper submitted by the United Kingdom of Great Britain and Northern Ireland on behalf of the European Union*, BWC/AD HOC GROUP/WP.272, 9 March 1998.

24. The text of Common Position (1999/346/CFSP) is available on the web site of the SIPRI Project on Chemical and Biological Warfare at http://projects.sipri.se/cbw/docs/btwc-EU-commpos.html.

25. The total number of working papers is 468, 105 of which were issued by the various friends of the Chair and not by states or groups of states.

26. See *Working paper submitted by the European Union*, Document BWC/CONF.V/COW/WP.23, Geneva, 27 November 2001; subsequent quotes taken from this document.

27. See J. Rissanen, 'Continued Turbulence over BWC Verification' in T. Findlay and O. Meier (eds), *Verification Yearbook 2002* (London: VERTIC, 2002).

28. See M. I. Chevrier, 'Waiting for Godot or Saving the Show? The BWC Review Conference Reaches Modest Agreement', in *Disarmament Diplomacy*, No.68 (December 2002/January 2003) 1–16.

29. See the *Final Document* of the Fifth Review Conference, Document BWC/CONF.V/17, Geneva 2002, pp.3f, at http://www.opbw.org/rev_cons/5rc/docs/rev_con_docs/i_docs/BWC-CONF.V-17-(final_doc).pdf

30. See D. Feakes, 'The European Union's Role in CBW Disarmament and Non-Proliferation', *The Chemical and Biological Weapons Conventions Bulletin*, Issue No.44 (June 1999) 4–9.

31. See M. Krepon, A. Smithson and J. Parachini, *The Battle to Obtain U.S. Ratification of the Chemical Weapons Convention*, Report No.35, Washington, DC: The Henry L. Stimson Center, July 1997.

32. See A. Kelle and K. Höhl, *Die Multilaterale Rüstungskontrolle von Chemischen Waffen am Scheideweg – Das Chemiewaffen-Übereinkommen und seine erste Überprüfungskonferenz*, HSFK-Report Nr.15, Frankfurt/Main (December 2003).

33. On this issue see M. Wheelis, 'Non-lethal Chemical Weapons – a Faustian Bargain', *Issues in Science and Technology* (Spring 2003) 74–8; M. Dando, 'Scientific and Technological Change and the Future of the CWC: the Problem of Non-Lethal Weapons', *Disarmament Forum*, No.4 (2002) 33–44.

34. See ICRC statement at http://www.icrc.org/Web/eng/siteeng0.nsf/html/5M4BGC ?OpenDocument
35. See D. Ozga, 'The Reluctant Giant of Arms Control', *Security Dialogue*, 34 (2003) 87–102.
36. For example, N. Tannenwald, 'U.S. Arms Control Policy in a Time Warp', *Ethics and International Affairs*, 15 (2001) 51–70.
37. See P. Bracken, 'Thinking (Again) About Arms Control', *Orbis*, 48 (2004) 149–59.
38. See the contributions in J. A. Larsen (ed.), *Arms Control: Cooperative Security in a Changing Environment* (Boulder, CO: Lynne Rienner, 2002).
39. See A. Kelle, 'Strengthening the Effectiveness of the BTW Control Regime – Feasibility and Options', *Contemporary Security Policy*, 24 (2003) 95–132.
40. See H. Müller, 'The Internalization of Principles, Norms and Rules by Governments: The Case of Security Regimes', in V. Rittberger (ed.) *Regime Theory and International Relations* (Oxford: Clarendon Press, 1993) 361–88.
41. See A. Hyde-Price, *Power and Authority in the European Security System*, presentation to the workshop 'European Security and Defense Policy: Towards Comprehensive Security', organized by the European Forum, Stanford University, 20–21 March 2002.
42. D.N. Nelson, *New Dimensions of Transatlantic Relations*, presentation to the workshop 'European Security and Defense Policy: Towards Comprehensive Security', organized by the European Forum, Stanford University, 20–21 March 2002.

14

What Future for Europe's Security and Defense Policy? Five Scenarios for the Year 2020

Heiko Borchert and Daniel Maurer

The struggle against terrorism, the near-breakdown of the transatlantic partnership over the War on Iraq, and the difficulties in adopting the draft treaty for a European constitution make it hard to envisage alternative future developments of Europe's Security and Defense Policy (ESDP). It seems as if the basic parameters of the international order established since the end of the Second World War are undergoing fundamental change, while a joint vision of the future international order and a common understanding of how to proceed are missing. Situations like this provide ample risks and opportunities. Ignoring the forces of change or believing in the existence of an auto-pilot that will bring international relations back to normalcy would be wrong. Rather, we contend that it is important to identify the key drivers shaping the future and to think about a range of possible outcomes. To this purpose our paper presents five scenarios for the future of the European Union (EU) in general and the ESDP in particular.

Exploring scenarios does not prescribe the future. Rather, such an exploration is intended to make decision-makers aware of alternative futures and their implications.[1] Our scenarios (See Figure 14.1) are based on three building blocks: first, an analysis of various studies dealing with long-term developments in such diverse areas as politics, society, economy, technology and ecology provided the general background. Second, we identified different influencing factors – such as the role of international security institutions, the behavior of state actors, and the growing importance of non-state actors – that make up the general international framework in which the European Union (EU) operates. Third, EU-specific variables, such as the main political motives for cooperation, the geographical scope of the Union, its institutional development, as well as military and non-military tasks and capabilities were summarized in an additional group of scenario variables.

The key features of the scenarios lead to different outcomes as summarized in Table 14.1. To complement our scenario descriptions, we also provide brief analyses of each scenario's risks and opportunities and discuss their

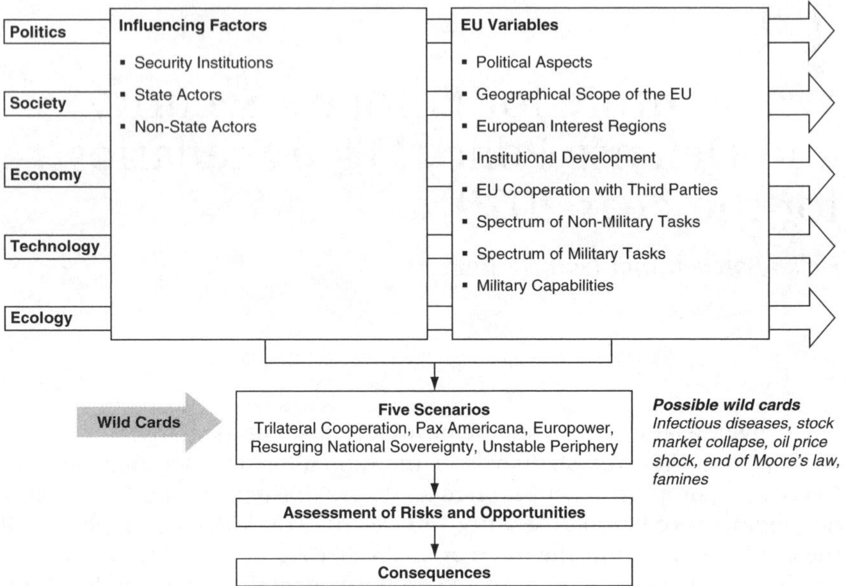

Figure 14.1   Main scenario elements

most important consequences. We show how each scenario will impact upon the need for conflict prevention, conflict management, and post-conflict stabilization. We also look at the division of labor among international organizations in executing these tasks and debate what potential zones of turmoil are most likely to see international interventions. Depending on the degree of multinational or supra-national cooperation, some of the scenarios also require the examination of the possible implications for the reform of national and international security institutions.

Scenario 1: trilateral cooperation and the triumph of multilateralism

The main feature of this scenario is the strong multilateral commitment of the international community, which strengthens international institutions. The boon for multilateralism is that it is based on mutual cooperation between the United States, the EU, and Russia. Together they decide to transfer NATO and the Organization for Security and Cooperation in Europe (OSCE) into a new Northern Hemisphere Alliance (NHA), in order to provide stability and prosperity around the world. Mutual understanding among the three also furthers the United Nations (UN), which – thanks to reforms – becomes more efficient and effective in accomplishing its tasks. As the major

Table 14.1 Key drivers and outcomes of the five ESDP scenarios

Scenario	Key Drivers	Outcome
Trilateral Cooperation	– US support for multilateralism	– Sustainable world order thanks to close US–EU–Russian cooperation
	– Cooperative Russian foreign policy	– NATO and OSCE transformed into Northern Hemisphere Alliance
	– Successful EU reform	– EU enlargement proceeds as foreseen
Pax Americana	– US 'velvet unilateralism' favors bilateral relationships and ad hoc-coalitions	– Unstable international environment
	– Frictions between transatlantic partners	– NATO transformed into toolbox
		– EU enlargement delayed and restricted to today's candidates
		– Artificial separation between CFSP and ESDP
Europower	– Good EU–US and EU–Russian relationship	– EU becomes fully-fledged supranational community (three pillars abolished)
	– Successful EU reform (convention adopted)	– EU has strong and well-balanced military and civilian capabilities
	– Successful ESDP operations bolster European confidence	– Enlargement proceeds as envisaged and includes Turkey
	– NATO becomes less effective	
Resurging National Sovereignty	– Severe and sustained economic downturn	– EU enlargement renders decision-making more difficult
	– US feels vulnerable and becomes only selectively engaged internationally	– Directorate of leading states takes over and pushes EU institutions back
	– EU military failure barely avoided	
	– Cleavages between EU members	
Unstable Periphery	– Global economic crisis	– Crisis of confidence in international politics weakens multilateral framework
	– Transatlantic relationship breaks down in spirit	– EU enlargement restricted to today's candidates
	– Turmoil in Europe's neighborhood; security concerns spur European integration	– Military and police capabilities of the Union receive substantial boost

coordination platform between the NHA and other regional organizations, the UN plays a key role in spurring regional cooperation, to the benefit of global multilateralism.

International stability reigns. Thanks to joint efforts via the NHA and the UN, the United States, the EU, and Russia are successful at preventing conflicts and avoiding the escalation of conflicts into crisis. Non-state actors also play a key role in maintaining stability. They have established themselves as key actors in the field of early warning and mediation, provide the international community with useful on-the-spot information for early warning, and helping to calm tensions between conflicting parties.

The EU is more integrated than it is today. The Council of Ministers remains key, but the European Commission and the European Parliament have more to say because of increased co-decision-making powers. Common Foreign and Security Policy (CFSP) issues are decided by qualified majority, whereas different majorities are needed for various ESDP issues. The President of the Council takes on the role of Europe's foreign minister and represents the Union in the UN Security Council and in the NHA. Enlargement proceeds as foreseen and results in a Union of 35 members comprising all of today's candidates, the remaining Balkan states, Norway, and Iceland. Furthermore, the Union gives greater recognition to the strategic importance of the Near and Middle East, the Caucasus, and Central Asia and becomes a welcome partner there. The trilateral cooperation among the EU, Russia, and the United States also contributes towards the harmonization of political and economic initiatives intended to empower those regions.

As a peaceful power anchored within the NHA, the EU has a balanced mix of military and non-military capabilities. An intervention force of 200,000 troops exists that covers all Petersberg tasks[2] and provides collective defense. Within the EU it assists civilian agencies at both national and European levels for the purpose of civil protection or border control. In the non-military field, Europe's capabilities have advanced, thanks to the pooling of resources and competencies in the fields of reconstruction, police, rule of law, and civil administration. The Union has its own budget to finance operations in these areas, and close cooperation with the UN, the United States, and Russia helps advance development policy.

Consequences

In this scenario, globalization has prompted the leading international actors to establish a collaborative framework to promote a stable international environment. Because the international community succeeds in preventing conflicts, the escalation of looming crises can be avoided. A high degree of political, economic, and societal interdependence among the members of the NHA leads to converging risk assessments, which facilitates cooperation.[3] To avoid the impression of a 'northern fortress in the making', it will be essential for the NHA to cooperate closely with other regional organizations. If that occurs, we expect that cooperation with the NHA will trigger domestic reform in partnering regions, thus stabilizing the periphery.

The key characteristic of this scenario is the spread of the zone of stability that covers the Northern hemisphere. This affects the need for and the conduct of prevention, conflict-management, and stabilization operations. Within the NHA the international community will focus primarily on stabilization operations on its outskirts, where newly established democracies come into being. To this end, international joint endeavors benefit from the smooth interplay between the political and the military capabilities of the NHA and the economic core competencies of the EU. The NHA and the EU will field joint missions that help advance regional stabilization and development programs. This is a major step forward, especially with regard to reforming the security sectors of these countries, disarming, demobilizing, and reintegrating former warring fractions, and strengthening democratically controlled institutions. At the heart of the NHA the importance of defense will drop, while it remains important at the borders with the new neighbors of the NHA, for example in Central Asia, North Africa, and the Near and Middle East.

Outside the NHA things will look different. A strong multilateral world order will give preference to preventive joint actions via international organizations. Where these are successful, the NHA and the UN will succeed in projecting stability and prosperity. However, there may be pockets of crisis that do not respond to this tactic. In these cases the international community has the will and the necessary means to intervene, with force if necessary. We assume that the NHA will be the instrument of first choice to deal with such challenges at the global level. The EU, by contrast, will be able to shoulder all military contingencies that have lower deployability requirements and will thus become a provider of regional stability.

Stability and prosperity alter the international agenda. The importance of fighting terrorism or the proliferation of weapons of mass destruction (WMD) will diminish, because the most important root causes – economic underdevelopment, corruption, bad governance, political instability, the disregard of democratic principles, or state failure – can be addressed with success. That is why *Trilateral Cooperation* helps establish the idea of 'human security' (individual welfare) as the corner stone of international politics. In Europe some pressing problems will be alleviated as well. Institutional competition between NATO and the EU is no longer as contentious as today, because NATO is substantially transformed and the EU has enhanced some of its capabilities. Furthermore, all three partners of the NHA agree on a comprehensive security approach that blends hard and soft power capabilities. This cushions burden-sharing discussions, which tend to focus all too readily on the hard power side of the equation while neglecting soft power issues.

Scenario 2: Pax Americana and a fragile unipolar world order

Thanks to robust economic growth and unmatched military capabilities, the United States dominates international politics. Washington's 'velvet unilateralism' respects international organizations, as long as they serve American interests. A web of close bilateral relationships and ad-hoc coalitions help enlarge the America's room for maneuver. In Europe, the United Kingdom, Spain, Italy, and Turkey are amongst its closest allies. Moscow and Washington have agreed on a strategic partnership. US aid supports Russia's economic recovery and its admission to the World Trade Organization. In turn, Washington receives exclusive access to Russian oil reserves and other natural resources. The new strategic partnership also works as an effective mechanism for containing the rise of 'would be' great powers in East Asia and helps forge new alliances in the Middle East.

In contrast, US–European relations remain rocky. US military supremacy, higher defense spending, and technological progress have reduced the reliance of the United States on third parties (for instance, for host nation support) in favor of 'go it alone' tactics. This policy engenders criticism in diplomatic circles, in the media, and by non-governmental actors and increases the number of attacks on US facilities and military bases, mainly in the Near and Middle East. These events harden America's policy of 'preemptive action' against any nation that is suspected of supporting terrorists. Washington's policy drives a wedge between EU members, one that hampers their willingness and ability to cooperate. Although most European governments criticize Washington, they are too weak and too disunited to counterbalance the hegemon.

On the one hand, the European force of 60,000 troops has not yet achieved in full all of its capability goals and it can thus only take on low-end Petersberg tasks (mainly humanitarian relief, rescue, and peace-keeping missions; stabilization tasks can only partially be tackled). The EU continues to depend on NATO, especially in the fields of crisis management and intervention. However, US force transformation has led to a comprehensive overhaul of the Alliance into a flexibly deployable, global intervention force made up of modular components. On the other hand, EU members agree on setting up a pool of police forces and merging the civil experts databases of the Union, the OSCE, and the UN. Although these measures facilitate the preparation of joint missions, their impact is limited due to continuing US–European disagreement over how to deal with zones of turmoil.

International disagreement also hampers Europe's integration process. Only after delays does the Union admit 10 new members. The second pillar remains intergovernmental, with the Council of Ministers as the most important decision-making body. CFSP issues can be decided by majority voting, but ESDP decisions still require unanimity. EU members appoint the President of the Council, who represents the Union at the UN, but not at

NATO. The resulting artificial separation between the CFSP and ESDP is accepted, particularly by those countries that themselves have strong military capabilities and good bilateral relations with Washington.

Consequences

Pax Americana yields ambivalent results: although the US hegemon provides stability, its actions cause asymmetric risks and provoke violent conflicts. The unipolar dominance of the US and its reliance on military power put the legitimacy of US leadership at risk. Attacks on US targets will also hurt America's allies. Therefore, the risk assessments of the US and its allies on the one hand and those of other European countries will diverge, thus making it more difficult to agree on joint actions. Given Washington's interest in security, we assume that there will be a growing US tendency to interfere with the domestic affairs of its allies, in order to accomplish its foreign policy goals. In the long run, this may hamper US soft power and further accentuate Washington's legitimacy crisis. However, failure to provide accurate intelligence, as witnessed in the aftermath of the war on Iraq, could make it difficult to justify the policy of preemption.

The emphasis of *Pax Americana* is on conflict management, especially for the purpose of fighting terrorism. NATO might benefit from the US preference to act with coalitions of the willing, because it can help prepare military forces to achieve the necessary degree of interoperability. The EU's military dimension, by contrast, will face tough times. Disagreement among EU members will make it more difficult to reach agreement on the Union's transformation agenda and might thus hamper activities aimed at overcoming European capability shortfalls. Therefore, it is no surprise that the scenario envisages EU military activities only for lower-scale Petersberg tasks. Defense is not a European Union task, but remains confined to NATO. The transformation of the Alliance brought about by the fight against terrorism, however, puts a question mark after the readiness and willingness of Alliance members (especially the US) to live up to their common defense requirements.[4] This outcome is disadvantageous for Europeans, because their mutual disagreement means that each nation must shoulder a larger part of the burden, as efficient cooperative solutions cannot be achieved.

Transatlantic disagreement makes it more difficult to reach accord on conflict prevention and post-conflict stabilization. Europeans will face tough decisions about the risks entailed in acting as the stabilization force in those conflicts where the US has initially intervened. Independent European prevention and stabilization activities are limited in scope because of diverging US–European interests. Europe's leeway as a whole will be limited to playing a niche role, while some individual European countries team up with the United States, also by providing niche capabilities for the hegemon. The US–Russian strategic partnership could aggravate this situation if it undermines European influence in potential zones of instability, such as the Caucasus or Russia's former 'near abroad'. This could drastically reduce the value of European integration as an instrument of structural prevention.

Scenario 3: Europower and the success of a comprehensive security approach

This scenario describes the advent of Europe as a leading political, economic, and military power, one that acts in favor of a strong multilateral world order and rules-based international politics. Apart from occasional differences, the transatlantic relationship evolves smoothly, and relations with other leading states, such as Russia or China, are also good. Current transatlantic differences will be overcome in the second decade, because ESDP makes substantial progress and launches successful operations in the Balkans and in Africa.

The EU implements a comprehensive security approach and works closely with the UN and the OSCE. The UN focuses on conflict prevention and development policy, and the OSCE pays special attention to furthering Central Asia's transition to democracy, stability, and prosperity.[5] NATO, in contrast, is of diminished importance in this scenario. Transatlantic differences hinder the Alliance's ability to act, and the admission of new candidates has rendered decision-making more difficult. Furthermore, effective cooperation between the EU, the OSCE and the UN – in tandem with non-governmental actors – proves extremely successful in preventing conflicts and containing crises, thus reducing the need for military intervention.

The EU becomes a fully-fledged supranational community. The adoption of a European Constitution gives rise to greater organizational flexibility, by abolishing the Union's three-pillar structure. A new EU Foreign and Security Commissioner represents the Union and heads the new Foreign and Security Council. The European Parliament elects the European President, who has representative functions, while the President of the European Commission plays a stronger role as a 'European Head of Government'. The European Commission becomes the central institution, and all matters are decided by single or qualified majority voting.

In geographic terms the Union comprises today's candidate countries, Norway and Iceland, all of the remaining Balkan states, and Turkey. In addition, the EU establishes a 'Trilateral Security Council' with Russia and Ukraine and adopts common strategies for North Africa and the Near and Middle East. In order to play a more global role, the EU builds up a balanced mix of military and non-military capabilities. In the civilian sector, the EU puts a major emphasis on conflict prevention, for which it uses all available instruments, especially economic 'carrots and sticks'. The Euro-Army, which is fully integrated and comprises 300,000 troops, comes under the leadership of the EU Foreign and Security Council. It handles a challenging spectrum of tasks, including collective defense, all Petersberg tasks, and subsidiary operations at the request of civilian authorities within Europe (for the purpose of emergency relief, border control, and other purposes). The European Head-quarters is responsible for both planning and operating integrated military and civilian contingencies. The European Procurement Agency, a security budget, a joint intelligence committee, and joint nuclear access – in coop-eration with the United Kingdom and France – round off the Union's secur-ity profile.

Consequences

Although the *Europower* scenario has a unipolar tendency, it differs substan-tially from *Pax Americana*. The EU's adherence to rules-based international politics, its emphasis on multilateralism, and a blended mix of military and civilian instruments help avoid the creation of the risky international envir-onment that characterizes *Pax Americana*. Additionally, active EU engage-ment in favor of conflict prevention reduces the Union's exposure to asymmetric risks. The admission of Turkey, as well as the existence of the Trilateral Security Council, helps project stability to potential pockets of crisis in Europe's neighborhood, thus avoiding the spill over of conflicts from these regions into the Union itself.

In this scenario the military and the non-military arms of Europe's security policy are fully fledged and cover all relevant capabilities. 'Constructive duplication' of capabilities between NATO and the EU thus becomes a reality.[6] Crucial areas in North Africa, the Near and Middle East, the Caucasus, and Central Asia benefit, as they receive tailored support and development assistance through close EU–UN–OSCE cooperation. This helps combine and harmonize UN and OSCE activities that favor democratic institutions and the rule of law with economic programs issued by the EU. As structural prevention takes root in these regions, the need to intervene militarily or to field stabilization operations diminishes.

Beyond the EU's zone of influence, however, military instruments remain important. Therefore, it is vital that EU–NATO and EU–US relationships be developed harmoniously.[7] This will not be easy, as the scenario assumes a reversal of today's situation, with the EU taking the lead over NATO. How-ever, even in the most optimistic scenario and provided that the new EU Procurement Agency and national defense establishments find effective ways of cooperating with each other, it will take the Union years to over-come existing military shortcomings. Therefore, the interim period is cru-cial: the EU has to depend on NATO (and thus on US support) until it has the necessary capabilities. If both sides fail to achieve consensus, this scenario will probably slip in the direction of *Pax Americana*.

As in the *Trilateral Cooperation* scenario, military deployments are also possible within the EU. This is envisaged in the draft European Convention as part of the solidarity clause, which foresees support for EU members in case of terrorist attacks.[8] This can be interpreted as the first building block of a European approach to homeland security. Domestic military operations at the request of civilian authorities will, however, require a reform of the domestic security competencies with regard to the division of labor between police and military forces. Together with an increased level of police cooperation, this development could help overcome the artificial gap between the second and the third pillar of the EU security policy.[9] As an instrument to prevent crisis and provide stability, police forces gain greater importance both outside and within the EU. This should be more clearly reflected in current discussions. This scenario suggests that the Union's institutional set-up will change fundamentally, thereby influencing national security sectors as well. The scenario foresees a more integrated approach to security policy, *inter alia* by merging military and civilian planning activities in a joint European Headquarters.[10] If this is the case, national security institutions and processes – ranging from planning staffs in the Ministries of Defense and Foreign Affairs, to national intelligence agencies and national procurement establishments, as well as the respective political oversight bodies – will have to be adapted as well. Today's segmented approach to security policy will have to be replaced by a more functional approach that cuts across organizational stovepipes – i.e., existing organizational boundaries – and gives rise to 'network-centric security policy'.[11] This approach will help realign tasks, competencies, and capabilities to make them comensurate with the new security demands. At the same time, the plea for more integration will also require reform of EU institutions, by redesigning key processes in order to guarantee the smooth interplay of all actors involved.

Scenario 4: Resurging national sovereignty and Europe at a standstill

In this scenario, severe world economic problems that endure for years, the near-failure of a EU military operation in the Balkans, and substantial frictions among EU member states lead to the collapse of the European integration process. Support for international organizations is nothing but an empty promise, because the international community is neither willing nor able to cooperate. US isolationism is a particular problem. Terrorist attacks create a feeling of being vulnerable anywhere and anytime, which drastically reduces Washington's preparedness to take the lead in international politics. In addition, new problems in South-East Asia and a severe economic downturn in Latin America shift the attention of the United States away from Europe. Other regional powers try to size the opportunity and to leverage their position.

The EU is weak. The European Council cancels the European Stability and Growth Pact and agrees on increasing public debts to fight the sluggish European economy and to beef-up military capabilities. In addition, the Heads of States and Governments also agree to postpone the next round of enlargement. This engenders heavy criticism by admission candidates, leads to a rift between old and new members, and helps spur the impact of right-wing political parties. After admitting today's candidates, enlargement is stopped. At the same time, a European military operation in the Balkans is on the verge of collapsing. US support, which was requested by the new NATO members, helps avoid the worst, but the credibility of the EU as a trustworthy international actor is severely damaged. To make matters worse, EU members cannot agree on a US plan to rescue Latin American economies by providing help through international financial institutions. This prompts unilateral action by Washington to bail out these economies.

Confidence in the EU plunges to an all time low and leads France, the United Kingdom, Germany, and Italy to step in to 'save' the Union. This 'Group of Four' (G-4) establishes a power directorate. The Council of Ministers is strengthened by returning to unanimity and by containing the influence of the European Commission and the European Parliament. The CFSP ceases to exist as such, because the member states return to a level of minimal political information sharing and coordination not witnessed since the early days of European Political Cooperation. Military tasks are no longer part of the Union's business. International operations take place either under the leadership of ad-hoc coalitions or the G-6 (G-4 plus Spain and Poland).

Consequences

This scenario lacks any drivers for stability. Whether the G-6 can ameliorate the situation depends on the worldview of the beholder. Advocates of a neo-realist or an intergovernmental worldview surely interpret the G-6 as a force for stabilization. In their view, *Kerneuropa*, or Core Europe, is the ultimate guarantor of effective cooperation and stability, because the nation state is the primary source of stabilization. But on the contrary, we expect rough times. In our interpretation, the G-6 will potentially separate European states from each other, increase differences, and thus make it more difficult to reach agreement on common solutions. While violent military conflicts in the Union are not a realistic option for the time frame analyzed, they might explode in surrounding states and regions.

Given this more critical interpretation, we contend that this scenario comes with the most severe consequences for the EU. As this scenario stresses, the classical aspects of state sovereignty, and all significant impulses for international politics, derive from the major powers and directorates. This undermines the value of international institutions in general and the EU in particular. International action is reactive and focuses on conflict management only. Due to a lack of agreement and willingness to cooperate, conflict prevention and post-conflict stabilization cease to play a meaningful role. This initiates a vicious circle in which the lack of prevention almost automatically produces the need for intervention and possibly also for pre-emption. There might, however, be a need for niche activities that help advance confidence and security-building measures. The OSCE might be better equipped to handle this job than the EU, given its broader spectrum of 55 participating states and its well-developed array of instruments.[12]

Military cooperation in Europe and among transatlantic partners will become more difficult as interoperability requirements diverge. In its most extreme form, Europe may see the rise of three different interoperability standards: the United States will define requirements for the coalitions it is willing to lead. These contingencies will focus on the fight against terrorism and WMD non-proliferation and might also include interventions for the purpose of regime change. The key areas of intervention are the Middle East and South West Asia. Requirements for mobility and sustainability will increase drastically, thus reducing the prospect for European participation. The G-6, which is the only potential European partner or leader for international operations, can hardly meet these requirements and will concentrate on lesser contingencies that do not require major expeditionary capabilities. The rest of Europe must decide if it wants to follow the United States or the G-6 or end up with standards of its own. It goes without saying that this development seriously hampers the defense commitments of the transatlantic community. Together with *Unstable Periphery, Resurging National Sovereignty* is the only case study in which defense gains in importance. However, neither NATO nor the EU is really fit to deal with this challenge, thus forcing individual nations to increase national defense capacities.

Scenario 5: Unstable periphery and 'Fortress Europe'

Europe's periphery is unstable. Conflicts that break out in North Africa, in the Caucasus, and in the Near and Middle East are the result of an explosive mixture of economic underdevelopment, demographic pressure, and ethnic-religious fundamentalism. International organizations remain ineffective in addressing the root causes, because support is lacking. Faith has been lost in the UN due to corruption scandals and allegations of misconduct and fraud. As a result, public opinion turns from skepticism into widespread distrust, which affects all international institutions. Participating states of the OSCE, to take one example, decide to suspend the organization's activities in the field of conflict prevention and to freeze the funds allocated for such activities.

The United States shifts its attention to the Asian–Pacific basin and is not interested in the conflicts on Europe's border. Widespread dissent between non-EU members and EU/NATO members leads to mutual recriminations and obstructionism. The transatlantic relationship breaks down in spirit. The only thing that interests Washington with regard to the future of NATO is the extent to which it will contribute to handling problems in Asia. Russia is in a very difficult situation, as it needs to cope with domestic upheaval, economic problems, and conflicts in neighboring regions (Ukraine,

Moldova, South Caucasus, Central Asia). However, growing uncertainties in the Arabian Peninsula serve to increase the importance of Russia's natural resources. This improves US–Russian relations; in particular. Moscow and Washington agree not to interfere in each other's regions of interest.

Europe fails to deal with the increasing flow of migrants from the Mediterranean. EU members fail in their attempts at integrating people from the new conflict regions. As these minorities are themselves well organized and radicalized, increasingly violent confrontations are possible. Thus, the risk of societal instability and terrorist activities is on the rise. Instead of addressing the root causes, European governments focus on fighting the symptoms by toughening border controls and immigration acts. 'Fortress Europe' becomes a reality.

Europe's integration process slows down. After admitting today's candidates, there is no second round of enlargement. Inter-governmentalism continues to reign in the CFSP, and the Council of Ministers remains key. The ESDP requires unanimity, while CFSP matters can be decided by qualified majority. The theoretical gain in flexibility is, however, offset by the fact that the external representation of the EU remains heterogeneous. This unsatisfactory outcome is the result of the EU member states' desires to determine the foreign and security policy agendas on their own. Europe becomes a 'security state'. People are increasingly anxious, political right-wing parties gain in importance, and the number of terrorist attacks on European and national targets grows. Conflict prevention fails, thus rendering economic aid and non-military instruments of conflict management ineffective. In contrast, Europe's military and police capabilities receive a substantial boost. A European Police Headquarters and a Police Academy are established. The EU has a defense budget and can dispose over an intervention force of 200,000 troops for all Petersberg tasks, the fight against terrorism, and to guarantee of law and order within the EU. A European Missile Defense system is being built.

Consequences

Unstable Periphery is the most turbulent of all of the scenarios, with the EU having to tackle traditional and asymmetric risks. Its response is similar to the US reaction in *Pax Americana*, in that Europe beefs-up its military capabilities and strengthens its police forces. Again, the result is ambivalent: The feeling of increased security comes with serious civil liberties curtailments. This in turn puts at risk the legitimacy of the European integration process. In addition, the advent of the 'European security state' stirs conflicts, because it toughens European immigration regulations and could lead to interventions abroad. The lack of any preventive policies increases the vulnerability of the EU.

Security is the top issue in this scenario, but the emphasis is on military and police cooperation only. Direct threats to the security of Europe give rise to traditional concepts of 'national security' at the expense of other approaches like 'human security', which dominates in the *Trilateral Cooperation* scenario. The reduction in soft power capabilities and the EU's shift in favor of a more reactive policy approach diminishes the value of preventive diplomacy, development cooperation, human rights policy, and post-conflict stabilization.

With the US concentration on the Asian–Pacific region, the transatlantic link epitomized by NATO has lost importance. Therefore, Europe must defend itself. Unlike in the *Europower* scenario, however, the EU has neither established its own headquarters nor does it have its own military forces. The lower degree of integration and the multinational character of these forces increase the need to achieve interoperability and standardization. To this end, it is possible that the EU will try to take operational control of NATO's European headquarters, in order to benefit from its well established structures, processes, and planning capabilities. Assuming that this does not mean that the EU becomes powerful enough to counterbalance or challenge the US, it is feasible that Washington might not oppose such a step.

In order to fight the crises in its neighborhood, the EU will become more interventionist. Whereas Europe follows global interests in the *Trilateral Cooperation* and *Europower* scenarios, the scope of action in the *Unstable Periphery* scenario will be limited to the Union's periphery. Portions of the Balkans and Turkey will remain outside the EU, and cooperation agreements with potential zones of conflicts in the Caucasus, the Near and Middle East, and North Africa do not exist. These areas thus become zones of strategic concern for Europe. In order to project stability into these regions, EU member states will have to pay more attention to increasing the fighting power of their military forces and to ensuring it has the capability to rapidly deploy, sustain, and protect such expeditionary forces.

Europe's focus on military and police security will also affect national security policies. In the *Europower* scenario, the increased level of supranationality in turn required members to adjust their national security institutions. In the *Unstable Periphery* scenario the pressure stems from the need to effectively fight the looming crises that surround Europe. As the Union provides security, it will require its members to share an equal burden. This will also hold true for potential candidates for admission. Given our risk assessment, we contend that would-be members of the Union will come under pressure to align their security establishment and to act in solidarity with the EU prior to joining it.

Conclusions

At present, international relations show clear signs of both the *Pax Americana* and *Unstable Periphery* scenarios. Both of these scenarios illustrate the risks entailed in a transatlantic divorce and the dominance of a hegemon that is not benevolent. Besides global developments that affect Europe, the future of Europe's integration process depends above all on the ability of the big EU members to mend fences over a number of issues related to the financing of common activities, enlarging the Union, and reforming its institutions. If this is not the case, the *Resurging of National Sovereignty* scenario hints at a possible outcome.

Unlike other commentators who are more pessimistic, we believe that the situations described in the *Europower* or *Trilateral Cooperation* scenarios should and can be achieved. To this end, Europe's broad understanding of security policy, the aim of balancing military and non-military capabilities, the European security strategy, the adoption of a solidarity clause and structured defense cooperation, the institutional innovations foreseen in the draft EU constitution – such as the appointment of an EU Foreign Minster and the establishment of the European Agency for Procurement, Defense Capabilities and Research – and provisions for closer cooperation between the EU and NATO, the OSCE, and the UN[13] are all welcome steps in the right direction. In order to expand these initial successes and overcome existing shortcomings, the EU and its members should address the following issues specifically:

First, the European security strategy should fully embrace the notions of network-centric security policy and effects-based operations. While most of today's security demands are network centric, existing policies, processes, and structures are organized along organizational stovepipes rather than functional considerations. The multi-faceted character of the new security risks requires a more integrated approach that puts prime emphasis on a comprehensive analysis, provision, and development of security policy capabilities. Effects-based operations (EBO) are the primary mode of conduct, because they start from comprehensive analysis of political, military, economic, social, infrastructural, and informational aspects.[14] The EU and its members are well equipped to comply with this requirement and to provide the necessary instruments to conduct EBO. In order to fully leverage this potential, national and European security sectors need to be transformed, thereby paving the way for smooth interaction among and between the security sector, the corporate sector, and non-governmental organizations.

Second, the broad guidelines for Europe's key capabilities must be defined at the political level. Capabilities mirror political ambitions. Although it is possible to identify the key capabilities that the European security strategy tacitly refers to, it would be wise to address this task explicitly. So far, the EU's Capability Development Mechanism is restricted to the military–technical level.[15] Assuming that armaments cooperation will receive a boost from the new European Defence Agency, a political mechanism will be indispensable in developing military and non-military capabilities that are in line with the EU's overall political ambitions. That is why the European Heads of State and Governments, the Commission, and the High Representative should play a stronger role in defining Europe's strategic capabilities. This requires the establishment of an appropriate mechanism at the political level to define the broad outlook that can be translated into long-term planning guidelines.

Third, the European security strategy should be more precise on when, where, and how to combine the EU's impressive array of political, economic, and military instruments. So far, the strategy is too vague on the operational interplay of its various instruments, thus making it more difficult to agree on concrete steps for their advancement. One challenge is regional, in the sense that the EU must look beyond the first round of enlargement to regions such as the Southern Caucasus, Africa, Central Asia, or the Far East, where new opportunities and risks might potentially arise that endanger stability and prosperity. The other challenge is conceptual and stems from the need to combine the various instruments for conflict prevention, conflict management, and post-conflict stabilization in a more coherent way. As our discussion of the *Europower* scenario underlines, this could be achieved through wide-ranging institutional reforms and strategic partnerships with other international organizations.

Fourth, European states should address more seriously the issues of pooling their resources and agreeing on a division of labor (role specialization).[16] Both approaches provide for a more effective and efficient use of scarce resources, while also bolstering existing strengths and improving coherence in addressing capability shortfalls. In order to unleash their potential, joint planning mechanisms should be strengthened and the competencies of European institutions expanded. Most importantly, role specialization and the pooling of resources should not be confined to the military sector alone, but should cover all security sector actors and the relevant partners in other ministries (such as the ministries of foreign affairs and interior) and in the corporate sector.

Notes

1. P. Schwartz, *The Art of the Long View. Planning for the Future in an Uncertain World* (New York: Currency Doubleday, 1995).
2. Originally, these tasks included (1) humanitarian and rescue, (2) peacekeeping, and (3) combat forces in crisis management, including peacemaking. The Draft Treaty establishing a European constitution has added joint disarmament operations, military advice and assistance tasks, and post-conflict stabilization, which can contribute to the fight against terrorism. See: Article III-210, Draft Treaty establishing a Constitution for Europe, CONV 850/03, Brussels, 18 July 2003, <http:// european-convention.eu.int/docs/Treaty/cv00850.en03.pdf> (accessed 20 January 2004).
3. On the role of threat perceptions, see S. Penksa's contribution in this volume.
4. Anti- and counter-terrorist capabilities redefine the purpose of defense in shifting the front lines from territorial defense to global contingencies. This will affect doctrine, organization, training, material, leadership, personnel, and facilities. One of the most visible changes, the reform of the military posture of the US

overseas, is already underway. See: K. M. Campbell and C. J. Ward, 'New Battle Stations?' *Foreign Affairs*, No. 82 (3) (September/October 2003) 95–103.
5. On the OSCE's role in Central Asia, see also the contribution by T. Hopmann in this volume.
6. K. Schake, *Constructive Duplication: Reducing EU Reliance on US Military Assets* (London: Centre for European Reform, 2002).
7. For more on this, see also the contributions by H. Gärtner and R. Karp in this volume.
8. Article I-42, Draft Treaty Establishing a Constitution for Europe (see note 2 above).
9. A. Townsend, *Guarding Europe* (London: Centre for European Reform, 2003); J. D. Occhipinti, *The Politics of EU Police Cooperation. Toward a European FBI?* (Boulder/London: Lynne Rienner Publishers, 2003), pp. 119–88.
10. 'EU Operational Planning. The Politics of Defence,' *IISS Strategic Comments*, December 2003.
11. For more on this, see H. Borchert (ed.), *Vernetzte Sicherheit. Leitbild der Sicherheitspolitik im 21. Jahrhundert [Network Centric Security. Leitmotif for Security Policy in the 21st Century]* (Hamburg/Berlin/Bonn: Mittler, 2004).
12. The OSCE's most important instruments of preventive diplomacy include the High Commissioner on National Minorities, the Representative on Freedom of the Media, long-term missions, and a broad spectrum of rules, norms, and principles for military and non-military confidence and security-building measures.
13. EU–NATO Declaration on ESDP, Press Release (2002)142, Brussels, 16 December 2002, <http://www.nato.int/docu/pr/2002/p02-142e.htm>; EU–OSCE cooperation in conflict prevention, crisis management and post-conflict rehabilitation, General Affairs Council, 14486/03 (Presse 319), Brussels, 17 November 2003, pp. I–III, <http://ue.eu.int/pressData/en/gena/77929.pdf>; The European Union and the United Nations: The choice of multilateralism, COM(2003) 526 final, Brussels, 10 September 2003, <http://europa.eu.int/comm/external_relations/un/docs/com03_526en.pdf> (accessed 3 January 2004).
14. E. A. Smith, *Effects Based Operations. Applying Network Centric Warfare in Peace, Crisis, and War* (Washington, DC: CCRP Publications, 2003).
15. Achievement of the Headline Goal: Review Mechanism for Military Capabilities, Appendix to Annex I to Annex VI, EU Presidency Conclusions, Nice European Council, 7–9 December 2000, reprinted in: M. Rutten, *From St-Malo to Nice. European Defence: Core Documents*, Chaillot Papers 47 (Paris: EU Institute for Security Studies, 2001), pp. 181–5.
16. EU Ministers acknowledged the benefits of role specialization in their May 2003 statement on EU military capabilities, and the European Parliament advocates pooling as the preferred method to advance the EU's space policy. See: Declaration on EU Military Capabilities, 2509th Meeting of the General Affairs and External Relations Council, 9379/03 (Presse 138), Brussels, 19–20 May 2003, pp. 13–15, esp. p. 14, <http://ue.eu.int/pressData/en/gena/75857.pdf> (accessed 4 February 2004); European Parliament resolution on the Action Plan for Implementing the European Space Policy, PS-TA-PROV (2004) 0054, Strasbourg, 29 January 2004, Para. 2.

Conclusions and Recommendations

Ian M. Cuthbertson and Heinz Gärtner

After the collapse of the Soviet Union, it quickly became clear that the international system was destined for the foreseeable future to be dominated by the sole remaining superpower, the United States. While some commentators in both Europe and North America were concerned over this unipolar situation, if only because the global system had never had to cope with such a state of affairs before, the actual behavior of the United States gave little cause for concern. The care taken to assemble a broad coalition to wage the First Gulf War, leadership in humanitarian missions in Somalia and the Balkans, areas where the US had no strategic interests at stake, and such symbolic acts as the America's return to full membership in UNESCO suggested that if the world had gained a sole hegemon, it was a benign one. Indeed, President George W. Bush, while a candidate, went so far as to speak of the importance of the US being 'humble' in its conduct of foreign policy.[1]

The US and Europe after 9/11

Even the immediate aftermath of 9/11 did little to dispel that image. The outpouring of international support for the war on terrorism, ranging from the participation of allies in the war in Afghanistan to intelligence sharing on terrorist subjects, with European allies, Russia, adversaries such as Iran and many others contributing information and expertise, and with the wholehearted involvement of institutions ranging from the UN and NATO, all gave the impression that the US was continuing to operate as *primus inter pares*. It took the build up to, and the launching of, the invasion of Iraq to dispel that comforting myth. The war in Iraq exposed a deep and profound cleavage between the world views of the United States and those of its traditional allies, a fundamental difference of outlook on the nature of the evolving international system and the role of power in it.

For Europeans, it is a system of laws and rules, one in which peace and order in the world depends on all states working cooperatively within multilateral institutions to ensure the proper implementation of international laws. For the US, always profoundly skeptical about the utility of the vast majority of multilateral institutions and well aware that many international laws are honored more in the breach than in the observance by what it had already labeled 'rogue states,' the European view seemed utopian and ill suited to a nation at war. For Americans, security rested on military power, not treaties, and it was not prepared to have its national security compromised by other states, countries that did not share its threat perceptions or risk assessments, dictating how or where its military power could be used. As Robert Kagan has put it: 'On major strategic and international questions today, Americans are from Mars and Europeans are from Venus: they agree on little and understand on another less and less.'[2] But if the Western alliance is to survive and, indeed, prosper, ways have to be found to bridge this widening division of perceptions and expectations. This book has been an exploration of some of the ways in which this might be done.

With the end of the Cold War, it became clear to both the United States and the Europeans that, absent any credible threat of a large-scale conventional attack, in the future the security of NATO countries was no longer going to rest primarily on military power. The disappearance of the Warsaw Pact, the collapse of the Soviet Union and the descent into chaos that marked both the economic and military situations in NATO's former adversaries, coupled with the political rapprochement that blossomed after the fall of communism, meant that there was no credible risk of any kind of conventional attack happening against NATO in the foreseeable future. Indeed, in the only military crisis Europe has had to face in the past decade, the various conflicts in the Balkans, even Serbia at its most aggressive never harbored any delusions about invading neighboring states, be they neutral or NATO countries.[3]

Even as the potency of NATO members military instruments remained intact, as evidence by their part in the easy victory in the Gulf War, for Europeans, it became a truism that real security lay not in military power but in the strengthening of political integration and economic cooperation, the more efficient usage of natural resources, the provision of better social welfare policies and the promotion of deeper understandings between nations and peoples by a more thorough appreciation of each other cultures and history. As history had ended[4] and the global triumph of democracy seemed assured, their vision became one of a world in which security rested on common values and the globalization of the market economy, and the integration that would automatically follow in the wake of these two seemingly unstoppable trends. While Americans were never as convinced that the military instrument had lost its usefulness and potency, they also seemed to feel, like Europeans, that it had had its day as the preeminent guarantor of stability and national security. And after all, it was as much American economic muscle and cultural influence as it was military strength that made the US the sole hegemon, and, therefore, it was not as if the US was going to suffer if military power was relegated to a lesser standing in determining ranking in global power and security.[5]

It thus became close to being conventional wisdom that ensuring stability and security would in future require a sophisticated blend of military and civilian strategies, an approach that would stress cooperation and integration, and from the European perspective, promote the model of regional and international integration that Western Europe had been pursuing through the EU for four decades.[6] The events of 9/11, however, showed that much of the thinking that dismissed military power as a vital instrument of state policy and security and that had sought to reshape security doctrine along purely civilian grounds had been, at best, premature. For both the EU and the United States, 9/11 proved to be as major a turning point in reshaping strategic doctrine as those they had experienced at the end of the Cold War. There were, overnight, major shifts in threat assessment, in strategic focus, and in the dynamics of transatlantic relations.[7]

As Susan E. Penksa in her chapter, 'Defining the Enemy: EU and US Threat Perceptions After 9/11,' points out, after 9/11, there was a fundamental reassessment of threat perceptions on both sides of the Atlantic. While there was a consensus on core dangers, the 'triple threat' from terrorism, weapons of mass destruction and failed states, there the commonality of views ended. Europeans, as had been the case before 9/11, continued to place importance on a more comprehensive range of dangers, ranging from organized crime and mass migration, to endemic contagious diseases. Americans, from their perspective of being at much more imminent risk from the consequences of the three core dangers, were no longer prepared to accept such a comprehensive list of challenges, some of which they viewed as minor compared to the dangers by which they now felt imperiled.

After the first attack on the continental United States since the nineteenth century, it was natural for Americans to concentrate on homeland defense and the projection of military power abroad as the best guarantors of their security. European states, however, perhaps in part because their own territories seemed to be in less imminent danger, continued to take a more holistic view in their threat assessments and stuck to their beliefs that the risks that faced them were not as clear cut as the 'triple threat', but were more diffuse and mutually reinforcing. In the view of the EU as an institution, echoing the views of most of its member states, only a comprehensive strategy that embraced the full range of civil and military instruments could act as an effective defense against such diverse threats. A diversion in strategic outlook has thus developed between the EU and US, and more recently, among EU members themselves.

But that does not mean that the various viewpoints cannot be harmonized. In the broader perspective, the differences are more of emphasis than of fundamental opinion and they do not reach a level where they should be either irreversible or sufficiently significant so as to impact seriously the long-term transatlantic relationship or to act as a serious brake on further European integration in foreign and security policy. What is needed to overcome existing divisions is greater creativity in the dialogue on these issues and a real commitment to find a workable and effective consensus on solutions to the challenges that the West as a whole faces. At root, both the EU and US share a similar assessment of just how dangerous, deadly and destabilizing the common challenges they face have been allowed to become. After 9/11 and the bombings in Madrid in Spring 2004, they share a common personification of the enemy, in the shape of terrorist organizations such as al Qaeda and its network of affiliated organizations.[8] The challenge for the US, EU and NATO is to build on their common values and interests and embark on a reinvigorated effort to strengthen and broaden transatlantic cooperation across the two pillars on which so much of international peace, security and stability rests.

It will not, however, be an easy task to meld the differing outlooks of all of the parties, national and institutional, involved in this critical debate. The prevailing strategic paradigm in the United States makes military strategy to a great degree independent of political policy making. In this regard, the American traditional of bringing overwhelming military force to bear in any conflict and then using it to not only defeat but totally destroy the enemy is once more the predominant voice in US policy making. The more calibrate approach to the use of military power that was seen in the 1990s, from the lack of heavy armor in Somalia and the refusal to use ground combat forces in the Balkans, to the use of stand-off weapons as a response to terrorist attacks, are widely judged in both political and military circles in the United States to be not merely failures, but an abdication of responsibility.[9] But an outlook in which the nature of war-making is increasing divorced from the political and strategic objectives that its is meant to be furthering may be an increasing liability in the more nuanced interventions that to a large extent mark the use of military power in the contemporary world.

The use of force has become increasingly delegitimized in modern international relations, to the extent that the use off military power is now supposed to be constrained to the use of a proportionate response to a specific provocation or threat. The American propensity, in the eyes of many people, for using disproportionate force based on insufficient threat, thus undercuts its claim to be acting in a moral manner. Thus, as Jan Willem Honig points out in his chapter, 'A Revolution in Strategy? Conducting War in an Age of Rogues,' despite 9/11 and the dangers that terrorism obviously poses, the challenge remains for the actual method of use of the military instrument to be subordinated to remain subordinate to the larger political objectives it is trying to further. Neither the desire for victory nor the needs of force protection can be allowed to dictate the manner in which military power is finally put to use. If, as Clausewitz claimed, war is merely the continuation of politics by other means, then it is long-term political objectives, not the short-term military considerations, which must drive strategy when military power is used.

In the face of the continuing success of terrorists in carrying out major acts of terror on a global scale, this will not be an easy restriction to get the United States government, its military advisors or its citizens, to embrace. Facing an enemy who appears to be intent on waging total war, and whose aim appears to be to inflict the maximum amount of carnage on innocent civilians and property that it can achieve, the claim by those at most risk is that, in the word of the British Admiral, Jackie Fisher, 'Moderation in war is imbecility.'[10] And for Europeans in particular, the idea that the battle against terrorism perhaps cannot be the type of limited war that they have grown accustomed to in the years since 1945 is hard to accept. Always far more comfortable with the idea that the use of state violence is an immoral act whose wrongness is only mitigated by a need to achieve an even greater social good, the US return to a concept of total war leaves them restless and alienated. Yet from the American perspective, no other approach is acceptable. As the bomb attacks in Madrid illustrated, despite all of the major efforts to improve security against terrorist attacks by major Western states, all are still highly vulnerable to catastrophic terrorism.

EU–US responses to terrorism

The reality is that far from being destroyed or even crippled, al Qaeda has devolved into a kind of franchise operation, one in which a loosely affiliated network of local Islamic fundamentalist terrorist organisations embrace the rhetoric of the movement while largely running their own operations. It appears that, unlike in the past when the al Qaeda leadership were closely involved at all stages of the planning and implementation of major operations, now they merely provide strategic guidance and some of the financing necessary to ensure success. The capture of so many of the first generation of the al Qaeda leadership has also meant that operational control has devolved onto a younger group of terrorist, who exercise power from the field not from any centralized location. Thus the dangers posed by what Friedrich Steinhäusler in his chapter, 'Strategic Terrorism: Threats and Risk Assessment,' terms 'strategic terrorism' remains very real, and this was amply demonstrated by the ability of the terrorists to launch synchronized attacks in a major European capital despite the fact that their infrastructure and personnel have been under heavy attack from police, intelligence agencies and military forces for the three and a half years since 9/11.

In response to this continued global scale threat, it has become obvious that still more has to be done to improve intelligence gathering on the logistical activities and technical progress being made by terrorist organizations worldwide. Only with such information is it then possible to assess properly the real operational capabilities of those terrorist groups who are committed to carrying out acts of catastrophic terrorism. As Madrid has shown, more also needs to be done to improve the physical protection of vulnerable and sensitive areas national infrastructure, such as transportation networks. The kind of effort put into air transport security after 9/11 needs to be expanded to cover all public forms of transportation.

This kind of major effort is necessary, despite the expense and disruption that these kinds of measures inevitably involve, because in today's world, we are faced with a clear trend towards the use of greater and more indiscriminate violence by a whole host of religiously and ethnically motivated terrorists. At a time when purely political ideology has largely disappeared as a motivator for terrorism, it is these simpler and more potent ideologies that have emerged to fill the vacuum. These are threats that governments throughout the world, following the example of the United States after 9/11, need to treat with the seriousness they deserve. New passive counter-terrorism measures against terrorism, from better trained first-responders, through the procurement of new emergency and rescue equipment, to the continuous mounting of large-scale training exercises and the stockpiling of antidotes to chemical and biological weapons, a particular need given the possible use of weapons of mass destruction, need to be extensively implemented. A valuable first step towards the rationalization of all of this disparate activity is the setting up of an effective European wide agency to coordinate contingency planning and resource allocations for civil defense, as well as the development of disaster protocols and specific resources to meet both natural and man-made events.

However, as Ian M. Cuthbertson stresses in his chapter, 'Peering into the Abyss: Understanding and Combating NBC Terrorism,' the West also needs to recognize and accept that even if fully implemented and wholly effective, such passive defenses can only serve to mitigate a terrorist attack, particularly one involving the use of a nuclear, radiological, chemical or biological weapon, not prevent it. For prevention, we need to look elsewhere, to more pro-active measures. There are a number of ways in which enhancements and alterations in a wide variety of Western policies would serve to develop the attitudes, tools and plans that would allow Western nations to tackle more effectively the threats that arise from both the possibilities and realities of terrorism in general and the threat posed by NBC weapons in particular. Perhaps most critical is the abandonment of the policy that unalloyed pre-emption is the unilateral prerogative of the United States. Such a mindset undermines the long established international standards of behavior and experience has amply demonstrated that this emphasis on pre-emption also fatally undermines Western political and popular cohesion.

What is needed instead is for the EU and NATO (if it adopts this strategy) to set clear guidelines for the use of pre-emptive or preventive force (in the case of the EU) in the war on terrorism and for there to be quickly developed a set of comprehensive and effective pre-emptive capabilities that are capable of responding to any and all incipient acts of NBC terrorism, as soon as they are detected and confirmed. It is clear that what is required is a much wider range of intelligence gathering and analysis assets, unconventional military capabilities and law enforcement efforts and options, ones that are seen as innovative, proportionate, and discriminate responses to real threats. If such capabilities are seen as capable, useable and proportionate to the threat, then Western publics and their political representatives are much more likely to be supportive of their aggressive use. If they are interpreted as unethical and ineffective half-measures, they will receive less support and it will be difficult to marshal the political will actually to deploy them in action.

Western nations also need to face up to the morally and politically sensitive idea that there needs to be a fundamental re-examination of and possible revision to the range of civil liberty protections afforded to suspected terrorist groups and their individual members and supporters. To date, Western governments have only begun fully and properly to explore their options with regard to the most imaginative methods available for the prevention of terrorist attacks, and so far they have tended towards adopting only the most publicly acceptable and politically palatable methods for use when investigating terrorist suspects.[11] The circumspect approach by European governments, and their reliance on a patchwork of different laws and regulations, means it is too easy for terrorists in general, and their more passive support infrastructure in particular, to find undisturbed havens in areas where law enforcement is lax or under resourced. In particular, the wide variety of strategies taken by law enforcement and intelligence agencies have not adequately addressed the seriousness of the consequences of failure should they not detect and prevent a terrorist attack that employs an NBC weapon.

It is not as if there is not already a firm foundation on which to build such far-reaching measures. The response of the United States to the events of 9/11 is well known and Europe's response to terrorism was equally swift and multifaceted. With the creation of the European Security Strategy, a comprehensive political framework has been established that correctly puts terrorism into a threat context that also includes weapons of mass destruction, organized crime and failing states, and recognizes all of them as major threats to European and international security. To meet these dangers, there are a number of political steps that need to be taken, most important of which is healing the rift between the US and some of its major European allies over the war on Iraq. Georg Witschel, in his chapter, 'The European Response to Terrorism,' speaking from the centre of the European decision-making process, draws attention to the urgent need for closer and more rigorous attention to be given to European attitudes towards state sponsorship of terrorism, and the political will summoned to move beyond words to actual deeds by invoking the various counter-terrorism clauses that have been included in international treaties, so to give a clear warning signal to a third state that may be sponsoring terrorism.

More also has to be done to cut off the access of terrorists to financial and other economic resources. Despite major improvements, European intelligence, police and judicial cooperation in bodies such as Europol, Eurojust, the Joint Situation Centre and other bodies still need to be significantly improved. In addition to the better protection of international transportation links mentioned above, the quality of border controls also needs further improvements, including the enhancement of capacities for the identification of terrorists and the detection of terrorist devices at land, sea and air border entry points. Finally, a sustained dialogue with the Muslim world and – for Europe a particularly important part of it – the Arab countries and societies that border the Mediterranean, is an imperative if the root causes of radical Islamic terrorism are going to be identified and removed. All of these steps are necessary because, as the West's experience to date amply demonstrates, preventing and combating terrorism is a long-term task, one that will require systematic and sustained efforts for the foreseeable future.

Unilateralism and multilateralism

A major part, however, of coming properly to grips with terrorism lies in first resolving the issues that bedevil the West as it seeks a unified front in facing the danger. As discussed above the decision of the United States to adopt a largely unilateralist approach to many of the facets of directly confronting terrorism is a decision that undercuts the multilateralist approach which has underpinned much of Europe's approach to international relations over at least the last 25 years. The existence of a unipolar world, one in which there is no effective balance to American power, a situation that is welcomed and apparently reveled in by a Republican controlled administration and legislature, has been a hard reality for a number of European states to adjust to. It is a difficulty they share with many liberal internationalists in both the political and academic worlds in the United States itself. All of these group believe that it is the responsibility of the US as the unipolar power to subordinate its capabilities to the constraints of international institutions and laws and to seek the approval and support of friends and allies before engaging in courses of action that would see the use of America's overwhelming strength.

The underlying assumption of such an approach to the use of American capabilities is that this power can best serve international peace and security if it is channeled and constrained. With such a mindset, the next step is to believe that it is up to the US to show restraint and for it to the voluntarily reject the unique opportunities that its unrivaled supremacy could provide it with. From this perspective, the United States should be modest, not despite of its great power, but because of it. For the US, the advantages of exercising restraint are held up to be the greater likelihood that its actions will receive international approval and support. Experience in Iraq has amply demonstrated that democracy cannot be imposed and that the US acting alone or in concert with only a close group of allies lacks legitimacy, not least among the populations it is trying to assist.

An approach that involves more of America's friends and allies would help achieve the goal that the US has laid out, but only if it is a full partnership and not the use of smaller powers as window dressing to disguise the reality of US unilateralism. As Regina Karp details in her chapter on 'Transatlantic Relations after 9/11 and Iraq: Continuities and Discontinuities,' whether sufficient trust in US intentions can be generated for offers of assistance to be proffered remains a major question. And whether or not the US is even seriously interested in constraining its own prerogatives remains to be seen. However, all parties to this debate need to engage in it with the knowledge that the shape of its final resolution will to a large extent define the nature of the transatlantic relationship for the foreseeable future and go a long way towards determining what the European Union and NATO will contribute to building a higher level of international peace and stability.

Not all of the signs for a happy outcome to this debate are auspicious. There are many who still believe that a stable and peaceful world can best be achieved through the untrammeled use of American power, and that a Pax Americana, one that rests on the strong pillars of American economic, military and political power, offers the most robust prospects to the many security challenges facing the international system, not least of which is the specter of NBC terrorism. If, as we propose, the best approach is for unilateralism to be rejected by the US as its preferred mode of behavior, then what other options are available to it? NATO's long history of consensual decision-making and actions, and the willingness of NATO's member states to accept American leadership of the Alliance means that it remains, after the United Nations, the best model for embedding the world's sole hegemon in a multilateral decision-making process. It also needs to be acknowledged that, despite the primacy that the UN enjoys as a security institution in most of the international community, US policy-makers from across the political spectrum have consistently displayed a low level of confidence in its utility and effectiveness in this critical area. When these attitudes are compared to the esteem that NATO continues to generate amongst policy-makers and opinion formers in the United States, in the short term it may be NATO that has the greater utility and offers a wider range of possibilities in this critical role.[12]

But NATO, at the very least, has a history of strength continuity and purpose on which to fall back. That its image for the last decade resembles more a Potemkin village than the cohesive, integrated military and political Alliance of earlier years is something that can still be changed. In his chapter, 'Three Fictions of Transatlantic Relations,' Daniel Nelson makes it very clear that failure to return real substance to the rhetoric of Alliance consultation is to stare weakness, disjunction and retreat in the face. The missteps of American policy before and after the invasion of Iraq shows that this is no abstract danger, even if in some quarters there remains denial that the course America chose to steer was not the best of the various options available to it or that closer cooperation with allies, who shared a commonality of aims if not methods, might have produced a happier outcome at less cost in blood and treasure for all involved.

If Europe is also to fulfill what it believes to be its destiny, then it must pursue unity, a coherent identity and a level of political and military cohesion that at least begins to approach the levels of its economic strengths. If the Euroatlantic community of nations is going to cooperate on the same basis on which it has always operated, as a liberal, pluralist, multilateralist collective, then the shortcomings of expediency and unilateralism must finally be accepted by the United States, while Europe needs to realize, in a dangerous world, it is the reality of American power, not wishful thinking, that keeps barbarism at bay. On the basis of the mutual recognition of both sides' strengths and weaknesses, perhaps the rhetoric of NATO can be given a new reality.

EU–NATO: a qualified division of labor

The structure is already in place. NATO's strategic partnership with the European Union has been formalized in the *Berlin Plus* arrangements, which provides for 'separable but not separate' EU forces. A qualified division of labor in the military and political fields, one in which Europe and the US, EU and NATO concentrate on capabilities where each has a comparative advantage is not only a feasible but vitally necessary concept. Other types of divisions of labor have already emerged. One is geographical, as in the case of Afghanistan, which is the main priority for NATO, with the possibility of heavier involvement in Iraq still a possibility, while the EU is focused almost entirely on the Balkans, with missions in Africa only just beginning to emerge as competitors for resources. As Heinz Gärtner points out in his chapter, 'NATO and EU: Duplication or Division of Labor?' functional specializations are also emerging, where NATO involvement in the Middle East is based on the Alliance offering countries throughout the region a range of military cooperation programs, including training for peacekeeping missions, border security and counter-terrorism. NATO has also focused on promoting political reforms that would result in effective civilian control over regional militaries, essentially an expansion of the original PfP program into a new region of the world. The EU, meanwhile, is seeking to expand its existing network of trade and development agreements along the Mediterranean periphery, to achieve free-trade arrangements by the end of the decade.

Beyond this type of role specialization and burden sharing, there is also a clear consensus among at least some of the EU member states and the US on the need to develop more coordinated and where possible common force planning and strategies. Such harmonized capabilities would make it much quicker and easier in the future if there was a need to build for ad-hoc coalitions of the willing that would require access to the full panoply of NATO and EU economic, military and human assets to tackle threats, even pre-emptively, from such things as terrorism or failed states. Such an approach would be in line with the often-expressed ambition that both NATO and the EU build coherent, transparent and mutually reinforcing capabilities.

Gärtner also stresses that success in implementing such a qualified division of labor between NATO and the EU would have the effect of leaving the US with its current capability to fight high-tech, high-intensity, high-speed wars, while in areas it has shown itself to be less effective, such as nation building, peacekeeping and postwar reconstruction efforts, Europeans would be able to play to their strengths in the softer areas of power projection. The US would therefore continue to be able to largely do all they want to, while the Europeans would focus on areas where their expertise represents a value-added contribution, not just an afterthought to American power. As all parties would have a moral and financial stake in any operation, risk and responsibility would also be more evenly shared, not only directly, as in the dangers of suffering casualties, but also at the more existential of shared responsibility for success or failure.

Such EU–US cooperation in the field of crisis management and the acceptance of the concept of a qualified division of labor would also help defuse much of the unilateralism–multilateralism debate, because the complementariness of capabilities would necessitate real consultation and agreement before an action was launched. Those favoring a multilateral approach to conflict prevention, from early resolution to full-blown war fighting, would at last have something they could offer, in terms of critical capabilities, to restrain the American urge towards unilateral action. The US, on the other hand, despite its decisive military victories in Afghanistan and Iraq, has become much more aware that a lasting peace and the nation building that are fundamental to such a condition are best achieved through multilateral efforts. Not wishing to be left again with the kind of long-term commitments that it is burdened with in Iraq in particular, deployments that tie down its troops and drain American military readiness, the US is much less likely to launch its troops into action without the support of the allies, absent which there is little prospect of long term resolution of the problem.

And as Christian Tuschhoff forcefully underlines in his chapter, 'NATO Cohesion from Afghanistan to Iraq,' despite legitimate concerns in many quarters that 9/11 had marginalized NATO, the Alliance has provided an indispensable command function in both Afghanistan and Iraq. As the

Alliance attempts to shake of the divisions that bedeviled it in the run up to the invasion of Iraq, it may now be ready to move forward and fulfill the at least some of the roles set out above. Based on extensive prior consultations of what the Alliance's response to terrorism should be, NATO immediately responded to the 9/11 attacks, by invoking the collective defense provisions of Article 5 of its founding treaty. The United States welcomed this early and unambiguous support from its major allies not for military but for political reasons as it prepared to wage the new war on terrorism. However, the US also bypassed NATO's command because it did not want the European allies involved in the US command structure. Later, the US submitted a list of requests to NATO on how it could most effectively assist the war effort against international terrorism. And despite the disruptions and disagreements caused within the Alliance by the invasion of Iraq, NATO's general capabilities, such as its decision-making procedures and the smooth functioning of NATO's institutional assets, which still provide worthwhile ties among the allies. These in turn continue to affect significantly the attitudes and behavior of member states and help shape both their policies and politics.

NATO had also prepared militarily for a wide range of contingencies that were encompassed by terrorist attacks. NATO has already begun a fundamental restructuring of its armed forces and command structures, and a similar process is already underway in terms of wide-reaching modernization to the armed forces and command structures of individual member states to address the many deficiencies that remain. NATO is thus working hard to prove itself relevant, in terms of both its political and military value, in the post-9/11 era. It is seeking to shape long-term military modernization in individual states in accordance with its revised threat assessment after 9/11 and based on the new strategic concepts that grew out of the need to fight what is sure to be a long war against international terrorism. That NATO was riven by dissent, weak, divided and indecisive in the face of the very public wrangling between its major members in the run up to the war in Iraq was the result of having no contingency plans in place that envisaged such a major step for the Alliance and then trying to make policy on the run. For the future, as the experience of 9/11 amply demonstrates, the Alliance works best when major political decisions are taken in advance, all possible problems are aired and explored and decisions are taken and positions agreed that allow authority to be pre-delegated to military commanders to meet the specified challenges. This is the approach NATO needs to adopt if it is going to stay vibrant and relevant in the post-9/11 world.

The importance of NATO as a common security organization staying relevant, indeed central, to the Euroatlantic relationship and to the international strategic scene as a whole is hard to over stress. While Europe itself is no longer a realm of intense security competition and naked power politics, neither has it emerged as an oasis of Kantian 'perpetual peace' and multilateral cooperation. Rather, Europe remains an 'anarchic society' based on a mix of power and authority. Thus Europe's democracies must continue to build aggressively on their recent history of acting cooperatively and consensually whenever possible, while being willing and able to use military force coercively to back up when necessary. NATO, acting in concert with the EU, at a time when this institution, even as the first civilian and military crisis-management missions signify the coming of age of the ESDP, is still trying to find its voice in foreign policy, defence affairs and on security issues generally, would seem to still be the best available option.

The EU as a security policy actor

But it must also be remembered that the authority and ability of the European Union as a security-policy actor remains in question not only because of differences among the member states, but also because of the continued dominance of the voice of the United States on matters of international security. Despite this, the US desire to see the EU take an ever increasing role in difficult post-conflict, low-intensity stabilization tasks in Europe and beyond has undoubtedly created additional missions for the ESDP to take on and master, a task that will be made easier as the implications of the ESDP for NATO's competences and capabilities are increasingly overcome by new collaborative arrangements.

As the global security order evolves, so too are the roles of the EU and US changing. As he makes clear in his chapter 'The European "Centaur": Power and Authority in Europe's Society of States,' Adrian Hyde-Price believes that for the EU, in particular, the need is to build a more comprehensive range of non-military capabilities and stress the strategy of effective multilateralism both to enhance its own authority in international affairs and to give greater legitimacy to its policies. But the EU also has to adjust its thinking, doctrine and capabilities to reflect the reality that it is seeking to operate in an international environment in which the use of force as a crisis management tool remains top on the list of US preferences, and where EU capabilities remain a pale shadow over the overwhelming US power in the military arena. And as Kari Möttölä, explains in his chapter 'The European Union and Crisis Management,' an absolute division of labour between the US and EU is neither acceptable nor practical, and full symmetry in military assets is not truly practicable given America's clear commitment to maintaining its superiority. Thus, building more rounded crisis intervention capabilities would allow the EU to leverage more effectively the strategic advantages that its multi-faceted functions could allow it to play in international relations.

Indeed, as there is a greater understanding and acceptance across the board of both the roots and causes of terrorism, and the wide range of policies, military, law enforcement, economic and societal that are needed to combat its growth and operations, the value and utility of multifaceted, multilateral institutions such as the EU and the OSCE will inevitably increase. This case is well made by P. Terrence Hopmann in his detailed description of the role and capabilities of the OSCE in particular, where he stresses how in turn this growing realization of the potentials of a range of institutions allows them to play a more central role in enhancing the safety and security of individuals, peoples and states throughout the world. In addition to these advantages, of taking on fuller crisis management responsibilities, as the case of NATO and the OSCE have amply demonstrated, preparing for and implementing these types of missions will also bring greater coherence and consistency to the EU's internal decision-making process, and force it to find the correct balance between the priorities and preferences of individual member states and the EU as an institution.

Part of promoting the multilateral agenda, as opposed to the unilateralism or bilateralism increasingly favored by the US, lies in enforcing the strictures of international law as a restraint on all states, even the most powerful. One of the most critical elements in international law when it comes to the area of international security lies in the various multilateral arms control and disarmament agreements that have been signed over the past 40 years and which have become one of the cornerstones of much of the international security system. In his chapter, 'Multilateral Arms Control as a Response to NBC Proliferation – A New Transatlantic Divide?' Alexander Kelle leaves the reader in little doubt that Europe is the stronger supporter of all arms control and disarmament measures, in particular those seeking to limit the proliferation of NBC weapons. In sharp contrast, the US is, at best, a reluctant adherent and harbors deep skepticism about the effectiveness of the treaty regimes to which it is a party. This is coupled with a deep belief that the critical advantages the US enjoys across the board in military power must not be compromised by legally binding multilateral arms control agreements by which the US, a nation of laws, is bound, but which its adversaries continue to flout. In the face of this American recalcitrance, Europe has remained totally committed to multilateral NBC arms control, despite the many shortcomings that have been revealed in the verification provisions of a number of the most critical treaties, in particular the NPT. Part of this continue adherence to multilateral treaty regimes is due to the simple reality that for European countries, unilateralist opportunities of the sort faced by the US to carry out end runs around treaty regimes to achieve national security objectives in the area of NBC weapons proliferation simply do not present themselves.[13]

For Kelle, however, that is only part of the explanation for the Europe's normatist stance towards multilateral arms control regimes. Europeans have long been conditioned to viewing arms control as an important tool of their overall security policy and to their definition of their national security interests. Part of what causes them to embrace multilateral arms control through this prism is that European states have become accustomed to internalizing the rules and regulations issued from Brussels by the EU. As Europeans see things, the institution building processes that were used to create transparency, predictability and security within Europe can also be used to achieve the same on a wider playing field through the successful implementation of multilateral arms control regimes, which will see problem states alter the behavior under the normative pressures exerted by other parties to the various treaty regimes. Thus, from the European perspective, it is the United States, by failing to participate in the normative process that these treaties are seeking to establish, that is refusing to behave like a civilized state in the area of NBC arms control.

Given the perception of failure that characterizes multilateral arms control and disarmament in the US policy debate, and Europe's strong attachment to these regimes despite their obvious shortcomings, what can be done to strengthen these treaties? First, an intensified transatlantic dialogue about the essential nature and importance of arms control is necessary. Americans need to recognize that strong European support for multilateral NBC arms control is bedrock of their international security policy. Europeans need to accept that if multilateral arms control measures are again to feature as a tool of US security policy, a serious, and not merely cosmetic, regime of verification measures based on real world conditions and concerns must become a part of all multilateral NBC arms control and disarmament agreements.

What then needs to be done in order to make Europe a more equal partner in its security relationship with the US, and how can it be done without placing further strains on the transatlantic relationship? In their chapter, 'What Future for Europe's Security and Defense Policy? Five Scenarios for the Year 2020,' Heiko Borchert and Daniel Maurer explore the highly complex nature of the new risk environment and conclude that it requires a more integrated approach to the elucidation and implementation of security policy, one that places the emphasis on comprehensive and fully integrated capabilities. Drawing on both their prior experiences and temperaments, Borchert and Maurer believe that both the EU as an institution, and its individual member states, are well equipped to meet these requirements and build such capabilities In order to take fully advantage of these potentials, however, greater integration and cohesion must be quickly achieved, both at the national and EU level, of the security sector, business and commerce and civil society as a whole.

It is a truism that capabilities mirror political ambitions and vice-versa. It is of critical importance that new military and non-military capabilities are quickly developed and procured that can give credibility to any greater voice in the security field which the EU asserts for itself. New defense spending and a commitment to reform military establishments and strategies, without duplicating those of the US, are part of the equation, as are more integrated and rounded capabilities in the plethora of areas that combine to give a credible capability in the area of non-military power projection and interventions. But political will is necessary to galvanize both existing institutions and the new bodies that are being created to assist in European integration in this area, and move them beyond talking and planning into actual long-term actions.

Any new European security strategy also needs to define in advance the kind of scenarios it is willing to play out, both in terms of the geographical focus of such operations and the range of assets which Europe is prepared to deploy to meet different threat assessments. The relative weight which each of these different assets will be accorded in a range of different risk scenarios also needs to be determined. Such planning is especially critical for the EU, as it has clearly and repeatedly demonstrated that both the institution itself, and consultations amongst its constituent states, cannot be done quickly. Predetermined actions in face of anticipated scenarios, of the type Borchert and Maurer carefully detail, ones in which each country and institution can bring specific capabilities to the table based on a pre-agreed division of labor, thus becomes a failsafe that ensures a initial swift and integrate European response, even as consultations take place on longer term actions.

Many of these ideas, proposals and recommendations are broad and ambitious proposals, but terrorist attacks against Western targets, sooner or later involving the using of NBC weapons, are coming. The ability of Western countries to survive such assaults, both individually and collectively, will be determined by the steps that are taken now.

Notes

1. Vice President Gore And Governor Bush, Second Presidential, 11 October 2000, http://www.hideinplainwebsite.com/seconddebate.htm
2. Kagan, Robert, *Of Paradise and Power: America and Europe in the New World Order* (Knopf, New York, 2003), p. 3.
3. Silber, Laura & Little, Allen, *Yugoslavia: Death of a Nation* (TV Books, New York, 1996), contains a detailed history of both Serb aggression and Nato's reaction. It highlights the limited geographical aims wit which President Milosovic pursued his genocidal war.
4. It seems that the claims of F. Fukuyama in *The End of History and the Last Man* (Free Press, New York, 1992), have been overtaken by events.
5. Kagan, Robert, 'U.S. Dominance: Is It Good for the World?: The Benevolent Empire' *Foreign Policy*, Summer, 1998.
6. Holmes, Peter & Young, Alasdair R., *Exporting Rules: The European Union as a Model for International Regimes.* Paper to the ECSA Sixth Biennial Conference, Pittsburgh 2–5 June 1999.
7. Tenet, George J., *Worldwide Threat: Covering Dangers in a Post 9/11 World*, Remarks delivered by the Director, Central Intelligence Agency as testimony before the US Senate Committee on Armed Services, Washington, DC, March 19, 2002 http://usembassy.state.gov/bogota/wwws2415.shtml

8. Lobjakas, Ahto, *EU: Ministers Agree On Steps To Counter Terrorism*. Radio Free Europe/Radio Liberty, Friday, 19 March 2004. http://www.rferl.org/featuresarticle/2004/3/60F49235-087B-44BD-A52C-5E780855F3C5.html

9. Walter, Barbara F., & Snyder, Jack, *Civil Wars, Insecurity, and Intervention*. Columbia University Press, New York, 1999.

10. Hanson, Victor Davis, *At War – What Are We Made Of?: The Guts to Resist Evil National Review*, Washington, DC, 1 October 2001. This gives a good and concise insight into the fundamental difference in outlook that underin American and European thinking on this key issue.

11. Doyle, Charles, *The USA Patriot Act: A Legal Analysis*, Congressional Research Service, Washington, DC, 15 April 2002, In this report to the US Congress, the author gives a detailed and insightful description of the Patriot Act and its operation up to that date. In *Terrorism and Tyranny: Trampling Freedom, Justice, and Peace to Rid the War of Evil* by James Bovard (Palgrave Macmillan, London 2003), however, a much more scathing analysis is delivered on both the act itself and the government thinking that underpins it.

12. The *UN, THE EU, NATO AND OTHER REGIONAL ACTORS: Partners in Peace?* A conference report from a meeting hosted by the European Union Institute for Security Studies, the International Peace Academy and the French Ministry of Defence's Directorate of International Security. While the report is an excellent exposition of European thinking on these institutions, the absence of any skeptical American voice is striking and leaves the reader with a sense of unreality about the deliberations that underpin the report. http://www.ipacademy.org/PDF_Reports/BACKGROUNDER.pdf

13. The more forceful position taken by the major European powers in face of reliable reports that Iran is moving rapidly towards achieving a nuclear weapons capability, coupled with Iran's repeated flouting of IAEA injunctions may presage a shift by the Europeans the more robust American approach to these issues. Only time will tell.

Index